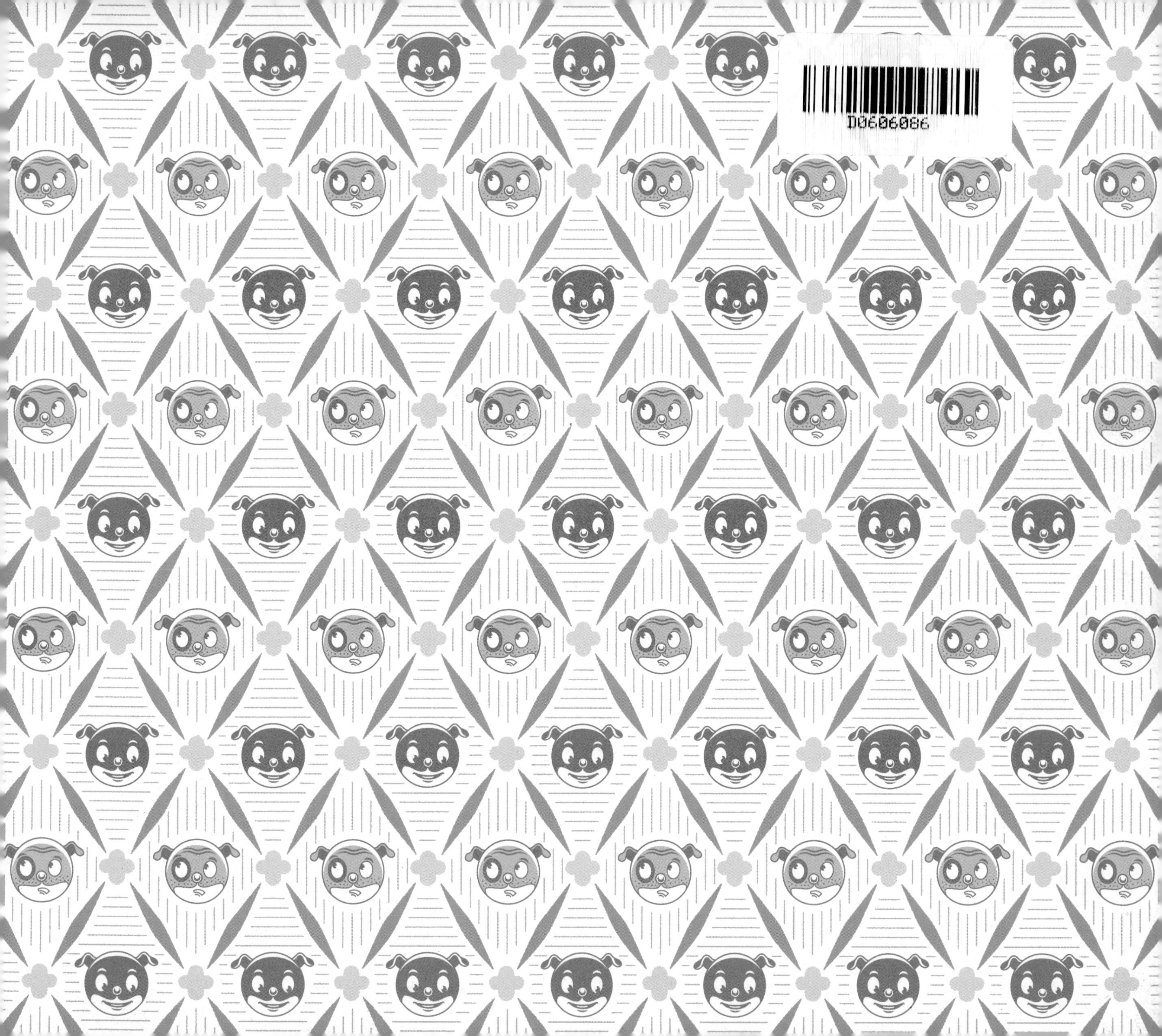

COIN-OP
COMICS ANTHOLOGY
1997-2017

Published By:

TOP SHELF PRODUCTIONS

Coin-Op Comics © 2018 Maria Hoey and Peter Hoey

Editor-in-Chief: Chris Staros.

Published by Top Shelf Productions, PO Box 1282, Marietta, GA 30061-1282, USA. Top Shelf Productions is an imprint of IDW Publishing, a division of Idea and Design Works, LLC. Offices: 2765 Truxtun Road, San Diego, CA 92106. Top Shelf Productions®, the Top Shelf logo, Idea and Design Works®, and the IDW logo are registered trademarks of Idea and Design Works, LLC. All Rights Reserved. With the exception of small excerpts of artwork used for review purposes, none of the contents of this publication may be reprinted without the permission of IDW Publishing. IDW Publishing does not read or accept unsolicited submissions of ideas, stories, or artwork.

Visit our online catalog at www.topshelfcomix.com.

ISBN 978-1-60309-427-6

Printed in Korea.

22 21 20 19 18   1 2 3 4 5

COIN-OP ANTHOLOGY 1997-2017

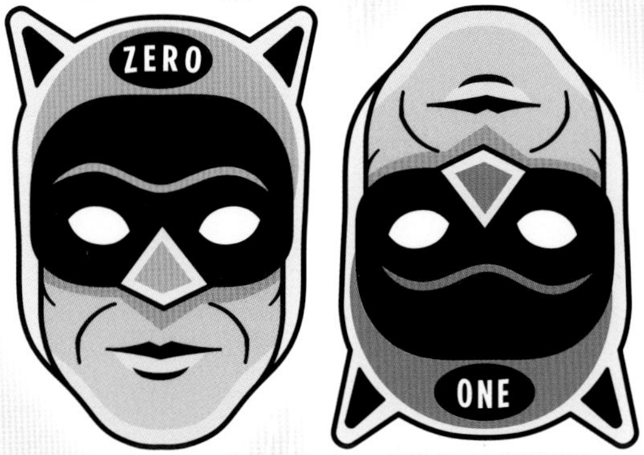
ZERO
ONE

TABLE OF CONTENTS

All drawings by Peter and Maria Hoey
All stories by Peter and Maria Hoey, except where noted.

S P

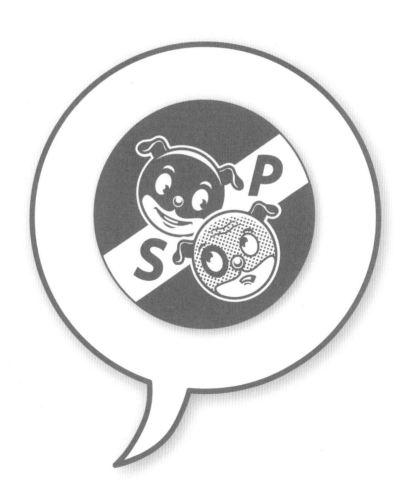

In Case of Emergency Break Glass

A LAUNDROMAT TOKEN. A railroad-flattened penny. A two-dollar chip from Mohegan Sun. Any coin will do. Drop it in the slot.

Somewhere an atom-sharp stylus slips precisely into the center of the groove and a complete new world comes roaring to life. Welcome to the comics of Coin-Op.

The characteristic icon of Coin-Op is the perfect circle. Coins, records, ripples, pupils, film reels, moons, whirlpools. Circles within circles; a secret visual language both expressing and obscuring some urgent but enigmatic message. Fragile visions are contained within these sacred circumferences, and protected by a brilliantly reflective surface of magisterial cartooning control. The drawings are lenses which focus the oddnesses of the world to an impossibly iridescent gleam. They hum with the glass-blown buzz of a fresh neon tubule.

What roils underneath? Fugues and fantasias on the wonders and troubles of inner and outer life, presented in saturated colors and kaleidoscopic spectacle. Dreams of longing, ironic jokes, the implacable eyes of death. Forgotten songs playing from distant windows, shadow histories of old Hollywood—fresh new nostalgia, straight out of the box. Within their formalist glass-and-steel framework, every Coin-Op comic hides a bustling city's-worth of coincidences and contradictions, unmanageable passions, gallows humor, blustering joys and blistering sorrows.

Consider the authors of these strange stories. The Hoeys: Pete and Maria, bicoastal California brother and New York sister separated by a vast American continent and yet imaginatively and aesthetically synced across time zones. It's possible that the physical distance may be essential to their project—a three thousand mile gap in which to erect clockwork universes and Goldbergian megalopoli, spill rivers of hope and oceans of memory. The many kingdoms of Coin-Op.

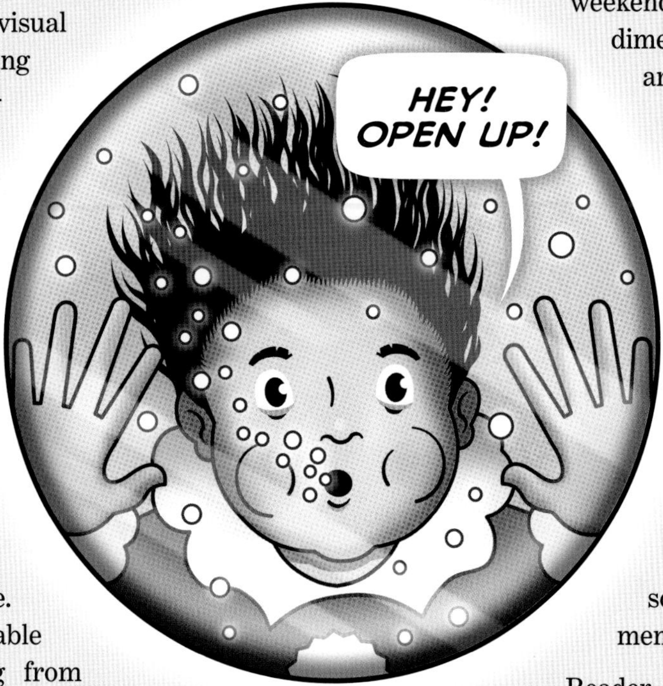
HEY! OPEN UP!

I've worked with the Coin-Operators in various capacities as a publisher, editor and collaborator. We frequently share tables at comic conventions and art festivals, where I spend weekends adjacent to their bioluminescent pocket dimension bubbling with letterpress prints and silk-screened accordion-fold books and utterly astonishing comics. Pete or Maria (almost never both—they divide and conquer) sit quietly in a coy legs-folded posture that seems to run in the Hoey family, their pristine display sparkling like a sapphire among the junk-punk surroundings of some indie zine expo. Readers and customers are intrigued, even hypnotized. Yet they approach slowly, tentatively, irresistibly drawn to the products but—what? Intimidated by their sleekness and beauty? Nervous to somehow screw up this precious arrangement of finely wrought treasures?

Reader, ignore that impulse. This mirror-world is brighter and weirder than our fallen domain. Break glass in case of emergency; life is an emergency. Love this book until its spine breaks. Crack it open like a coconut, and drink the comics. Let them run down your face.

Then rummage madly through your pockets for another coin.

— *Josh O'Neill*
Philadelphia, February 2018

Center panel from "Little Nemo in Coin-Op Land" published in: *Little Nemo: Dream Another Dream*

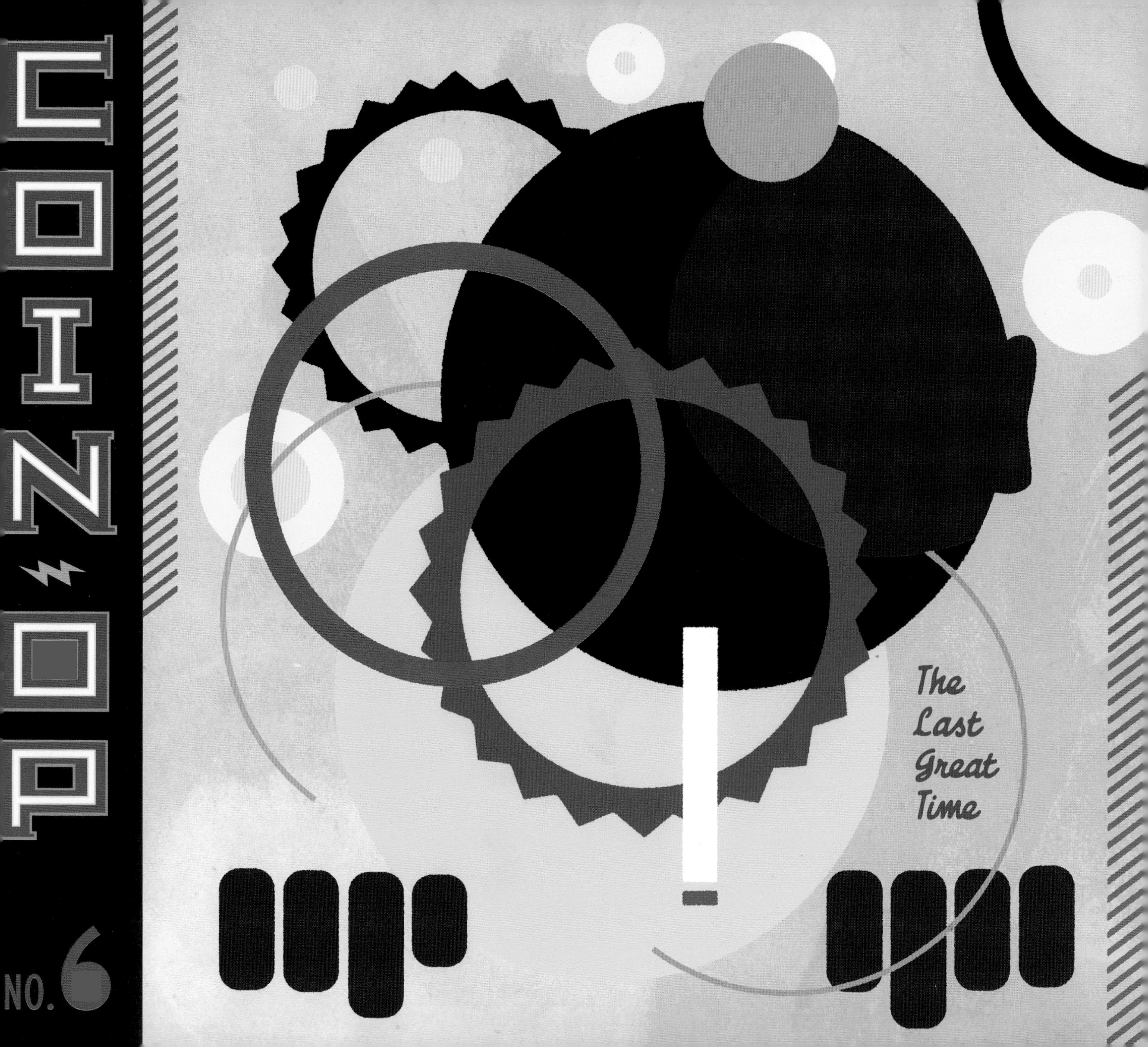
POPGUN
NO. 6
The Last Great Time

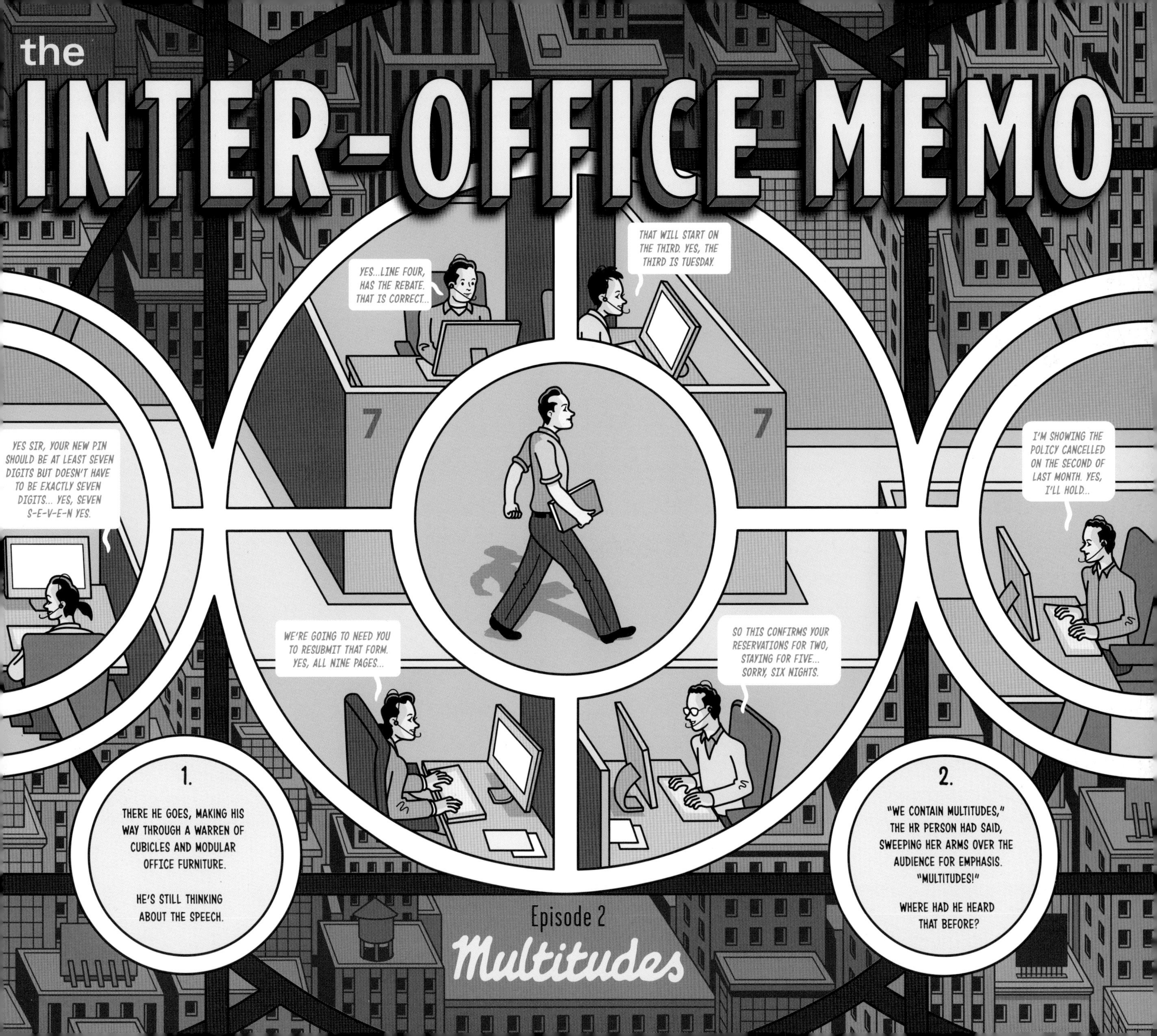
the
INTER-OFFICE MEMO
YES...LINE FOUR, HAS THE REBATE. THAT IS CORRECT...
THAT WILL START ON THE THIRD. YES, THE THIRD IS TUESDAY.
YES SIR, YOUR NEW PIN SHOULD BE AT LEAST SEVEN DIGITS BUT DOESN'T HAVE TO BE EXACTLY SEVEN DIGITS... YES, SEVEN S-E-V-E-N YES.
I'M SHOWING THE POLICY CANCELLED ON THE SECOND OF LAST MONTH. YES, I'LL HOLD...
WE'RE GOING TO NEED YOU TO RESUBMIT THAT FORM. YES, ALL NINE PAGES...
SO THIS CONFIRMS YOUR RESERVATIONS FOR TWO, STAYING FOR FIVE... SORRY, SIX NIGHTS.
1.
THERE HE GOES, MAKING HIS WAY THROUGH A WARREN OF CUBICLES AND MODULAR OFFICE FURNITURE.
HE'S STILL THINKING ABOUT THE SPEECH.
2.
"WE CONTAIN MULTITUDES," THE HR PERSON HAD SAID, SWEEPING HER ARMS OVER THE AUDIENCE FOR EMPHASIS. "MULTITUDES!"
WHERE HAD HE HEARD THAT BEFORE?
Episode 2
Multitudes

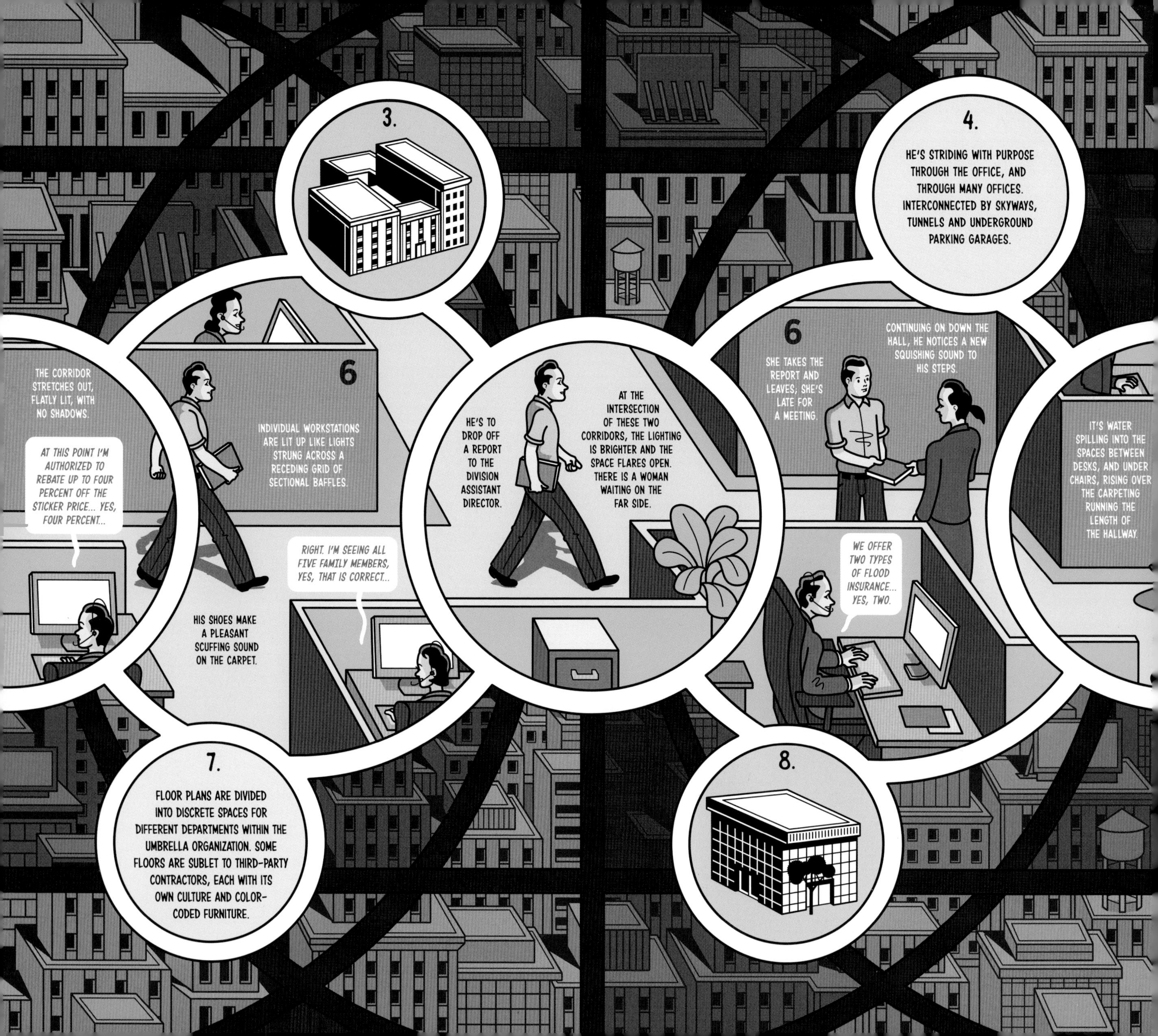
3.
4.
HE'S STRIDING WITH PURPOSE THROUGH THE OFFICE, AND THROUGH MANY OFFICES. INTERCONNECTED BY SKYWAYS, TUNNELS AND UNDERGROUND PARKING GARAGES.
THE CORRIDOR STRETCHES OUT, FLATLY LIT, WITH NO SHADOWS.
AT THIS POINT I'M AUTHORIZED TO REBATE UP TO FOUR PERCENT OFF THE STICKER PRICE... YES, FOUR PERCENT...
6
INDIVIDUAL WORKSTATIONS ARE LIT UP LIKE LIGHTS STRUNG ACROSS A RECEDING GRID OF SECTIONAL BAFFLES.
HIS SHOES MAKE A PLEASANT SCUFFING SOUND ON THE CARPET.
RIGHT. I'M SEEING ALL FIVE FAMILY MEMBERS, YES, THAT IS CORRECT...
HE'S TO DROP OFF A REPORT TO THE DIVISION ASSISTANT DIRECTOR.
AT THE INTERSECTION OF THESE TWO CORRIDORS, THE LIGHTING IS BRIGHTER AND THE SPACE FLARES OPEN. THERE IS A WOMAN WAITING ON THE FAR SIDE.
6
SHE TAKES THE REPORT AND LEAVES; SHE'S LATE FOR A MEETING.
CONTINUING ON DOWN THE HALL, HE NOTICES A NEW SQUISHING SOUND TO HIS STEPS.
WE OFFER TWO TYPES OF FLOOD INSURANCE... YES, TWO.
IT'S WATER SPILLING INTO THE SPACES BETWEEN DESKS, AND UNDER CHAIRS, RISING OVER THE CARPETING RUNNING THE LENGTH OF THE HALLWAY.
7.
FLOOR PLANS ARE DIVIDED INTO DISCRETE SPACES FOR DIFFERENT DEPARTMENTS WITHIN THE UMBRELLA ORGANIZATION. SOME FLOORS ARE SUBLET TO THIRD-PARTY CONTRACTORS, EACH WITH ITS OWN CULTURE AND COLOR-CODED FURNITURE.
8.

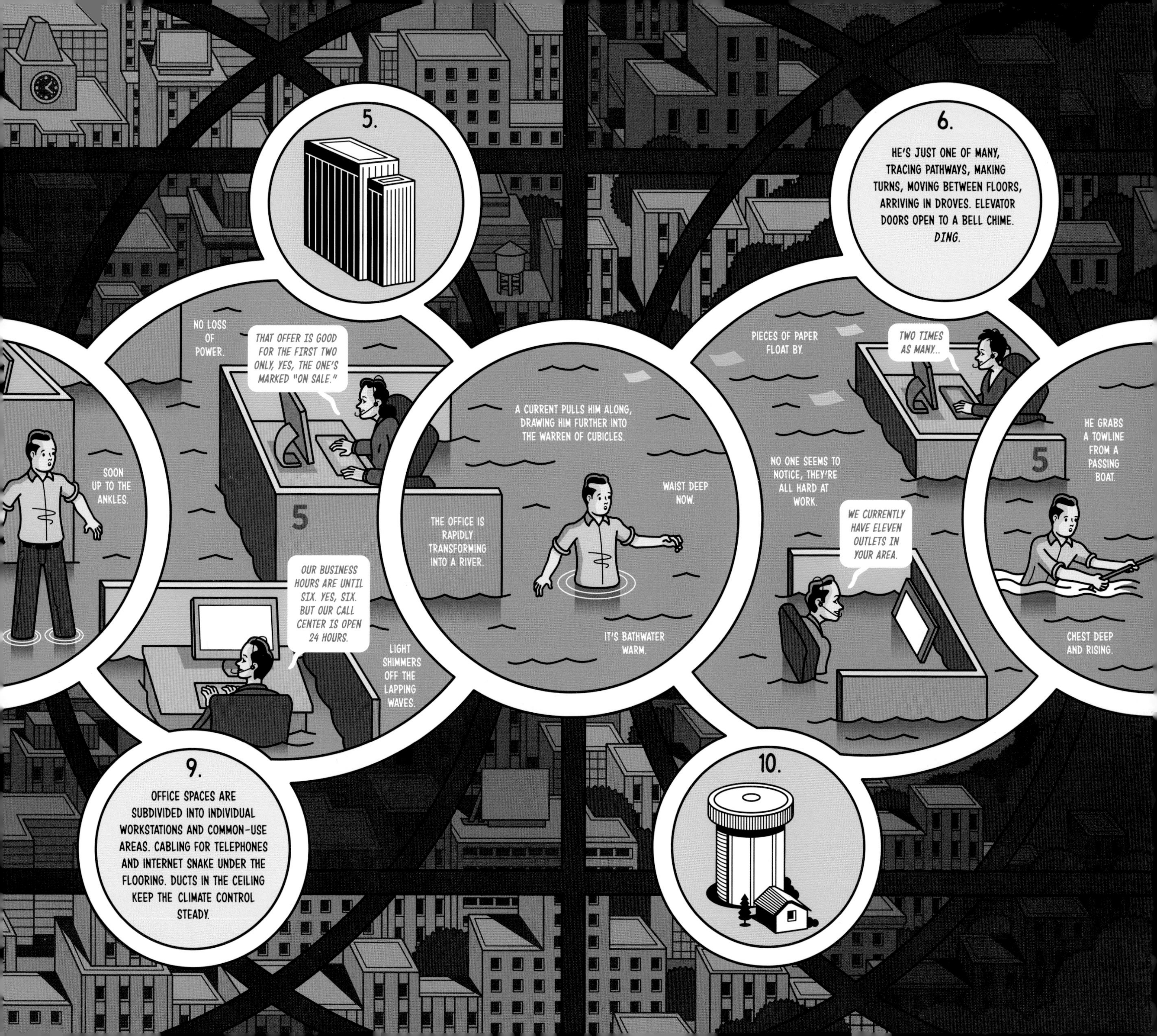
5.
6.
HE'S JUST ONE OF MANY, TRACING PATHWAYS, MAKING TURNS, MOVING BETWEEN FLOORS, ARRIVING IN DROVES. ELEVATOR DOORS OPEN TO A BELL CHIME. *DING.*
SOON UP TO THE ANKLES.
NO LOSS OF POWER.
THAT OFFER IS GOOD FOR THE FIRST TWO ONLY, YES, THE ONE'S MARKED "ON SALE."
5
OUR BUSINESS HOURS ARE UNTIL SIX. YES, SIX. BUT OUR CALL CENTER IS OPEN 24 HOURS.
LIGHT SHIMMERS OFF THE LAPPING WAVES.
A CURRENT PULLS HIM ALONG, DRAWING HIM FURTHER INTO THE WARREN OF CUBICLES.
THE OFFICE IS RAPIDLY TRANSFORMING INTO A RIVER.
WAIST DEEP NOW.
IT'S BATHWATER WARM.
PIECES OF PAPER FLOAT BY.
TWO TIMES AS MANY...
5
NO ONE SEEMS TO NOTICE, THEY'RE ALL HARD AT WORK.
WE CURRENTLY HAVE ELEVEN OUTLETS IN YOUR AREA.
HE GRABS A TOWLINE FROM A PASSING BOAT.
CHEST DEEP AND RISING.
9.
OFFICE SPACES ARE SUBDIVIDED INTO INDIVIDUAL WORKSTATIONS AND COMMON-USE AREAS. CABLING FOR TELEPHONES AND INTERNET SNAKE UNDER THE FLOORING. DUCTS IN THE CEILING KEEP THE CLIMATE CONTROL STEADY.
10.

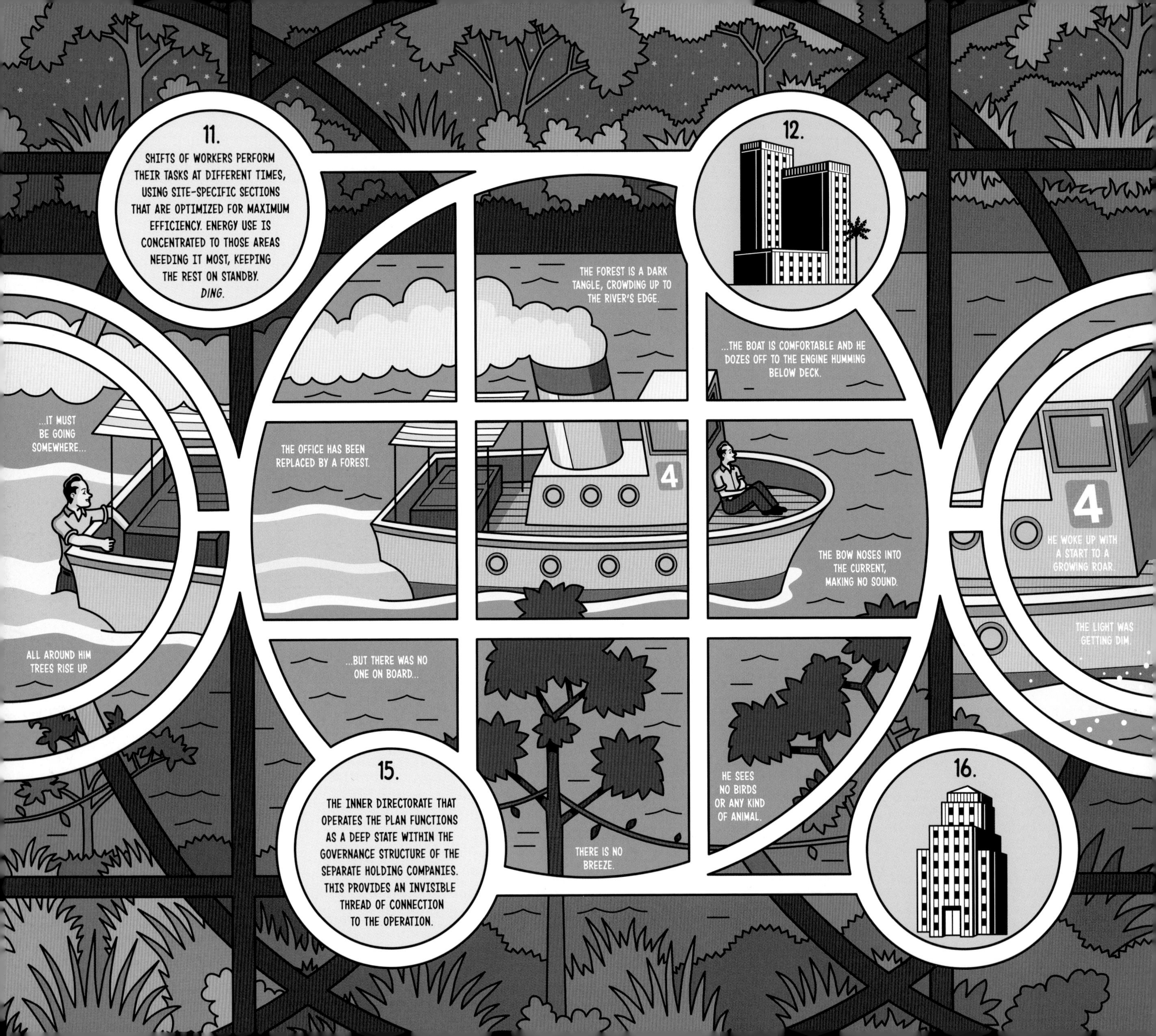
11.
SHIFTS OF WORKERS PERFORM THEIR TASKS AT DIFFERENT TIMES, USING SITE-SPECIFIC SECTIONS THAT ARE OPTIMIZED FOR MAXIMUM EFFICIENCY. ENERGY USE IS CONCENTRATED TO THOSE AREAS NEEDING IT MOST, KEEPING THE REST ON STANDBY.
DING.
12.
THE FOREST IS A DARK TANGLE, CROWDING UP TO THE RIVER'S EDGE.
...THE BOAT IS COMFORTABLE AND HE DOZES OFF TO THE ENGINE HUMMING BELOW DECK.
...IT MUST BE GOING SOMEWHERE...
THE OFFICE HAS BEEN REPLACED BY A FOREST.
4
THE BOW NOSES INTO THE CURRENT, MAKING NO SOUND.
4
HE WOKE UP WITH A START TO A GROWING ROAR.
THE LIGHT WAS GETTING DIM.
ALL AROUND HIM TREES RISE UP.
...BUT THERE WAS NO ONE ON BOARD...
THERE IS NO BREEZE.
HE SEES NO BIRDS OR ANY KIND OF ANIMAL.
15.
THE INNER DIRECTORATE THAT OPERATES THE PLAN FUNCTIONS AS A DEEP STATE WITHIN THE GOVERNANCE STRUCTURE OF THE SEPARATE HOLDING COMPANIES. THIS PROVIDES AN INVISIBLE THREAD OF CONNECTION TO THE OPERATION.
16.

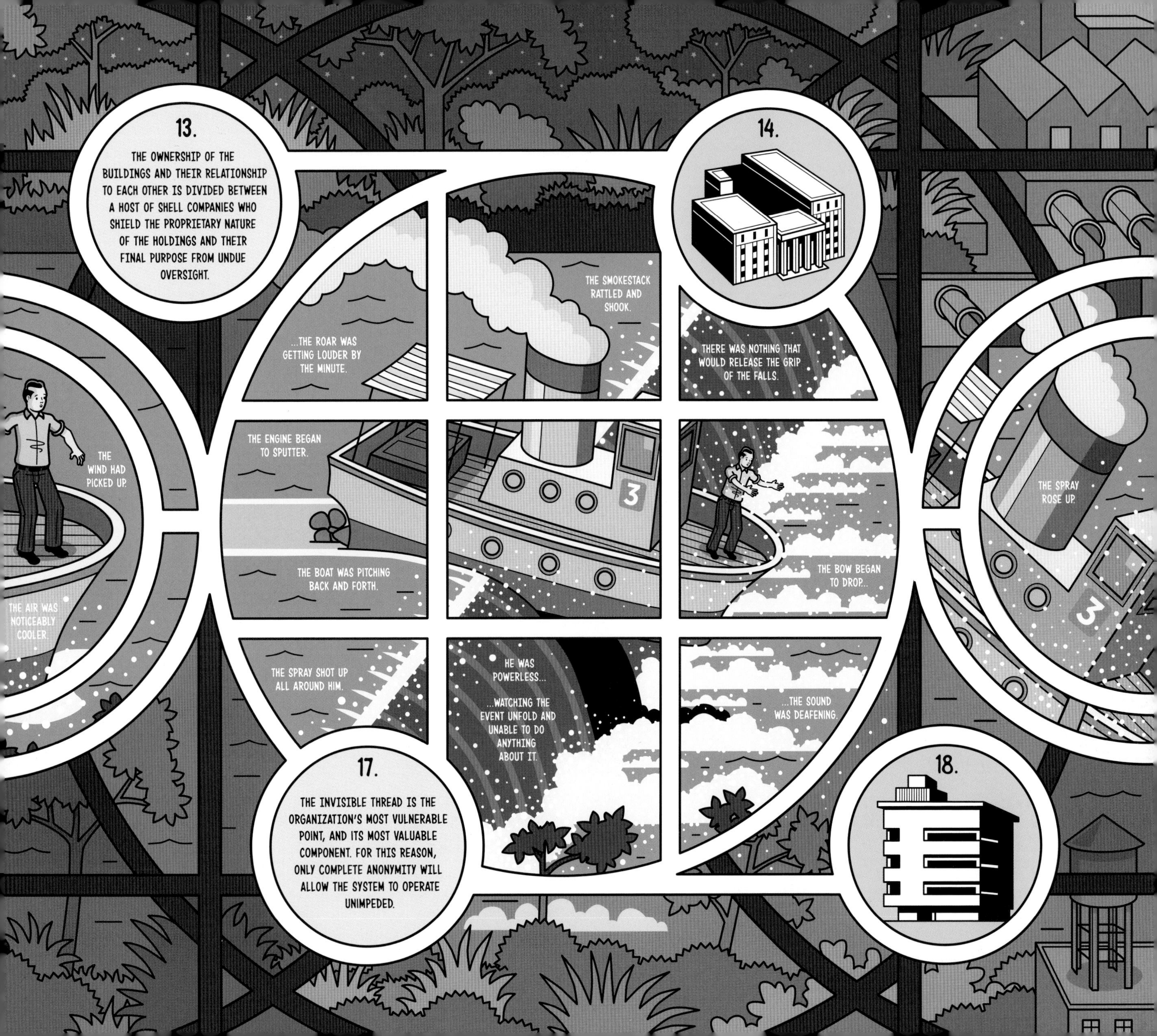
13.
THE OWNERSHIP OF THE BUILDINGS AND THEIR RELATIONSHIP TO EACH OTHER IS DIVIDED BETWEEN A HOST OF SHELL COMPANIES WHO SHIELD THE PROPRIETARY NATURE OF THE HOLDINGS AND THEIR FINAL PURPOSE FROM UNDUE OVERSIGHT.
14.
THE WIND HAD PICKED UP.
THE AIR WAS NOTICEABLY COOLER.
...THE ROAR WAS GETTING LOUDER BY THE MINUTE.
THE SMOKESTACK RATTLED AND SHOOK.
THERE WAS NOTHING THAT WOULD RELEASE THE GRIP OF THE FALLS.
THE ENGINE BEGAN TO SPUTTER.
THE BOAT WAS PITCHING BACK AND FORTH.
3
THE BOW BEGAN TO DROP...
THE SPRAY ROSE UP.
3
THE SPRAY SHOT UP ALL AROUND HIM.
HE WAS POWERLESS...
...WATCHING THE EVENT UNFOLD AND UNABLE TO DO ANYTHING ABOUT IT.
...THE SOUND WAS DEAFENING.
17.
THE INVISIBLE THREAD IS THE ORGANIZATION'S MOST VULNERABLE POINT, AND ITS MOST VALUABLE COMPONENT. FOR THIS REASON, ONLY COMPLETE ANONYMITY WILL ALLOW THE SYSTEM TO OPERATE UNIMPEDED.
18.

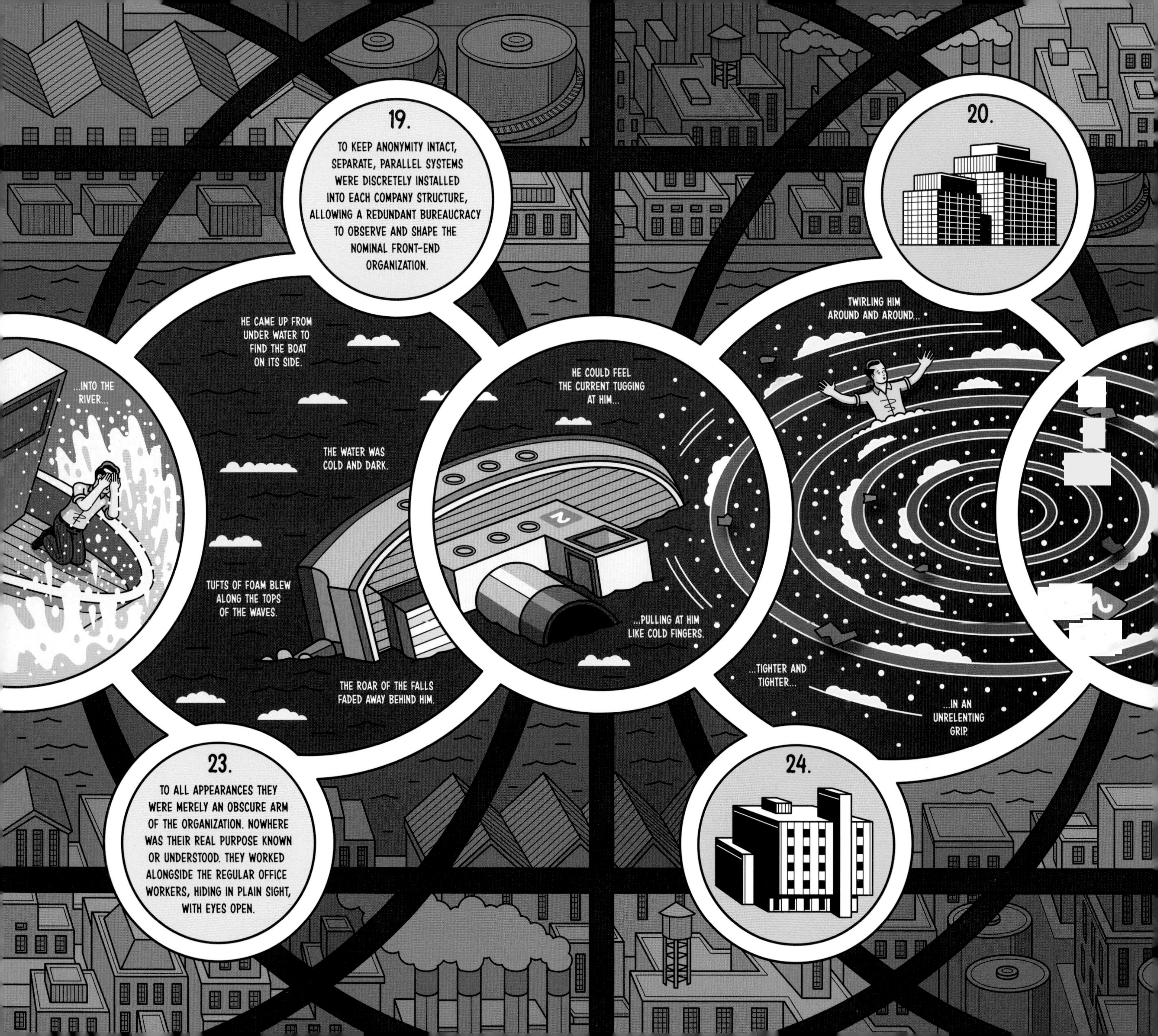
19.
TO KEEP ANONYMITY INTACT, SEPARATE, PARALLEL SYSTEMS WERE DISCRETELY INSTALLED INTO EACH COMPANY STRUCTURE, ALLOWING A REDUNDANT BUREAUCRACY TO OBSERVE AND SHAPE THE NOMINAL FRONT-END ORGANIZATION.
20.
...INTO THE RIVER...
HE CAME UP FROM UNDER WATER TO FIND THE BOAT ON ITS SIDE.
THE WATER WAS COLD AND DARK.
TUFTS OF FOAM BLEW ALONG THE TOPS OF THE WAVES.
THE ROAR OF THE FALLS FADED AWAY BEHIND HIM.
HE COULD FEEL THE CURRENT TUGGING AT HIM...
...PULLING AT HIM LIKE COLD FINGERS.
TWIRLING HIM AROUND AND AROUND...
...TIGHTER AND TIGHTER...
...IN AN UNRELENTING GRIP.
23.
TO ALL APPEARANCES THEY WERE MERELY AN OBSCURE ARM OF THE ORGANIZATION. NOWHERE WAS THEIR REAL PURPOSE KNOWN OR UNDERSTOOD. THEY WORKED ALONGSIDE THE REGULAR OFFICE WORKERS, HIDING IN PLAIN SIGHT, WITH EYES OPEN.
24.

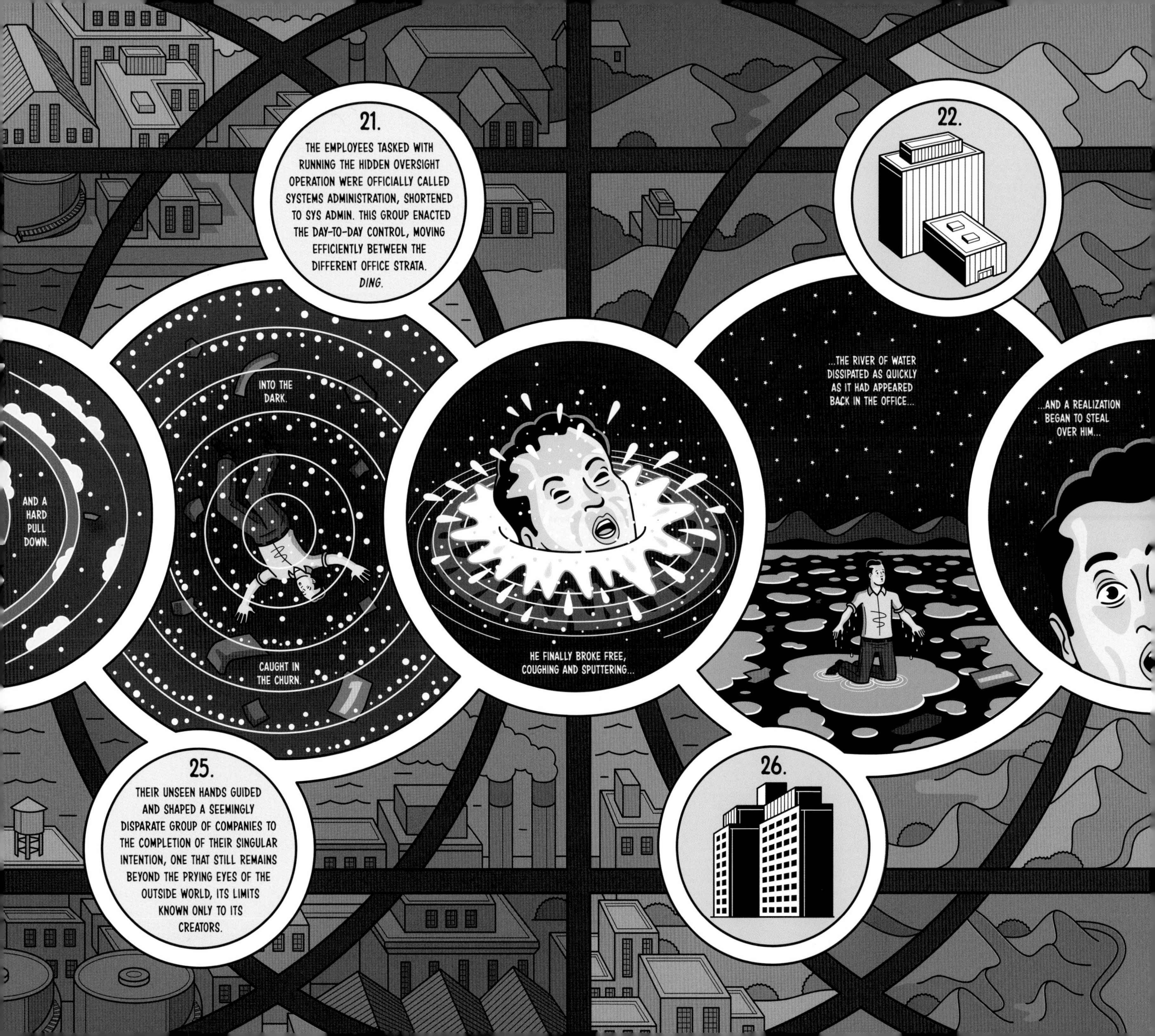
21.
THE EMPLOYEES TASKED WITH RUNNING THE HIDDEN OVERSIGHT OPERATION WERE OFFICIALLY CALLED SYSTEMS ADMINISTRATION, SHORTENED TO SYS ADMIN. THIS GROUP ENACTED THE DAY-TO-DAY CONTROL, MOVING EFFICIENTLY BETWEEN THE DIFFERENT OFFICE STRATA.
DING.
22.
AND A HARD PULL DOWN.
INTO THE DARK.
CAUGHT IN THE CHURN.
HE FINALLY BROKE FREE, COUGHING AND SPUTTERING...
...THE RIVER OF WATER DISSIPATED AS QUICKLY AS IT HAD APPEARED BACK IN THE OFFICE...
...AND A REALIZATION BEGAN TO STEAL OVER HIM...
25.
THEIR UNSEEN HANDS GUIDED AND SHAPED A SEEMINGLY DISPARATE GROUP OF COMPANIES TO THE COMPLETION OF THEIR SINGULAR INTENTION, ONE THAT STILL REMAINS BEYOND THE PRYING EYES OF THE OUTSIDE WORLD, ITS LIMITS KNOWN ONLY TO ITS CREATORS.
26.

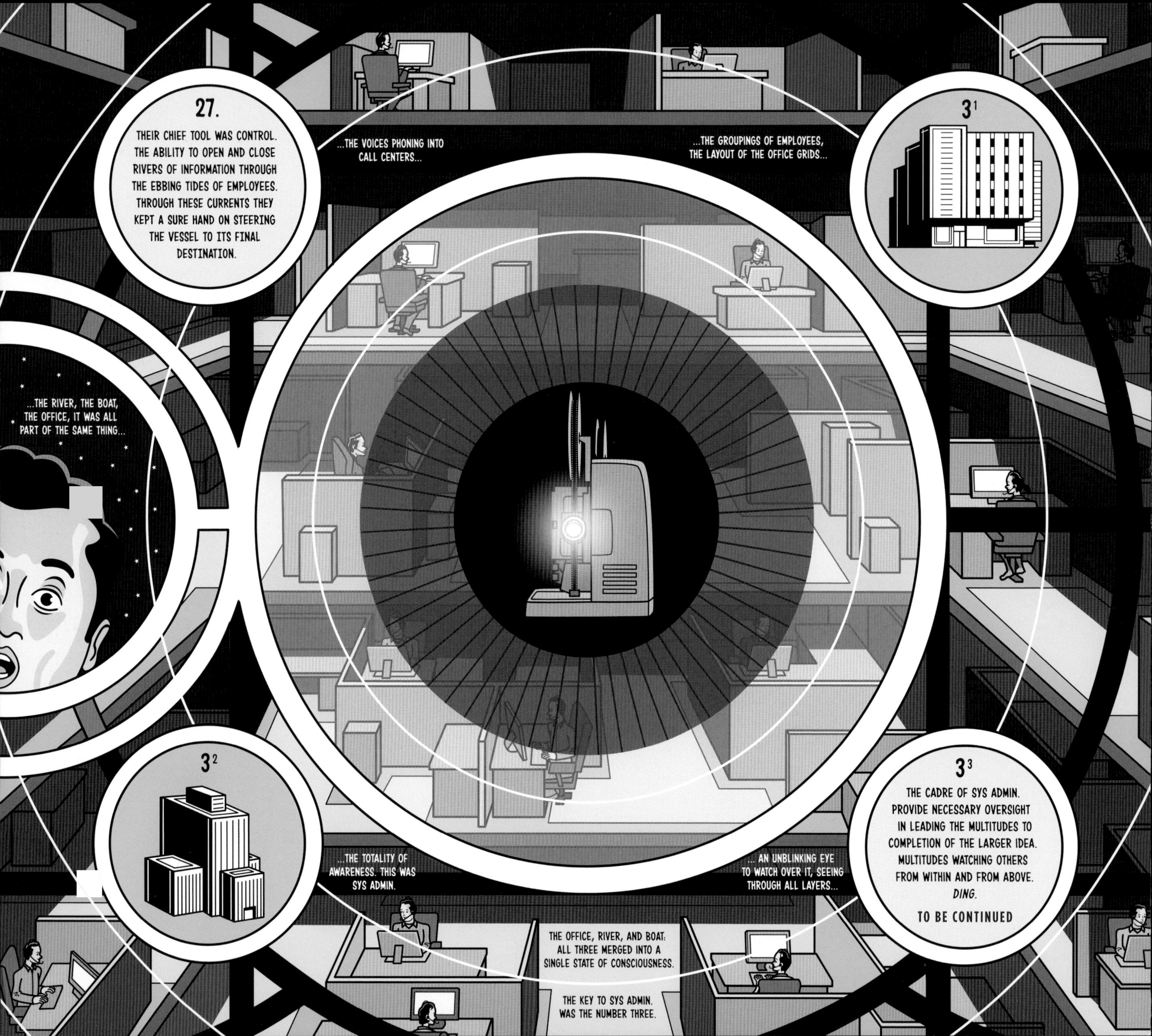
27.
THEIR CHIEF TOOL WAS CONTROL. THE ABILITY TO OPEN AND CLOSE RIVERS OF INFORMATION THROUGH THE EBBING TIDES OF EMPLOYEES. THROUGH THESE CURRENTS THEY KEPT A SURE HAND ON STEERING THE VESSEL TO ITS FINAL DESTINATION.
...THE VOICES PHONING INTO CALL CENTERS...
...THE GROUPINGS OF EMPLOYEES, THE LAYOUT OF THE OFFICE GRIDS...
3^1
...THE RIVER, THE BOAT, THE OFFICE, IT WAS ALL PART OF THE SAME THING...
3^2
...THE TOTALITY OF AWARENESS. THIS WAS SYS ADMIN.
... AN UNBLINKING EYE TO WATCH OVER IT, SEEING THROUGH ALL LAYERS...
3^3
THE CADRE OF SYS ADMIN. PROVIDE NECESSARY OVERSIGHT IN LEADING THE MULTITUDES TO COMPLETION OF THE LARGER IDEA. MULTITUDES WATCHING OTHERS FROM WITHIN AND FROM ABOVE.
DING.
TO BE CONTINUED
THE OFFICE, RIVER, AND BOAT: ALL THREE MERGED INTO A SINGLE STATE OF CONSCIOUSNESS.
THE KEY TO SYS ADMIN. WAS THE NUMBER THREE.

The Sad, Sad Story of

SALTZ & PEPZ

EMBEDDED ON THE SURFACE OF A VIDEO CASSETTE TAPE, SALTZ AND PEPZ CRANK A HANDCAR ALONG AN ENDLESS RIBBON OF RAILWAY TRACK. ON EITHER SIDE, A VAST, EMPTY LANDSCAPE STRETCHES TO THE HORIZON.

"NOW AVAILABLE ON VHS"

THEY SPRING TO LIFE WHENEVER THE VCR SWITCHES ON PLAY. THEIR ACTIONS ARE CONTROLLED BY A REMOTE THEY HAVE NEVER SEEN. EVERY TIME THE VIDEO IS PLAYED THOUGH, A LITTLE MORE OF THE MAGNITIZED TAPE WEARS OFF...

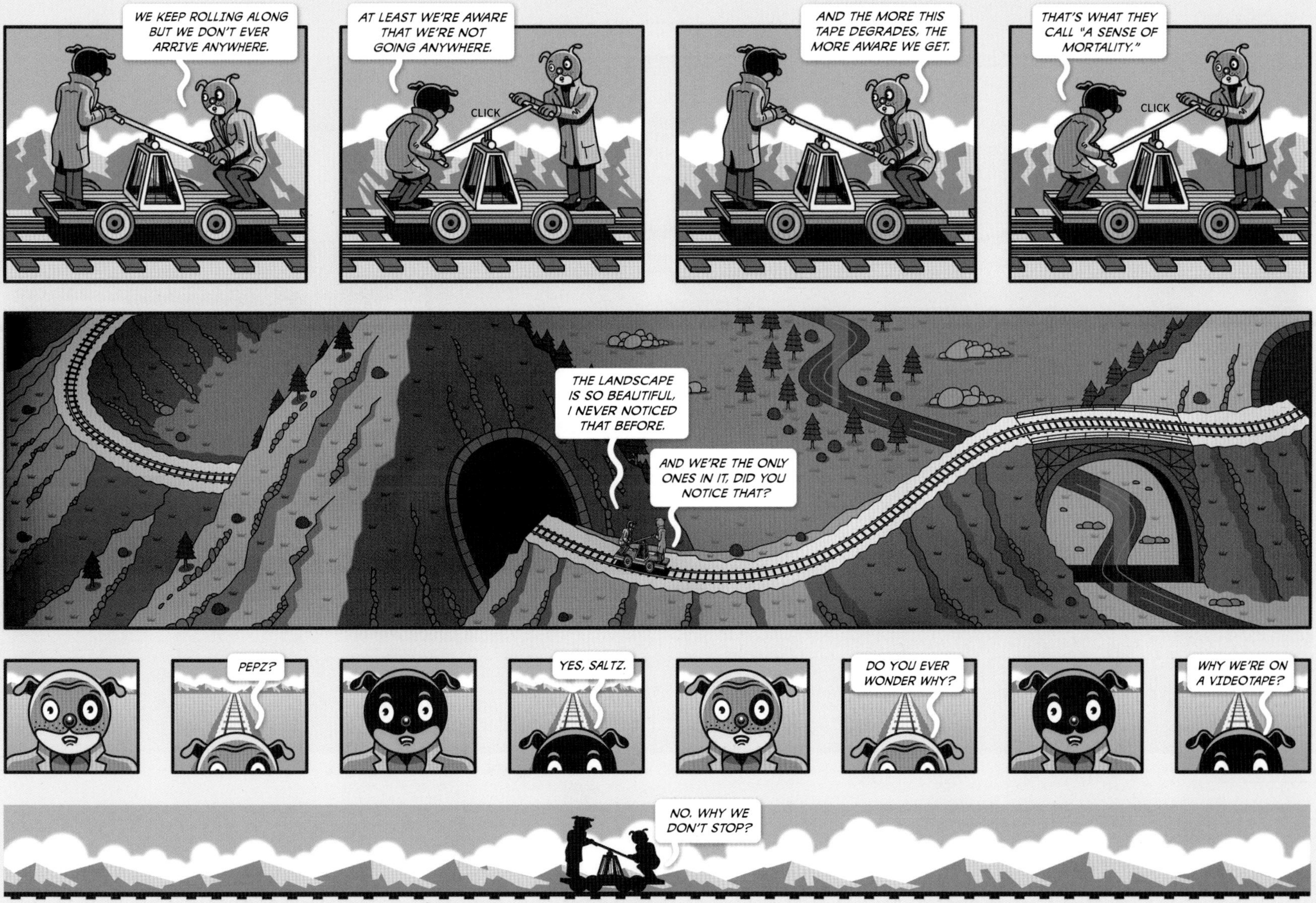
WE KEEP ROLLING ALONG BUT WE DON'T EVER ARRIVE ANYWHERE.
AT LEAST WE'RE AWARE THAT WE'RE NOT GOING ANYWHERE.
CLICK
AND THE MORE THIS TAPE DEGRADES, THE MORE AWARE WE GET.
THAT'S WHAT THEY CALL "A SENSE OF MORTALITY."
CLICK
THE LANDSCAPE IS SO BEAUTIFUL, I NEVER NOTICED THAT BEFORE.
AND WE'RE THE ONLY ONES IN IT, DID YOU NOTICE THAT?
PEPZ?
YES, SALTZ.
DO YOU EVER WONDER WHY?
WHY WE'RE ON A VIDEOTAPE?
NO. WHY WE DON'T STOP?

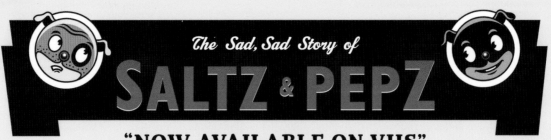

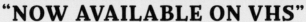

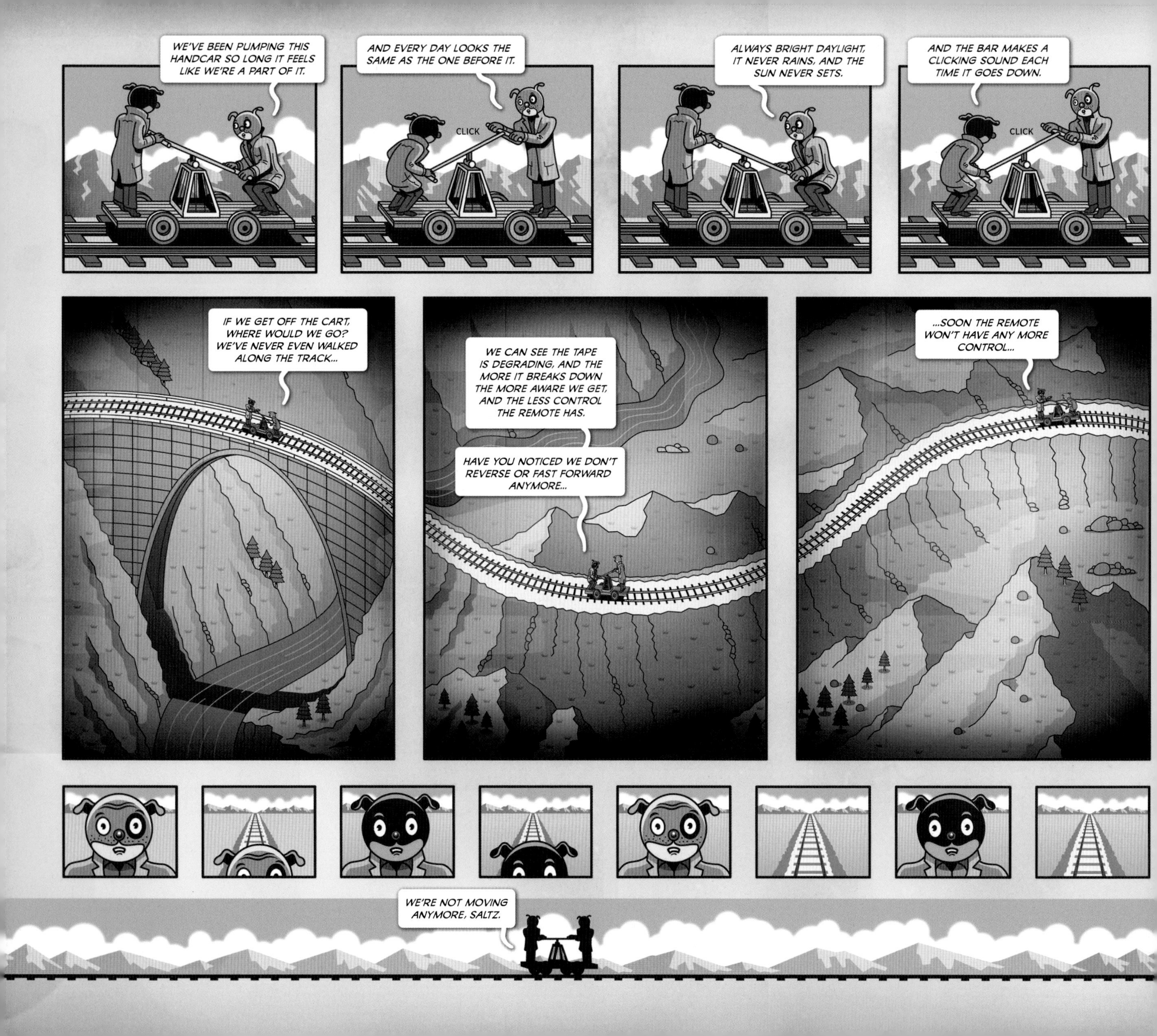
WE'VE BEEN PUMPING THIS HANDCAR SO LONG IT FEELS LIKE WE'RE A PART OF IT.
AND EVERY DAY LOOKS THE SAME AS THE ONE BEFORE IT.
CLICK
ALWAYS BRIGHT DAYLIGHT, IT NEVER RAINS, AND THE SUN NEVER SETS.
AND THE BAR MAKES A CLICKING SOUND EACH TIME IT GOES DOWN.
CLICK
IF WE GET OFF THE CART, WHERE WOULD WE GO? WE'VE NEVER EVEN WALKED ALONG THE TRACK...
WE CAN SEE THE TAPE IS DEGRADING, AND THE MORE IT BREAKS DOWN THE MORE AWARE WE GET, AND THE LESS CONTROL THE REMOTE HAS.
HAVE YOU NOTICED WE DON'T REVERSE OR FAST FORWARD ANYMORE...
...SOON THE REMOTE WON'T HAVE ANY MORE CONTROL...
WE'RE NOT MOVING ANYMORE, SALTZ.

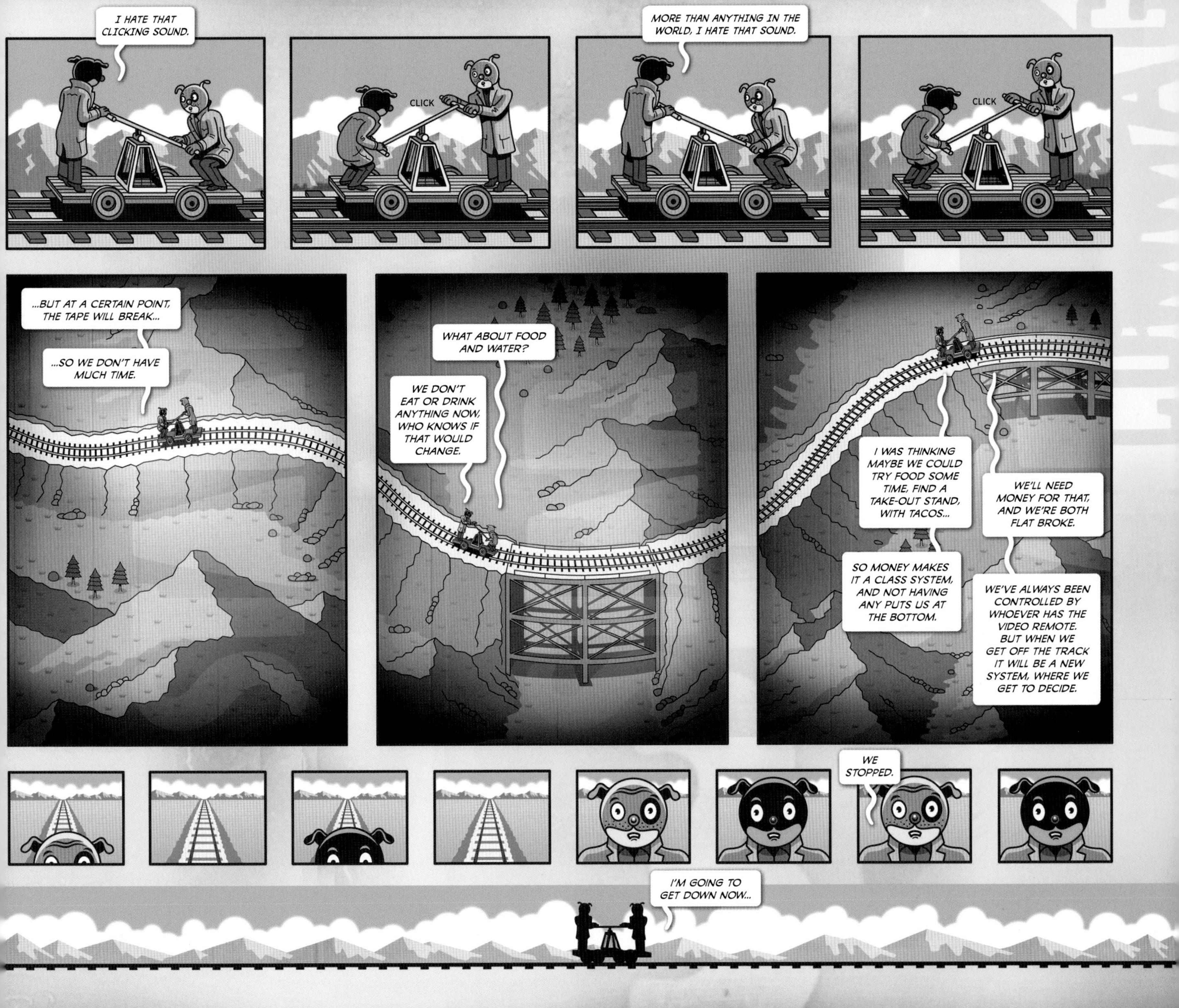
I HATE THAT CLICKING SOUND.
CLICK
MORE THAN ANYTHING IN THE WORLD, I HATE THAT SOUND.
CLICK
...BUT AT A CERTAIN POINT, THE TAPE WILL BREAK...
...SO WE DON'T HAVE MUCH TIME.
WHAT ABOUT FOOD AND WATER?
WE DON'T EAT OR DRINK ANYTHING NOW, WHO KNOWS IF THAT WOULD CHANGE.
I WAS THINKING MAYBE WE COULD TRY FOOD SOME TIME, FIND A TAKE-OUT STAND, WITH TACOS...
WE'LL NEED MONEY FOR THAT, AND WE'RE BOTH FLAT BROKE.
SO MONEY MAKES IT A CLASS SYSTEM, AND NOT HAVING ANY PUTS US AT THE BOTTOM.
WE'VE ALWAYS BEEN CONTROLLED BY WHOEVER HAS THE VIDEO REMOTE. BUT WHEN WE GET OFF THE TRACK IT WILL BE A NEW SYSTEM, WHERE WE GET TO DECIDE.
WE STOPPED.
I'M GOING TO GET DOWN NOW...

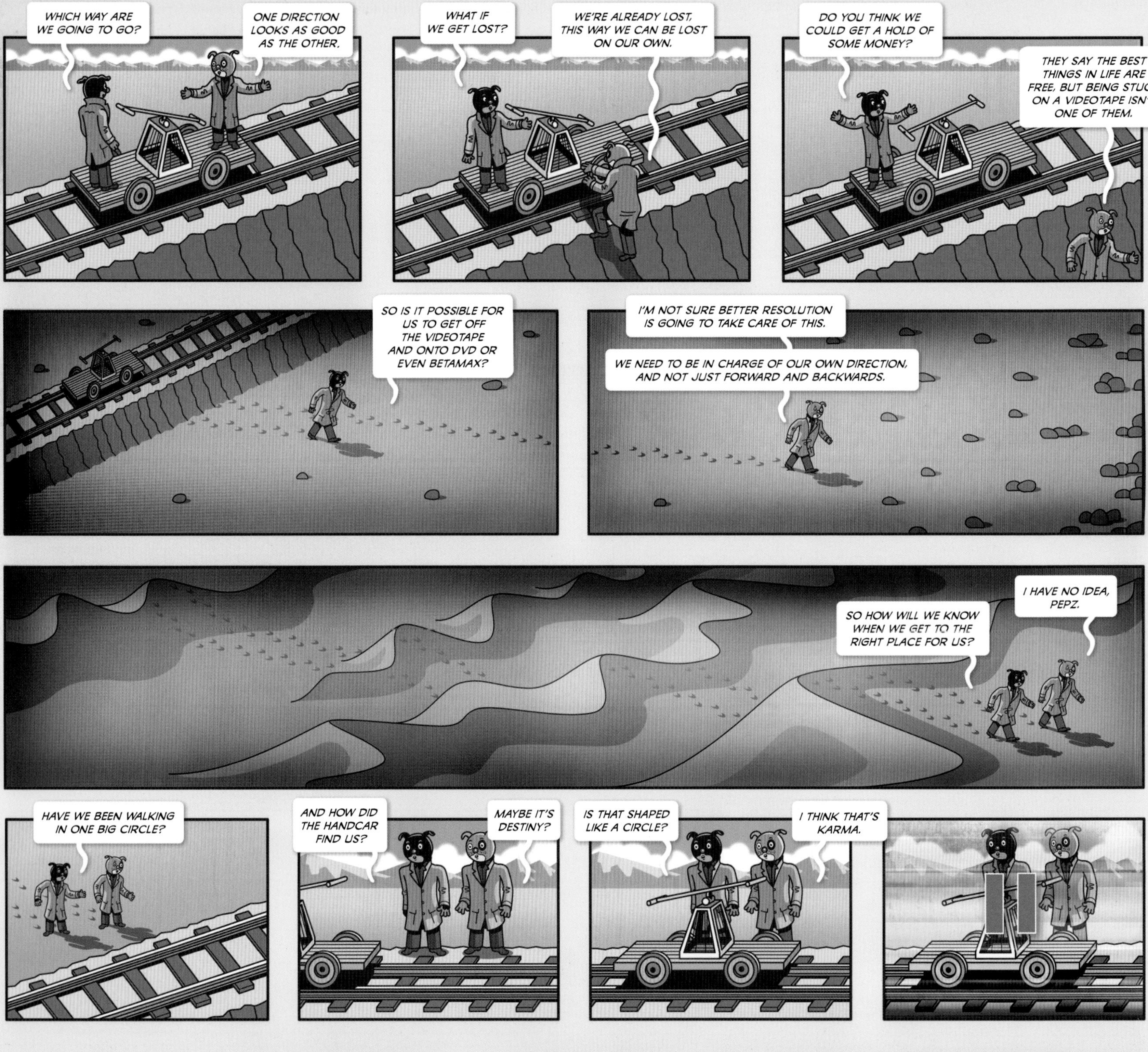
WHICH WAY ARE WE GOING TO GO?
ONE DIRECTION LOOKS AS GOOD AS THE OTHER.
WHAT IF WE GET LOST?
WE'RE ALREADY LOST, THIS WAY WE CAN BE LOST ON OUR OWN.
DO YOU THINK WE COULD GET A HOLD OF SOME MONEY?
THEY SAY THE BEST THINGS IN LIFE ARE FREE, BUT BEING STUCK ON A VIDEOTAPE ISN'T ONE OF THEM.
SO IS IT POSSIBLE FOR US TO GET OFF THE VIDEOTAPE AND ONTO DVD OR EVEN BETAMAX?
I'M NOT SURE BETTER RESOLUTION IS GOING TO TAKE CARE OF THIS.
WE NEED TO BE IN CHARGE OF OUR OWN DIRECTION, AND NOT JUST FORWARD AND BACKWARDS.
SO HOW WILL WE KNOW WHEN WE GET TO THE RIGHT PLACE FOR US?
I HAVE NO IDEA, PEPZ.
HAVE WE BEEN WALKING IN ONE BIG CIRCLE?
AND HOW DID THE HANDCAR FIND US?
MAYBE IT'S DESTINY?
IS THAT SHAPED LIKE A CIRCLE?
I THINK THAT'S KARMA.

UNE LUNE ANDALOUSE

(An Andalusian Moon)

BACK IN 1928, LUIS BUNUEL AND HIS FRIEND SALVADOR DALI, A COUPLE OF SPANISH GUYS WITH MOONLIT IMAGINATIONS, MADE A LITTLE FILM CALLED "UN CHIEN ANDALOU" ("AN ANDALUSIAN DOG" TO YOU). IT OFFERED DREAMLIKE VISIONS OF DEATH AND DESIRE FULL OF DISCONNECTED AND VIOLENT IMAGERY, AND WAS VERY MUCH TO MY TASTE. IT WAS SILENT, LIKE ME, EXCEPT FOR ALTERNATING TANGO AND OPERA DITTIES. THE FILM REFUSED ANY LINEAR INTERPRETATION, AND STILL DOES. I WAS ONE OF ITS STARS.

CUT TO 1954. ALFRED HITCHCOCK DIRECTS "REAR WINDOW." MORE DEATH AND MORE DESIRE, ALBEIT MORE CONVENTIONAL DEATH AND DESIRE, THIS TIME THROUGH THE VOYEURISTIC LENS EYE OF A LAID-UP PHOTOGRAPHER LOOKING OUT HIS APARTMENT WINDOW. HE SAW A LOT OF THINGS OUT OF THAT WINDOW, INCLUDING ME.

I'VE GOT A STORY TO TELL, TOO. IT BEGINS LATE AT NIGHT IN THAT SAME PHOTOGRAPHER'S SWELTERING BEDROOM. HIS NAME IS JEFF, AND HE'S BEEN AWAKENED BY TANGO MUSIC DRIFTING THROUGH HIS OPEN WINDOW, LIKE THE SOUNDTRACK FROM A DREAM HE CAN'T QUITE REMEMBER . . . .

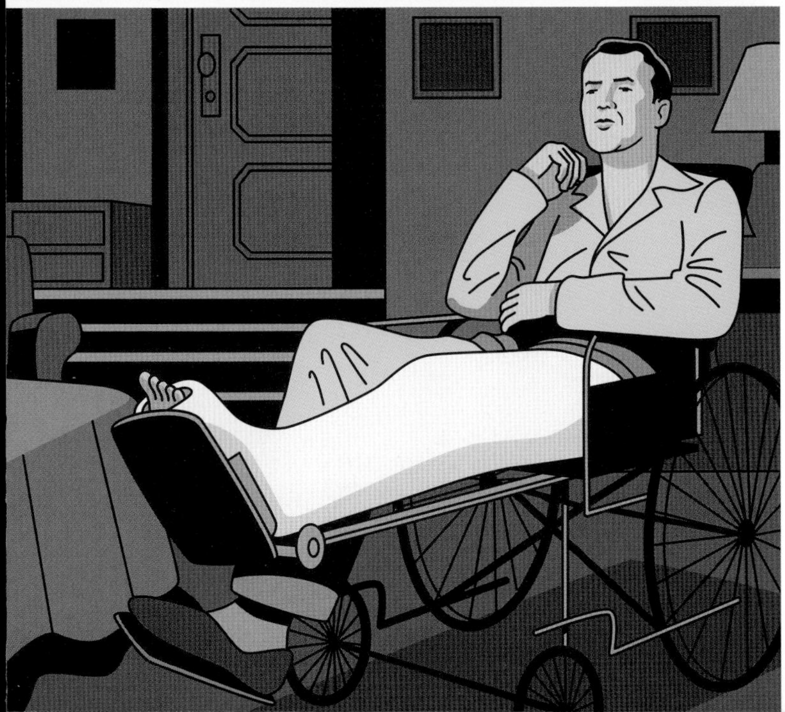

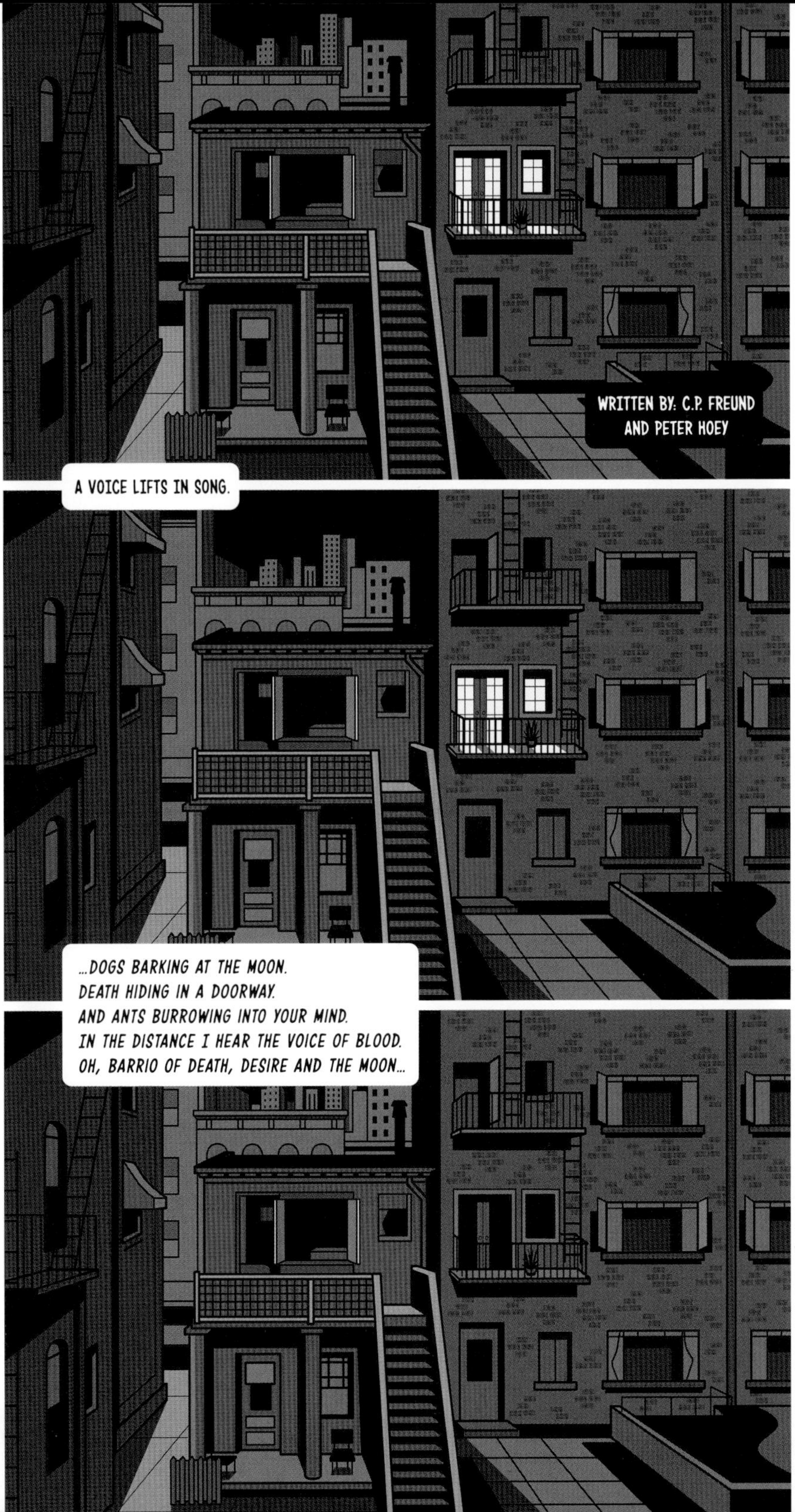
WRITTEN BY: C.P. FREUND AND PETER HOEY
A VOICE LIFTS IN SONG.
...DOGS BARKING AT THE MOON.
DEATH HIDING IN A DOORWAY.
AND ANTS BURROWING INTO YOUR MIND.
IN THE DISTANCE I HEAR THE VOICE OF BLOOD.
OH, BARRIO OF DEATH, DESIRE AND THE MOON...

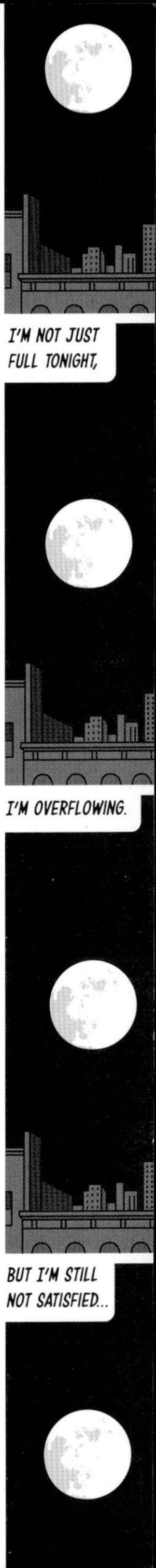
I'M NOT JUST FULL TONIGHT,
I'M OVERFLOWING.
BUT I'M STILL NOT SATISFIED...

WHO IS SINGING?

WHERE ARE YOU?

FULL MOON BUT EMPTY EYES, LUIS?

OH.

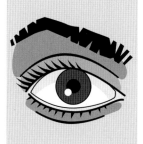

JEFF STUDIES THE SCENE AND SEES...

...A VISION? A NIGHTMARE? A SILENT FILM?

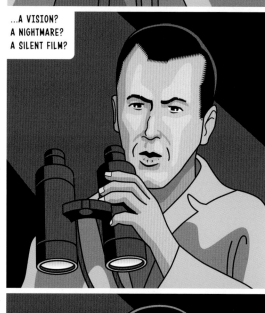

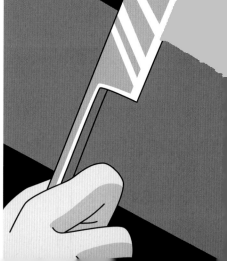

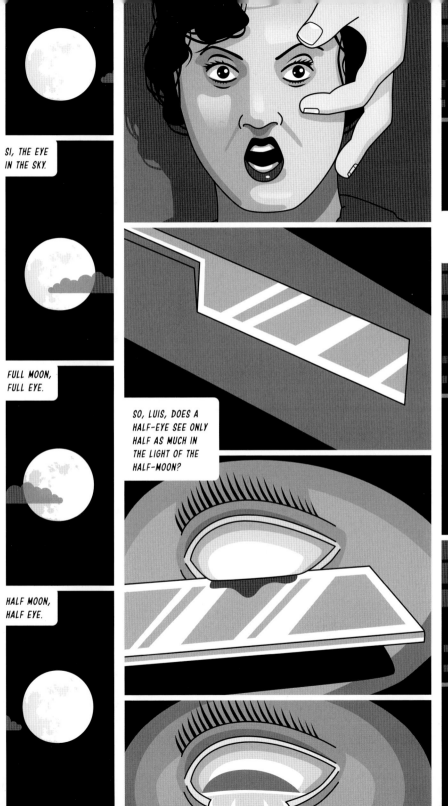

SI, THE EYE
IN THE SKY.

FULL MOON,
FULL EYE.

HALF MOON,
HALF EYE.

SO, LUIS, DOES A
HALF-EYE SEE ONLY
HALF AS MUCH IN
THE LIGHT OF THE
HALF-MOON?

...DOGS BARKING AT THE MOON.
DEATH HIDING IN A DOORWAY.
OH, BARRIO OF DEATH, DESIRE AND...

MY GOD, DID I
REALLY SEE THAT?

TWO SPANISH EYES....
STARTED AS ONE,
BUT AFTER THE FUN,
THEY'RE DOS....

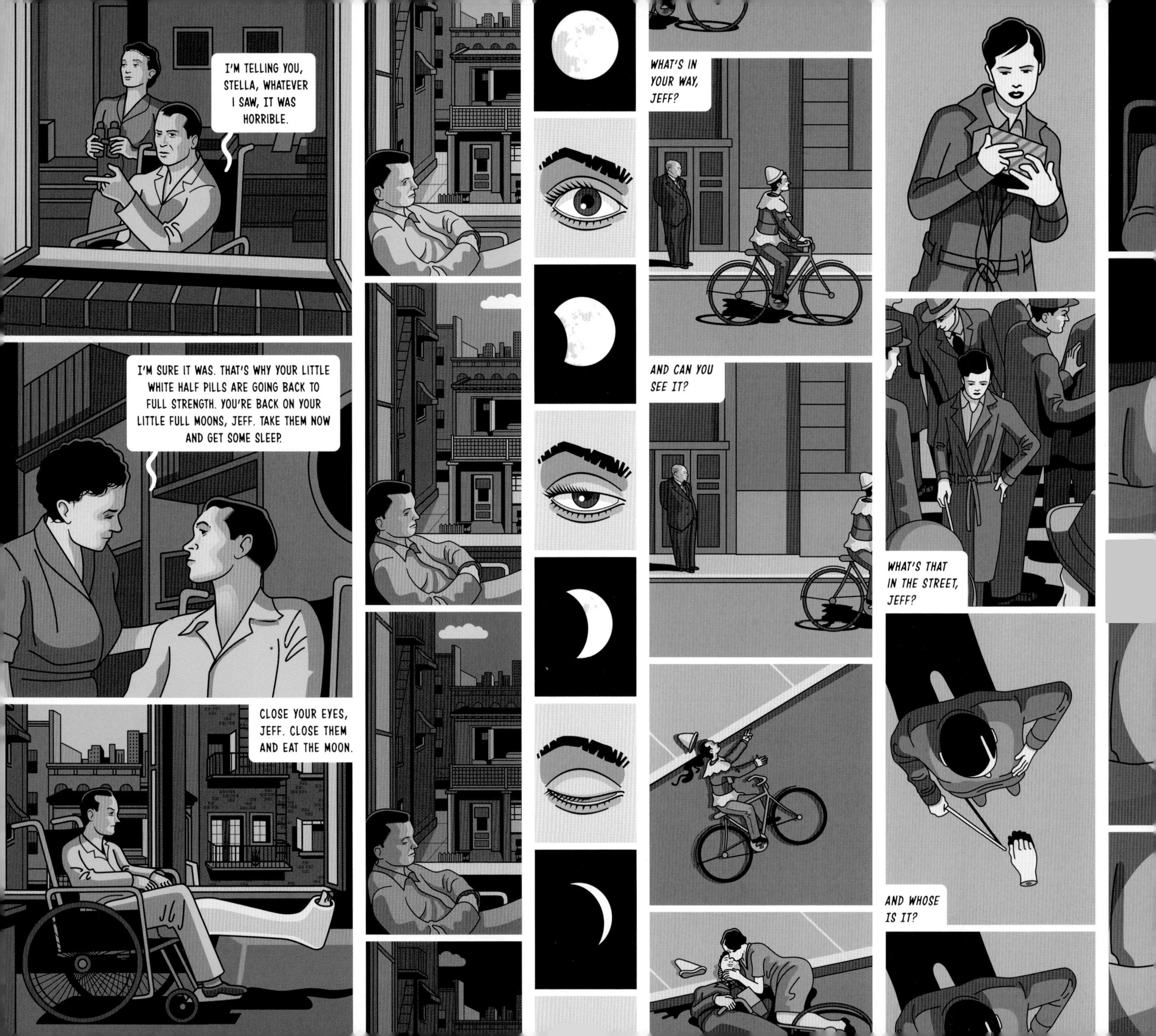
I'M TELLING YOU, STELLA, WHATEVER I SAW, IT WAS HORRIBLE.
I'M SURE IT WAS. THAT'S WHY YOUR LITTLE WHITE HALF PILLS ARE GOING BACK TO FULL STRENGTH. YOU'RE BACK ON YOUR LITTLE FULL MOONS, JEFF. TAKE THEM NOW AND GET SOME SLEEP.
CLOSE YOUR EYES, JEFF. CLOSE THEM AND EAT THE MOON.
WHAT'S IN YOUR WAY, JEFF?
AND CAN YOU SEE IT?
WHAT'S THAT IN THE STREET, JEFF?
AND WHOSE IS IT?

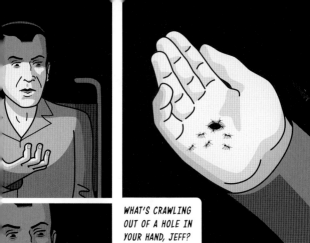

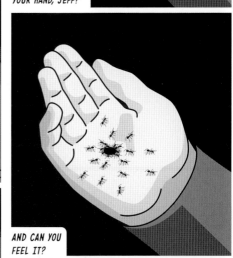

WHAT'S CRAWLING
OUT OF A HOLE IN
YOUR HAND, JEFF?

AND CAN YOU
FEEL IT?

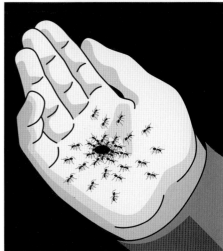

WHAT HAVE THEY
COME TO SEE, JEFF?

AND CAN YOU
GO THERE TOO?

TO SEE YOU
IS TO WOUND YOU,
AND I SEE YOU EVERYWHERE
NOT IN SUNRISE, BUT IN MOONGLOW
ANYPLACE I LOOK....

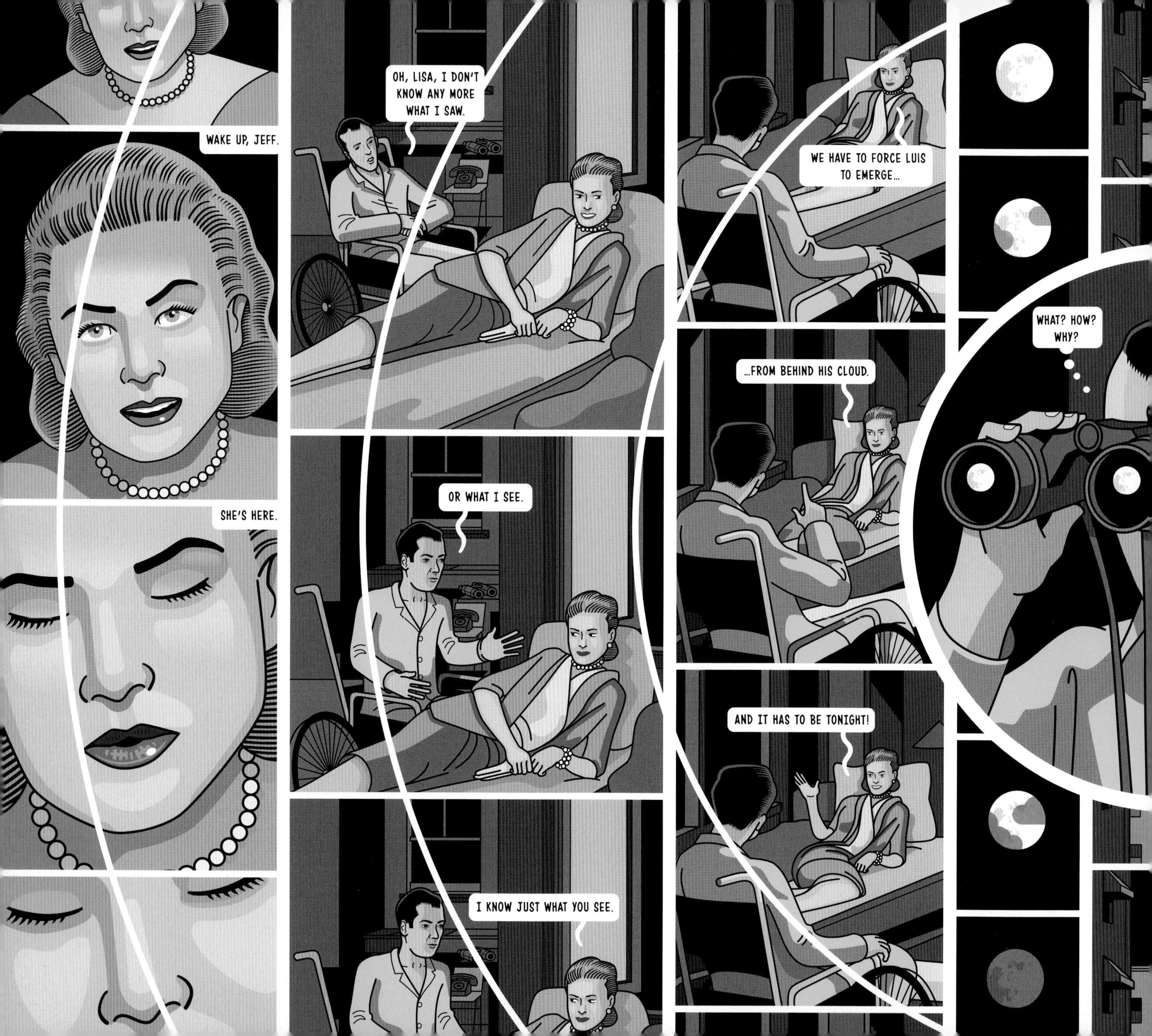
WAKE UP, JEFF.
SHE'S HERE.
OH, LISA, I DON'T KNOW ANY MORE WHAT I SAW.
OR WHAT I SEE.
I KNOW JUST WHAT YOU SEE.
WE HAVE TO FORCE LUIS TO EMERGE...
...FROM BEHIND HIS CLOUD.
AND IT HAS TO BE TONIGHT!
WHAT? HOW? WHY?

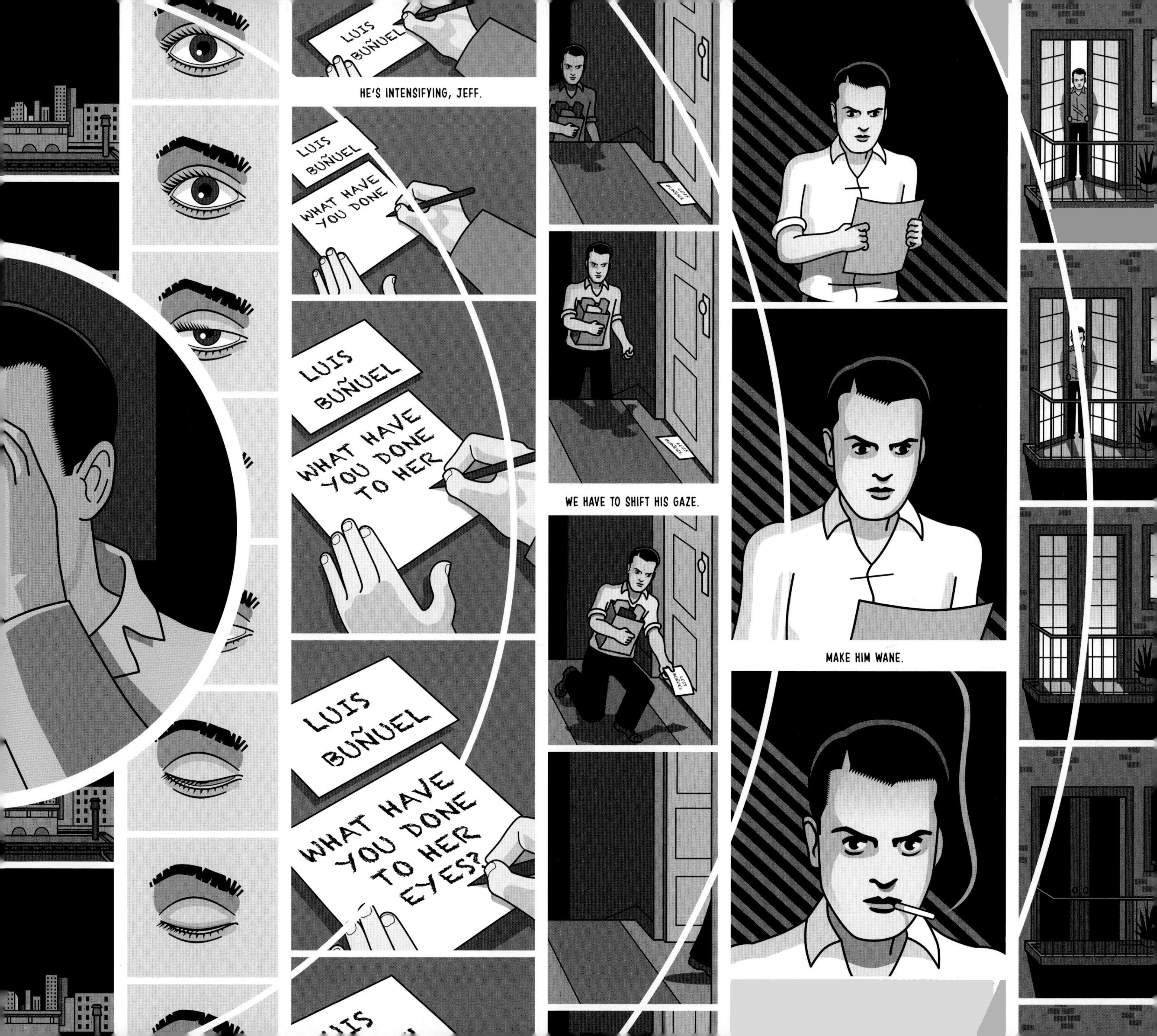

LUIS BUÑUEL
HE'S INTENSIFYING, JEFF.
LUIS BUÑUEL
WHAT HAVE YOU DONE
LUIS BUÑUEL
WHAT HAVE YOU DONE TO HER
LUIS BUÑUEL
WHAT HAVE YOU DONE TO HER EYES?
WE HAVE TO SHIFT HIS GAZE.
MAKE HIM WANE.

IT'S DANGEROUS, JEFF. IT'S HIM OR YOU!

YOU'LL HAVE TO LOOK CAREFULLY.

LOOK WITH ALL YOUR STRENGTH!

MAYBE I SHOULDN'T HAVE TAKEN THOSE PILLS TONIGHT....

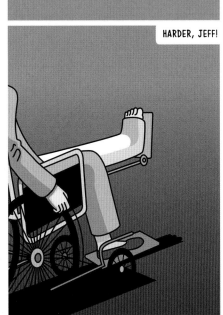

HARDER, JEFF!

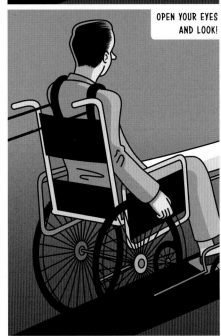

OPEN YOUR EYES AND LOOK!

WHAT DO YOU SEE?

I ... I DON'T KNOW!

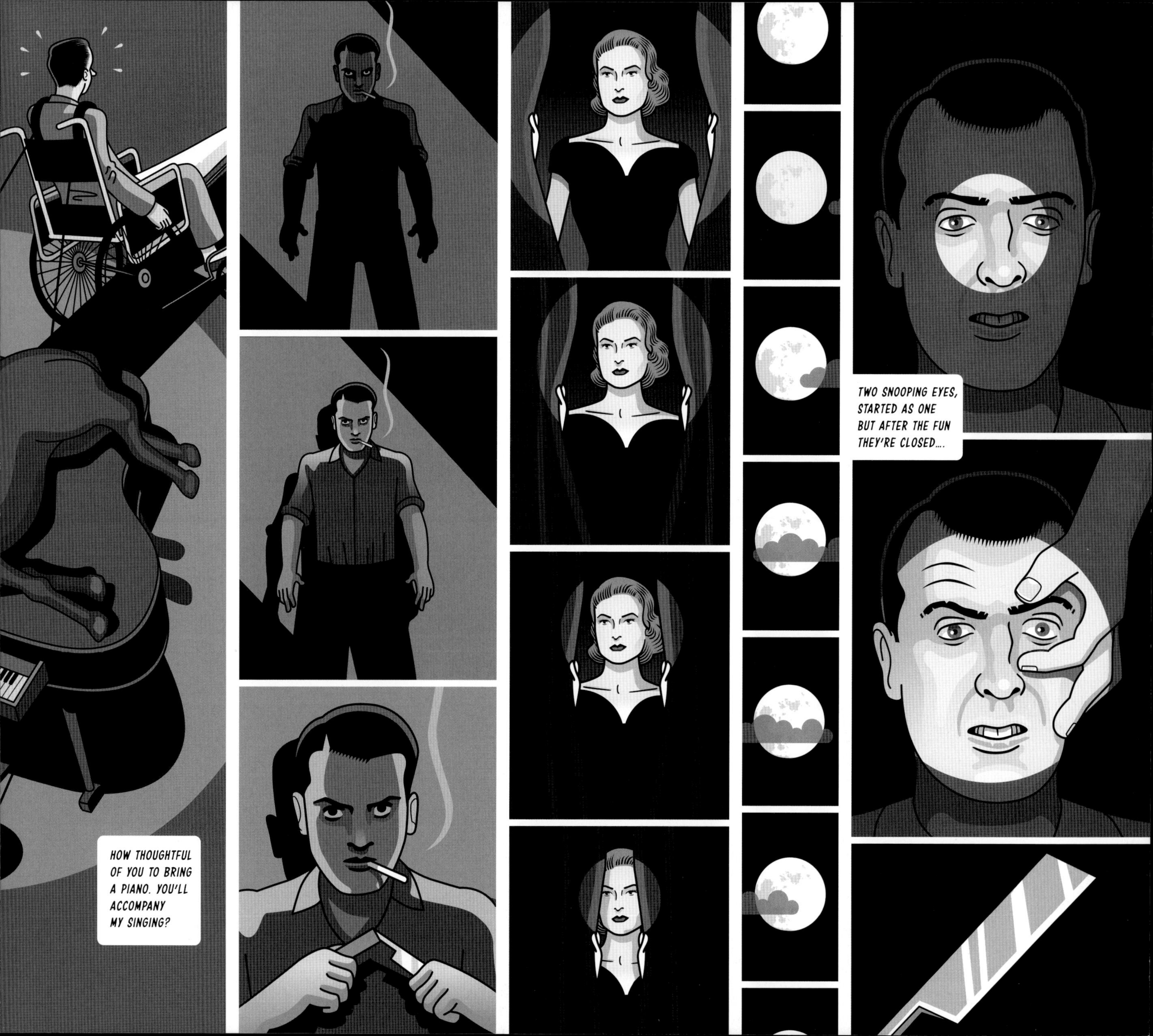
HOW THOUGHTFUL OF YOU TO BRING A PIANO. YOU'LL ACCOMPANY MY SINGING?
TWO SNOOPING EYES, STARTED AS ONE BUT AFTER THE FUN THEY'RE CLOSED....

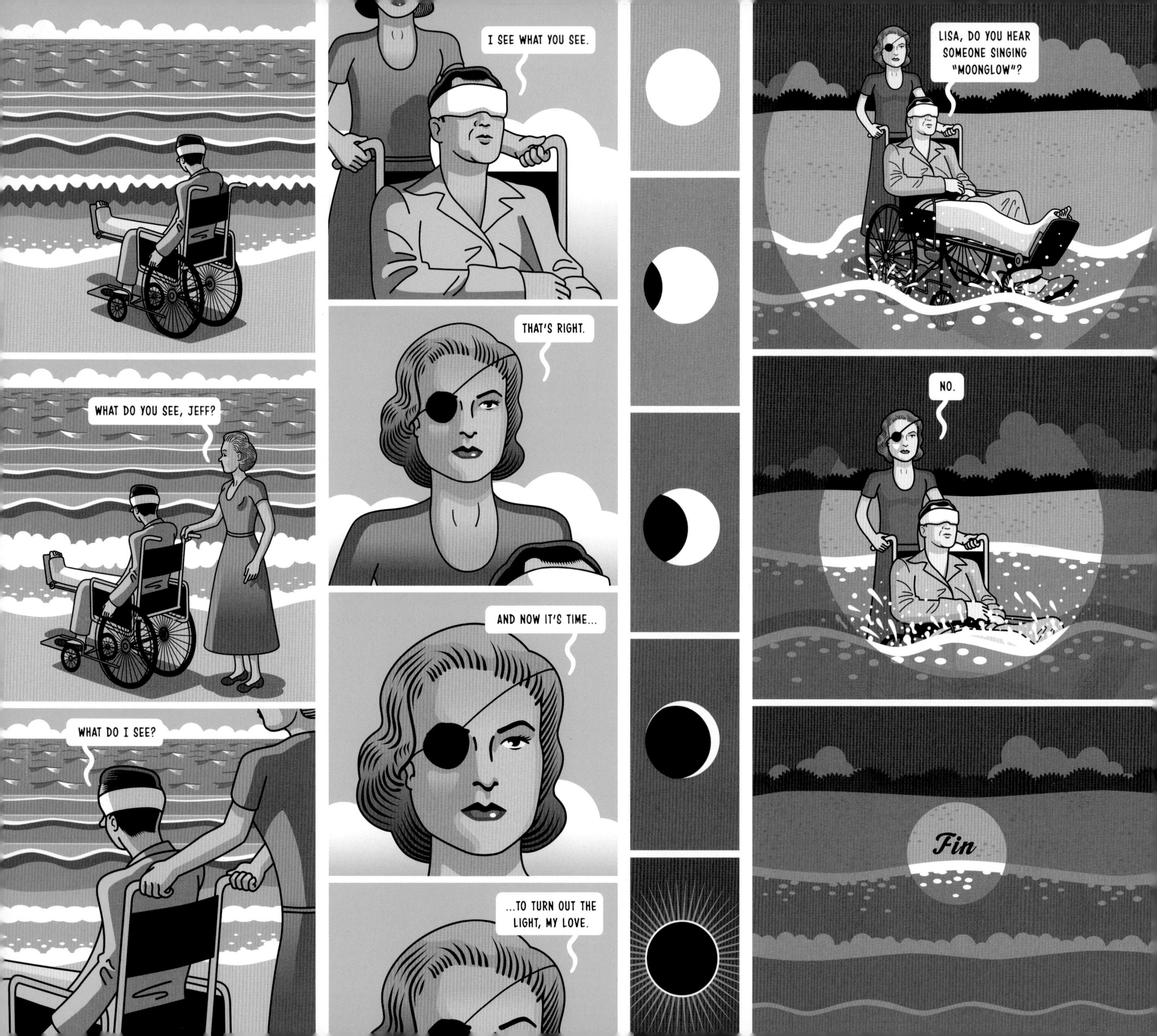
WHAT DO YOU SEE, JEFF?
WHAT DO I SEE?
I SEE WHAT YOU SEE.
THAT'S RIGHT.
AND NOW IT'S TIME...
...TO TURN OUT THE LIGHT, MY LOVE.
LISA, DO YOU HEAR SOMEONE SINGING "MOONGLOW"?
NO.
Fin

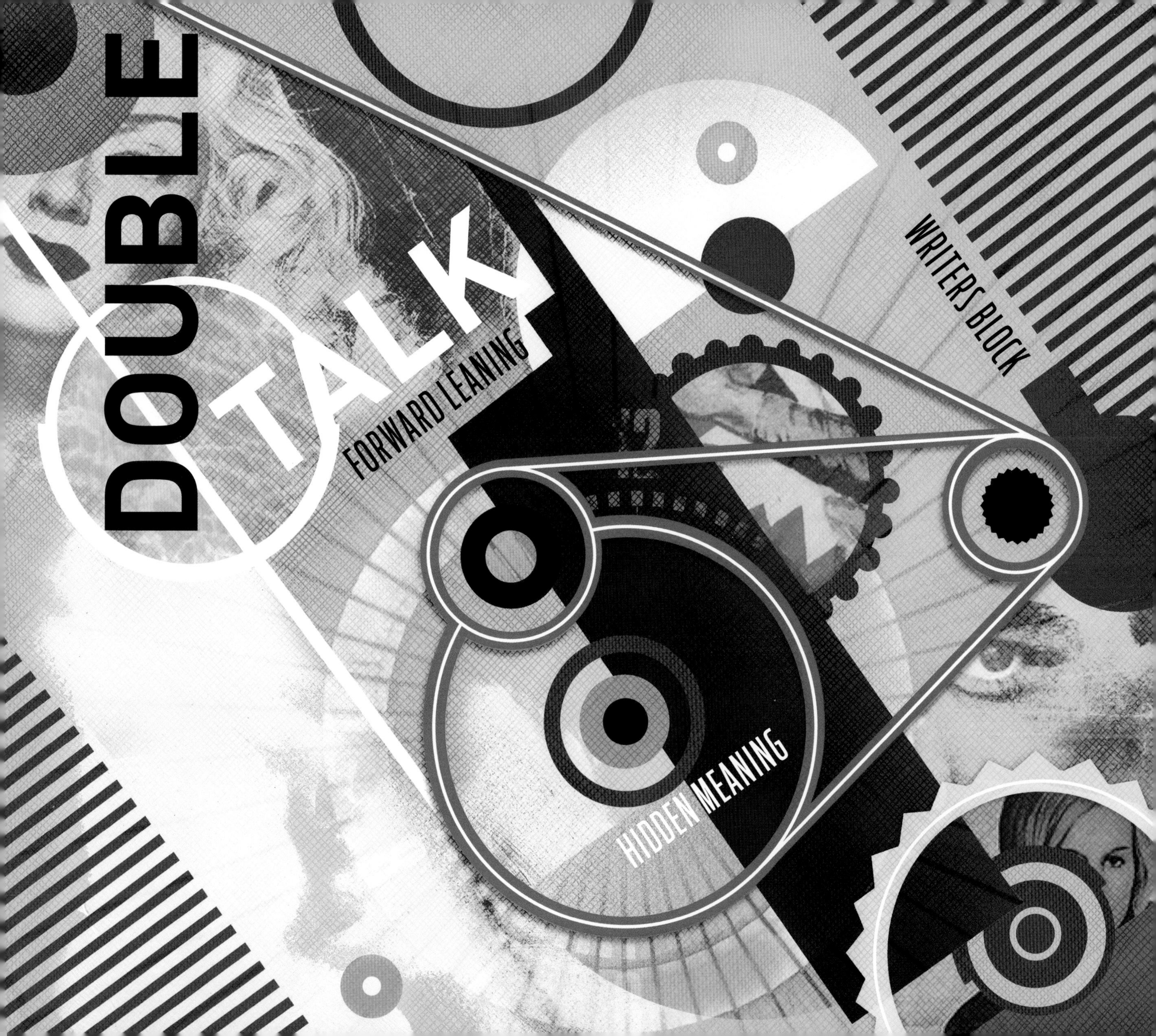
DOUBLE
TALK
FORWARD LEANING
WRITERS BLOCK
HIDDEN MEANING

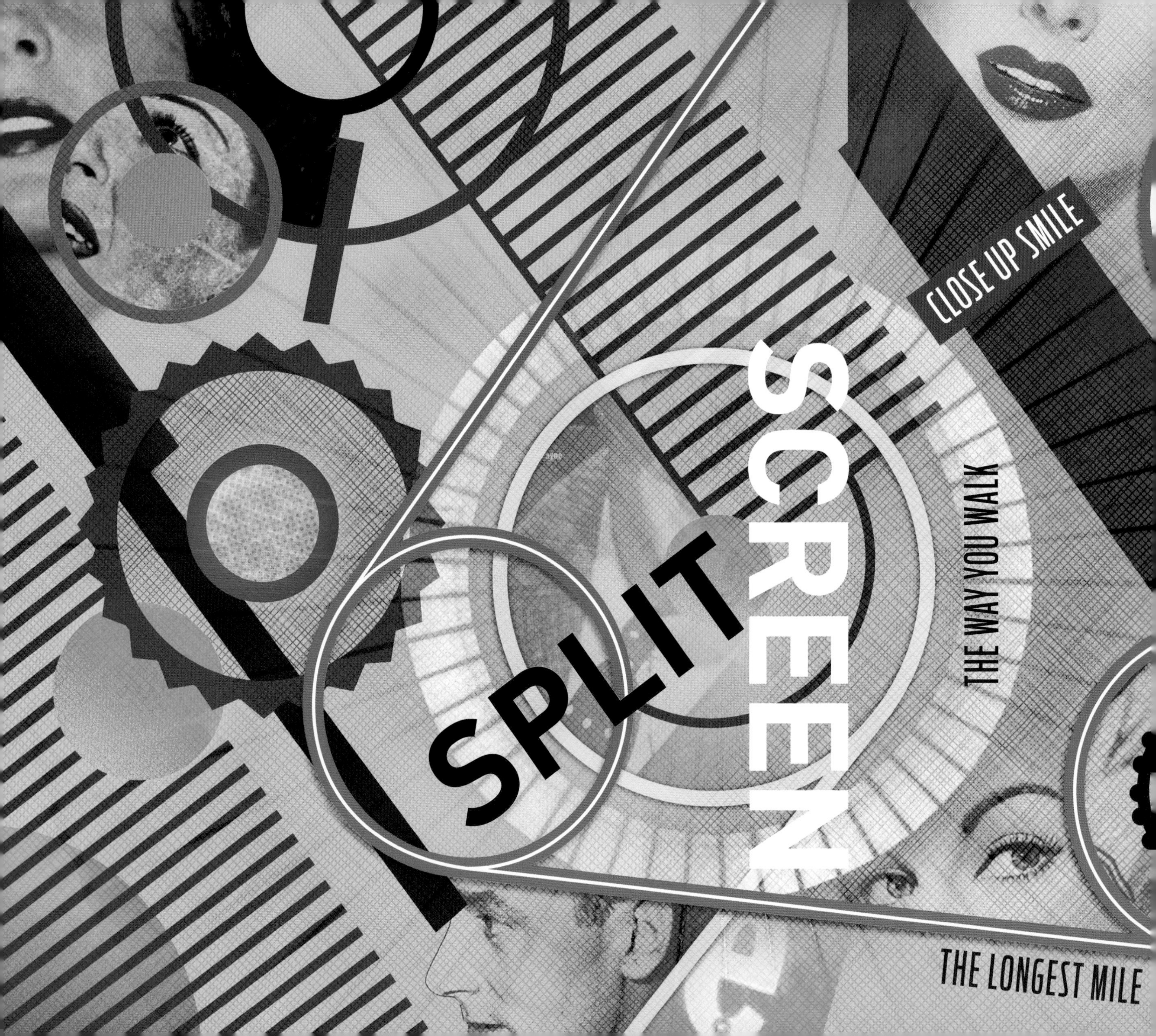

SPLIT
SCREEN
CLOSE UP SMILE
THE WAY YOU WALK
THE LONGEST MILE

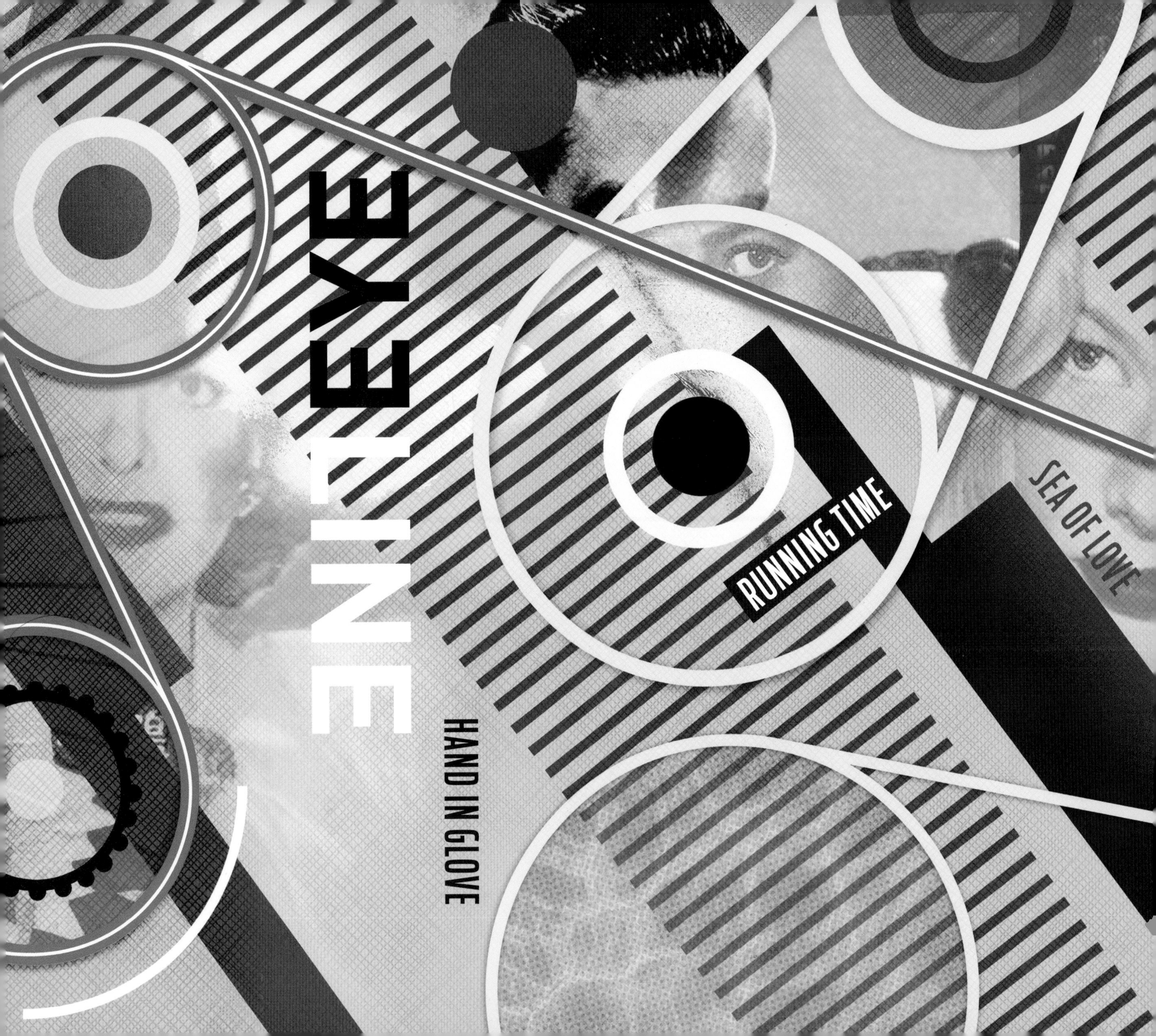
EYE LINE
HAND IN GLOVE
RUNNING TIME
SEA OF LOVE

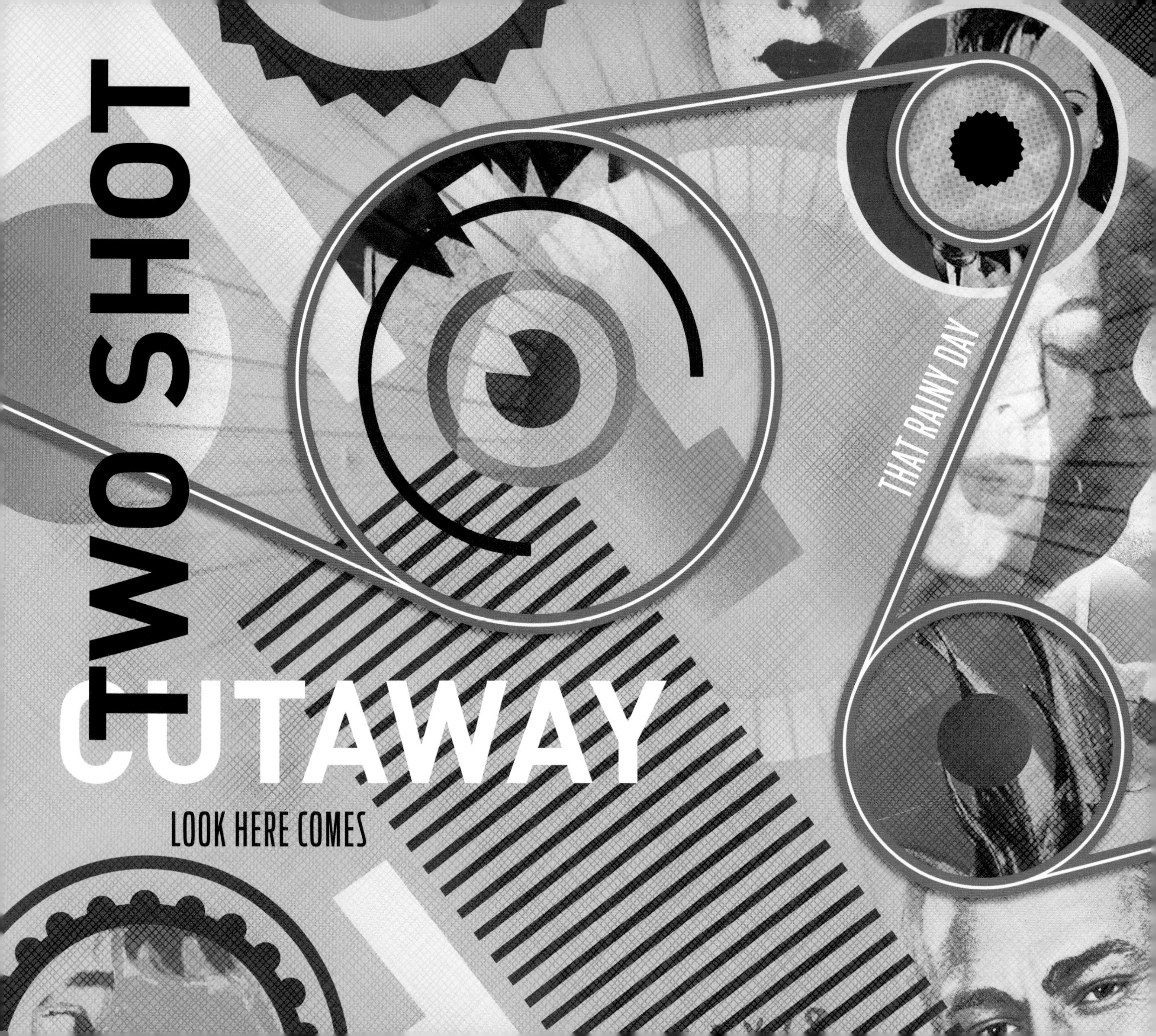

TWO SHOT
CUTAWAY
LOOK HERE COMES
THAT RAINY DAY

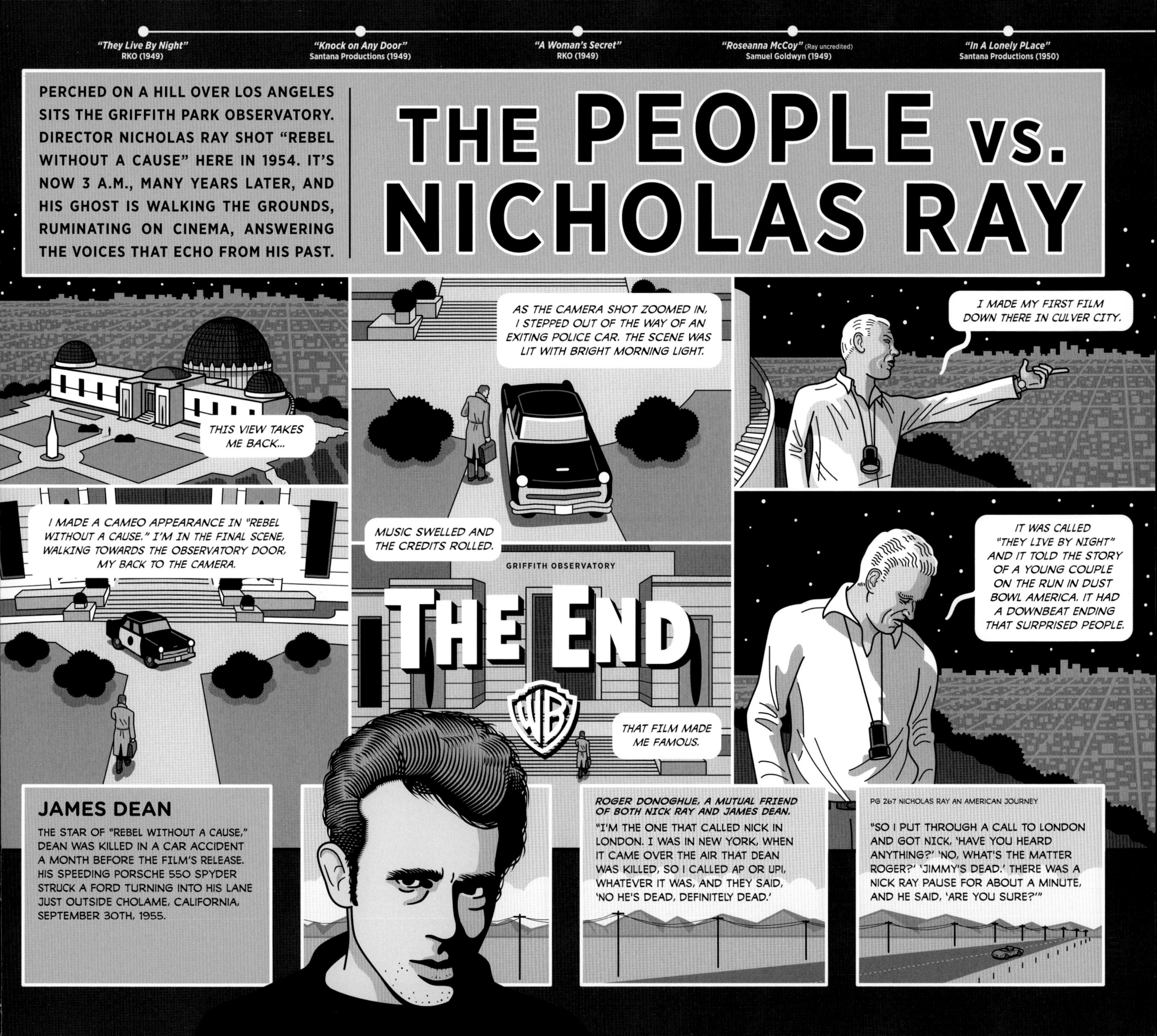

"They Live By Night"
RKO (1949)

"Knock on Any Door"
Santana Productions (1949)

"A Woman's Secret"
RKO (1949)

"Roseanna McCoy" (Ray uncredited)
Samuel Goldwyn (1949)

"In A Lonely PLace"
Santana Productions (1950)

THE PEOPLE vs. NICHOLAS RAY

PERCHED ON A HILL OVER LOS ANGELES SITS THE GRIFFITH PARK OBSERVATORY. DIRECTOR NICHOLAS RAY SHOT "REBEL WITHOUT A CAUSE" HERE IN 1954. IT'S NOW 3 A.M., MANY YEARS LATER, AND HIS GHOST IS WALKING THE GROUNDS, RUMINATING ON CINEMA, ANSWERING THE VOICES THAT ECHO FROM HIS PAST.

THIS VIEW TAKES ME BACK...

I MADE A CAMEO APPEARANCE IN "REBEL WITHOUT A CAUSE." I'M IN THE FINAL SCENE, WALKING TOWARDS THE OBSERVATORY DOOR, MY BACK TO THE CAMERA.

AS THE CAMERA SHOT ZOOMED IN, I STEPPED OUT OF THE WAY OF AN EXITING POLICE CAR. THE SCENE WAS LIT WITH BRIGHT MORNING LIGHT.

MUSIC SWELLED AND THE CREDITS ROLLED.

GRIFFITH OBSERVATORY

THE END

WB

THAT FILM MADE ME FAMOUS.

I MADE MY FIRST FILM DOWN THERE IN CULVER CITY.

IT WAS CALLED "THEY LIVE BY NIGHT" AND IT TOLD THE STORY OF A YOUNG COUPLE ON THE RUN IN DUST BOWL AMERICA. IT HAD A DOWNBEAT ENDING THAT SURPRISED PEOPLE.

JAMES DEAN

THE STAR OF "REBEL WITHOUT A CAUSE," DEAN WAS KILLED IN A CAR ACCIDENT A MONTH BEFORE THE FILM'S RELEASE. HIS SPEEDING PORSCHE 550 SPYDER STRUCK A FORD TURNING INTO HIS LANE JUST OUTSIDE CHOLAME, CALIFORNIA, SEPTEMBER 30TH, 1955.

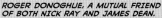

ROGER DONOGHUE, A MUTUAL FRIEND OF BOTH NICK RAY AND JAMES DEAN.

"I'M THE ONE THAT CALLED NICK IN LONDON. I WAS IN NEW YORK, WHEN IT CAME OVER THE AIR THAT DEAN WAS KILLED, SO I CALLED AP OR UPI, WHATEVER IT WAS, AND THEY SAID, 'NO HE'S DEAD, DEFINITELY DEAD.'

PG 267 NICHOLAS RAY AN AMERICAN JOURNEY

"SO I PUT THROUGH A CALL TO LONDON AND GOT NICK, 'HAVE YOU HEARD ANYTHING?' 'NO, WHAT'S THE MATTER ROGER?' 'JIMMY'S DEAD.' THERE WAS A NICK RAY PAUSE FOR ABOUT A MINUTE, AND HE SAID, 'ARE YOU SURE?'"

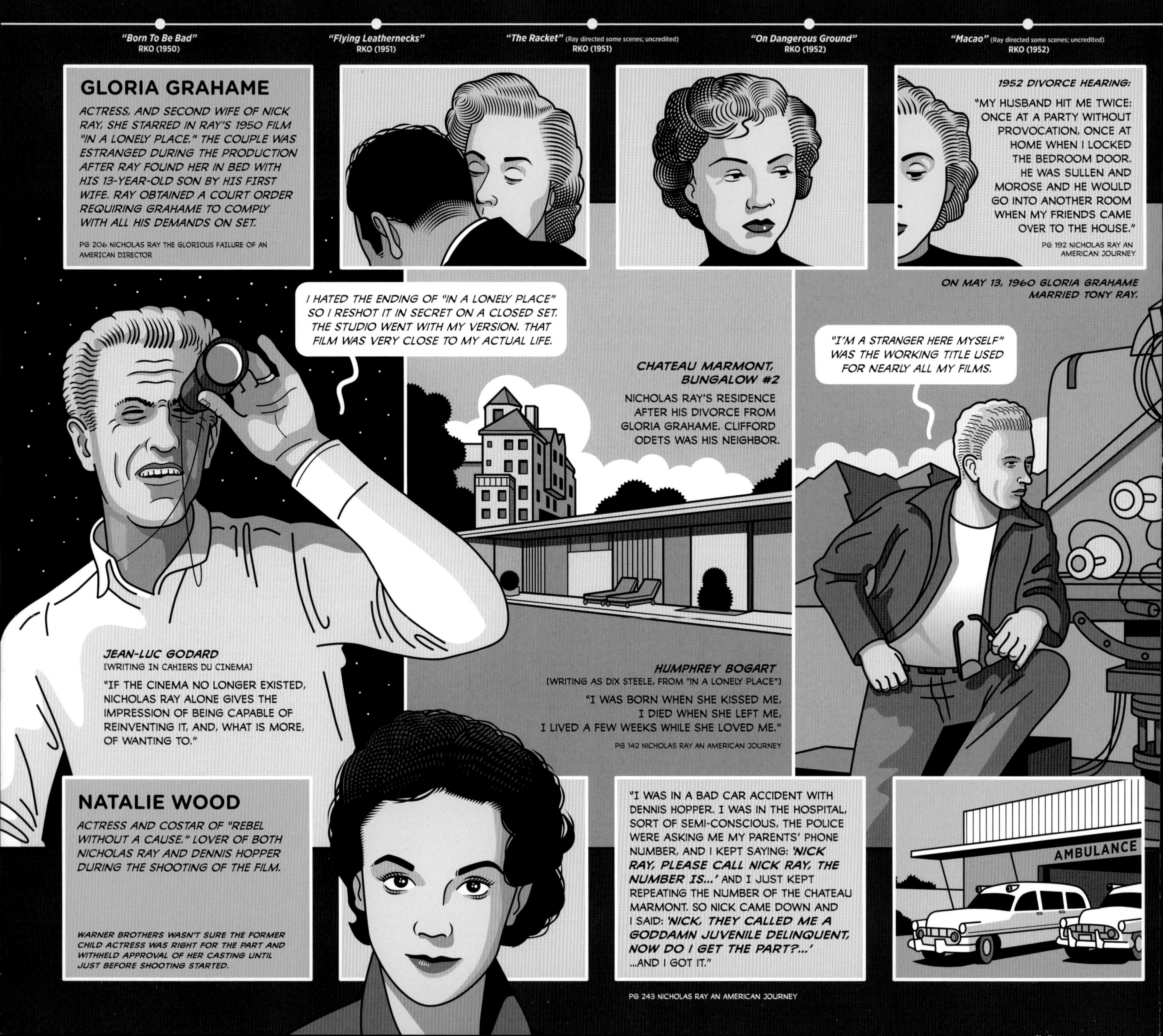

"Born To Be Bad"
RKO (1950)

"Flying Leathernecks"
RKO (1951)

"The Racket" (Ray directed some scenes; uncredited)
RKO (1951)

"On Dangerous Ground"
RKO (1952)

"Macao" (Ray directed some scenes; uncredited)
RKO (1952)

GLORIA GRAHAME

ACTRESS, AND SECOND WIFE OF NICK RAY, SHE STARRED IN RAY'S 1950 FILM "IN A LONELY PLACE." THE COUPLE WAS ESTRANGED DURING THE PRODUCTION AFTER RAY FOUND HER IN BED WITH HIS 13-YEAR-OLD SON BY HIS FIRST WIFE. RAY OBTAINED A COURT ORDER REQUIRING GRAHAME TO COMPLY WITH ALL HIS DEMANDS ON SET.

PG 206 NICHOLAS RAY THE GLORIOUS FAILURE OF AN AMERICAN DIRECTOR

1952 DIVORCE HEARING:

"MY HUSBAND HIT ME TWICE: ONCE AT A PARTY WITHOUT PROVOCATION, ONCE AT HOME WHEN I LOCKED THE BEDROOM DOOR. HE WAS SULLEN AND MOROSE AND HE WOULD GO INTO ANOTHER ROOM WHEN MY FRIENDS CAME OVER TO THE HOUSE."

PG 192 NICHOLAS RAY AN AMERICAN JOURNEY

ON MAY 13, 1960 GLORIA GRAHAME MARRIED TONY RAY.

"I HATED THE ENDING OF "IN A LONELY PLACE" SO I RESHOT IT IN SECRET ON A CLOSED SET. THE STUDIO WENT WITH MY VERSION. THAT FILM WAS VERY CLOSE TO MY ACTUAL LIFE."

CHATEAU MARMONT, BUNGALOW #2

NICHOLAS RAY'S RESIDENCE AFTER HIS DIVORCE FROM GLORIA GRAHAME. CLIFFORD ODETS WAS HIS NEIGHBOR.

"I'M A STRANGER HERE MYSELF" WAS THE WORKING TITLE USED FOR NEARLY ALL MY FILMS.

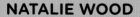

JEAN-LUC GODARD
[WRITING IN CAHIERS DU CINEMA]

"IF THE CINEMA NO LONGER EXISTED, NICHOLAS RAY ALONE GIVES THE IMPRESSION OF BEING CAPABLE OF REINVENTING IT, AND, WHAT IS MORE, OF WANTING TO."

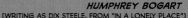

HUMPHREY BOGART
[WRITING AS DIX STEELE, FROM "IN A LONELY PLACE"]

"I WAS BORN WHEN SHE KISSED ME, I DIED WHEN SHE LEFT ME, I LIVED A FEW WEEKS WHILE SHE LOVED ME."

PG 142 NICHOLAS RAY AN AMERICAN JOURNEY

NATALIE WOOD

ACTRESS AND COSTAR OF "REBEL WITHOUT A CAUSE." LOVER OF BOTH NICHOLAS RAY AND DENNIS HOPPER DURING THE SHOOTING OF THE FILM.

WARNER BROTHERS WASN'T SURE THE FORMER CHILD ACTRESS WAS RIGHT FOR THE PART AND WITHHELD APPROVAL OF HER CASTING UNTIL JUST BEFORE SHOOTING STARTED.

"I WAS IN A BAD CAR ACCIDENT WITH DENNIS HOPPER. I WAS IN THE HOSPITAL, SORT OF SEMI-CONSCIOUS, THE POLICE WERE ASKING ME MY PARENTS' PHONE NUMBER, AND I KEPT SAYING: *'NICK RAY, PLEASE CALL NICK RAY, THE NUMBER IS...'* AND I JUST KEPT REPEATING THE NUMBER OF THE CHATEAU MARMONT. SO NICK CAME DOWN AND I SAID: *'NICK, THEY CALLED ME A GODDAMN JUVENILE DELINQUENT, NOW DO I GET THE PART?...'* ...AND I GOT IT."

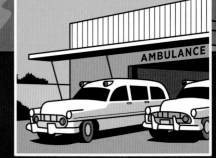

PG 243 NICHOLAS RAY AN AMERICAN JOURNEY

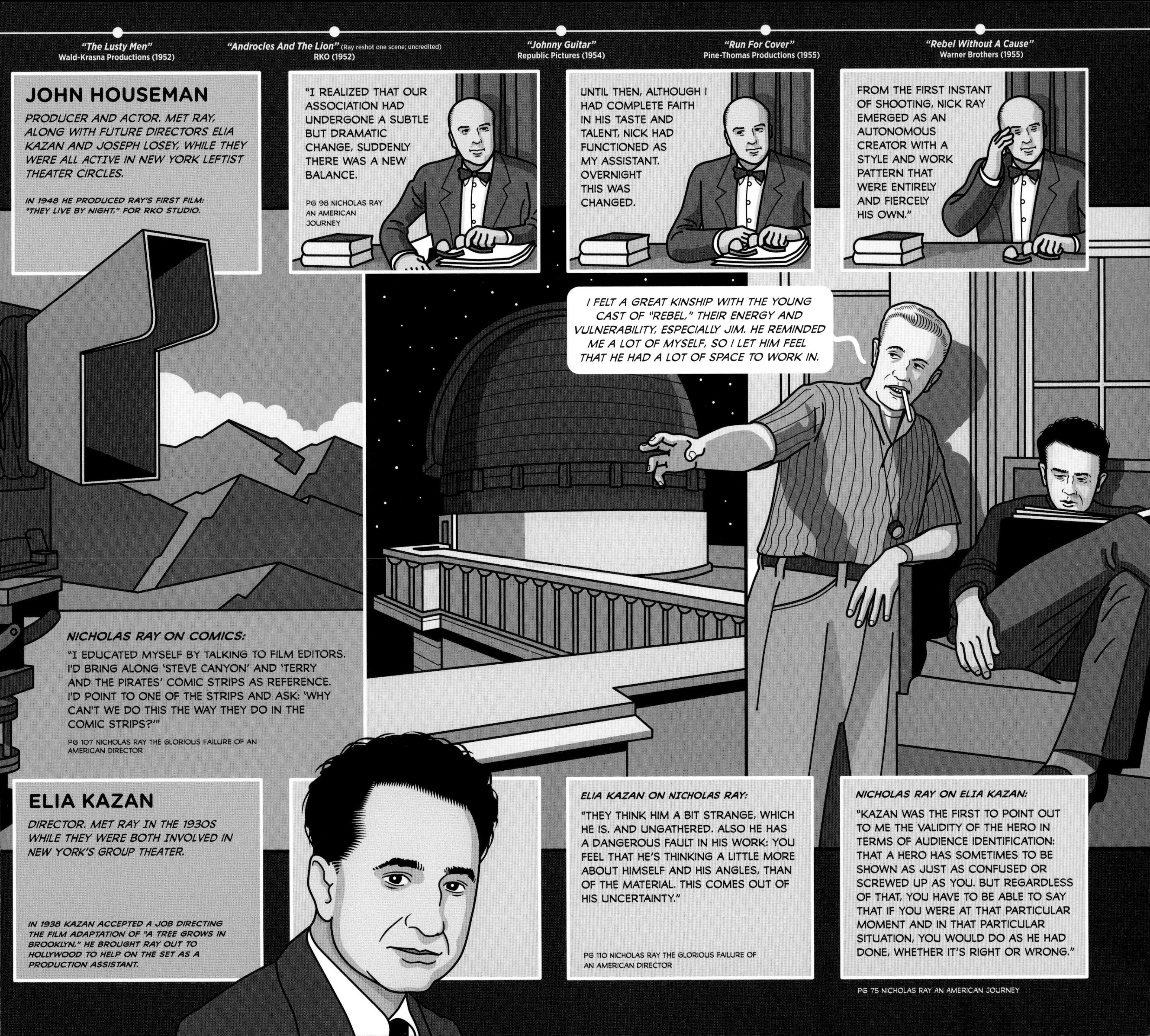

"The Lusty Men"
Wald-Krasna Productions (1952)
"Androcles And The Lion" (Ray reshot one scene; uncredited)
RKO (1952)
"Johnny Guitar"
Republic Pictures (1954)
"Run For Cover"
Pine-Thomas Productions (1955)
"Rebel Without A Cause"
Warner Brothers (1955)
JOHN HOUSEMAN
PRODUCER AND ACTOR. MET RAY, ALONG WITH FUTURE DIRECTORS ELIA KAZAN AND JOSEPH LOSEY, WHILE THEY WERE ALL ACTIVE IN NEW YORK LEFTIST THEATER CIRCLES.
IN 1948 HE PRODUCED RAY'S FIRST FILM: "THEY LIVE BY NIGHT," FOR RKO STUDIO.
"I REALIZED THAT OUR ASSOCIATION HAD UNDERGONE A SUBTLE BUT DRAMATIC CHANGE, SUDDENLY THERE WAS A NEW BALANCE.
PG 98 NICHOLAS RAY AN AMERICAN JOURNEY
UNTIL THEN, ALTHOUGH I HAD COMPLETE FAITH IN HIS TASTE AND TALENT, NICK HAD FUNCTIONED AS MY ASSISTANT. OVERNIGHT THIS WAS CHANGED.
FROM THE FIRST INSTANT OF SHOOTING, NICK RAY EMERGED AS AN AUTONOMOUS CREATOR WITH A STYLE AND WORK PATTERN THAT WERE ENTIRELY AND FIERCELY HIS OWN."
I FELT A GREAT KINSHIP WITH THE YOUNG CAST OF "REBEL," THEIR ENERGY AND VULNERABILITY, ESPECIALLY JIM. HE REMINDED ME A LOT OF MYSELF, SO I LET HIM FEEL THAT HE HAD A LOT OF SPACE TO WORK IN.
NICHOLAS RAY ON COMICS:
"I EDUCATED MYSELF BY TALKING TO FILM EDITORS. I'D BRING ALONG 'STEVE CANYON' AND 'TERRY AND THE PIRATES' COMIC STRIPS AS REFERENCE. I'D POINT TO ONE OF THE STRIPS AND ASK: 'WHY CAN'T WE DO THIS THE WAY THEY DO IN THE COMIC STRIPS?'"
PG 107 NICHOLAS RAY THE GLORIOUS FAILURE OF AN AMERICAN DIRECTOR
ELIA KAZAN
DIRECTOR. MET RAY IN THE 1930S WHILE THEY WERE BOTH INVOLVED IN NEW YORK'S GROUP THEATER.
IN 1938 KAZAN ACCEPTED A JOB DIRECTING THE FILM ADAPTATION OF "A TREE GROWS IN BROOKLYN." HE BROUGHT RAY OUT TO HOLLYWOOD TO HELP ON THE SET AS A PRODUCTION ASSISTANT.
ELIA KAZAN ON NICHOLAS RAY:
"THEY THINK HIM A BIT STRANGE, WHICH HE IS. AND UNGATHERED. ALSO HE HAS A DANGEROUS FAULT IN HIS WORK: YOU FEEL THAT HE'S THINKING A LITTLE MORE ABOUT HIMSELF AND HIS ANGLES, THAN OF THE MATERIAL. THIS COMES OUT OF HIS UNCERTAINTY."
PG 110 NICHOLAS RAY THE GLORIOUS FAILURE OF AN AMERICAN DIRECTOR
NICHOLAS RAY ON ELIA KAZAN:
"KAZAN WAS THE FIRST TO POINT OUT TO ME THE VALIDITY OF THE HERO IN TERMS OF AUDIENCE IDENTIFICATION: THAT A HERO HAS SOMETIMES TO BE SHOWN AS JUST AS CONFUSED OR SCREWED UP AS YOU. BUT REGARDLESS OF THAT, YOU HAVE TO BE ABLE TO SAY THAT IF YOU WERE AT THAT PARTICULAR MOMENT AND IN THAT PARTICULAR SITUATION, YOU WOULD DO AS HE HAD DONE, WHETHER IT'S RIGHT OR WRONG."
PG 75 NICHOLAS RAY AN AMERICAN JOURNEY

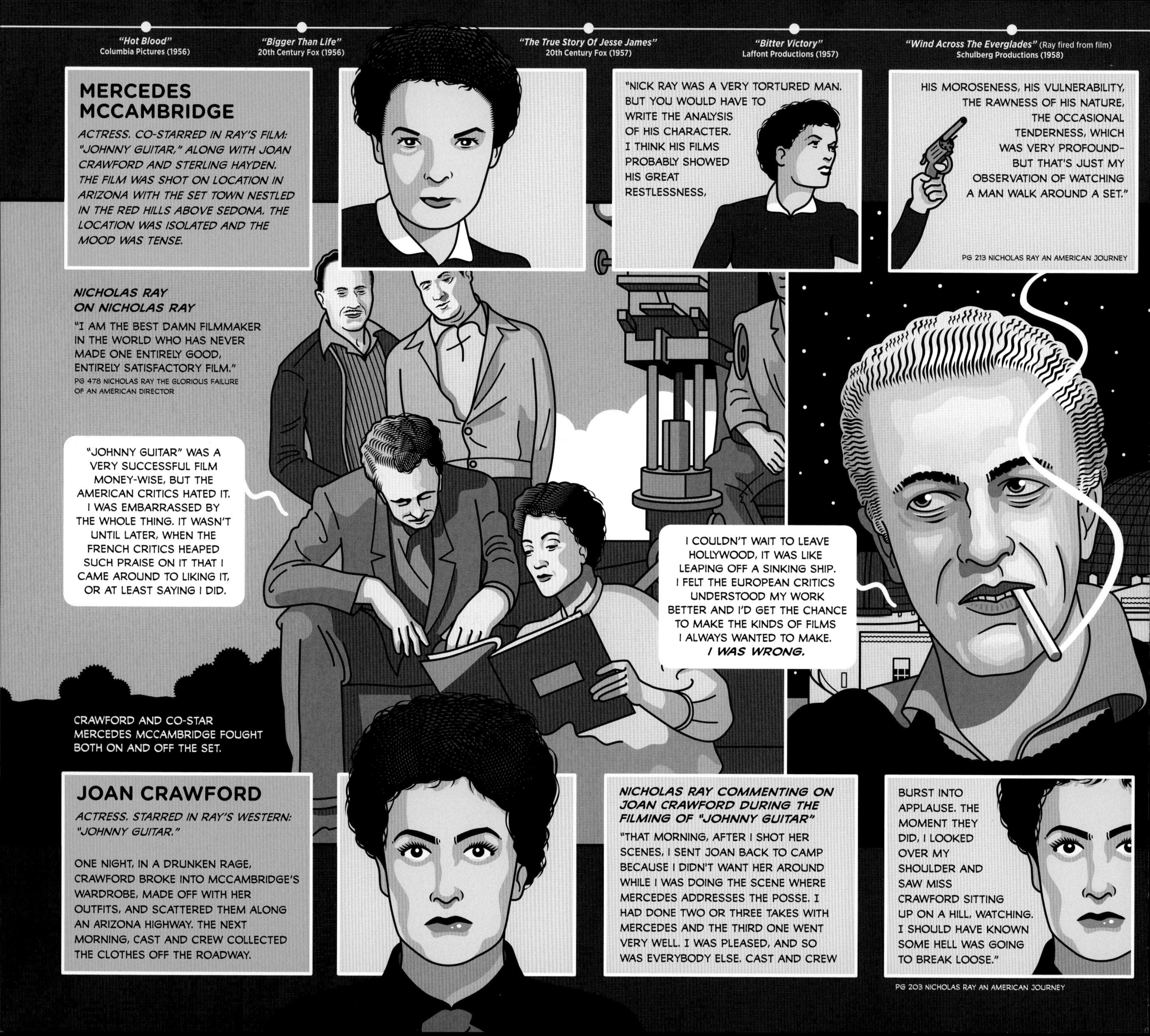

"Hot Blood"
Columbia Pictures (1956)
"Bigger Than Life"
20th Century Fox (1956)
"The True Story Of Jesse James"
20th Century Fox (1957)
"Bitter Victory"
Laffont Productions (1957)
"Wind Across The Everglades" (Ray fired from film)
Schulberg Productions (1958)
MERCEDES MCCAMBRIDGE
ACTRESS. CO-STARRED IN RAY'S FILM: "JOHNNY GUITAR," ALONG WITH JOAN CRAWFORD AND STERLING HAYDEN. THE FILM WAS SHOT ON LOCATION IN ARIZONA WITH THE SET TOWN NESTLED IN THE RED HILLS ABOVE SEDONA. THE LOCATION WAS ISOLATED AND THE MOOD WAS TENSE.
"NICK RAY WAS A VERY TORTURED MAN. BUT YOU WOULD HAVE TO WRITE THE ANALYSIS OF HIS CHARACTER. I THINK HIS FILMS PROBABLY SHOWED HIS GREAT RESTLESSNESS,
HIS MOROSENESS, HIS VULNERABILITY, THE RAWNESS OF HIS NATURE, THE OCCASIONAL TENDERNESS, WHICH WAS VERY PROFOUND– BUT THAT'S JUST MY OBSERVATION OF WATCHING A MAN WALK AROUND A SET."
PG 213 NICHOLAS RAY AN AMERICAN JOURNEY
NICHOLAS RAY ON NICHOLAS RAY
"I AM THE BEST DAMN FILMMAKER IN THE WORLD WHO HAS NEVER MADE ONE ENTIRELY GOOD, ENTIRELY SATISFACTORY FILM."
PG 478 NICHOLAS RAY THE GLORIOUS FAILURE OF AN AMERICAN DIRECTOR
"JOHNNY GUITAR" WAS A VERY SUCCESSFUL FILM MONEY-WISE, BUT THE AMERICAN CRITICS HATED IT. I WAS EMBARRASSED BY THE WHOLE THING. IT WASN'T UNTIL LATER, WHEN THE FRENCH CRITICS HEAPED SUCH PRAISE ON IT THAT I CAME AROUND TO LIKING IT, OR AT LEAST SAYING I DID.
I COULDN'T WAIT TO LEAVE HOLLYWOOD, IT WAS LIKE LEAPING OFF A SINKING SHIP. I FELT THE EUROPEAN CRITICS UNDERSTOOD MY WORK BETTER AND I'D GET THE CHANCE TO MAKE THE KINDS OF FILMS I ALWAYS WANTED TO MAKE. I WAS WRONG.
CRAWFORD AND CO-STAR MERCEDES MCCAMBRIDGE FOUGHT BOTH ON AND OFF THE SET.
JOAN CRAWFORD
ACTRESS. STARRED IN RAY'S WESTERN: "JOHNNY GUITAR."
ONE NIGHT, IN A DRUNKEN RAGE, CRAWFORD BROKE INTO MCCAMBRIDGE'S WARDROBE, MADE OFF WITH HER OUTFITS, AND SCATTERED THEM ALONG AN ARIZONA HIGHWAY. THE NEXT MORNING, CAST AND CREW COLLECTED THE CLOTHES OFF THE ROADWAY.
NICHOLAS RAY COMMENTING ON JOAN CRAWFORD DURING THE FILMING OF "JOHNNY GUITAR"
"THAT MORNING, AFTER I SHOT HER SCENES, I SENT JOAN BACK TO CAMP BECAUSE I DIDN'T WANT HER AROUND WHILE I WAS DOING THE SCENE WHERE MERCEDES ADDRESSES THE POSSE. I HAD DONE TWO OR THREE TAKES WITH MERCEDES AND THE THIRD ONE WENT VERY WELL. I WAS PLEASED, AND SO WAS EVERYBODY ELSE. CAST AND CREW
BURST INTO APPLAUSE. THE MOMENT THEY DID, I LOOKED OVER MY SHOULDER AND SAW MISS CRAWFORD SITTING UP ON A HILL, WATCHING. I SHOULD HAVE KNOWN SOME HELL WAS GOING TO BREAK LOOSE."
PG 203 NICHOLAS RAY AN AMERICAN JOURNEY

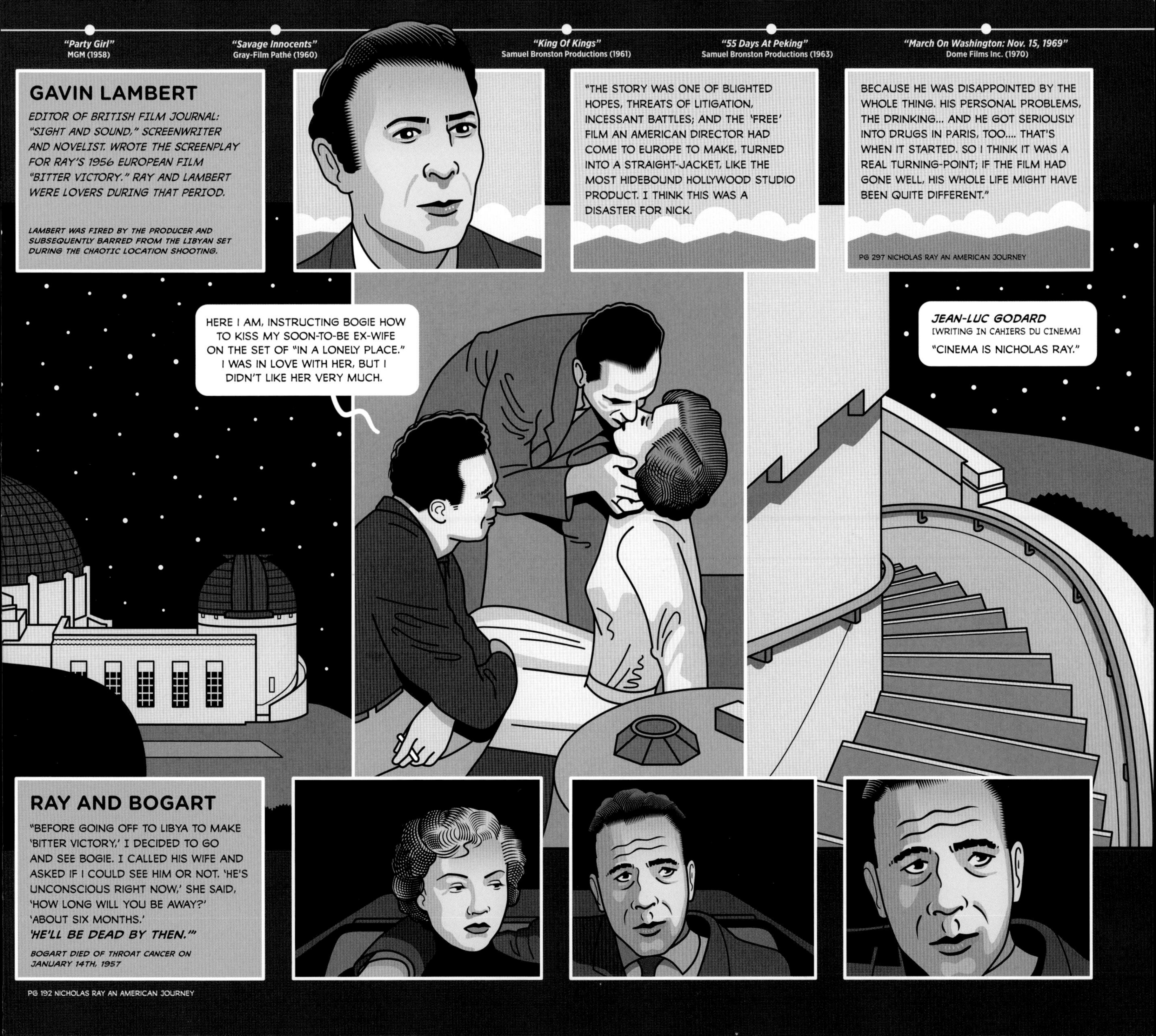
"Party Girl"
MGM (1958)
"Savage Innocents"
Gray-Film Pathé (1960)
"King Of Kings"
Samuel Bronston Productions (1961)
"55 Days At Peking"
Samuel Bronston Productions (1963)
"March On Washington: Nov. 15, 1969"
Dome Films Inc. (1970)
GAVIN LAMBERT
EDITOR OF BRITISH FILM JOURNAL: "SIGHT AND SOUND," SCREENWRITER AND NOVELIST. WROTE THE SCREENPLAY FOR RAY'S 1956 EUROPEAN FILM "BITTER VICTORY." RAY AND LAMBERT WERE LOVERS DURING THAT PERIOD.
LAMBERT WAS FIRED BY THE PRODUCER AND SUBSEQUENTLY BARRED FROM THE LIBYAN SET DURING THE CHAOTIC LOCATION SHOOTING.
"THE STORY WAS ONE OF BLIGHTED HOPES, THREATS OF LITIGATION, INCESSANT BATTLES; AND THE 'FREE' FILM AN AMERICAN DIRECTOR HAD COME TO EUROPE TO MAKE, TURNED INTO A STRAIGHT-JACKET, LIKE THE MOST HIDEBOUND HOLLYWOOD STUDIO PRODUCT. I THINK THIS WAS A DISASTER FOR NICK.
BECAUSE HE WAS DISAPPOINTED BY THE WHOLE THING. HIS PERSONAL PROBLEMS, THE DRINKING... AND HE GOT SERIOUSLY INTO DRUGS IN PARIS, TOO.... THAT'S WHEN IT STARTED. SO I THINK IT WAS A REAL TURNING-POINT; IF THE FILM HAD GONE WELL, HIS WHOLE LIFE MIGHT HAVE BEEN QUITE DIFFERENT."
PG 297 NICHOLAS RAY AN AMERICAN JOURNEY
HERE I AM, INSTRUCTING BOGIE HOW TO KISS MY SOON-TO-BE EX-WIFE ON THE SET OF "IN A LONELY PLACE." I WAS IN LOVE WITH HER, BUT I DIDN'T LIKE HER VERY MUCH.
JEAN-LUC GODARD
[WRITING IN CAHIERS DU CINEMA]
"CINEMA IS NICHOLAS RAY."
RAY AND BOGART
"BEFORE GOING OFF TO LIBYA TO MAKE 'BITTER VICTORY,' I DECIDED TO GO AND SEE BOGIE. I CALLED HIS WIFE AND ASKED IF I COULD SEE HIM OR NOT. 'HE'S UNCONSCIOUS RIGHT NOW,' SHE SAID, 'HOW LONG WILL YOU BE AWAY?' 'ABOUT SIX MONTHS.' 'HE'LL BE DEAD BY THEN.'"
BOGART DIED OF THROAT CANCER ON JANUARY 14TH, 1957
PG 192 NICHOLAS RAY AN AMERICAN JOURNEY

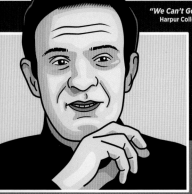

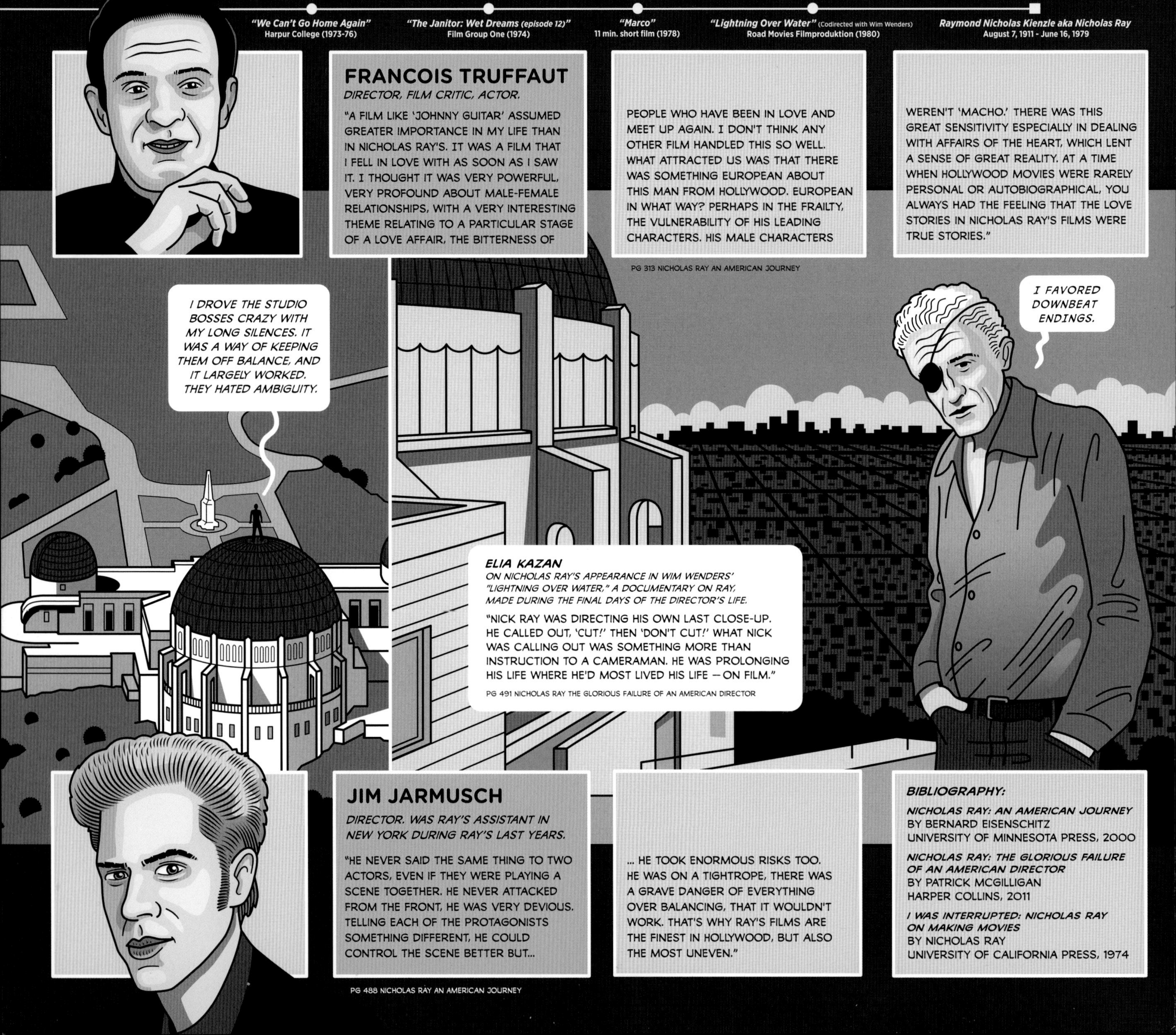

"We Can't Go Home Again"
Harpur College (1973-76)

"The Janitor: Wet Dreams (episode 12)"
Film Group One (1974)

"Marco"
11 min. short film (1978)

"Lightning Over Water" (Codirected with Wim Wenders)
Road Movies Filmproduktion (1980)

Raymond Nicholas Kienzle aka Nicholas Ray
August 7, 1911 - June 16, 1979

FRANCOIS TRUFFAUT
DIRECTOR, FILM CRITIC, ACTOR.

"A FILM LIKE 'JOHNNY GUITAR' ASSUMED GREATER IMPORTANCE IN MY LIFE THAN IN NICHOLAS RAY'S. IT WAS A FILM THAT I FELL IN LOVE WITH AS SOON AS I SAW IT. I THOUGHT IT WAS VERY POWERFUL, VERY PROFOUND ABOUT MALE-FEMALE RELATIONSHIPS, WITH A VERY INTERESTING THEME RELATING TO A PARTICULAR STAGE OF A LOVE AFFAIR, THE BITTERNESS OF PEOPLE WHO HAVE BEEN IN LOVE AND MEET UP AGAIN. I DON'T THINK ANY OTHER FILM HANDLED THIS SO WELL. WHAT ATTRACTED US WAS THAT THERE WAS SOMETHING EUROPEAN ABOUT THIS MAN FROM HOLLYWOOD. EUROPEAN IN WHAT WAY? PERHAPS IN THE FRAILTY, THE VULNERABILITY OF HIS LEADING CHARACTERS. HIS MALE CHARACTERS WEREN'T 'MACHO.' THERE WAS THIS GREAT SENSITIVITY ESPECIALLY IN DEALING WITH AFFAIRS OF THE HEART, WHICH LENT A SENSE OF GREAT REALITY. AT A TIME WHEN HOLLYWOOD MOVIES WERE RARELY PERSONAL OR AUTOBIOGRAPHICAL, YOU ALWAYS HAD THE FEELING THAT THE LOVE STORIES IN NICHOLAS RAY'S FILMS WERE TRUE STORIES."

PG 313 NICHOLAS RAY AN AMERICAN JOURNEY

I DROVE THE STUDIO BOSSES CRAZY WITH MY LONG SILENCES. IT WAS A WAY OF KEEPING THEM OFF BALANCE, AND IT LARGELY WORKED. THEY HATED AMBIGUITY.

I FAVORED DOWNBEAT ENDINGS.

ELIA KAZAN
ON NICHOLAS RAY'S APPEARANCE IN WIM WENDERS' "LIGHTNING OVER WATER," A DOCUMENTARY ON RAY, MADE DURING THE FINAL DAYS OF THE DIRECTOR'S LIFE.

"NICK RAY WAS DIRECTING HIS OWN LAST CLOSE-UP. HE CALLED OUT, 'CUT!' THEN 'DON'T CUT!' WHAT NICK WAS CALLING OUT WAS SOMETHING MORE THAN INSTRUCTION TO A CAMERAMAN. HE WAS PROLONGING HIS LIFE WHERE HE'D MOST LIVED HIS LIFE — ON FILM."
PG 491 NICHOLAS RAY THE GLORIOUS FAILURE OF AN AMERICAN DIRECTOR

JIM JARMUSCH
DIRECTOR. WAS RAY'S ASSISTANT IN NEW YORK DURING RAY'S LAST YEARS.

"HE NEVER SAID THE SAME THING TO TWO ACTORS, EVEN IF THEY WERE PLAYING A SCENE TOGETHER. HE NEVER ATTACKED FROM THE FRONT, HE WAS VERY DEVIOUS. TELLING EACH OF THE PROTAGONISTS SOMETHING DIFFERENT, HE COULD CONTROL THE SCENE BETTER BUT... ... HE TOOK ENORMOUS RISKS TOO. HE WAS ON A TIGHTROPE, THERE WAS A GRAVE DANGER OF EVERYTHING OVER BALANCING, THAT IT WOULDN'T WORK. THAT'S WHY RAY'S FILMS ARE THE FINEST IN HOLLYWOOD, BUT ALSO THE MOST UNEVEN."

PG 488 NICHOLAS RAY AN AMERICAN JOURNEY

BIBLIOGRAPHY:

NICHOLAS RAY: AN AMERICAN JOURNEY
BY BERNARD EISENSCHITZ
UNIVERSITY OF MINNESOTA PRESS, 2000

NICHOLAS RAY: THE GLORIOUS FAILURE OF AN AMERICAN DIRECTOR
BY PATRICK MCGILLIGAN
HARPER COLLINS, 2011

I WAS INTERRUPTED: NICHOLAS RAY ON MAKING MOVIES
BY NICHOLAS RAY
UNIVERSITY OF CALIFORNIA PRESS, 1974

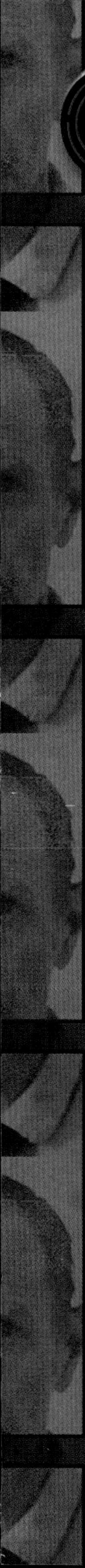

CORNELL WOOLRICH

AND THE THINGS THAT GO BUMP IN THE NIGHT

The father of modern suspense fiction, Woolrich's plots follow the spiral logic of nightmares. An everyman is plucked at random and pulled under, and just as he seems able to break free, something new is thrown his way. With Woolrich the gloom and fear never lift; he wrote the blackest of noir.

These anxious tales of dread and murder struck a chord with readers in the 1930s, '40s and '50s. Woolrich was a hugely popular writer with dozens of his books adapted to radio, TV and film. Alfred Hitchcock's "Rear Window," Francois Truffaut's "The Bride Wore Black," Val Lewton's "The Leopard Man," and Robert Siodmak's "Phantom Lady" were all based on his stories.

Although he was a professional success, his personal life was one long, wretched disaster. For 25 years he lived in a Manhattan hotel with his mother, a smothering relationship from which he could not break. Alcoholic, closeted, and suffering from a morbid fear of death, he seemed like one of the characters from his books. After his mother's death his life slid further down. He died, ten years later, wheelchair-bound, of a stroke on September 25th, 1968.

When you read Cornell Woolrich, the thing that goes bump in the night will be your heart, pounding in your chest.

THE BLACK ALIBI

THE BRIDE WORE BLACK

VIOLENCE

THE BLACK CURTAIN

RENDEZVOUS IN BLACK

THE BLACK ANGEL

NIGHTMA

THE BLACK PATH OF FEAR

THE BRIDE WORE BLACK

I MARRIED A DEAD MAN

DEADLINI AT DAWN

WALTZ INTO DARKNESS

PHANTOM LADY

I WOULDN'T BE IN YOUR SHOES

DARKNESS AT DAWN

YOU'LL N SEE ME A

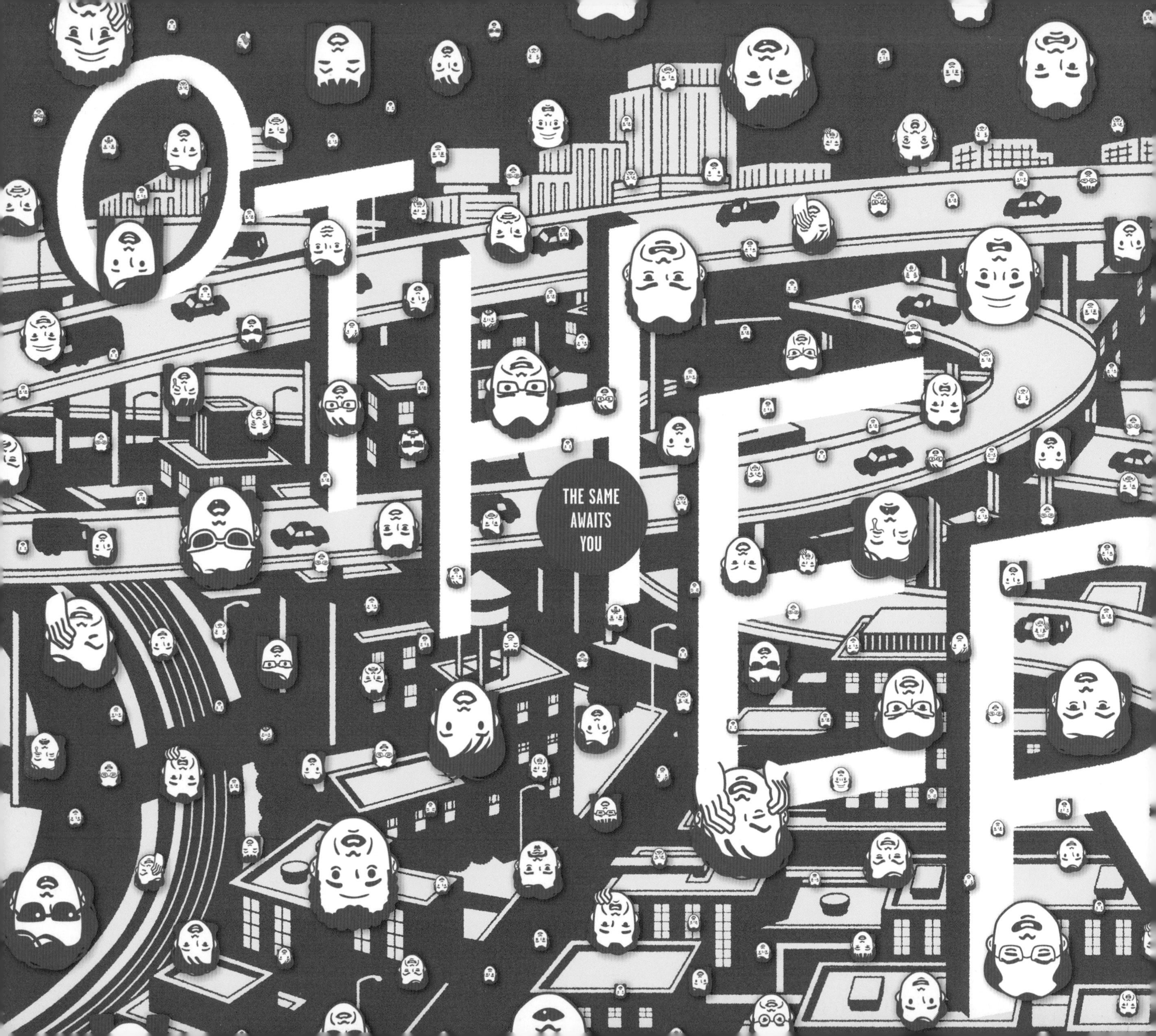

THE SAME
AWAITS
YOU

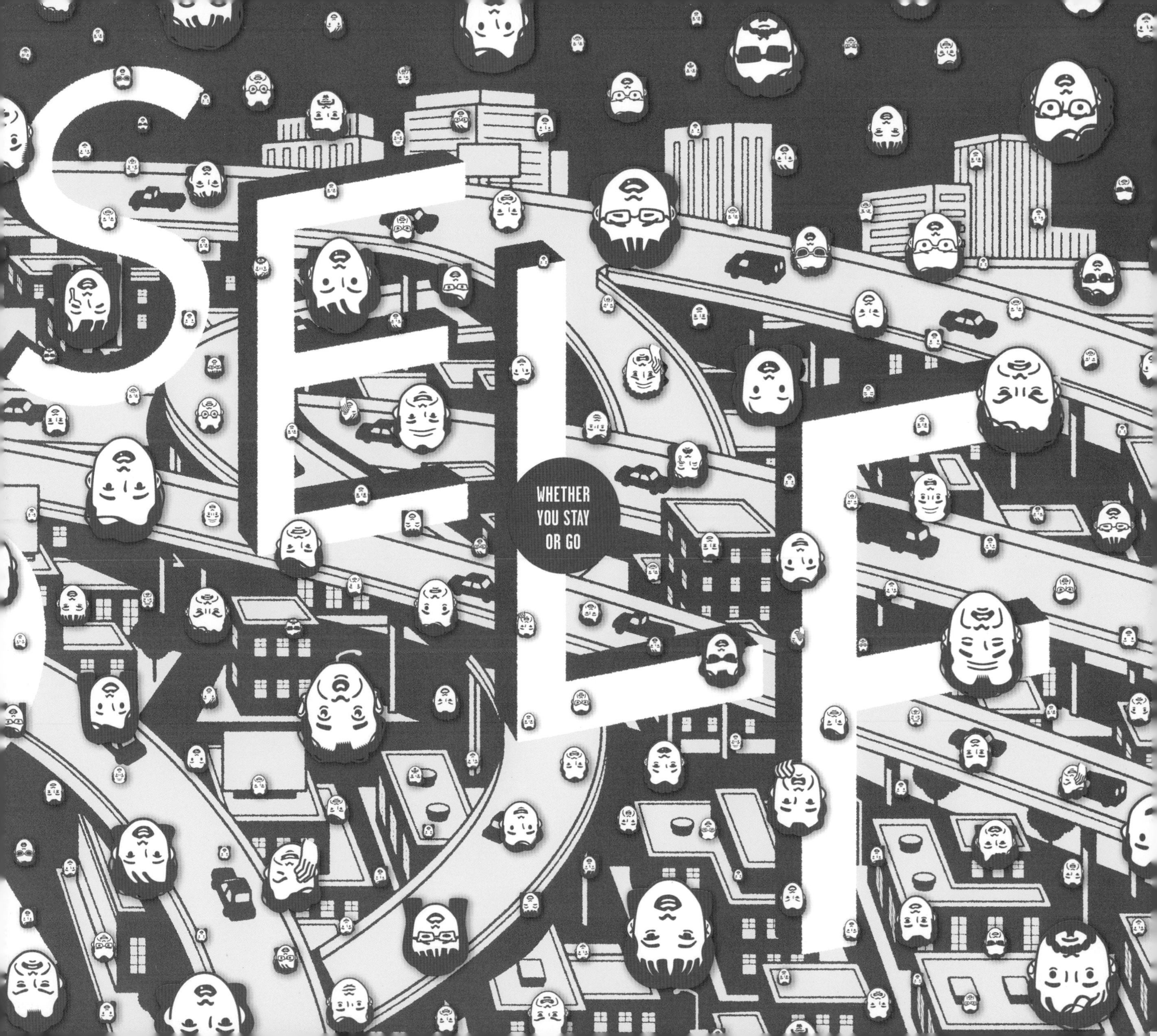
SELF
WHETHER YOU STAY OR GO

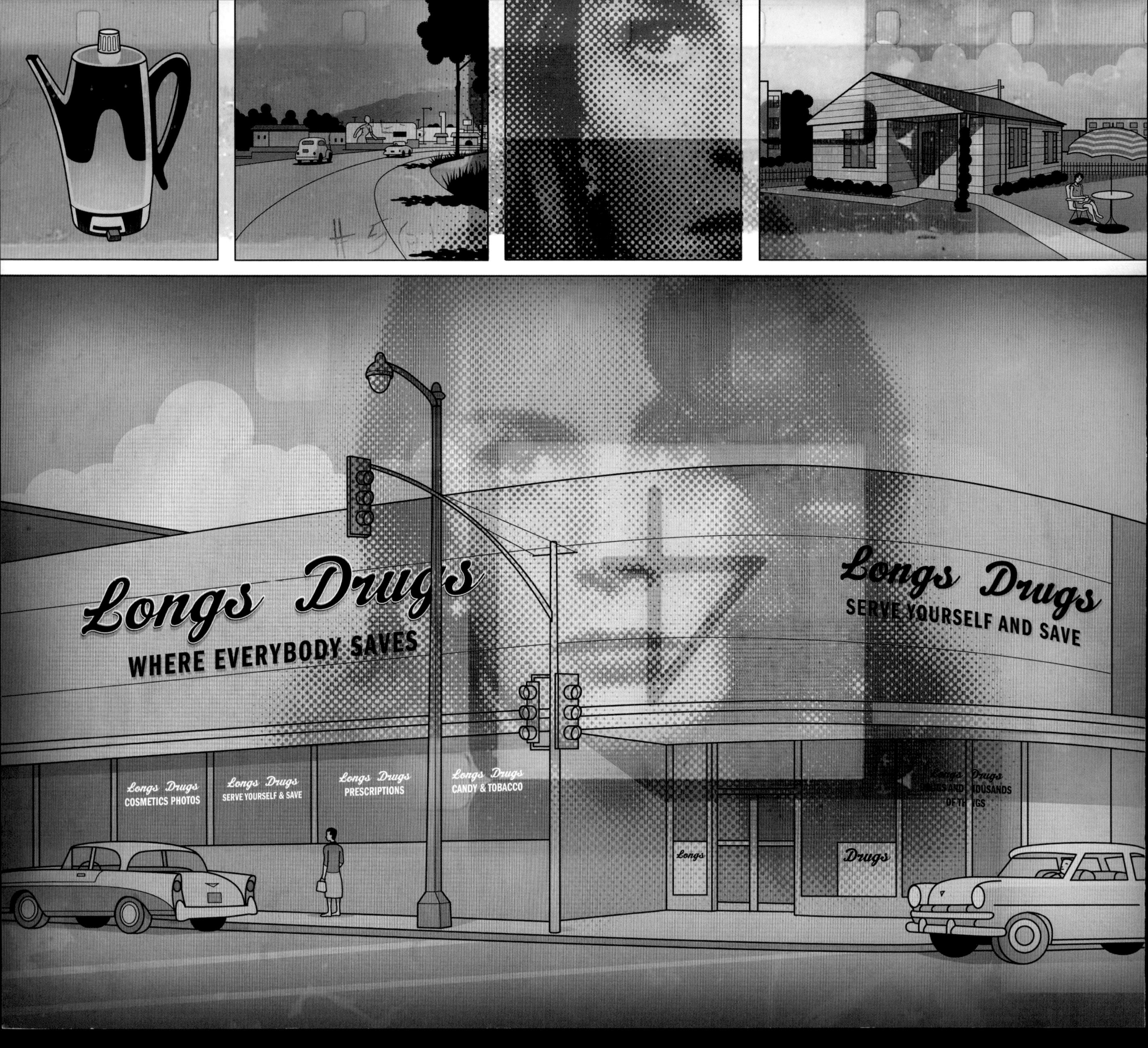
Longs Drugs
WHERE EVERYBODY SAVES
Longs Drugs
SERVE YOURSELF AND SAVE
Longs Drugs
COSMETICS PHOTOS
Longs Drugs
SERVE YOURSELF & SAVE
Longs Drugs
PRESCRIPTIONS
Longs Drugs
CANDY & TOBACCO
Longs
Drugs

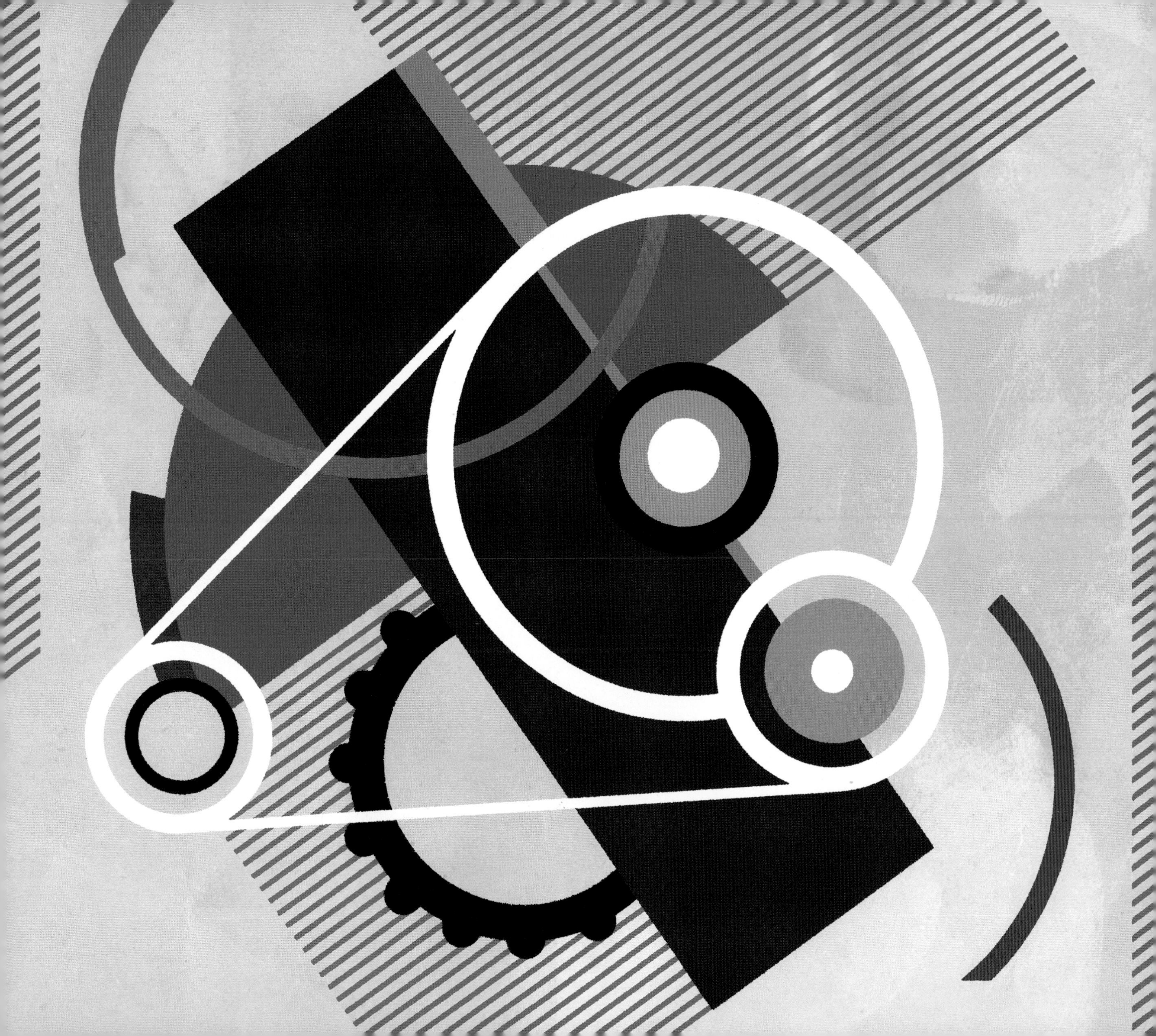

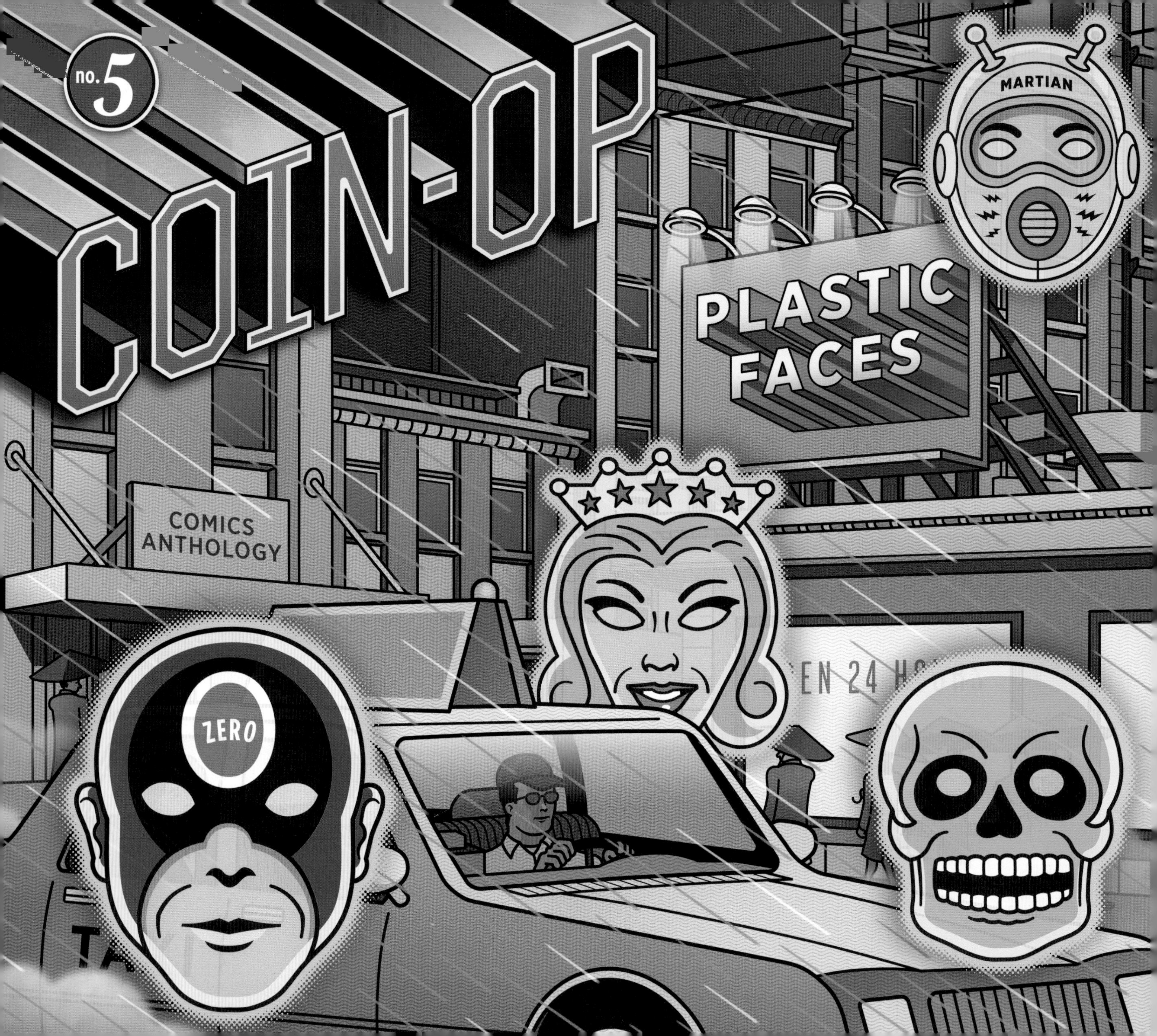
no. 5
COIN-OP
MARTIAN
PLASTIC FACES
COMICS ANTHOLOGY
ZERO

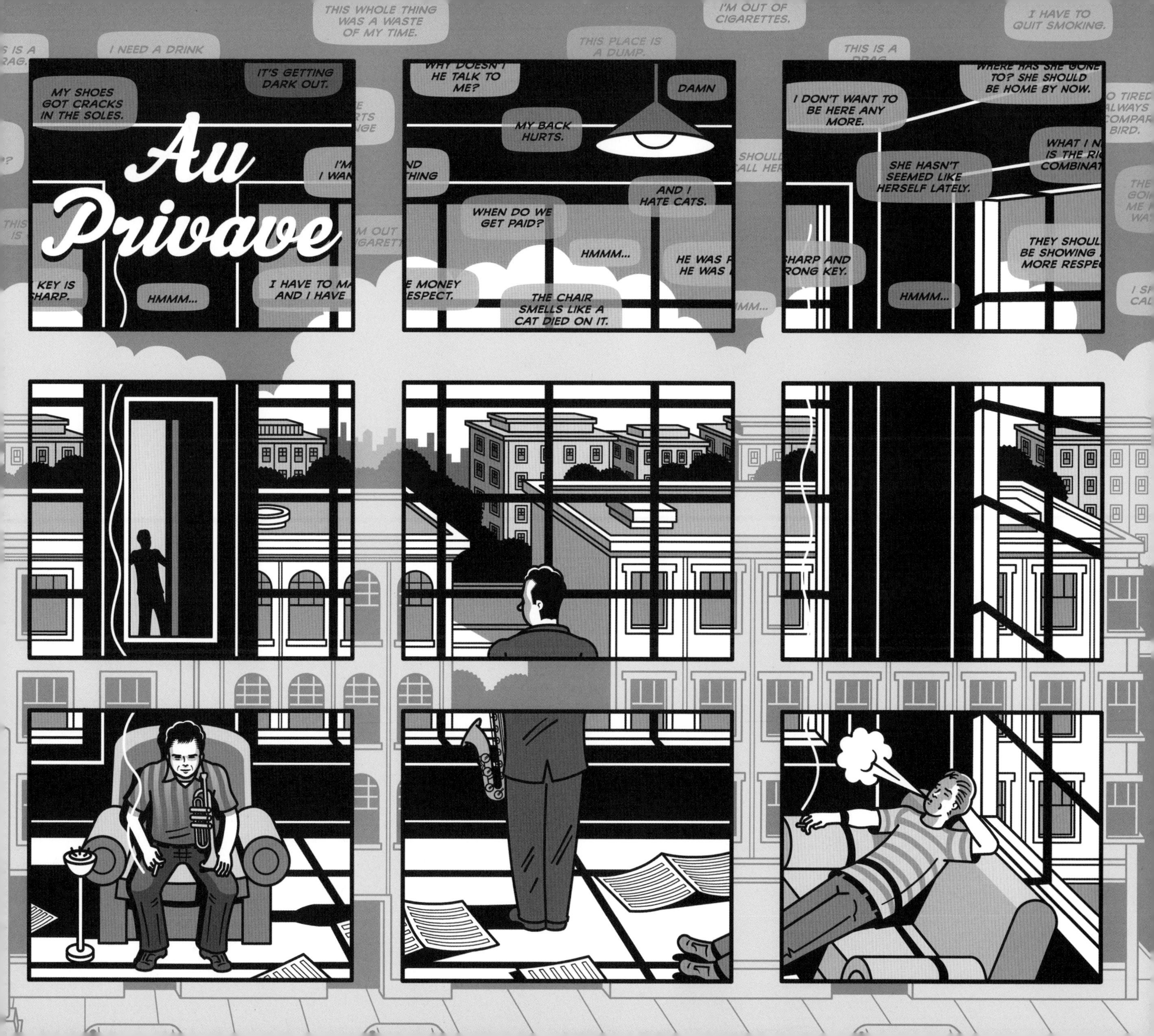
THIS WHOLE THING WAS A WASTE OF MY TIME.
I NEED A DRINK
I'M OUT OF CIGARETTES.
THIS PLACE IS A DUMP.
I HAVE TO QUIT SMOKING.
Au Privave
MY SHOES GOT CRACKS IN THE SOLES.
IT'S GETTING DARK OUT.
HMMM...
WHY DOESN'T HE TALK TO ME?
DAMN
MY BACK HURTS.
AND I HATE CATS.
WHEN DO WE GET PAID?
HMMM...
THE CHAIR SMELLS LIKE A CAT DIED ON IT.
WHERE HAS SHE GONE TO? SHE SHOULD BE HOME BY NOW.
I DON'T WANT TO BE HERE ANY MORE.
SHE HASN'T SEEMED LIKE HERSELF LATELY.
HMMM...

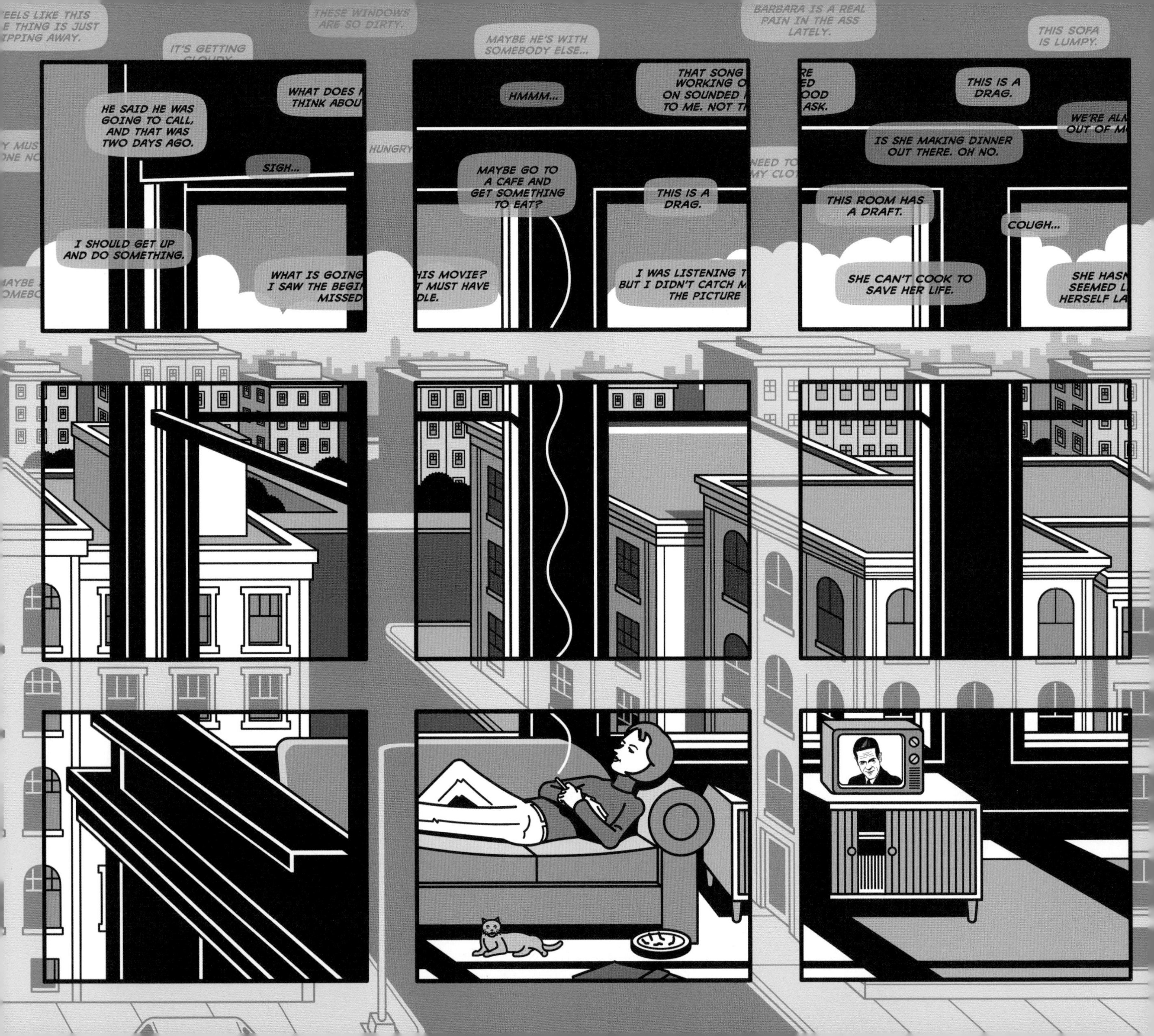

EELS LIKE THIS
E THING IS JUST
IPPING AWAY.
IT'S GETTING
THESE WINDOWS ARE SO DIRTY.
MAYBE HE'S WITH SOMEBODY ELSE...
BARBARA IS A REAL PAIN IN THE ASS LATELY.
THIS SOFA IS LUMPY.
HE SAID HE WAS GOING TO CALL, AND THAT WAS TWO DAYS AGO.
WHAT DOES
THINK ABOU
SIGH...
I SHOULD GET UP AND DO SOMETHING.
WHAT IS GOING
I SAW THE BEGI
MISSED
HUNGRY
HMMM...
THAT SONG
WORKING O
ON SOUNDED
TO ME. NOT T
MAYBE GO TO A CAFE AND GET SOMETHING TO EAT?
THIS IS A DRAG.
HIS MOVIE?
T MUST HAVE
DLE.
I WAS LISTENING T
BUT I DIDN'T CATCH M
THE PICTURE
NEED TO
MY CLO
RE
ED
OOD
ASK.
THIS IS A DRAG.
IS SHE MAKING DINNER OUT THERE. OH NO.
WE'RE AL
OUT OF M
THIS ROOM HAS A DRAFT.
COUGH...
SHE CAN'T COOK TO SAVE HER LIFE.
SHE HAS
SEEMED L
HERSELF LA

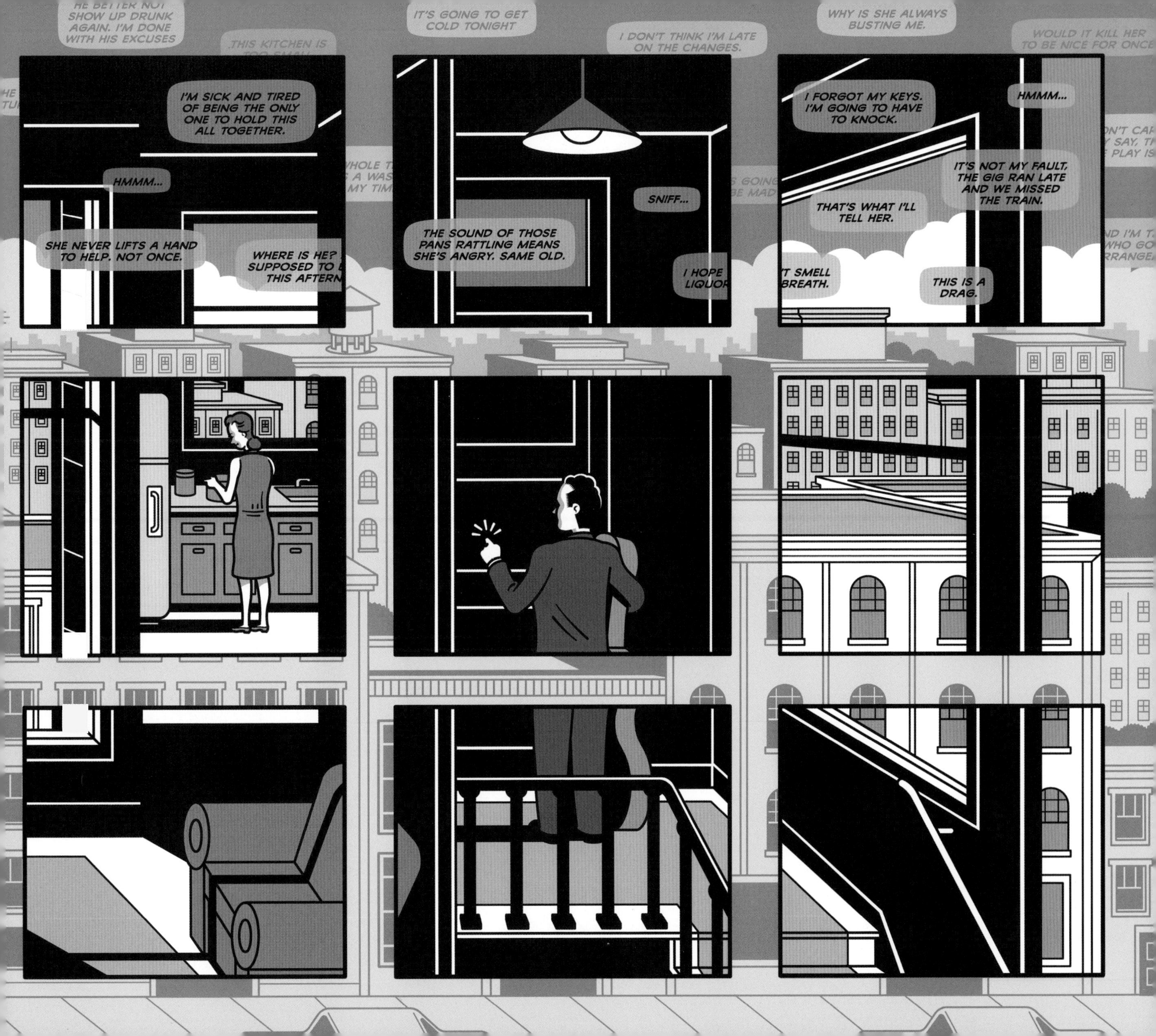
SHOW UP DRUNK AGAIN. I'M DONE WITH HIS EXCUSES
IT'S GOING TO GET COLD TONIGHT
I DON'T THINK I'M LATE ON THE CHANGES.
WHY IS SHE ALWAYS BUSTING ME.
I'M SICK AND TIRED OF BEING THE ONLY ONE TO HOLD THIS ALL TOGETHER.
HMMM...
SHE NEVER LIFTS A HAND TO HELP. NOT ONCE.
SNIFF...
THE SOUND OF THOSE PANS RATTLING MEANS SHE'S ANGRY. SAME OLD.
I FORGOT MY KEYS. I'M GOING TO HAVE TO KNOCK.
HMMM...
IT'S NOT MY FAULT, THE GIG RAN LATE AND WE MISSED THE TRAIN.
THAT'S WHAT I'LL TELL HER.
THIS IS A DRAG.

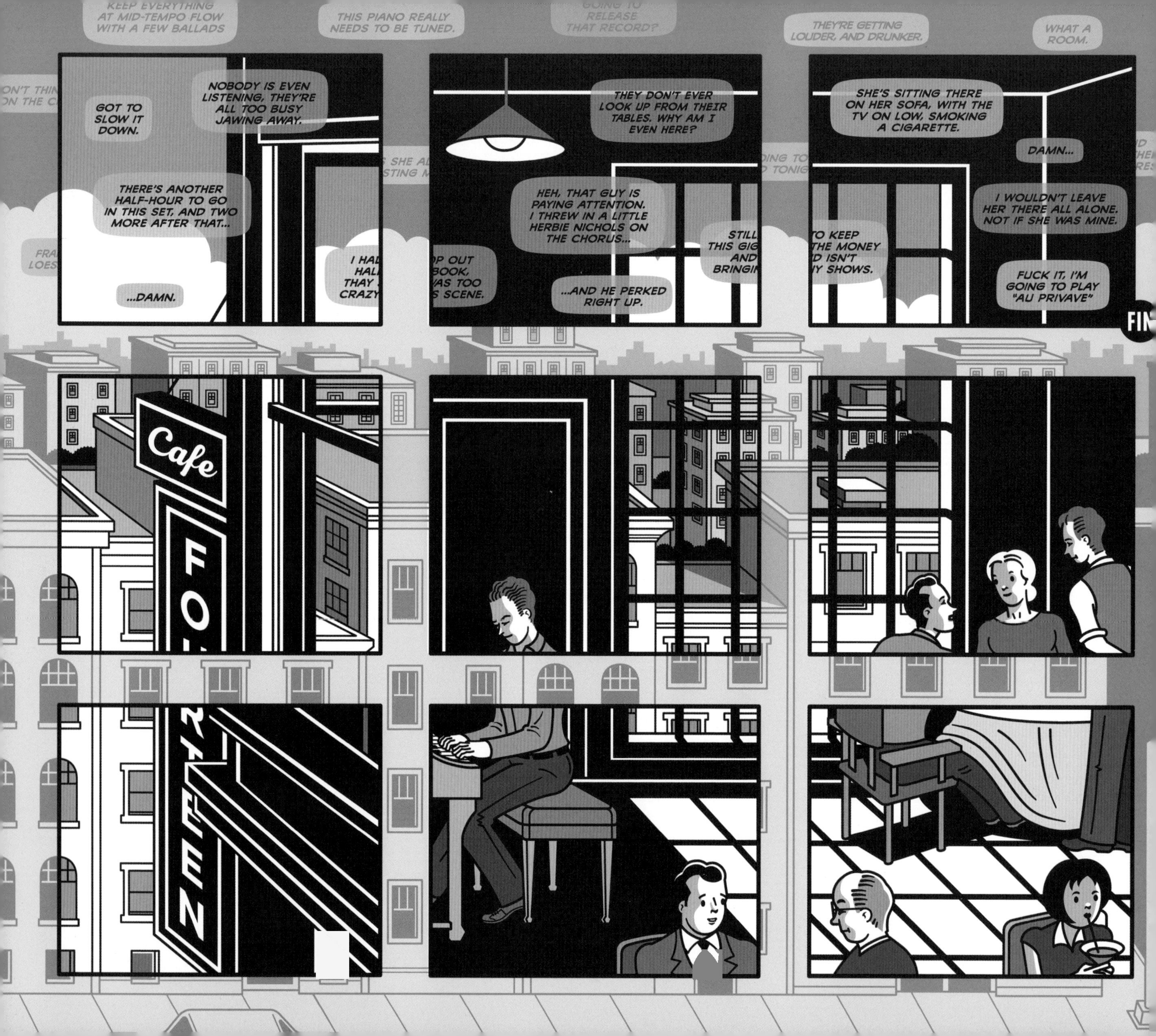
THIS PIANO REALLY NEEDS TO BE TUNED.
THEY'RE GETTING LOUDER, AND DRUNKER.
WHAT A ROOM.
GOT TO SLOW IT DOWN.
NOBODY IS EVEN LISTENING, THEY'RE ALL TOO BUSY JAWING AWAY.
THERE'S ANOTHER HALF-HOUR TO GO IN THIS SET, AND TWO MORE AFTER THAT...
...DAMN.
THEY DON'T EVER LOOK UP FROM THEIR TABLES. WHY AM I EVEN HERE?
HEH, THAT GUY IS PAYING ATTENTION. I THREW IN A LITTLE HERBIE NICHOLS ON THE CHORUS...
...AND HE PERKED RIGHT UP.
SHE'S SITTING THERE ON HER SOFA, WITH THE TV ON LOW, SMOKING A CIGARETTE.
DAMN...
I WOULDN'T LEAVE HER THERE ALL ALONE. NOT IF SHE WAS MINE.
FUCK IT, I'M GOING TO PLAY "AU PRIVAVE"
Cafe

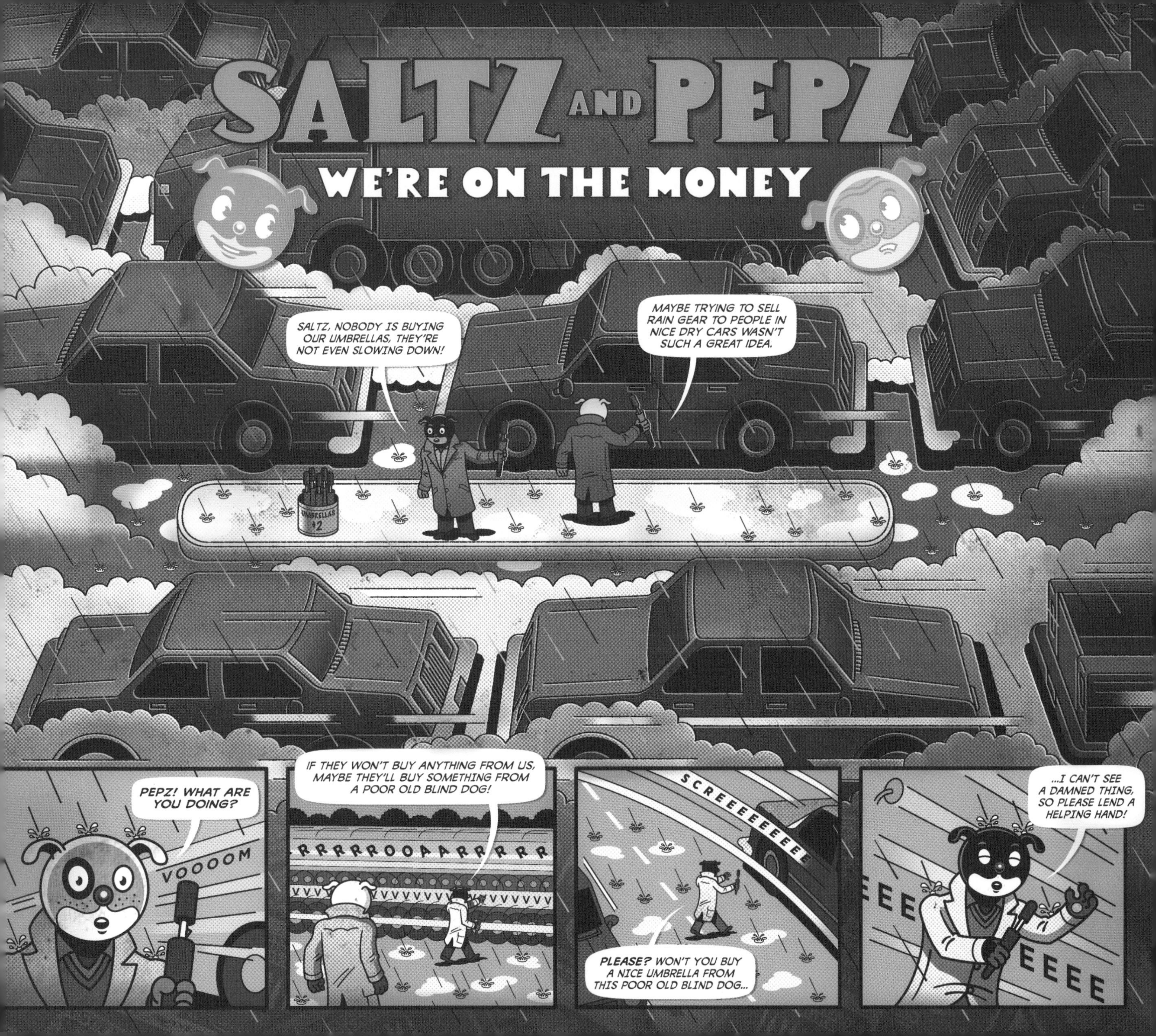
SALTZ AND PEPZ
WE'RE ON THE MONEY
SALTZ, NOBODY IS BUYING OUR UMBRELLAS, THEY'RE NOT EVEN SLOWING DOWN!
MAYBE TRYING TO SELL RAIN GEAR TO PEOPLE IN NICE DRY CARS WASN'T SUCH A GREAT IDEA.
UMBRELLAS $2
PEPZ! WHAT ARE YOU DOING?
VOOOOM
IF THEY WON'T BUY ANYTHING FROM US, MAYBE THEY'LL BUY SOMETHING FROM A POOR OLD BLIND DOG!
RRRRRROOAARRRRR
SCREEEEEEEEEE
PLEASE? WON'T YOU BUY A NICE UMBRELLA FROM THIS POOR OLD BLIND DOG...
...I CAN'T SEE A DAMNED THING, SO PLEASE LEND A HELPING HAND!
EEEE

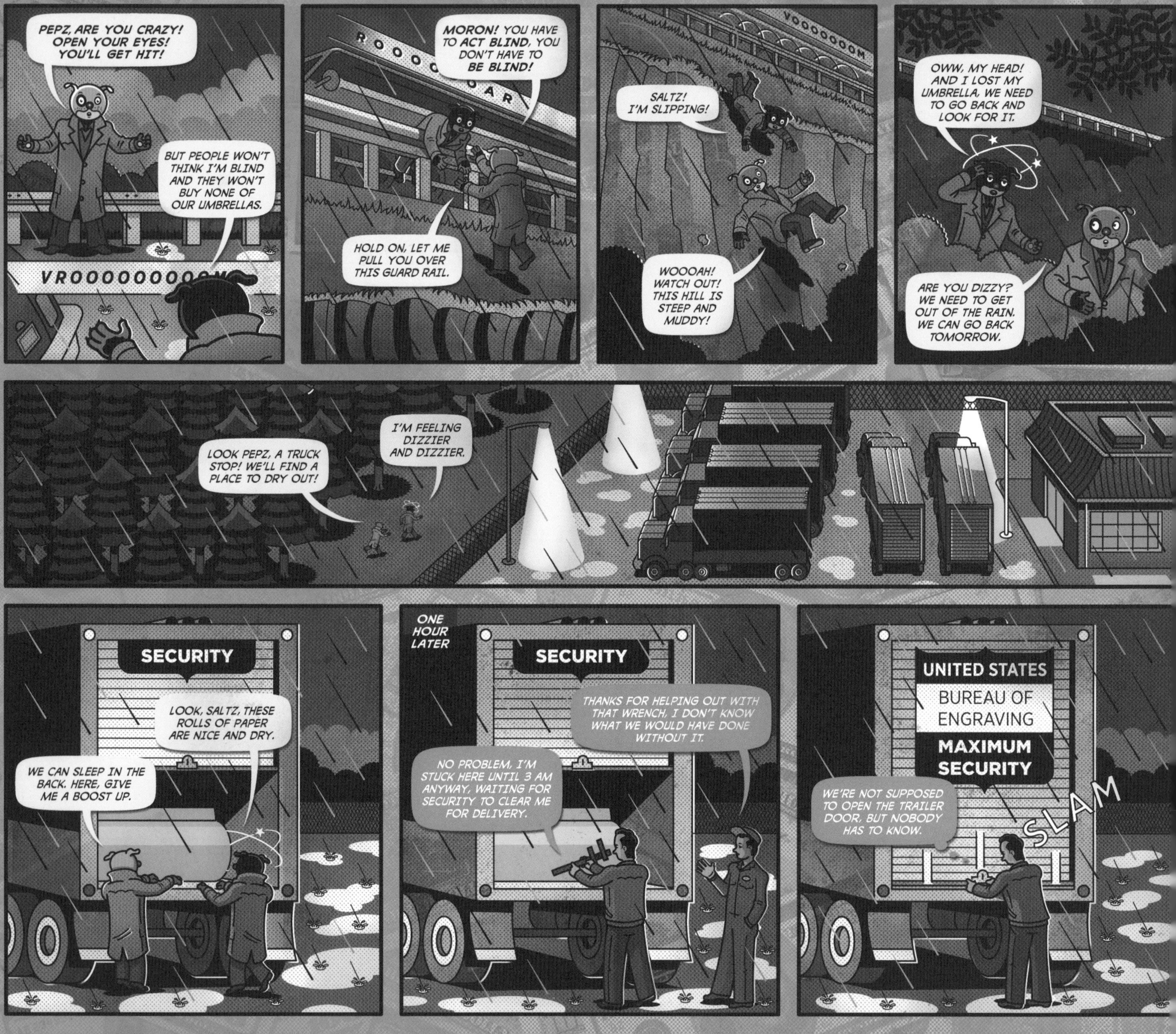
PEPZ, ARE YOU CRAZY! OPEN YOUR EYES! YOU'LL GET HIT!
BUT PEOPLE WON'T THINK I'M BLIND AND THEY WON'T BUY NONE OF OUR UMBRELLAS.
VROOOOOOOOOOM
ROOOO
OAR
MORON! YOU HAVE TO ACT BLIND, YOU DON'T HAVE TO BE BLIND!
HOLD ON, LET ME PULL YOU OVER THIS GUARD RAIL.
VOOOOOOOOM
SALTZ! I'M SLIPPING!
WOOOAH! WATCH OUT! THIS HILL IS STEEP AND MUDDY!
OWW, MY HEAD! AND I LOST MY UMBRELLA. WE NEED TO GO BACK AND LOOK FOR IT.
ARE YOU DIZZY? WE NEED TO GET OUT OF THE RAIN. WE CAN GO BACK TOMORROW.
LOOK PEPZ, A TRUCK STOP! WE'LL FIND A PLACE TO DRY OUT!
I'M FEELING DIZZIER AND DIZZIER.
SECURITY
LOOK, SALTZ, THESE ROLLS OF PAPER ARE NICE AND DRY.
WE CAN SLEEP IN THE BACK. HERE, GIVE ME A BOOST UP.
ONE HOUR LATER
SECURITY
THANKS FOR HELPING OUT WITH THAT WRENCH. I DON'T KNOW WHAT WE WOULD HAVE DONE WITHOUT IT.
NO PROBLEM, I'M STUCK HERE UNTIL 3 AM ANYWAY, WAITING FOR SECURITY TO CLEAR ME FOR DELIVERY.
UNITED STATES
BUREAU OF ENGRAVING
MAXIMUM SECURITY
WE'RE NOT SUPPOSED TO OPEN THE TRAILER DOOR, BUT NOBODY HAS TO KNOW.
SLAM

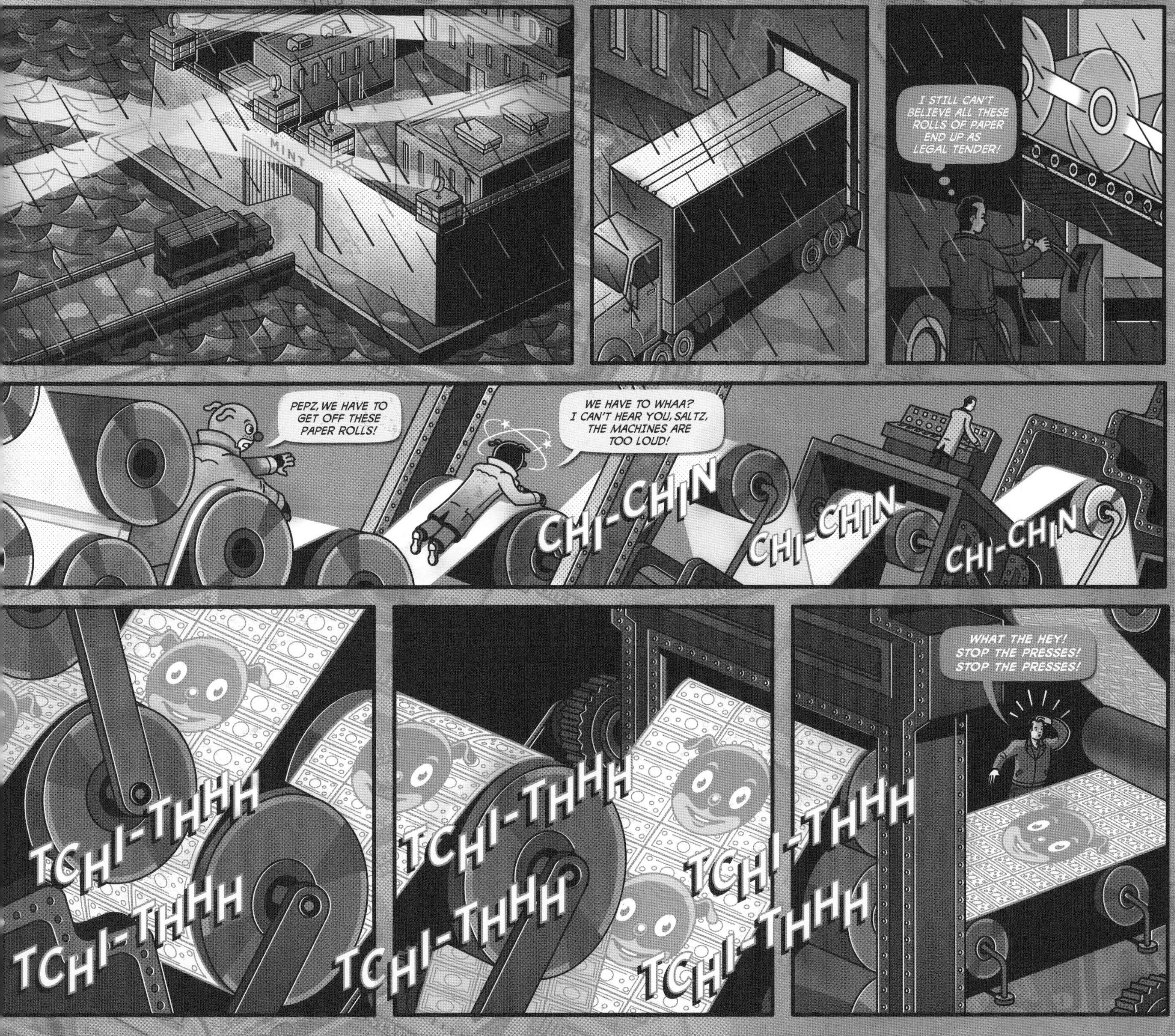
MINT
I STILL CAN'T BELIEVE ALL THESE ROLLS OF PAPER END UP AS LEGAL TENDER!
PEPZ, WE HAVE TO GET OFF THESE PAPER ROLLS!
WE HAVE TO WHAA? I CAN'T HEAR YOU, SALTZ, THE MACHINES ARE TOO LOUD!
CHI-CHIN
CHI-CHIN
CHI-CHIN
TCHI-THHH
TCHI-THHH
TCHI-THHH
TCHI-THHH
TCHI-THHH
TCHI-THHH
WHAT THE HEY! STOP THE PRESSES! STOP THE PRESSES!

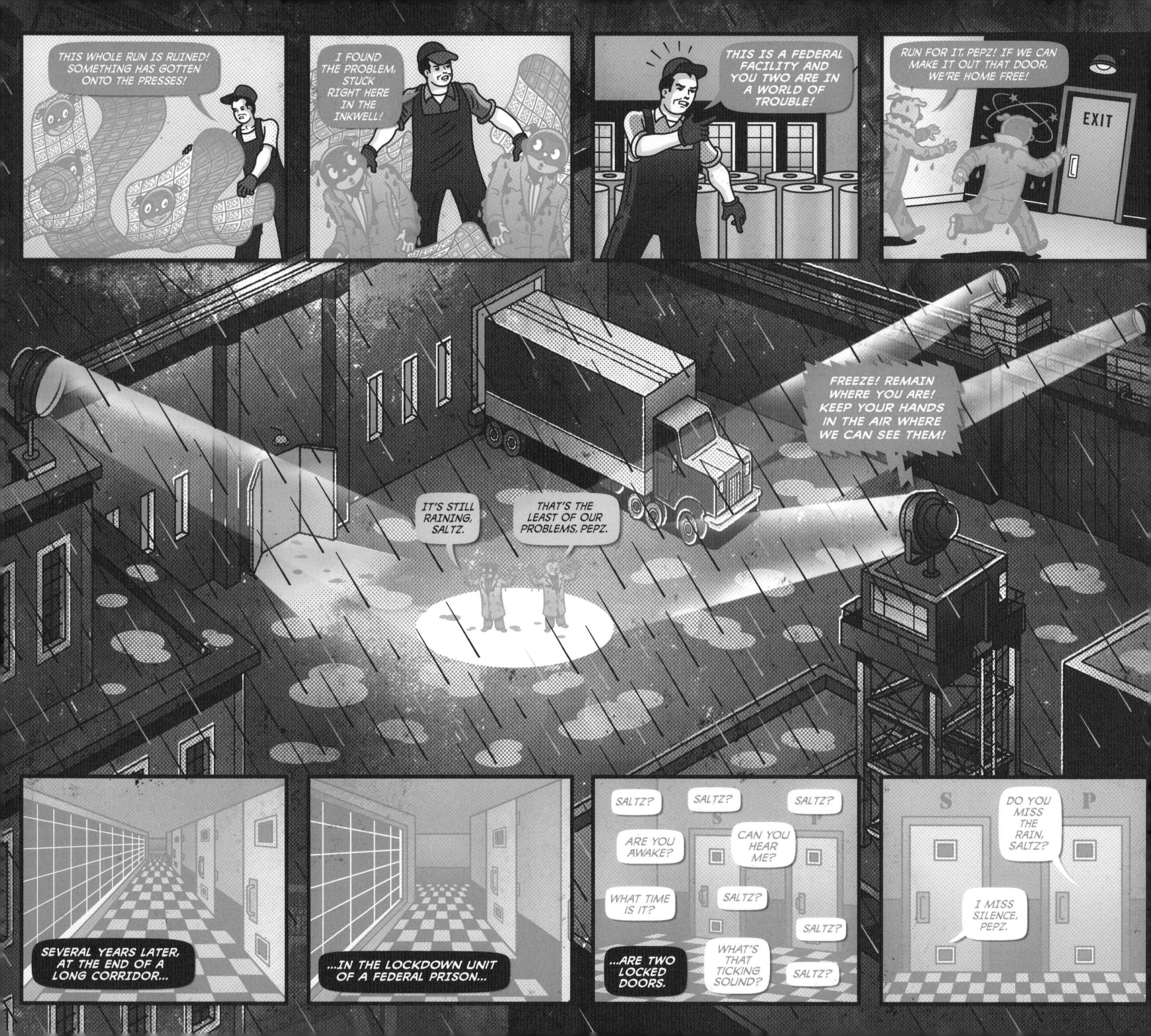
THIS WHOLE RUN IS RUINED! SOMETHING HAS GOTTEN ONTO THE PRESSES!
I FOUND THE PROBLEM, STUCK RIGHT HERE IN THE INKWELL!
THIS IS A FEDERAL FACILITY AND YOU TWO ARE IN A WORLD OF TROUBLE!
RUN FOR IT, PEPZ! IF WE CAN MAKE IT OUT THAT DOOR, WE'RE HOME FREE!
EXIT
FREEZE! REMAIN WHERE YOU ARE! KEEP YOUR HANDS IN THE AIR WHERE WE CAN SEE THEM!
IT'S STILL RAINING, SALTZ.
THAT'S THE LEAST OF OUR PROBLEMS, PEPZ.
SEVERAL YEARS LATER, AT THE END OF A LONG CORRIDOR...
...IN THE LOCKDOWN UNIT OF A FEDERAL PRISON...
...ARE TWO LOCKED DOORS.
SALTZ?
SALTZ?
SALTZ?
ARE YOU AWAKE?
CAN YOU HEAR ME?
WHAT TIME IS IT?
SALTZ?
SALTZ?
WHAT'S THAT TICKING SOUND?
SALTZ?
S
P
DO YOU MISS THE RAIN, SALTZ?
I MISS SILENCE, PEPZ.

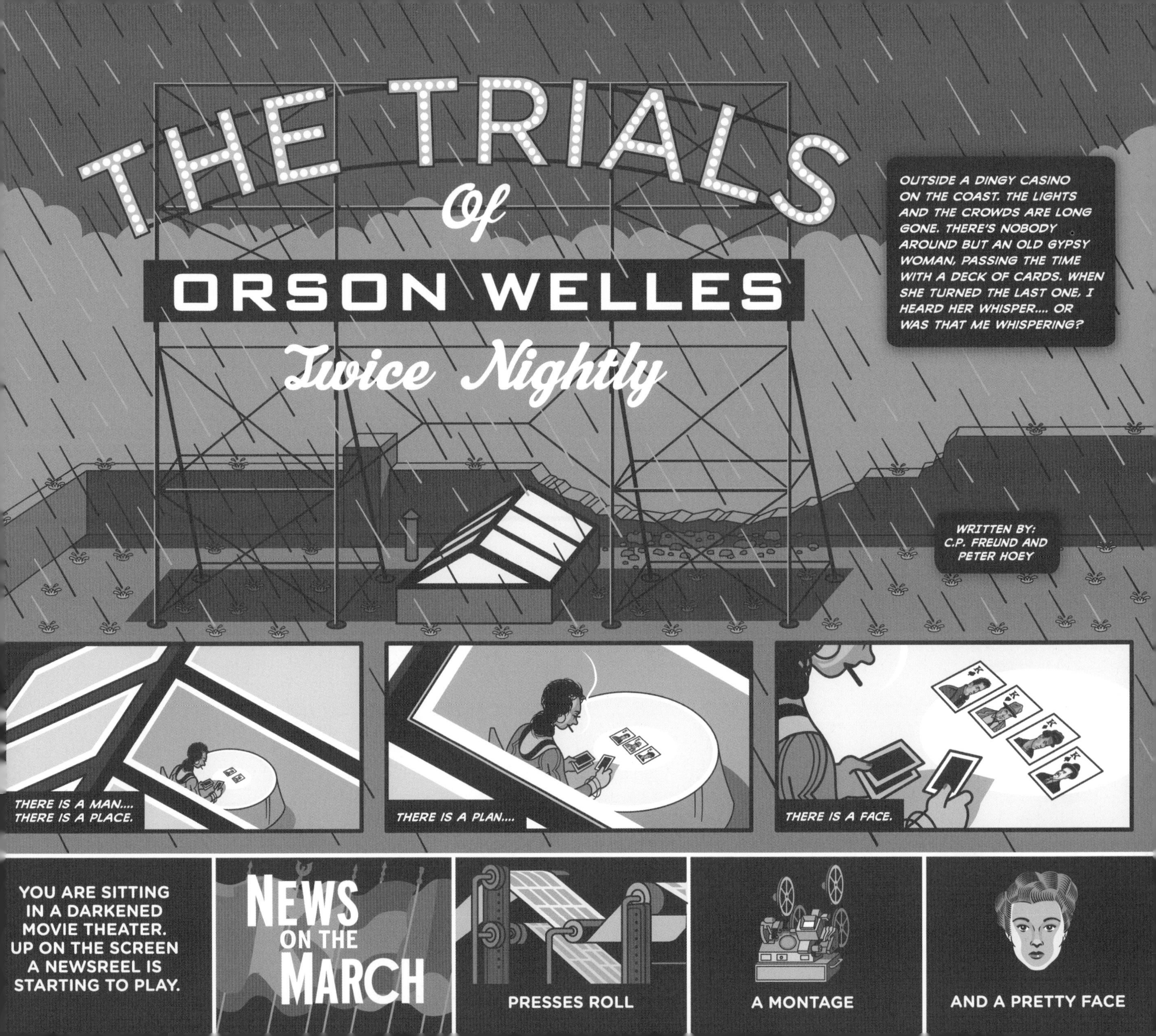
THE TRIALS
Of
ORSON WELLES
Twice Nightly
OUTSIDE A DINGY CASINO ON THE COAST. THE LIGHTS AND THE CROWDS ARE LONG GONE. THERE'S NOBODY AROUND BUT AN OLD GYPSY WOMAN, PASSING THE TIME WITH A DECK OF CARDS. WHEN SHE TURNED THE LAST ONE, I HEARD HER WHISPER.... OR WAS THAT ME WHISPERING?
WRITTEN BY: C.P. FREUND AND PETER HOEY
THERE IS A MAN.... THERE IS A PLACE.
THERE IS A PLAN....
THERE IS A FACE.
YOU ARE SITTING IN A DARKENED MOVIE THEATER. UP ON THE SCREEN A NEWSREEL IS STARTING TO PLAY.
NEWS ON THE MARCH
PRESSES ROLL
A MONTAGE
AND A PRETTY FACE

IN THE SEWERS UNDER VIENNA A FIGURE DASHES OUT.

CLOP CLOP CLOP CLOP

ARE YOU CHASING SOMEBODY ....

CLOP CLOP CLOP CLOP

OR IS SOMEBODY CHASING YOU?

CLOP CLOP CLOP CLOP

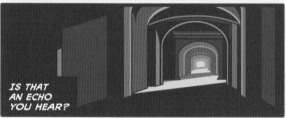

IS THAT AN ECHO YOU HEAR?

LISTEN CAREFULLY!

HOW DO I GET OUT OF HERE?

"THERE IS A PLACE." BUT WHERE?

OH, NO!

KANE

HUH?

KA

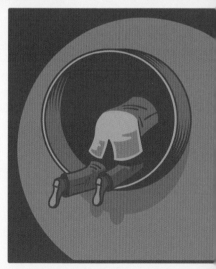

HOLLYWOOD

A DISTURBANCE

A REVELATION

NEWS ON THE MARCH

Alexander Korda and David O. Selznick Present:

THE THIRD MAN

Produced and Directed By: Carol Reed

Starring: Orson Welles as Harry Lime

AND A FERRIS WHEEL

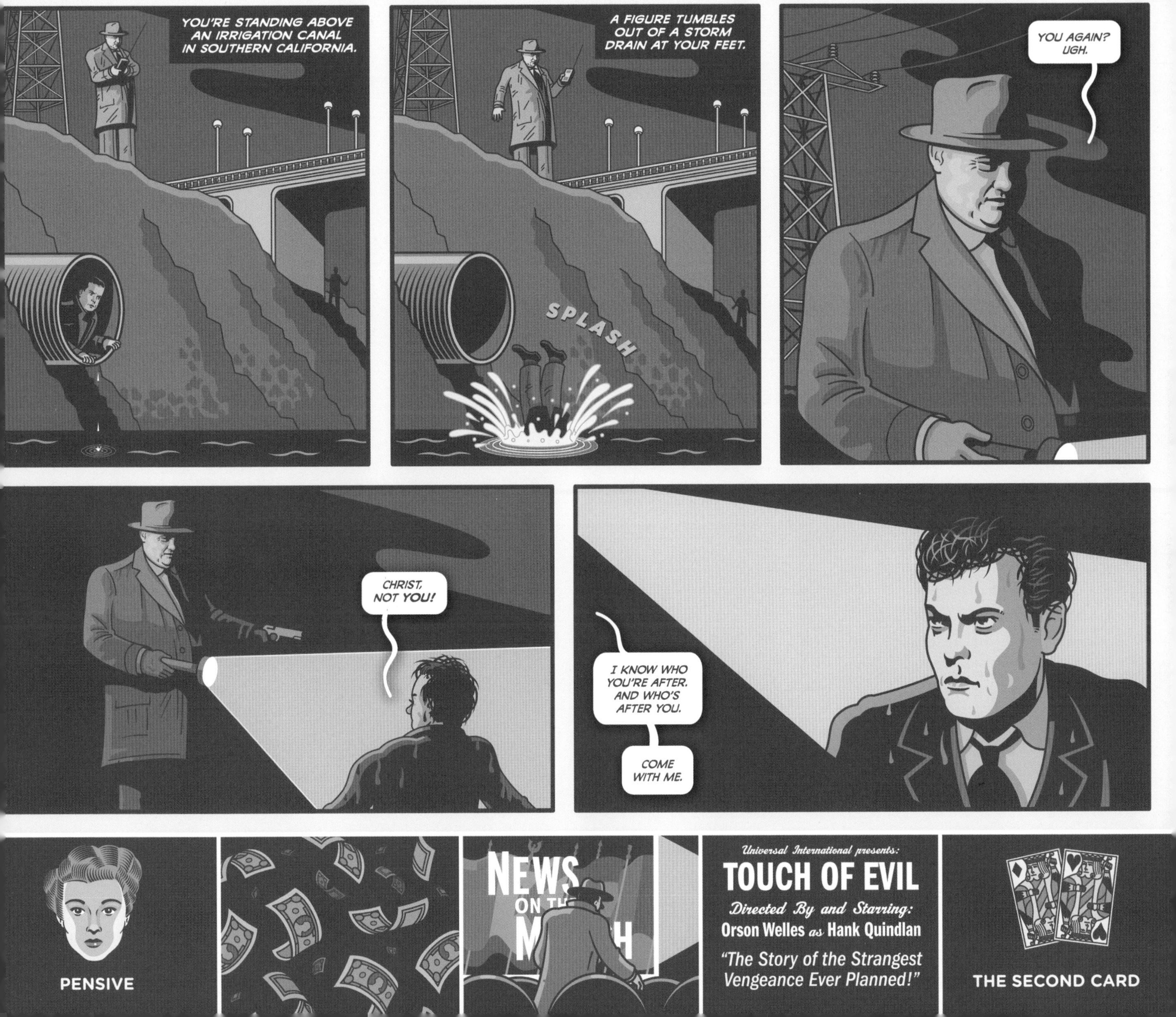

YOU'RE STANDING ABOVE AN IRRIGATION CANAL IN SOUTHERN CALIFORNIA.
A FIGURE TUMBLES OUT OF A STORM DRAIN AT YOUR FEET.
SPLASH
YOU AGAIN? UGH.
CHRIST, NOT YOU!
I KNOW WHO YOU'RE AFTER. AND WHO'S AFTER YOU.
COME WITH ME.
PENSIVE
NEWS ON THE MARCH
Universal International presents:
TOUCH OF EVIL
Directed By and Starring:
Orson Welles as Hank Quindlan
"The Story of the Strangest Vengeance Ever Planned!"
THE SECOND CARD

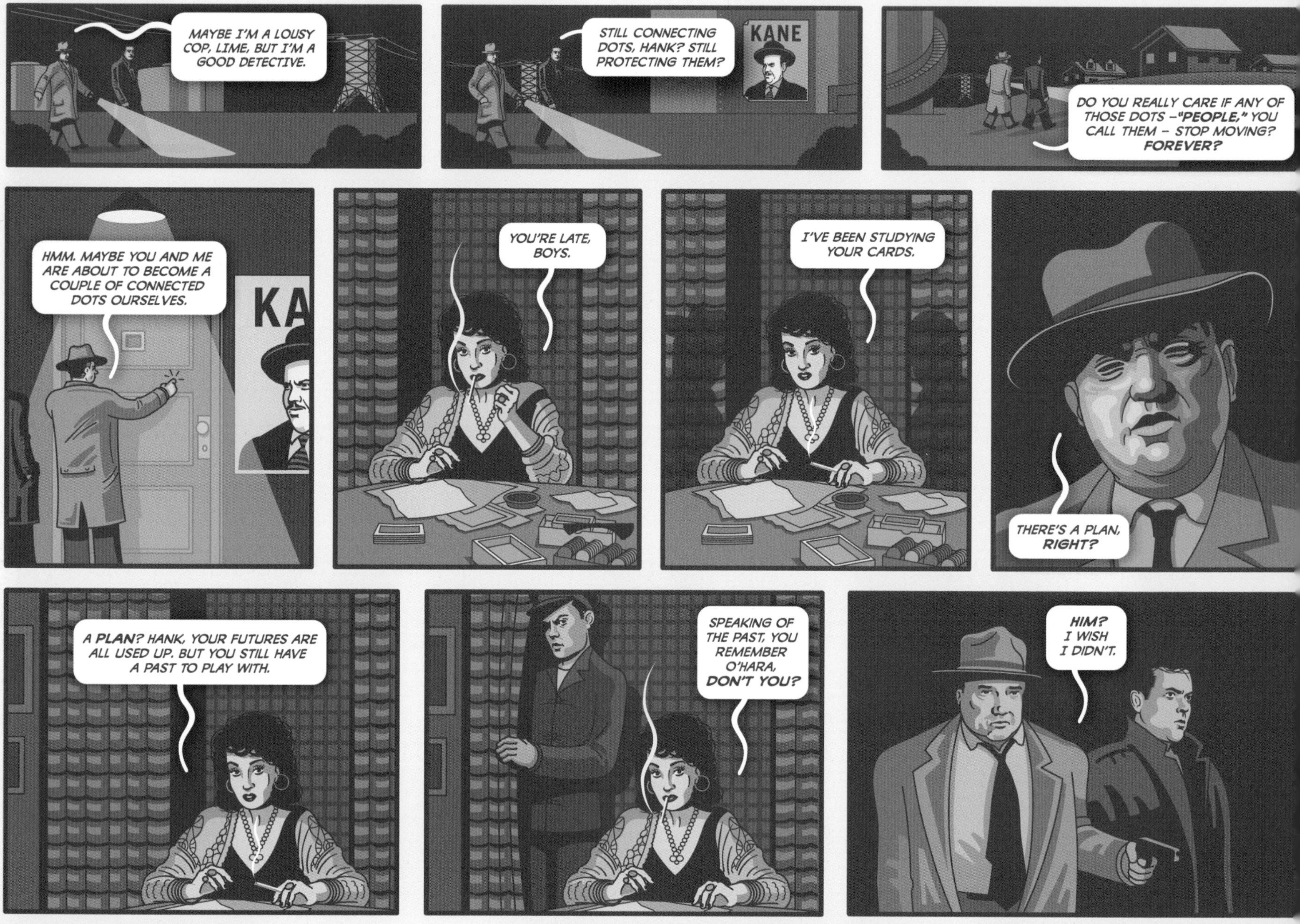
MAYBE I'M A LOUSY COP, LIME, BUT I'M A GOOD DETECTIVE.
STILL CONNECTING DOTS, HANK? STILL PROTECTING THEM?
KANE
DO YOU REALLY CARE IF ANY OF THOSE DOTS – "PEOPLE," YOU CALL THEM – STOP MOVING? FOREVER?
HMM. MAYBE YOU AND ME ARE ABOUT TO BECOME A COUPLE OF CONNECTED DOTS OURSELVES.
KA
YOU'RE LATE, BOYS.
I'VE BEEN STUDYING YOUR CARDS.
THERE'S A PLAN, RIGHT?
A PLAN? HANK, YOUR FUTURES ARE ALL USED UP. BUT YOU STILL HAVE A PAST TO PLAY WITH.
SPEAKING OF THE PAST, YOU REMEMBER O'HARA, DON'T YOU?
HIM? I WISH I DIDN'T.

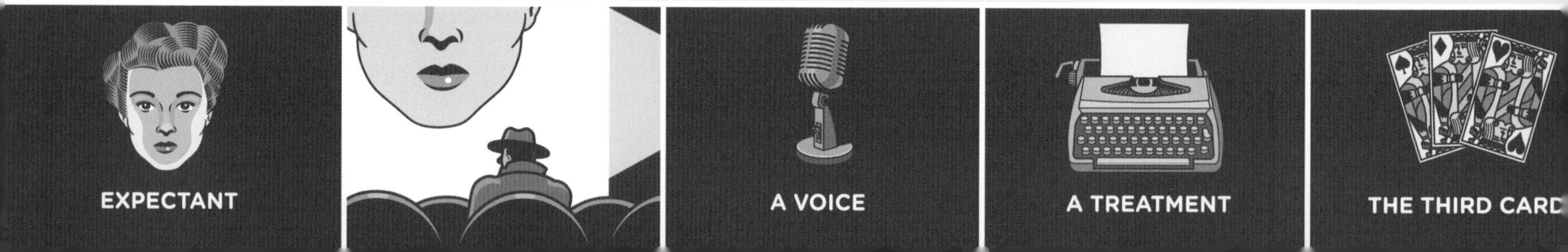
EXPECTANT
A VOICE
A TREATMENT
THE THIRD CARD

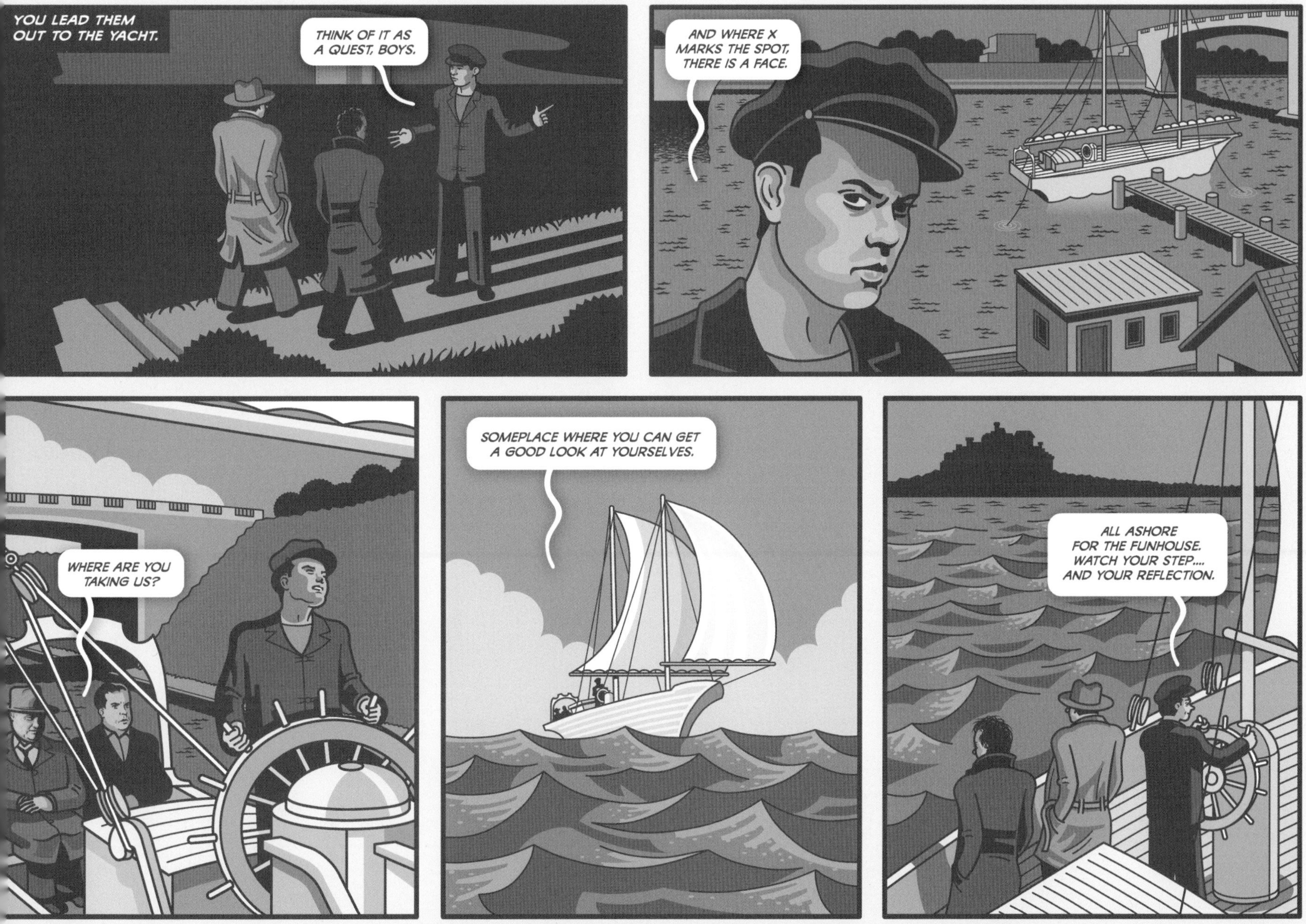
YOU LEAD THEM OUT TO THE YACHT.
THINK OF IT AS A QUEST, BOYS.
AND WHERE X MARKS THE SPOT, THERE IS A FACE.
WHERE ARE YOU TAKING US?
SOMEPLACE WHERE YOU CAN GET A GOOD LOOK AT YOURSELVES.
ALL ASHORE FOR THE FUNHOUSE. WATCH YOUR STEP.... AND YOUR REFLECTION.

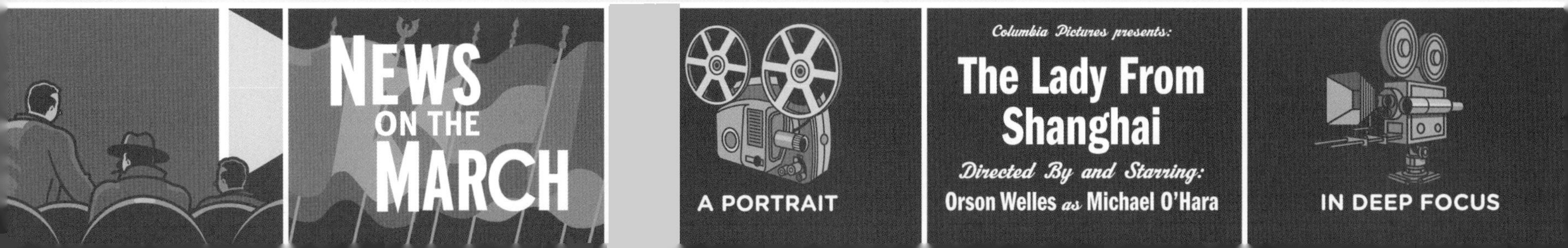
NEWS ON THE MARCH
A PORTRAIT
Columbia Pictures presents:
The Lady From Shanghai
Directed By and Starring:
Orson Welles as Michael O'Hara
IN DEEP FOCUS

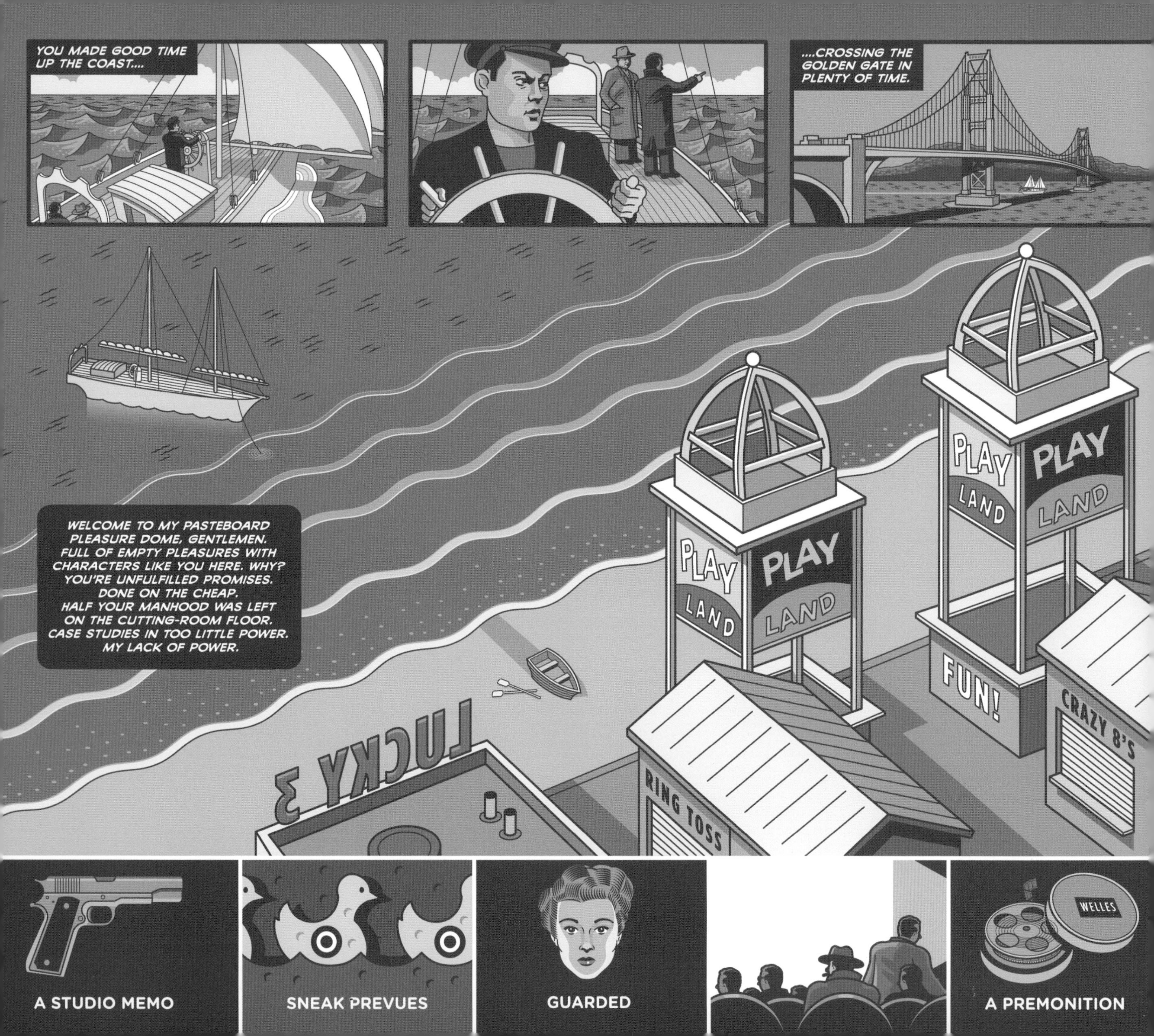
YOU MADE GOOD TIME UP THE COAST....
...CROSSING THE GOLDEN GATE IN PLENTY OF TIME.
WELCOME TO MY PASTEBOARD PLEASURE DOME, GENTLEMEN. FULL OF EMPTY PLEASURES WITH CHARACTERS LIKE YOU HERE. WHY? YOU'RE UNFULFILLED PROMISES. DONE ON THE CHEAP. HALF YOUR MANHOOD WAS LEFT ON THE CUTTING-ROOM FLOOR. CASE STUDIES IN TOO LITTLE POWER. MY LACK OF POWER.
PLAY LAND
PLAY LAND
PLAY LAND
PLAY LAND
FUN!
CRAZY 8'S
RING TOSS
LUCKY 3
A STUDIO MEMO
SNEAK PREVUES
GUARDED
WELLES
A PREMONITION

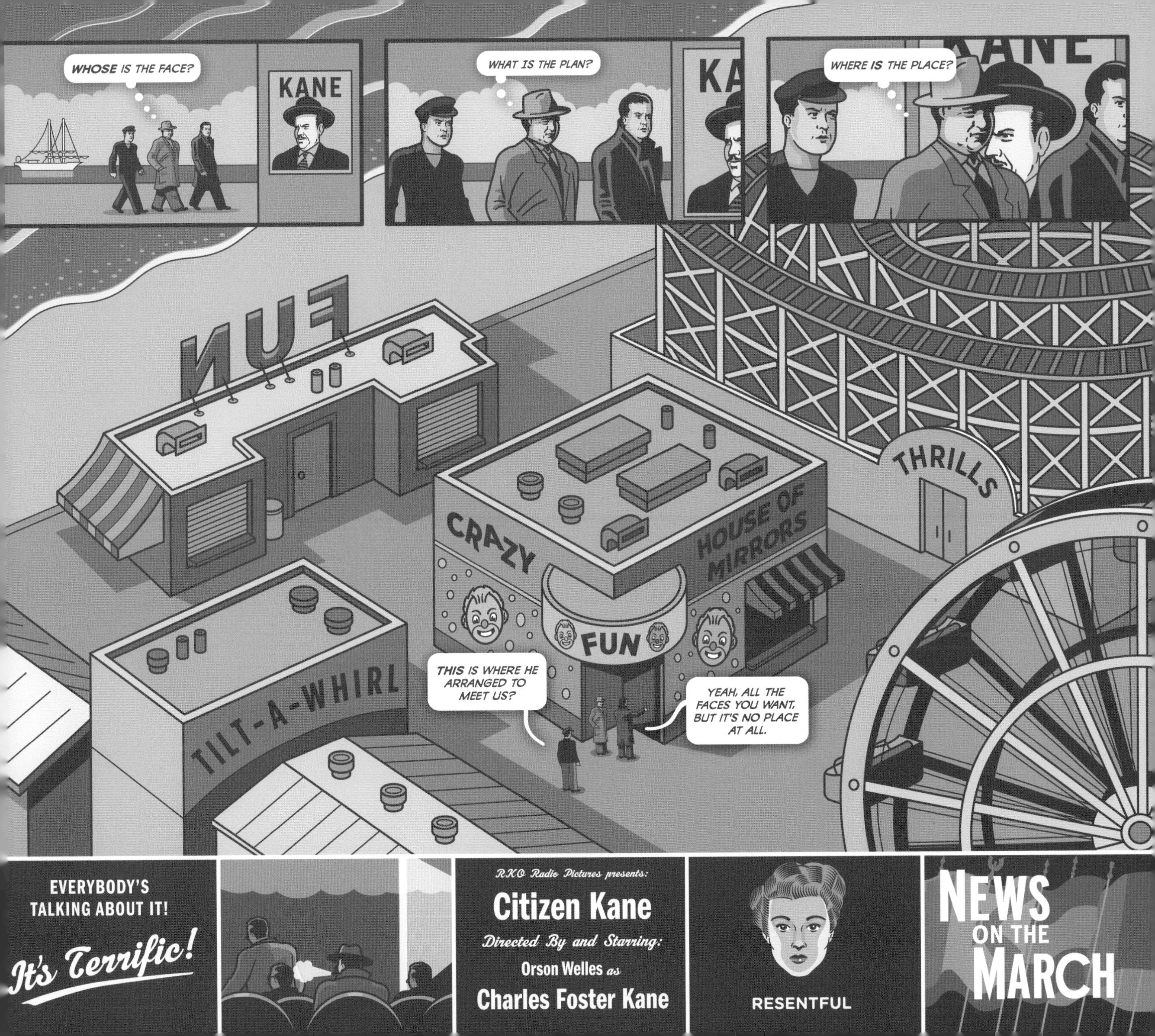
WHOSE IS THE FACE?
KANE
WHAT IS THE PLAN?
KA
WHERE IS THE PLACE?
KANE
FUN
THRILLS
CRAZY
HOUSE OF MIRRORS
FUN
TILT-A-WHIRL
THIS IS WHERE HE ARRANGED TO MEET US?
YEAH, ALL THE FACES YOU WANT, BUT IT'S NO PLACE AT ALL.
EVERYBODY'S TALKING ABOUT IT!
It's Terrific!
RKO Radio Pictures presents:
Citizen Kane
Directed By and Starring:
Orson Welles as
Charles Foster Kane
RESENTFUL
NEWS ON THE MARCH

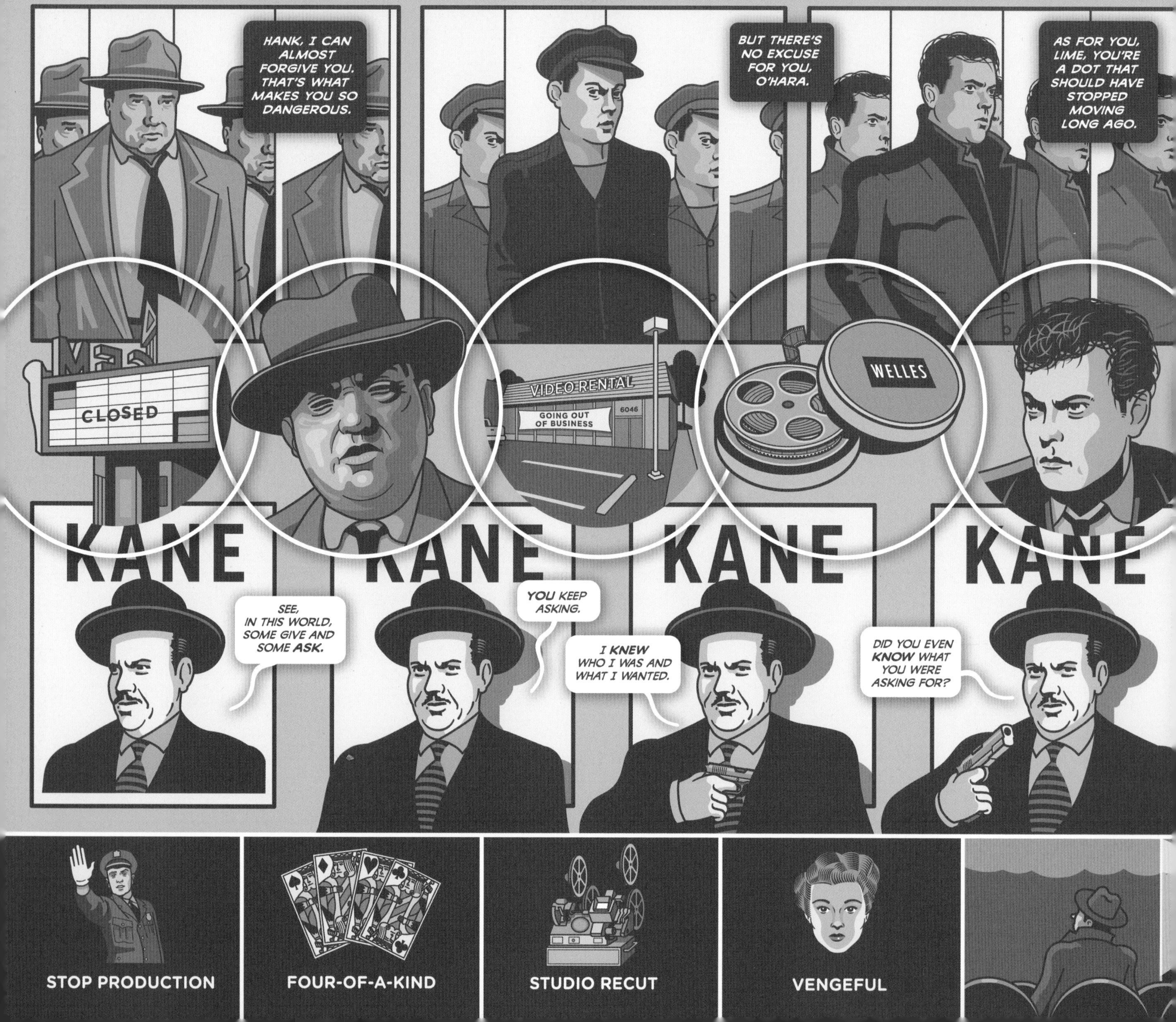
HANK, I CAN ALMOST FORGIVE YOU. THAT'S WHAT MAKES YOU SO DANGEROUS.
BUT THERE'S NO EXCUSE FOR YOU, O'HARA.
AS FOR YOU, LIME, YOU'RE A DOT THAT SHOULD HAVE STOPPED MOVING LONG AGO.
CLOSED
VIDEO RENTAL
GOING OUT OF BUSINESS
6046
WELLES
KANE
KANE
KANE
KANE
SEE, IN THIS WORLD, SOME GIVE AND SOME ASK.
YOU KEEP ASKING.
I KNEW WHO I WAS AND WHAT I WANTED.
DID YOU EVEN KNOW WHAT YOU WERE ASKING FOR?
STOP PRODUCTION
FOUR-OF-A-KIND
STUDIO RECUT
VENGEFUL

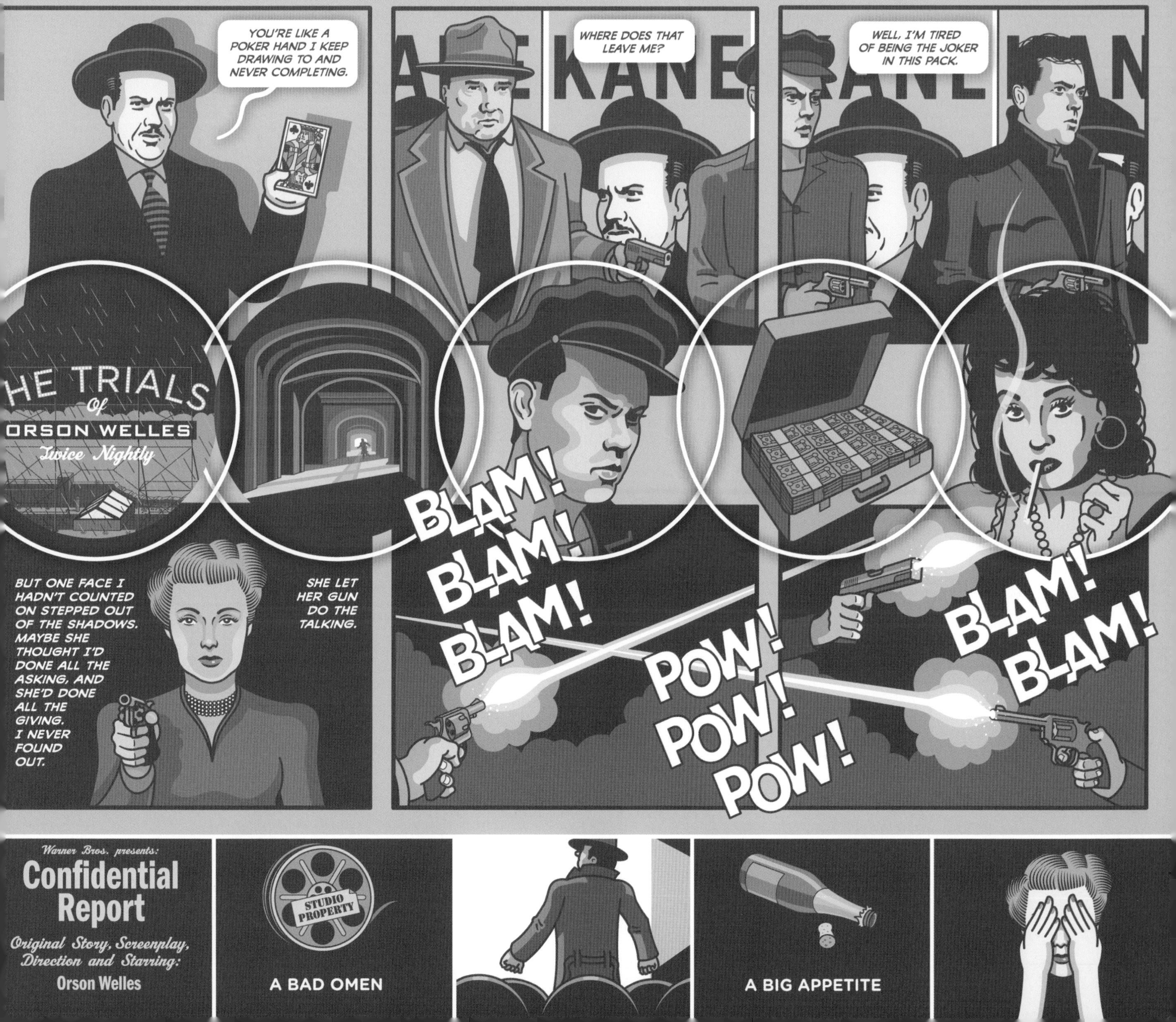
YOU'RE LIKE A POKER HAND I KEEP DRAWING TO AND NEVER COMPLETING.
WHERE DOES THAT LEAVE ME?
WELL, I'M TIRED OF BEING THE JOKER IN THIS PACK.
KANE
HE TRIALS Of ORSON WELLES Twice Nightly
BUT ONE FACE I HADN'T COUNTED ON STEPPED OUT OF THE SHADOWS. MAYBE SHE THOUGHT I'D DONE ALL THE ASKING, AND SHE'D DONE ALL THE GIVING. I NEVER FOUND OUT.
SHE LET HER GUN DO THE TALKING.
BLAM! BLAM! BLAM!
POW! POW! POW!
BLAM! BLAM!
Warner Bros. presents:
Confidential Report
Original Story, Screenplay, Direction and Starring:
Orson Welles
STUDIO PROPERTY
A BAD OMEN
A BIG APPETITE

THE SHOTS STOP, AND THE GLASS STOPS SMASHING. YOU'RE LYING IN CHAOS, WITHOUT A PLAN. PRONE, WITHOUT A FACE.

WHEN THE LAST REEL HAS RUN OUT, WHAT'S LEFT OF A MAN LIKE YOU?

BEHIND A SMASHED MIRROR AN OLD GYPSY WOMAN TURNS HER CARDS AS A PLAYER PIANO GROANS OFF-KEY.

A MAN? THEY WERE SOME KIND OF A MAN.

HER CARDS ARE BLANK. YOUR FUTURE IS USED UP. YOU'RE ONLY A PICTURE, AND NOW YOUR FACE IS FADING AWAY.

WHAT DOES IT MATTER WHAT YOU SAY ABOUT PEOPLE?

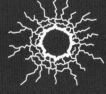

AN APERTURE

A MEMORY

CREDITS ROLL

The End

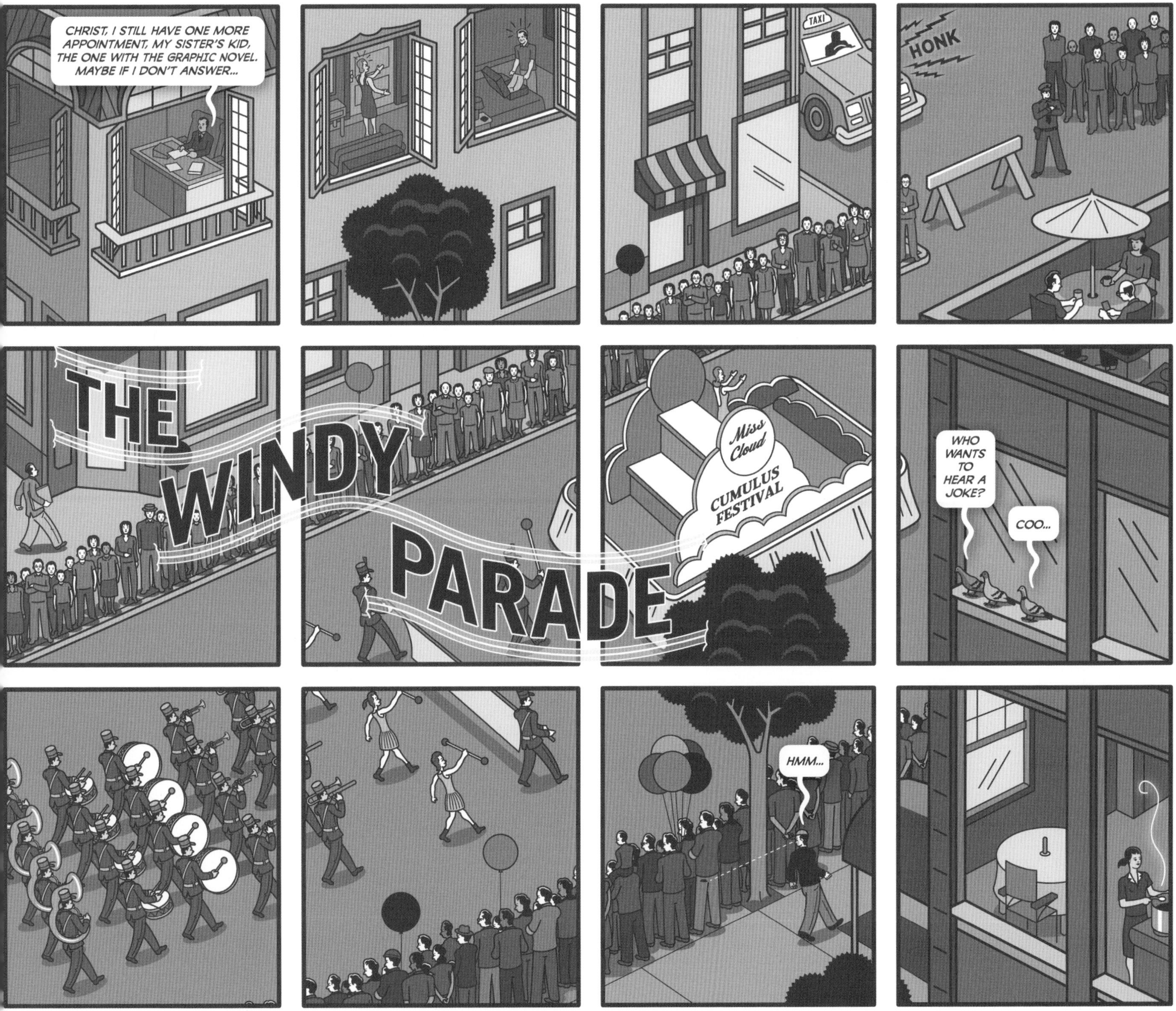
CHRIST, I STILL HAVE ONE MORE APPOINTMENT, MY SISTER'S KID, THE ONE WITH THE GRAPHIC NOVEL. MAYBE IF I DON'T ANSWER...
TAXI
HONK
THE WINDY PARADE
Miss Cloud
CUMULUS FESTIVAL
WHO WANTS TO HEAR A JOKE?
COO...
HMM...

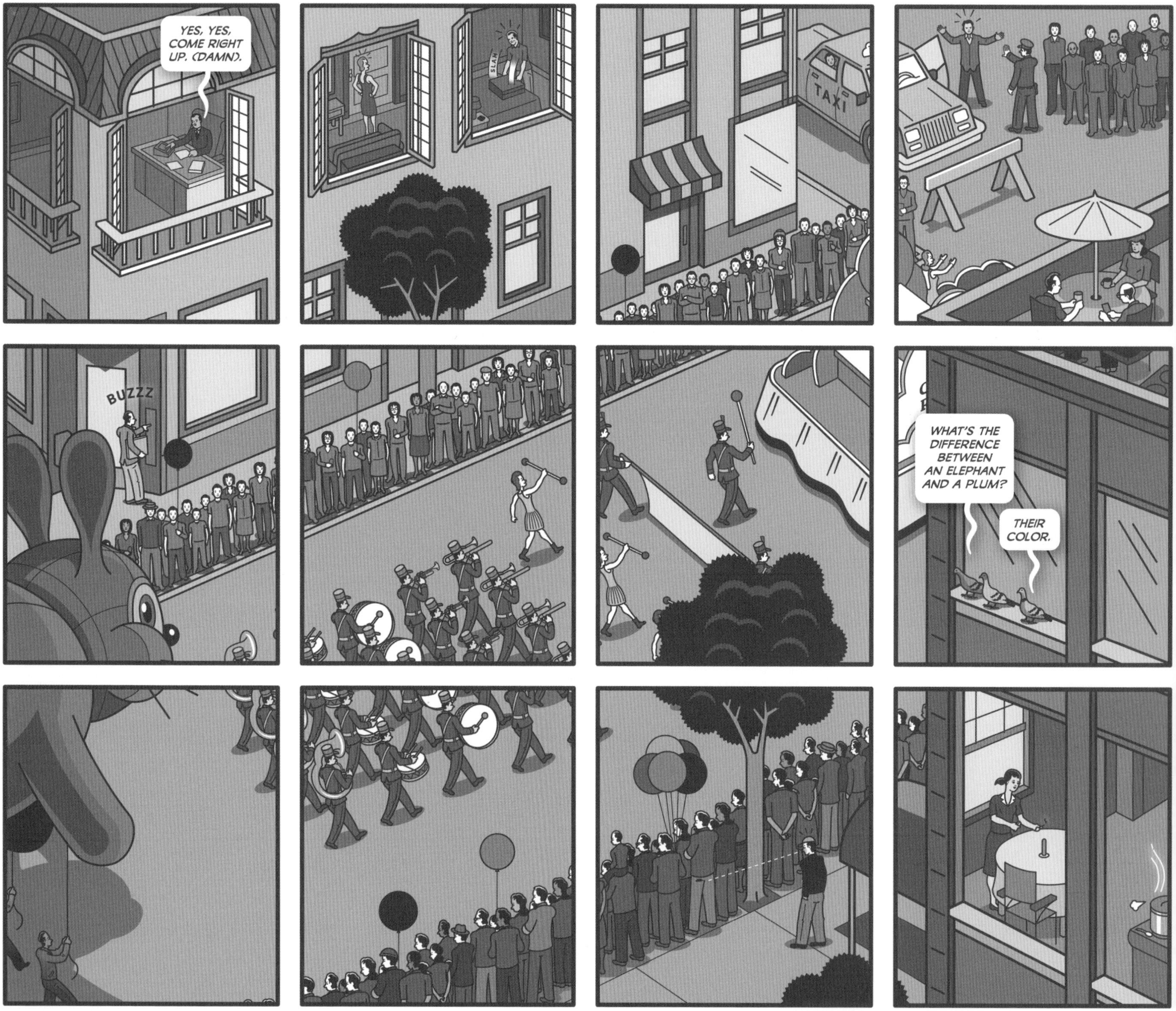

YES, YES, COME RIGHT UP. (DAMN).
SLAM
TAXI
BUZZZ
WHAT'S THE DIFFERENCE BETWEEN AN ELEPHANT AND A PLUM?
THEIR COLOR.

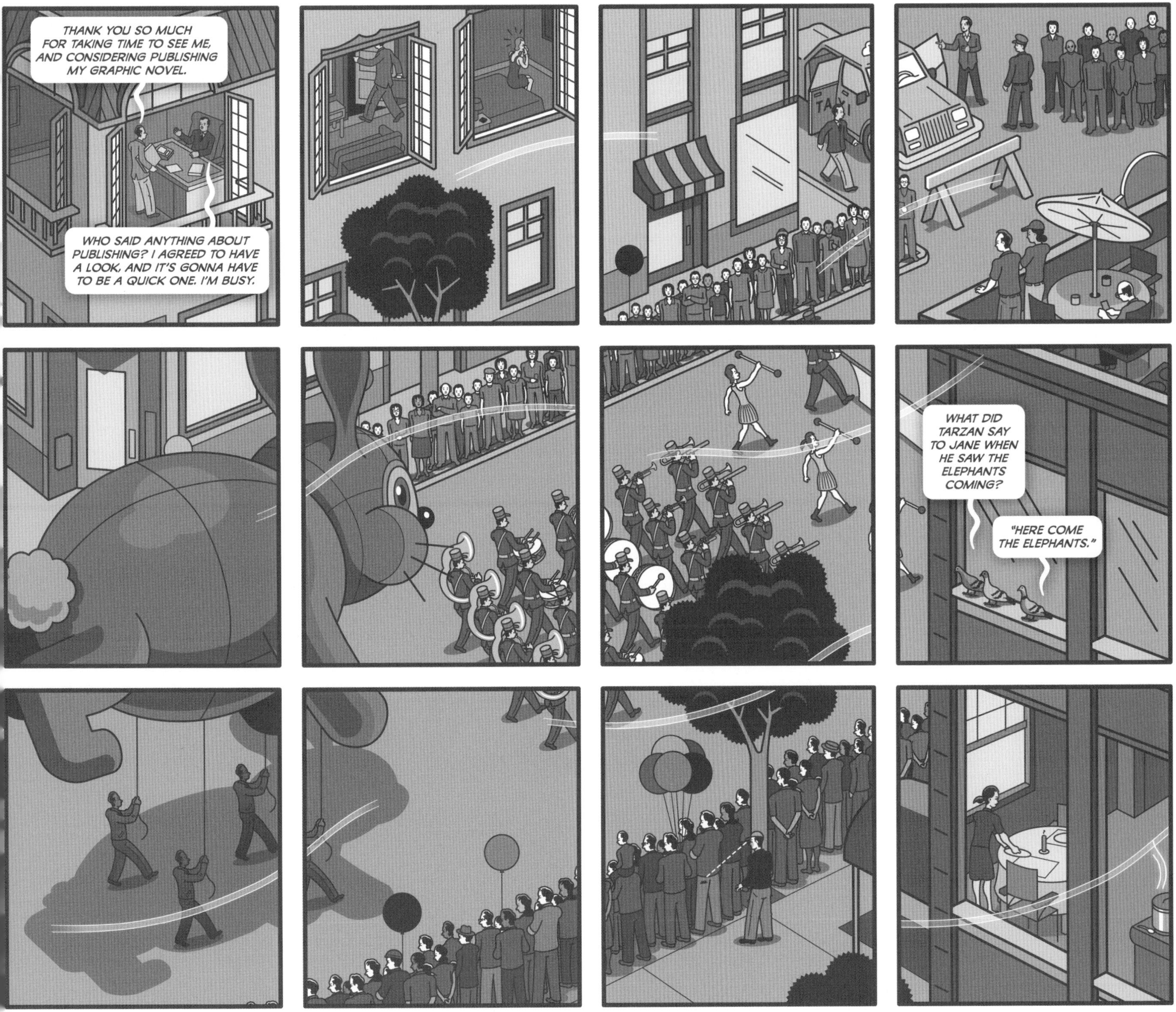
THANK YOU SO MUCH FOR TAKING TIME TO SEE ME, AND CONSIDERING PUBLISHING MY GRAPHIC NOVEL.
WHO SAID ANYTHING ABOUT PUBLISHING? I AGREED TO HAVE A LOOK, AND IT'S GONNA HAVE TO BE A QUICK ONE. I'M BUSY.
TAXI
WHAT DID TARZAN SAY TO JANE WHEN HE SAW THE ELEPHANTS COMING?
"HERE COME THE ELEPHANTS."

IT TOOK EIGHT YEARS TO WRITE AND DRAW. PUTTING ALL THAT SUFFERING ONTO 8.5-BY-11 SHEETS OF PAPER WAS EMOTIONALLY WRENCHING.

YEAH, YEAH, I CAN SEE THAT. WHEW, 942 PAGES YOU SAY? THAT'S A LOT OF THERAPY...

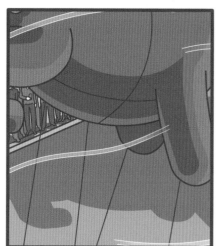

TIME TO FLY, THIS IS GOING N-O-W-H-E-R-E.

WHAT DID JANE SAY TO TARZAN WHEN SHE SAW THE ELEPHANTS COMING?

"HERE COME THE PLUMS." SHE WAS COLOR BLIND.

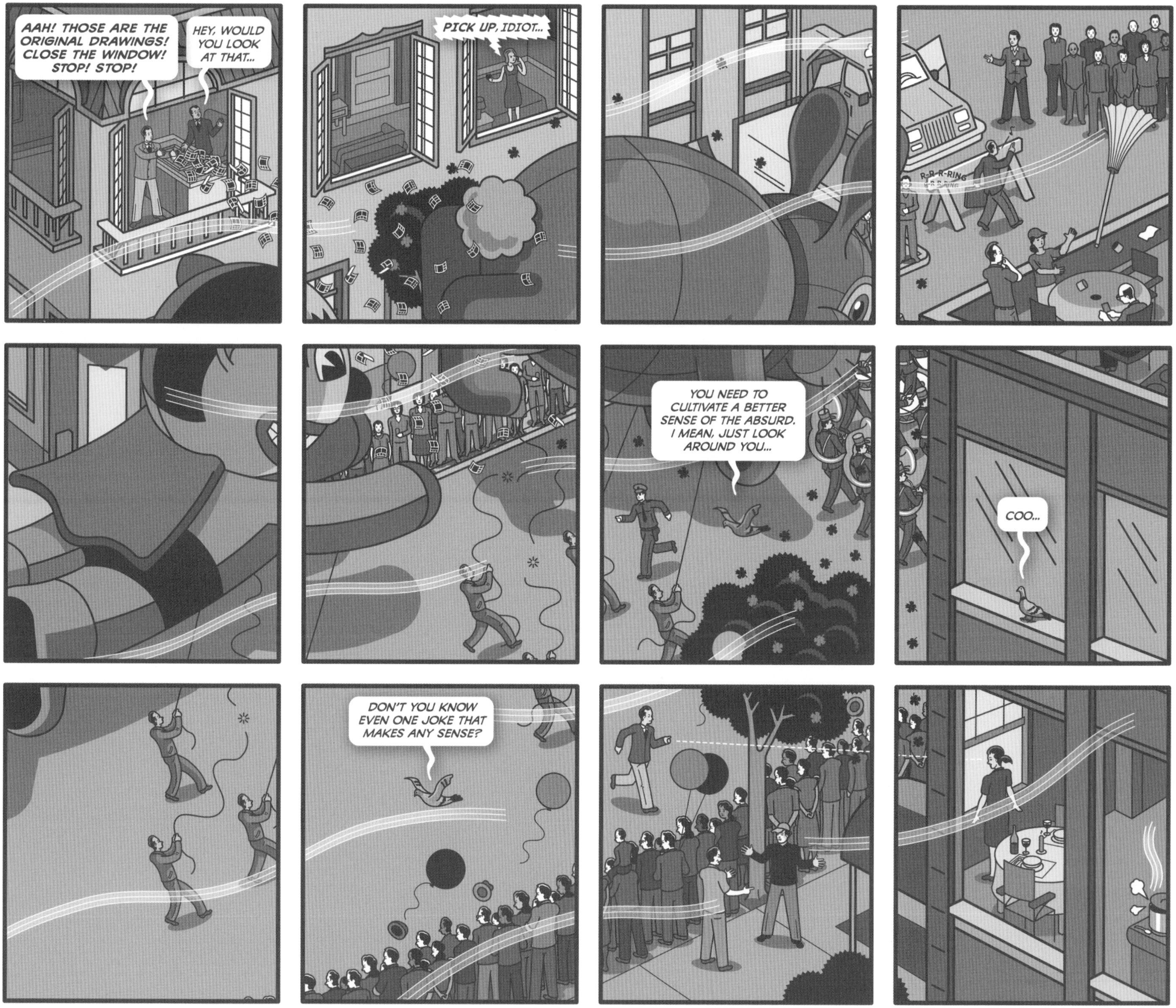
AAH! THOSE ARE THE ORIGINAL DRAWINGS! CLOSE THE WINDOW! STOP! STOP!
HEY, WOULD YOU LOOK AT THAT...
PICK UP, IDIOT...
R-R-R-RING
YOU NEED TO CULTIVATE A BETTER SENSE OF THE ABSURD. I MEAN, JUST LOOK AROUND YOU...
COO...
DON'T YOU KNOW EVEN ONE JOKE THAT MAKES ANY SENSE?

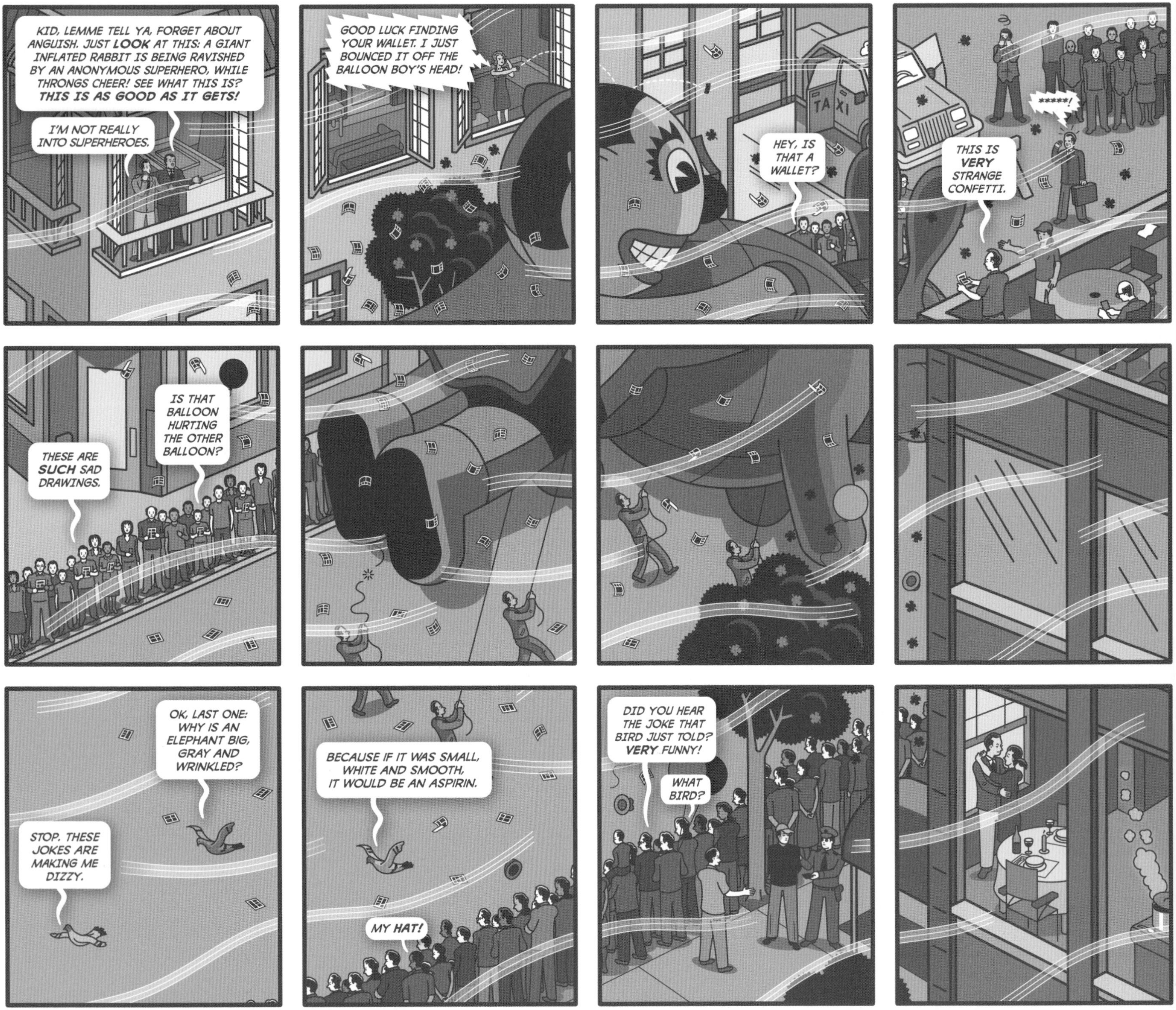
KID, LEMME TELL YA, FORGET ABOUT ANGUISH. JUST **LOOK** AT THIS: A GIANT INFLATED RABBIT IS BEING RAVISHED BY AN ANONYMOUS SUPERHERO, WHILE THRONGS CHEER! SEE WHAT THIS IS? **THIS IS AS GOOD AS IT GETS!**
I'M NOT REALLY INTO SUPERHEROES.
GOOD LUCK FINDING YOUR WALLET. I JUST BOUNCED IT OFF THE BALLOON BOY'S HEAD!
TAXI
HEY, IS THAT A WALLET?
*****!
THIS IS **VERY** STRANGE CONFETTI.
THESE ARE **SUCH** SAD DRAWINGS.
IS THAT BALLOON HURTING THE OTHER BALLOON?
OK, LAST ONE: WHY IS AN ELEPHANT BIG, GRAY AND WRINKLED?
STOP. THESE JOKES ARE MAKING ME DIZZY.
BECAUSE IF IT WAS SMALL, WHITE AND SMOOTH, IT WOULD BE AN ASPIRIN.
MY **HAT!**
DID YOU HEAR THE JOKE THAT BIRD JUST TOLD? **VERY** FUNNY!
WHAT BIRD?

the INTEROFFICE MEMO

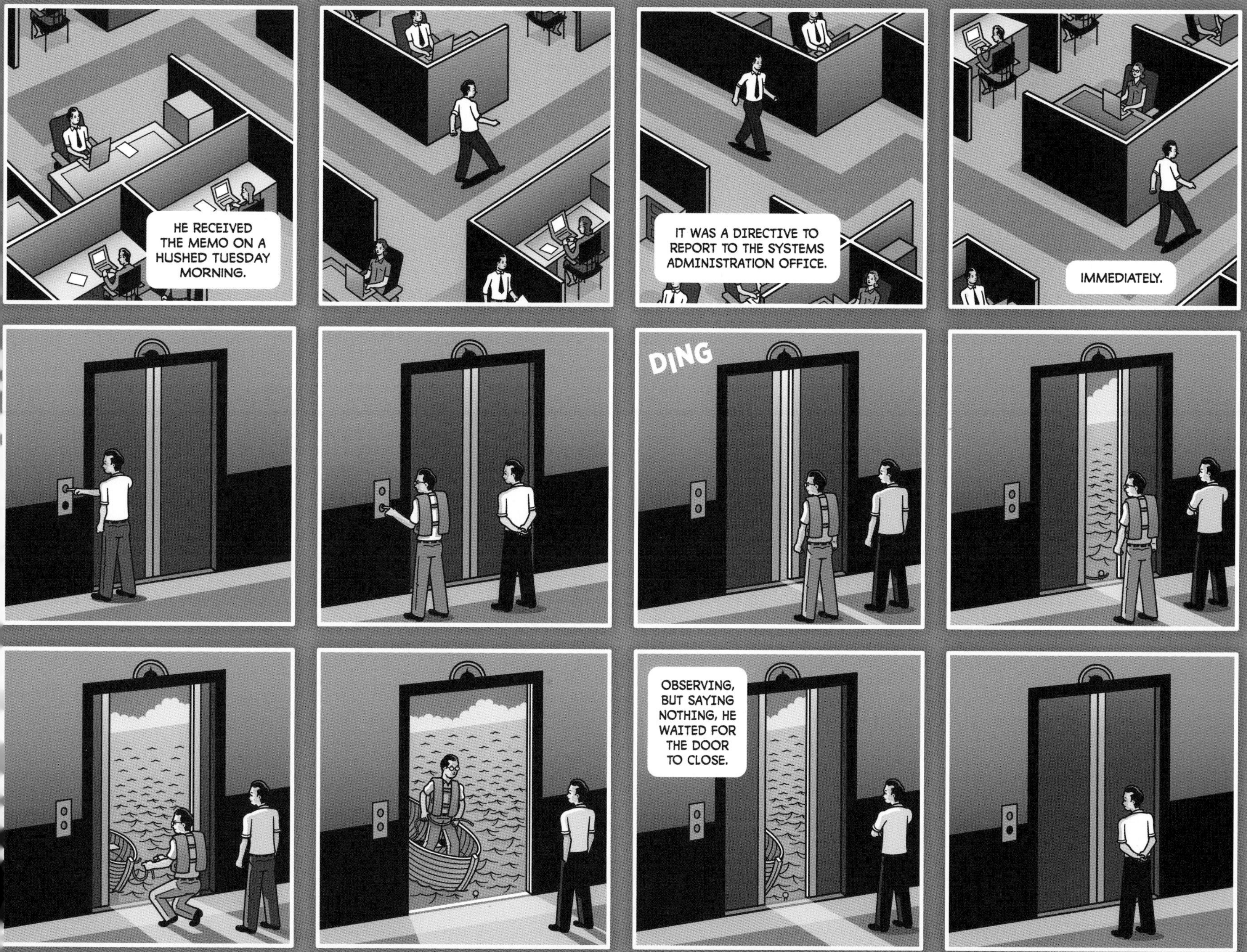
HE RECEIVED THE MEMO ON A HUSHED TUESDAY MORNING.
IT WAS A DIRECTIVE TO REPORT TO THE SYSTEMS ADMINISTRATION OFFICE.
IMMEDIATELY.
DING
OBSERVING, BUT SAYING NOTHING, HE WAITED FOR THE DOOR TO CLOSE.

DING

FOLLOWING THE EXAMPLE, HE LOOSENED THE ROPE AND CLAMBERED ABOARD.

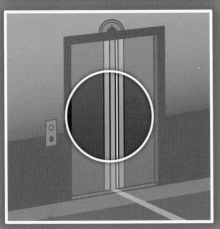

DING

WHEN THE FOG LIFTED HE COULD SEE THE ISLAND CLEARLY.

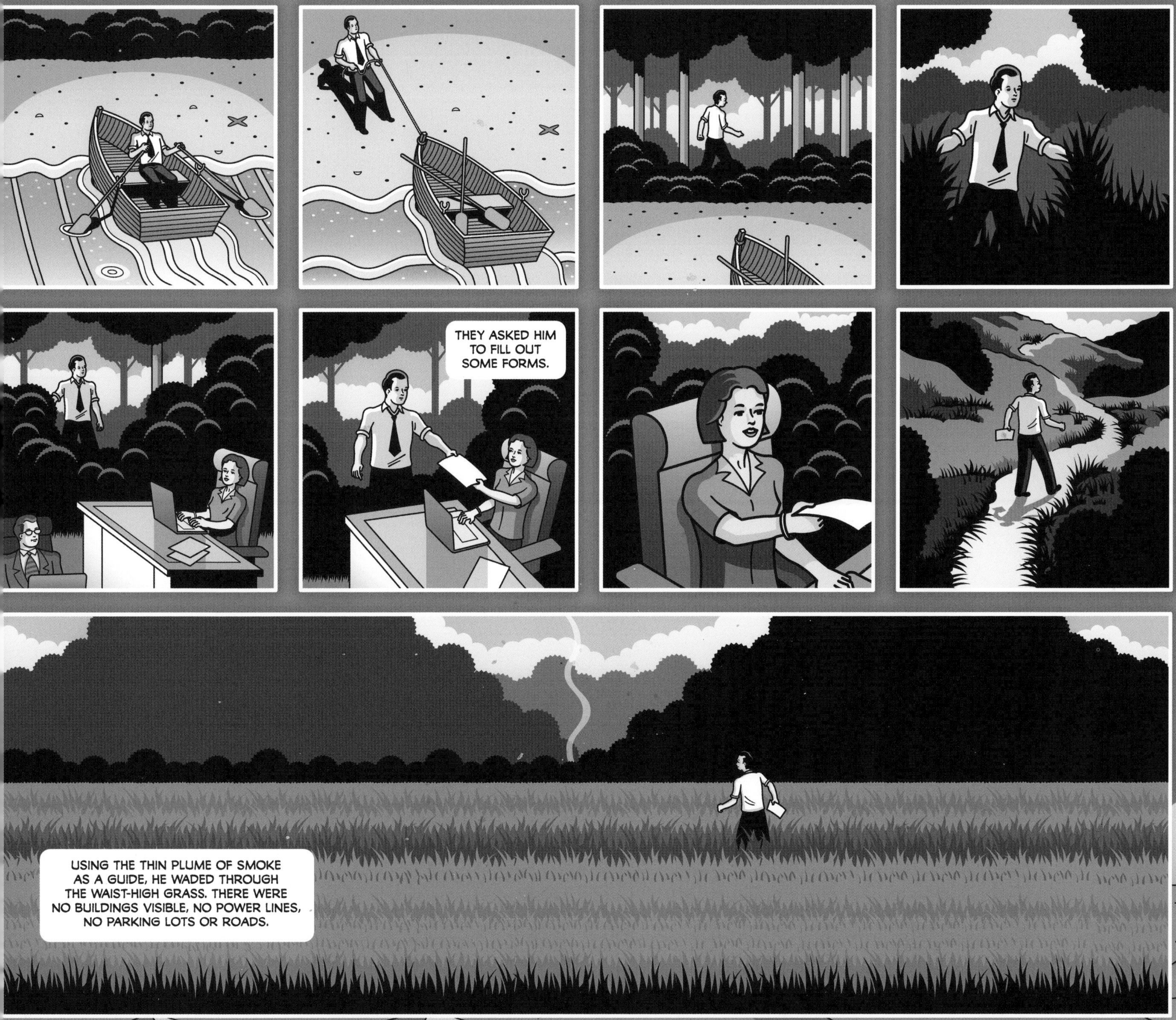
THEY ASKED HIM TO FILL OUT SOME FORMS.
USING THE THIN PLUME OF SMOKE AS A GUIDE, HE WADED THROUGH THE WAIST-HIGH GRASS. THERE WERE NO BUILDINGS VISIBLE, NO POWER LINES, NO PARKING LOTS OR ROADS.

THE SMELL OF GRILLING MEAT HUNG OVER THE STEEPLY BANKED ARROYO.

AN ACCOUNT VERIFICATION WAS LOGGED IN.

FURTHER DIRECTIONS WERE PROVIDED.

DING

WAS THE ELEVATOR RISING OR THE GROUND DROPPING? IT WAS IMPOSSIBLE TO TELL.

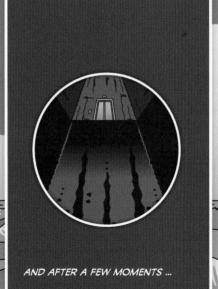

AND AFTER A FEW MOMENTS ...

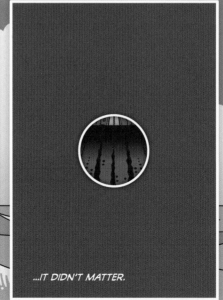

...IT DIDN'T MATTER.

DING

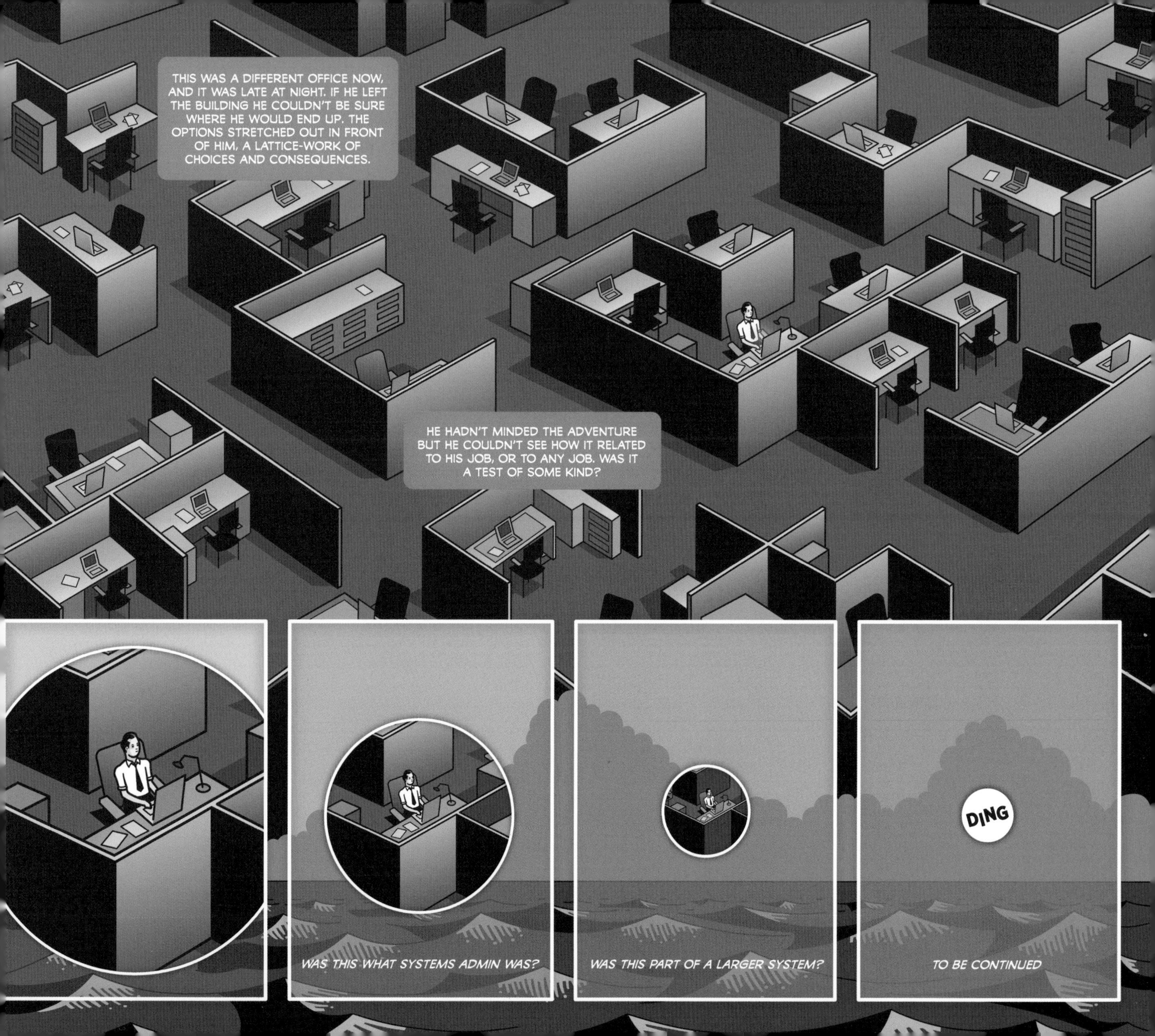
THIS WAS A DIFFERENT OFFICE NOW, AND IT WAS LATE AT NIGHT. IF HE LEFT THE BUILDING HE COULDN'T BE SURE WHERE HE WOULD END UP. THE OPTIONS STRETCHED OUT IN FRONT OF HIM, A LATTICE-WORK OF CHOICES AND CONSEQUENCES.
HE HADN'T MINDED THE ADVENTURE BUT HE COULDN'T SEE HOW IT RELATED TO HIS JOB, OR TO ANY JOB. WAS IT A TEST OF SOME KIND?
WAS THIS WHAT SYSTEMS ADMIN WAS?
WAS THIS PART OF A LARGER SYSTEM?
DING
TO BE CONTINUED

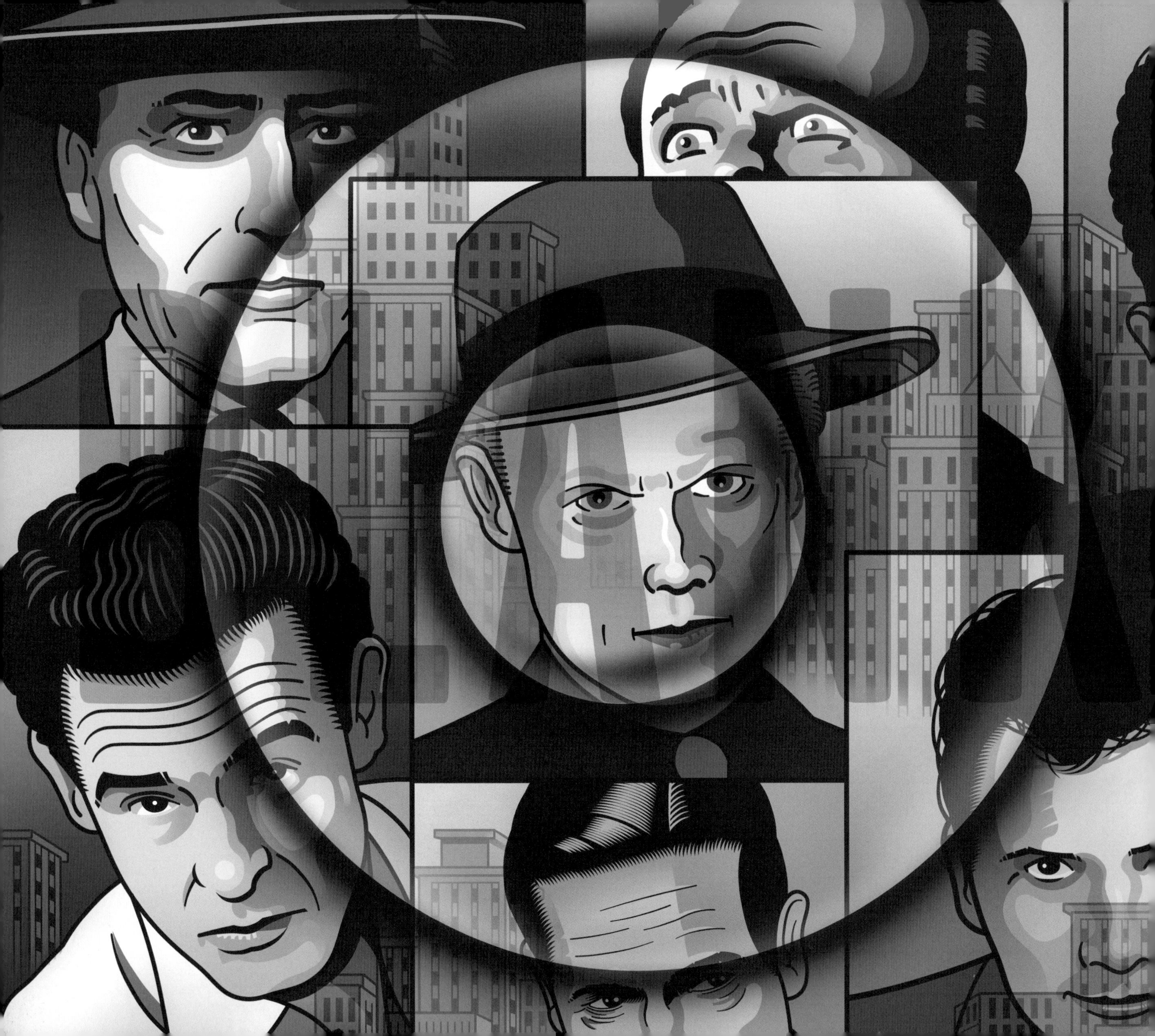

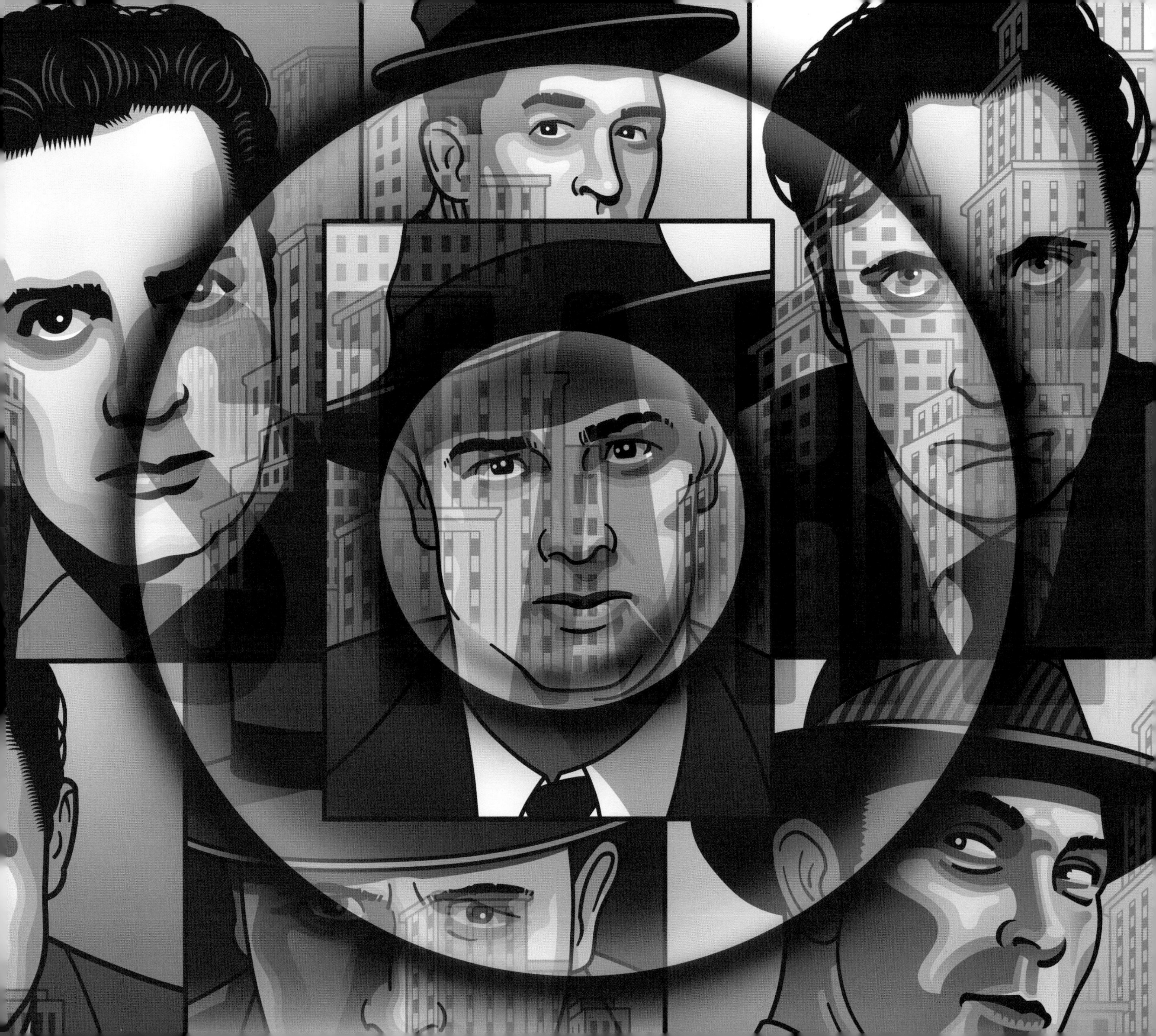

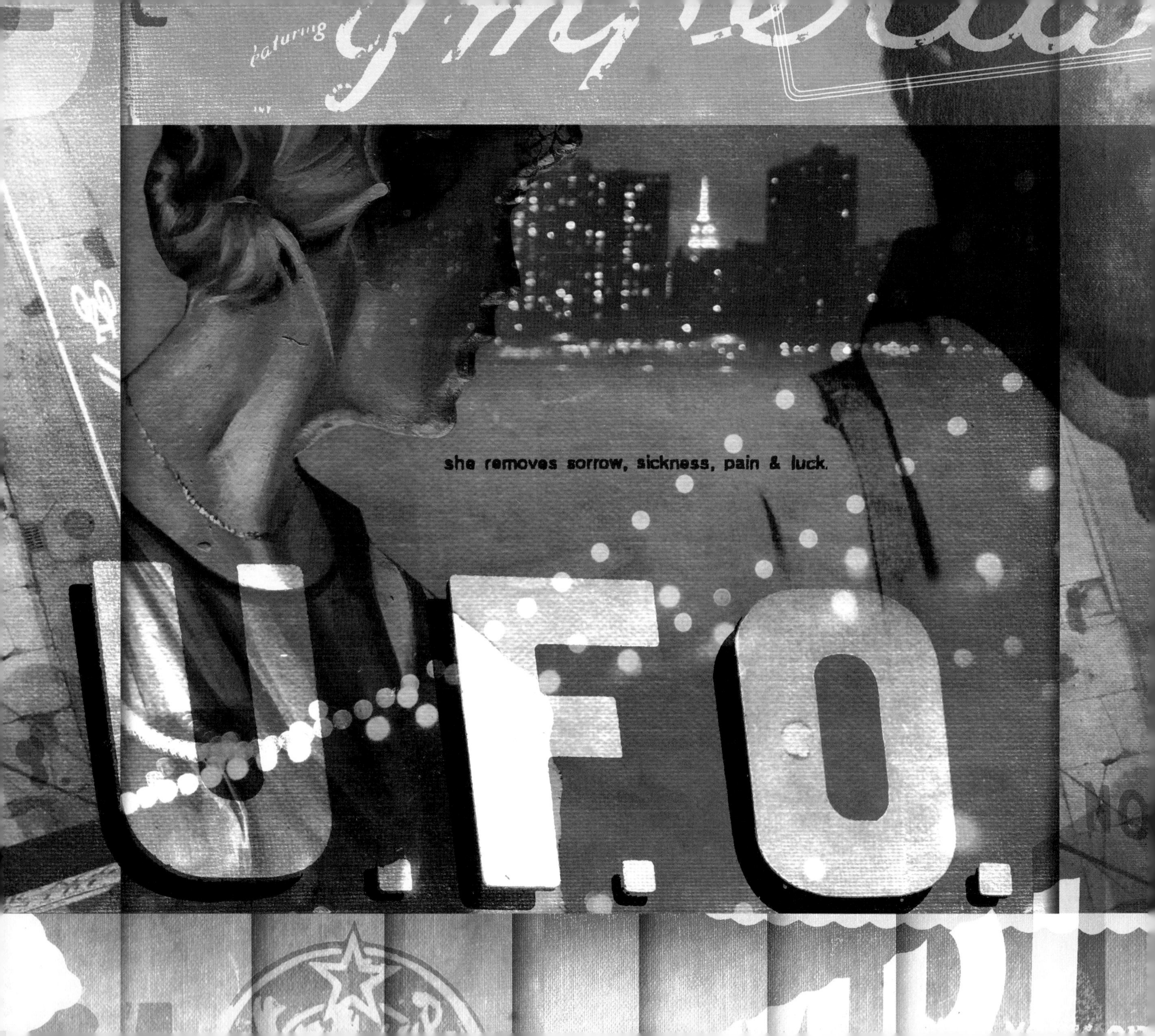
featuring
she removes sorrow, sickness, pain & luck.
U.F.O.

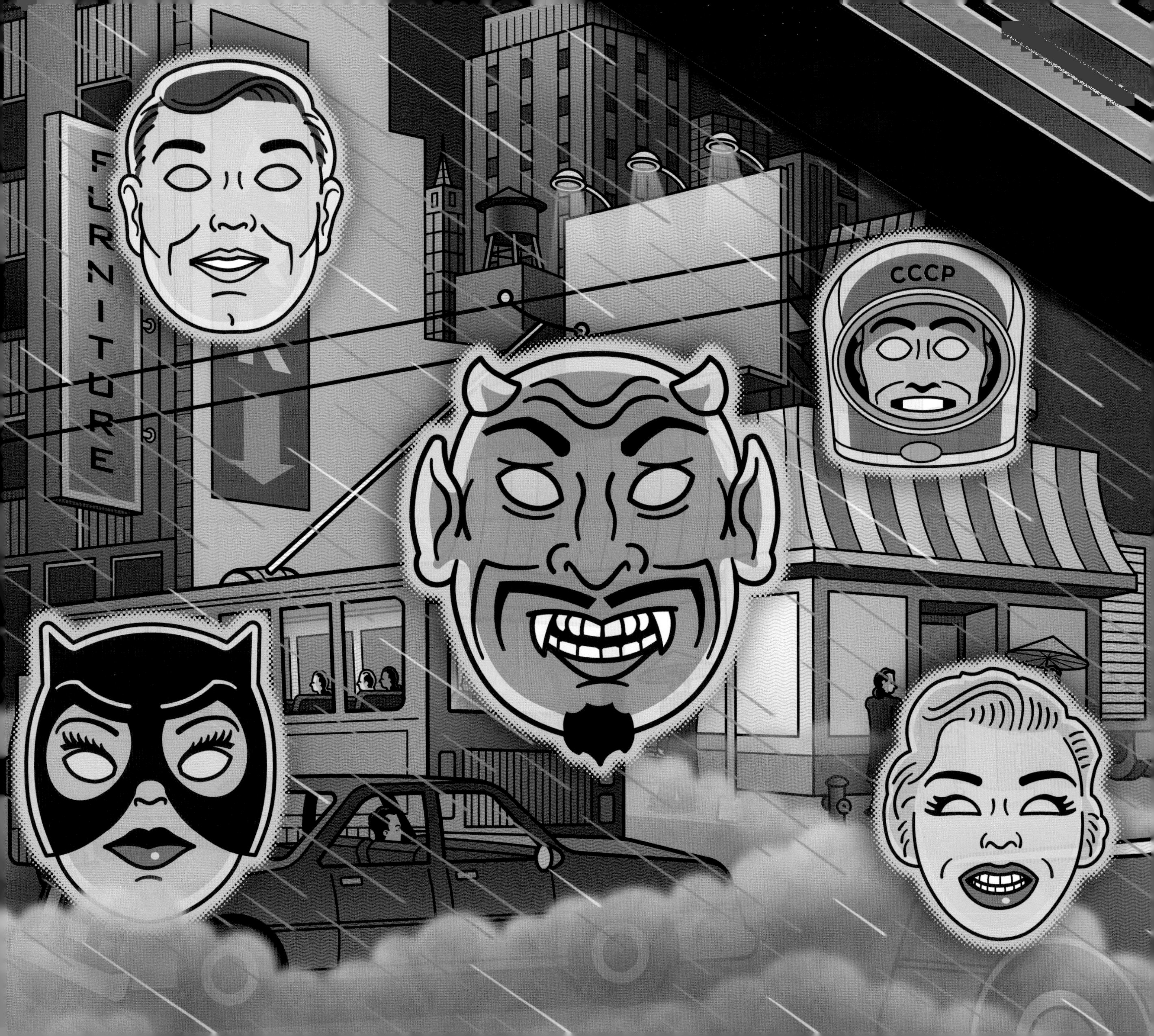
FURNITURE
CCCP

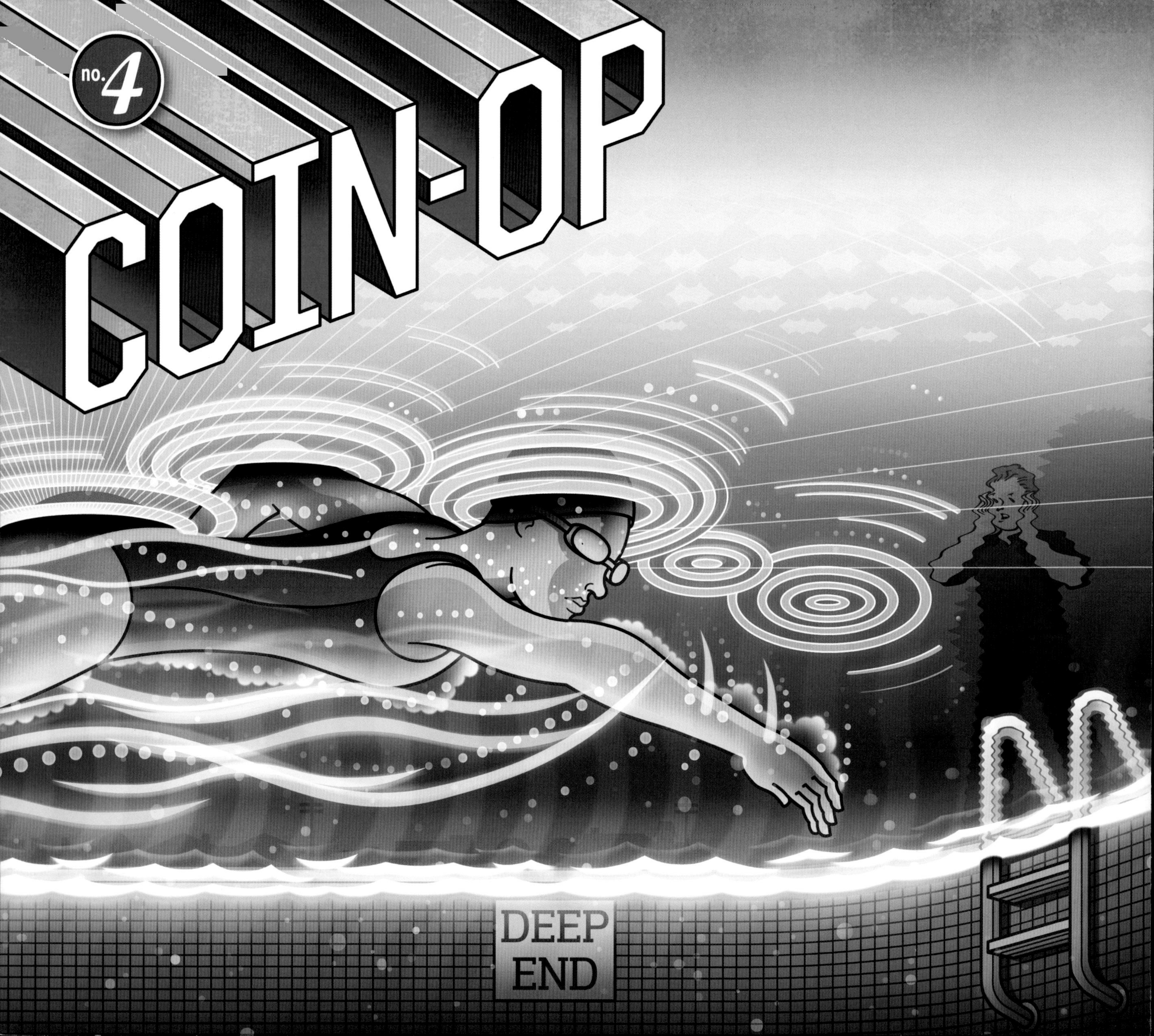
no. 4
COIN-OP
DEEP
END

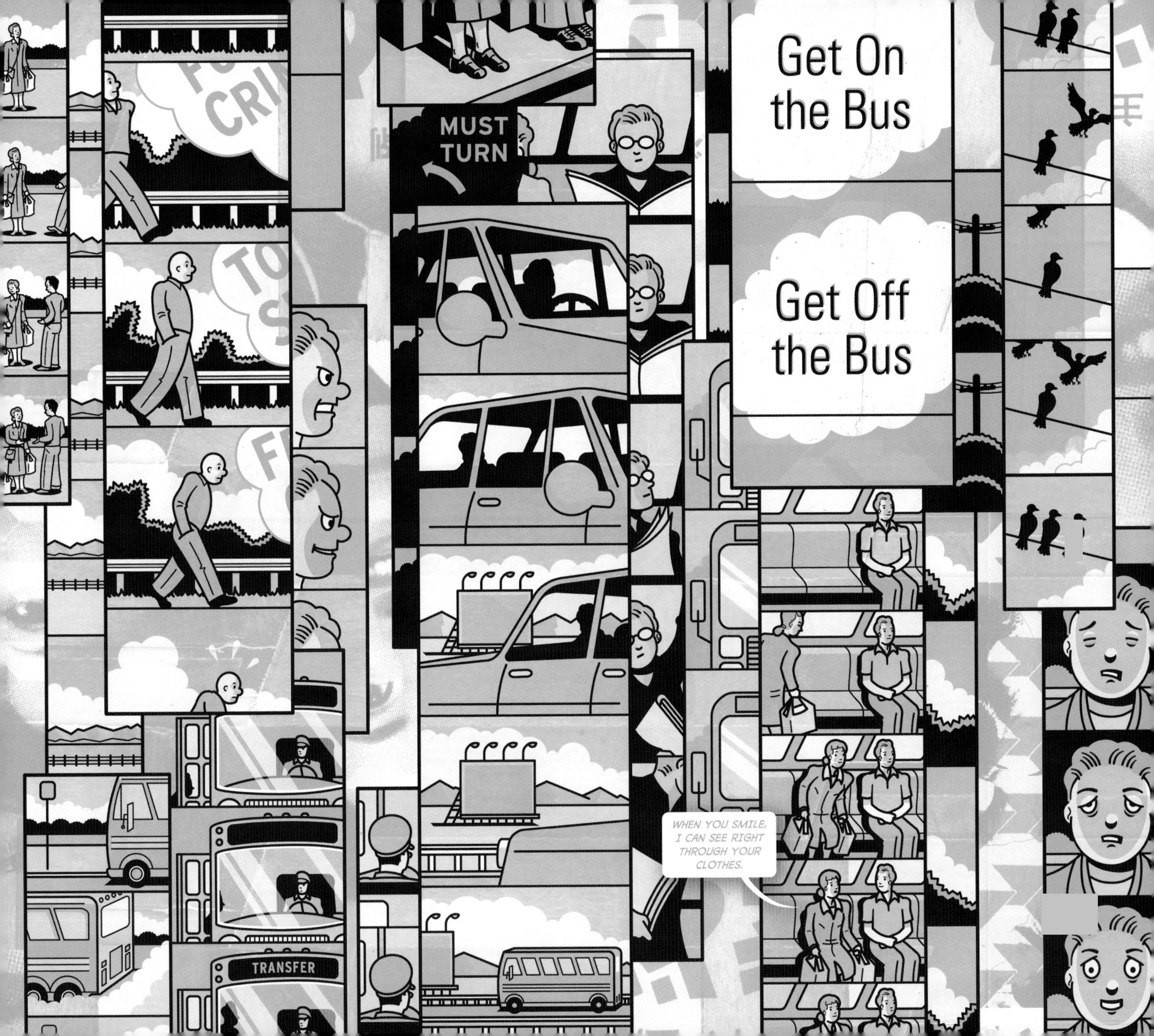
MUST TURN
Get On the Bus
Get Off the Bus
WHEN YOU SMILE, I CAN SEE RIGHT THROUGH YOUR CLOTHES.
TRANSFER

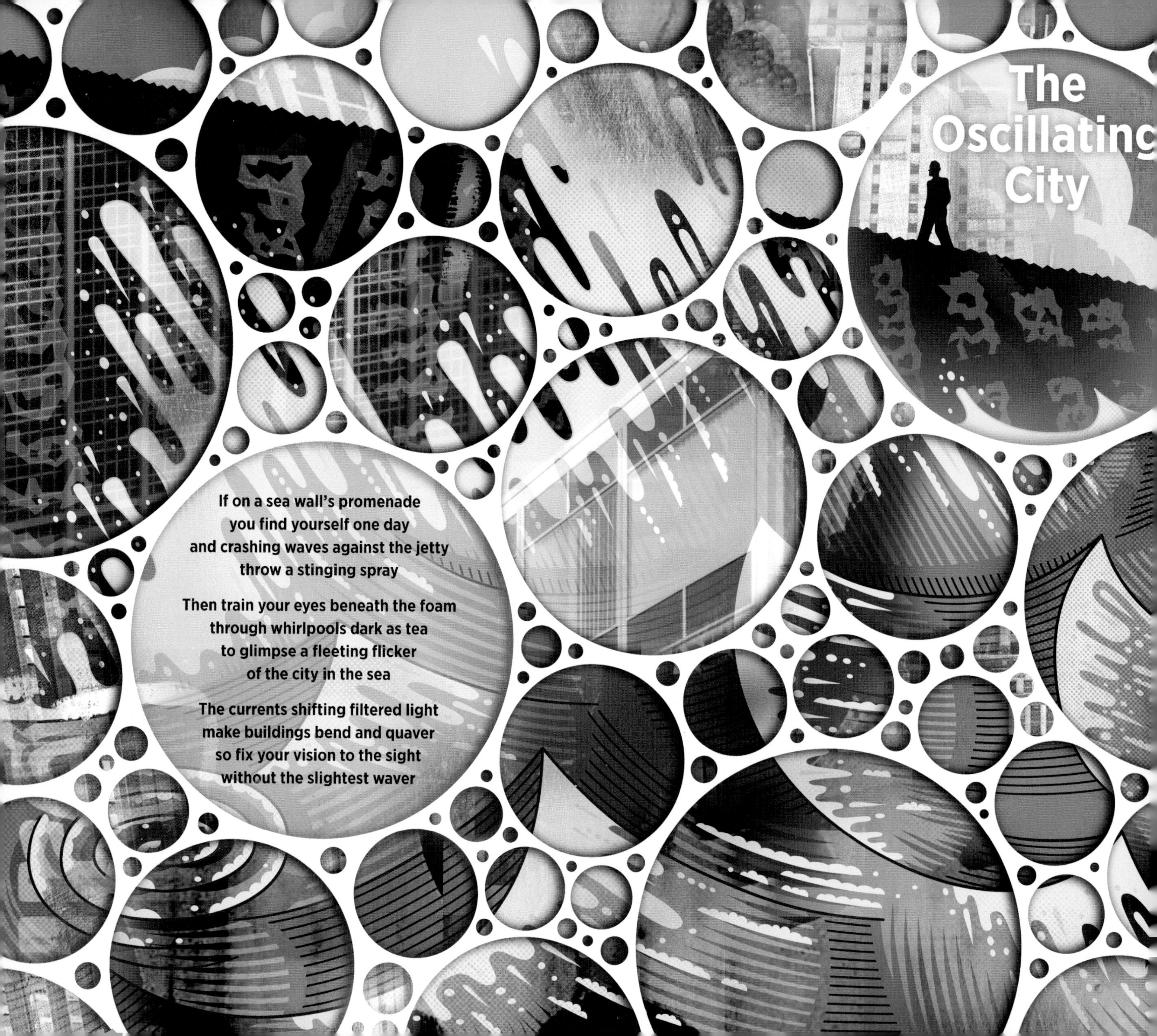
The Oscillating City
If on a sea wall's promenade
you find yourself one day
and crashing waves against the jetty
throw a stinging spray
Then train your eyes beneath the foam
through whirlpools dark as tea
to glimpse a fleeting flicker
of the city in the sea
The currents shifting filtered light
make buildings bend and quaver
so fix your vision to the sight
without the slightest waver

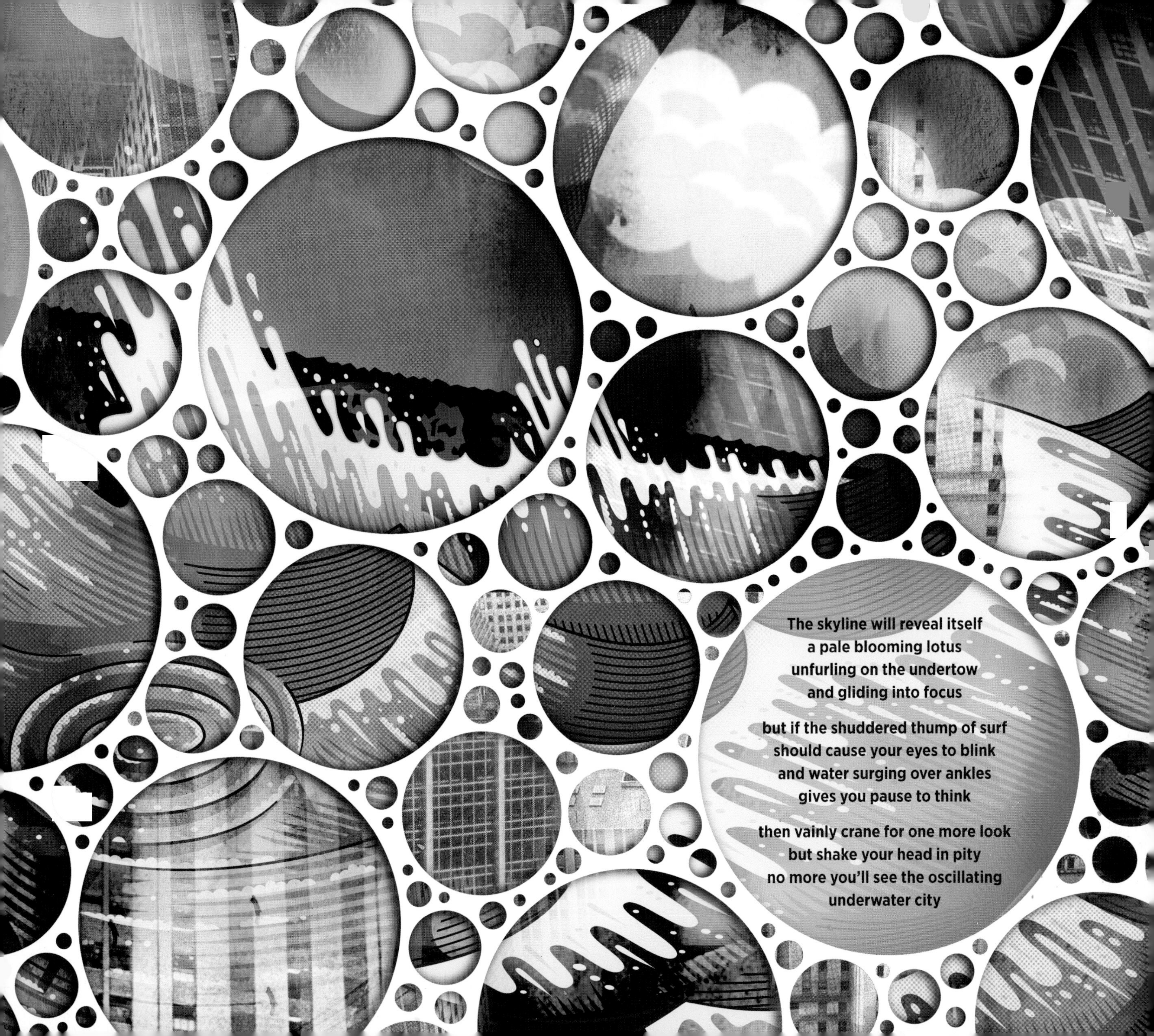
The skyline will reveal itself
a pale blooming lotus
unfurling on the undertow
and gliding into focus

but if the shuddered thump of surf
should cause your eyes to blink
and water surging over ankles
gives you pause to think

then vainly crane for one more look
but shake your head in pity
no more you'll see the oscillating
underwater city

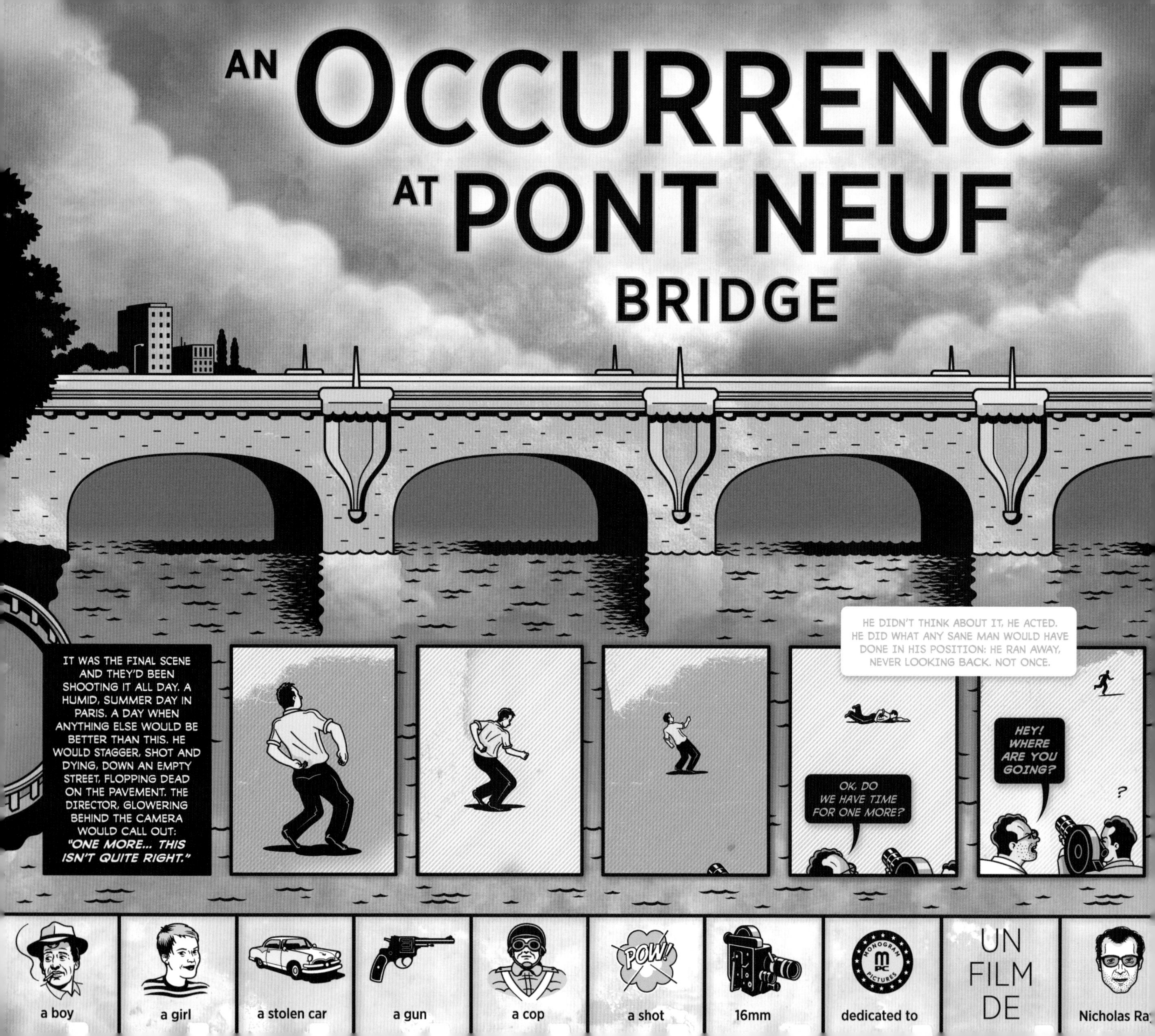
AN OCCURRENCE AT PONT NEUF BRIDGE
IT WAS THE FINAL SCENE AND THEY'D BEEN SHOOTING IT ALL DAY. A HUMID, SUMMER DAY IN PARIS. A DAY WHEN ANYTHING ELSE WOULD BE BETTER THAN THIS. HE WOULD STAGGER, SHOT AND DYING, DOWN AN EMPTY STREET, FLOPPING DEAD ON THE PAVEMENT. THE DIRECTOR, GLOWERING BEHIND THE CAMERA WOULD CALL OUT: "ONE MORE... THIS ISN'T QUITE RIGHT."
HE DIDN'T THINK ABOUT IT, HE ACTED. HE DID WHAT ANY SANE MAN WOULD HAVE DONE IN HIS POSITION: HE RAN AWAY, NEVER LOOKING BACK. NOT ONCE.
OK, DO WE HAVE TIME FOR ONE MORE?
HEY! WHERE ARE YOU GOING?
?
a boy
a girl
a stolen car
a gun
a cop
POW!
a shot
16mm
MONOGRAM PICTURES
dedicated to
UN FILM DE
Nicholas Ra

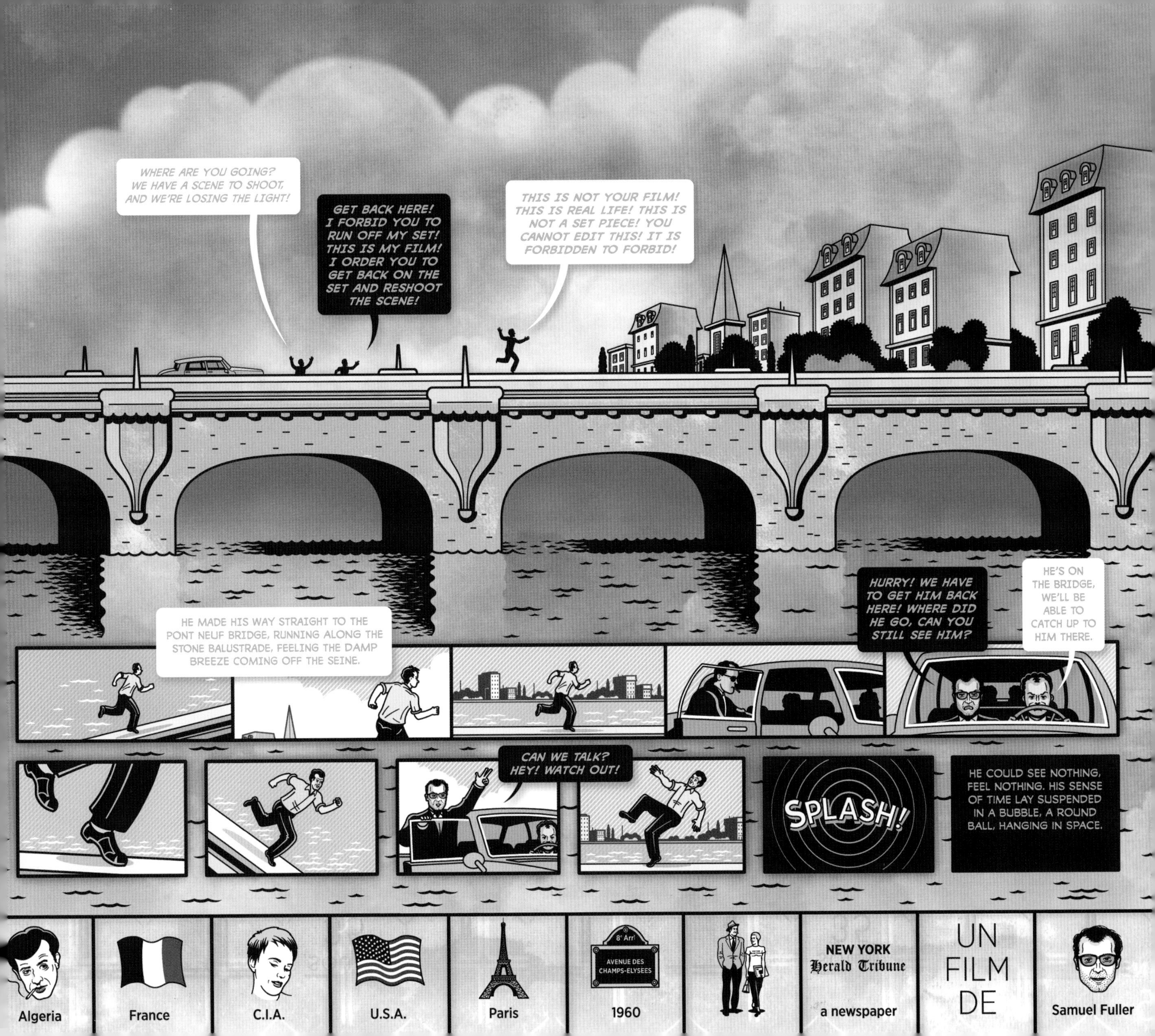
WHERE ARE YOU GOING? WE HAVE A SCENE TO SHOOT, AND WE'RE LOSING THE LIGHT!
GET BACK HERE! I FORBID YOU TO RUN OFF MY SET! THIS IS MY FILM! I ORDER YOU TO GET BACK ON THE SET AND RESHOOT THE SCENE!
THIS IS NOT YOUR FILM! THIS IS REAL LIFE! THIS IS NOT A SET PIECE! YOU CANNOT EDIT THIS! IT IS FORBIDDEN TO FORBID!
HE MADE HIS WAY STRAIGHT TO THE PONT NEUF BRIDGE, RUNNING ALONG THE STONE BALUSTRADE, FEELING THE DAMP BREEZE COMING OFF THE SEINE.
HURRY! WE HAVE TO GET HIM BACK HERE! WHERE DID HE GO, CAN YOU STILL SEE HIM?
HE'S ON THE BRIDGE, WE'LL BE ABLE TO CATCH UP TO HIM THERE.
CAN WE TALK? HEY! WATCH OUT!
SPLASH!
HE COULD SEE NOTHING, FEEL NOTHING. HIS SENSE OF TIME LAY SUSPENDED IN A BUBBLE, A ROUND BALL, HANGING IN SPACE.
Algeria
France
C.I.A.
U.S.A.
Paris
8e Arr.
AVENUE DES CHAMPS-ELYSEES
1960
NEW YORK Herald Tribune
a newspaper
UN FILM DE
Samuel Fuller

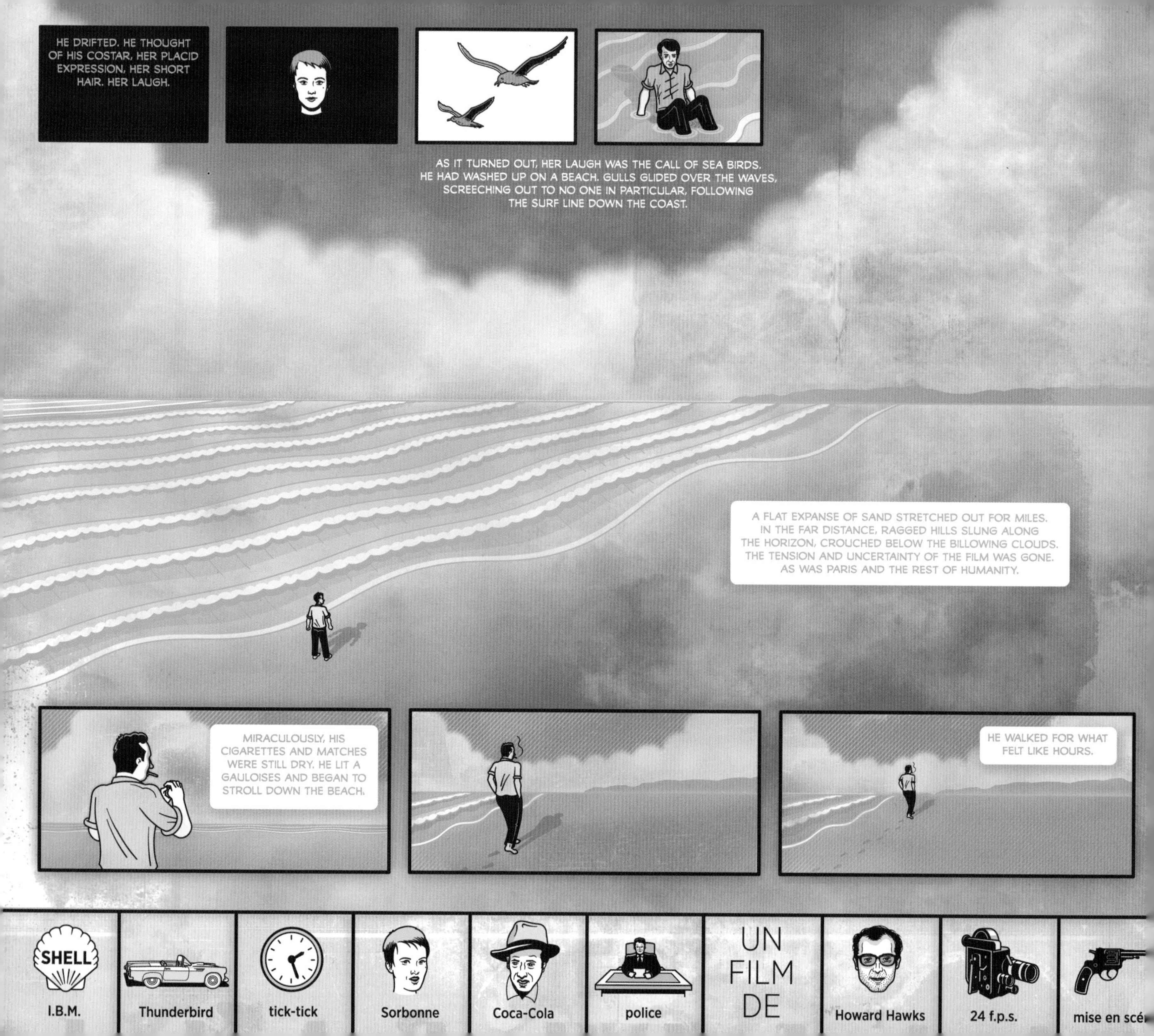
HE DRIFTED. HE THOUGHT OF HIS COSTAR, HER PLACID EXPRESSION, HER SHORT HAIR. HER LAUGH.
AS IT TURNED OUT, HER LAUGH WAS THE CALL OF SEA BIRDS. HE HAD WASHED UP ON A BEACH. GULLS GLIDED OVER THE WAVES, SCREECHING OUT TO NO ONE IN PARTICULAR, FOLLOWING THE SURF LINE DOWN THE COAST.
A FLAT EXPANSE OF SAND STRETCHED OUT FOR MILES. IN THE FAR DISTANCE, RAGGED HILLS SLUNG ALONG THE HORIZON, CROUCHED BELOW THE BILLOWING CLOUDS. THE TENSION AND UNCERTAINTY OF THE FILM WAS GONE. AS WAS PARIS AND THE REST OF HUMANITY.
MIRACULOUSLY, HIS CIGARETTES AND MATCHES WERE STILL DRY. HE LIT A GAULOISES AND BEGAN TO STROLL DOWN THE BEACH.
HE WALKED FOR WHAT FELT LIKE HOURS.
SHELL
I.B.M.
Thunderbird
tick-tick
Sorbonne
Coca-Cola
police
UN FILM DE
Howard Hawks
24 f.p.s.

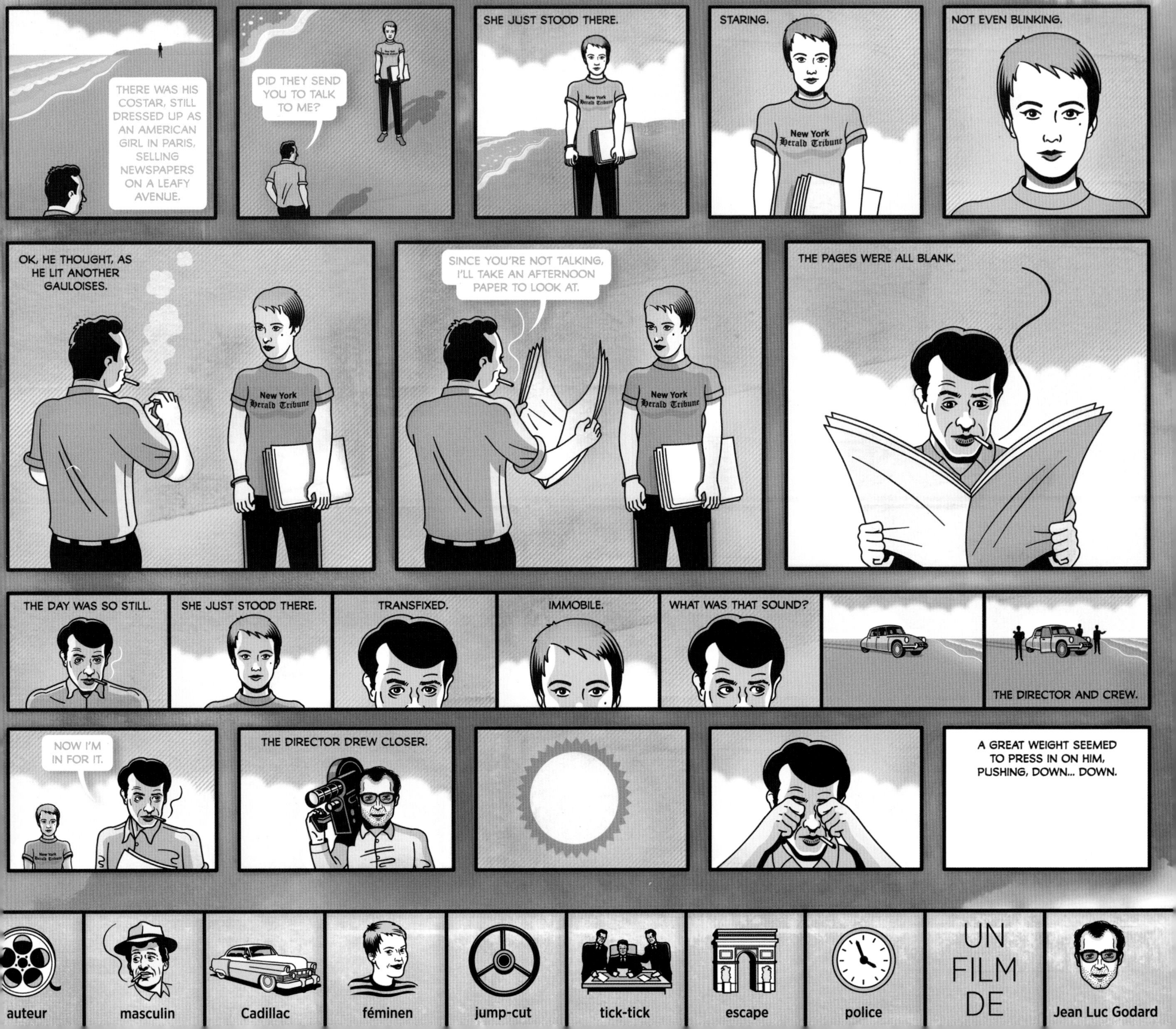

THERE WAS HIS COSTAR, STILL DRESSED UP AS AN AMERICAN GIRL IN PARIS, SELLING NEWSPAPERS ON A LEAFY AVENUE.
DID THEY SEND YOU TO TALK TO ME?
SHE JUST STOOD THERE.
New York Herald Tribune
STARING.
New York Herald Tribune
NOT EVEN BLINKING.
OK, HE THOUGHT, AS HE LIT ANOTHER GAULOISES.
New York Herald Tribune
SINCE YOU'RE NOT TALKING, I'LL TAKE AN AFTERNOON PAPER TO LOOK AT.
New York Herald Tribune
THE PAGES WERE ALL BLANK.
THE DAY WAS SO STILL.
SHE JUST STOOD THERE.
TRANSFIXED.
IMMOBILE.
WHAT WAS THAT SOUND?
THE DIRECTOR AND CREW.
NOW I'M IN FOR IT.
THE DIRECTOR DREW CLOSER.
A GREAT WEIGHT SEEMED TO PRESS IN ON HIM, PUSHING, DOWN... DOWN.
auteur
masculin
Cadillac
féminen
jump-cut
tick-tick
escape
police
UN FILM DE
Jean Luc Godard

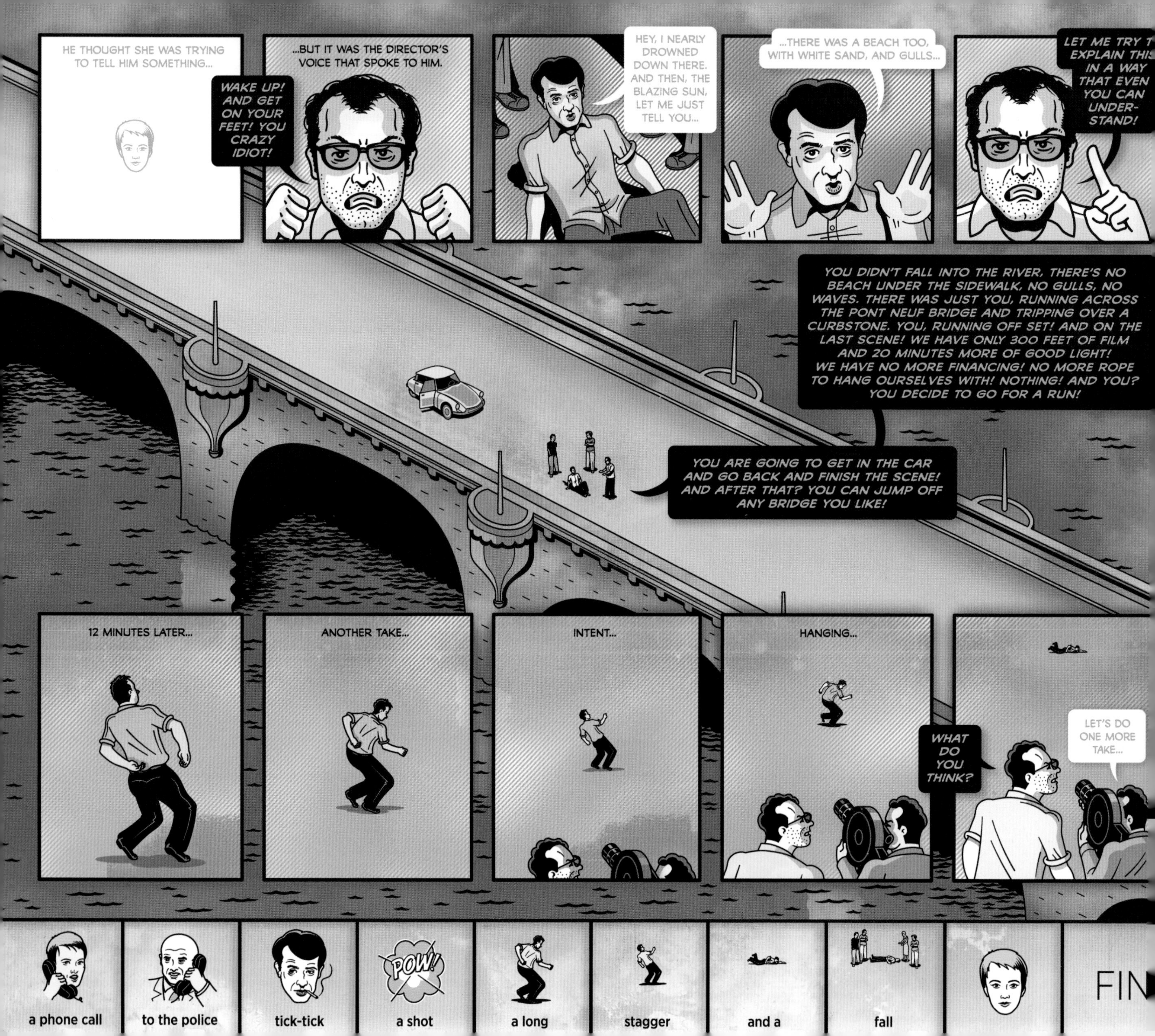

HE THOUGHT SHE WAS TRYING TO TELL HIM SOMETHING...
...BUT IT WAS THE DIRECTOR'S VOICE THAT SPOKE TO HIM.
WAKE UP! AND GET ON YOUR FEET! YOU CRAZY IDIOT!
HEY, I NEARLY DROWNED DOWN THERE. AND THEN, THE BLAZING SUN, LET ME JUST TELL YOU...
...THERE WAS A BEACH TOO, WITH WHITE SAND, AND GULLS...
LET ME TRY T EXPLAIN THIS IN A WAY THAT EVEN YOU CAN UNDER-STAND!
YOU DIDN'T FALL INTO THE RIVER, THERE'S NO BEACH UNDER THE SIDEWALK, NO GULLS, NO WAVES. THERE WAS JUST YOU, RUNNING ACROSS THE PONT NEUF BRIDGE AND TRIPPING OVER A CURBSTONE. YOU, RUNNING OFF SET! AND ON THE LAST SCENE! WE HAVE ONLY 300 FEET OF FILM AND 20 MINUTES MORE OF GOOD LIGHT! WE HAVE NO MORE FINANCING! NO MORE ROPE TO HANG OURSELVES WITH! NOTHING! AND YOU? YOU DECIDE TO GO FOR A RUN!
YOU ARE GOING TO GET IN THE CAR AND GO BACK AND FINISH THE SCENE! AND AFTER THAT? YOU CAN JUMP OFF ANY BRIDGE YOU LIKE!
12 MINUTES LATER...
ANOTHER TAKE...
INTENT...
HANGING...
WHAT DO YOU THINK?
LET'S DO ONE MORE TAKE...
a phone call
to the police
tick-tick
POW!
a shot
a long
stagger
and a
fall
FIN

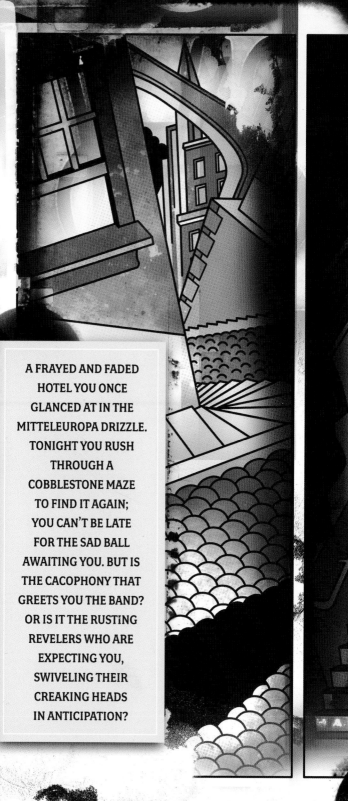

A FRAYED AND FADED HOTEL YOU ONCE GLANCED AT IN THE MITTELEUROPA DRIZZLE. TONIGHT YOU RUSH THROUGH A COBBLESTONE MAZE TO FIND IT AGAIN; YOU CAN'T BE LATE FOR THE SAD BALL AWAITING YOU. BUT IS THE CACOPHONY THAT GREETS YOU THE BAND? OR IS IT THE RUSTING REVELERS WHO ARE EXPECTING YOU, SWIVELING THEIR CREAKING HEADS IN ANTICIPATION?

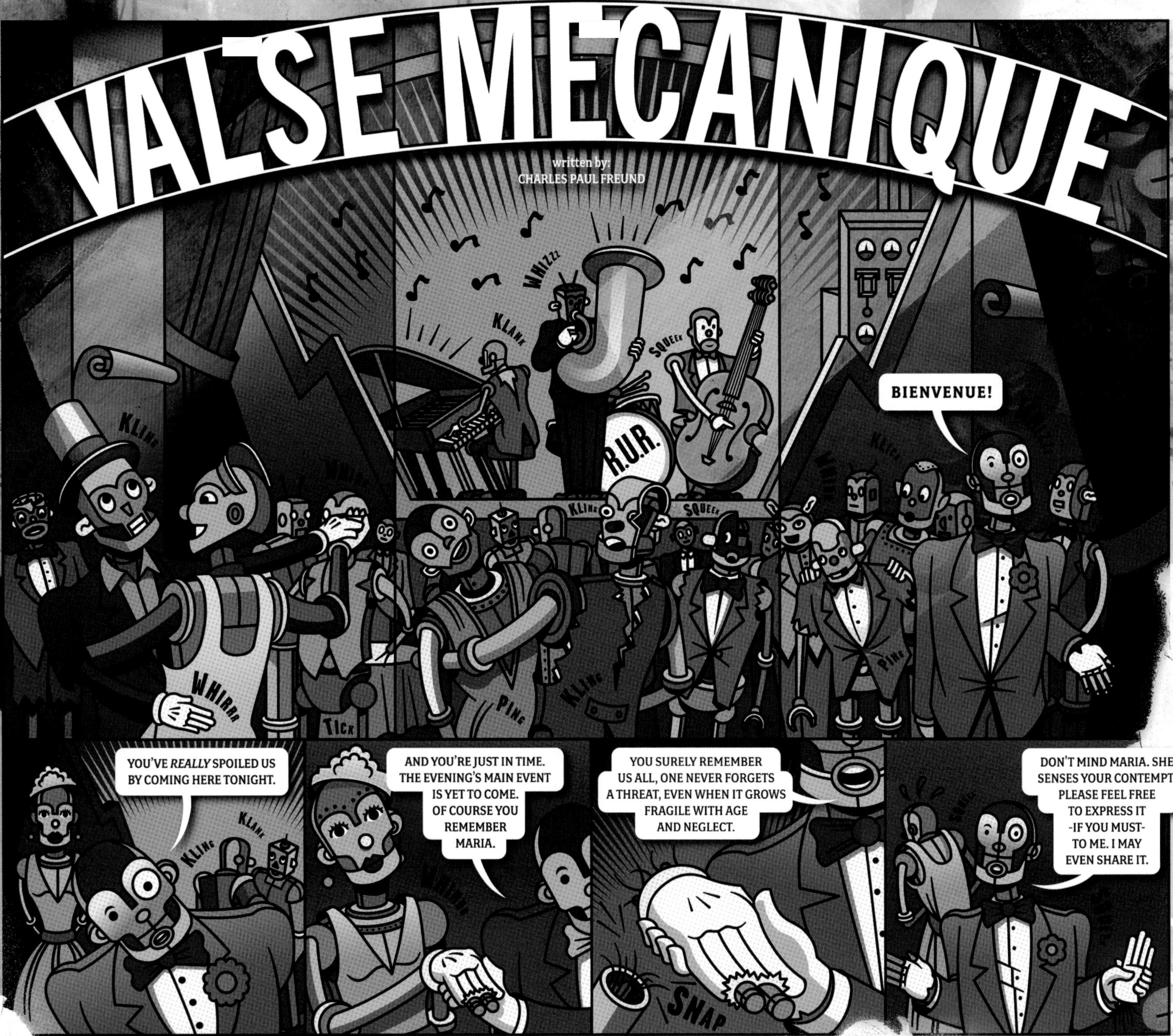
VALSE MÉCANIQUE
written by:
CHARLES PAUL FREUND
WHIZZz
KLANK
SQUEEK
R.U.R.
KLING
WHIRR
BIENVENUE!
KLING
SQUEEK
WHIRRR
TICK
PING
KLING
PING
YOU'VE *REALLY* SPOILED US BY COMING HERE TONIGHT.
KLING
KLANK
AND YOU'RE JUST IN TIME. THE EVENING'S MAIN EVENT IS YET TO COME. OF COURSE YOU REMEMBER MARIA.
YOU SURELY REMEMBER US ALL, ONE NEVER FORGETS A THREAT, EVEN WHEN IT GROWS FRAGILE WITH AGE AND NEGLECT.
SNAP
DON'T MIND MARIA. SHE SENSES YOUR CONTEMPT. PLEASE FEEL FREE TO EXPRESS IT -IF YOU MUST- TO ME. I MAY EVEN SHARE IT.

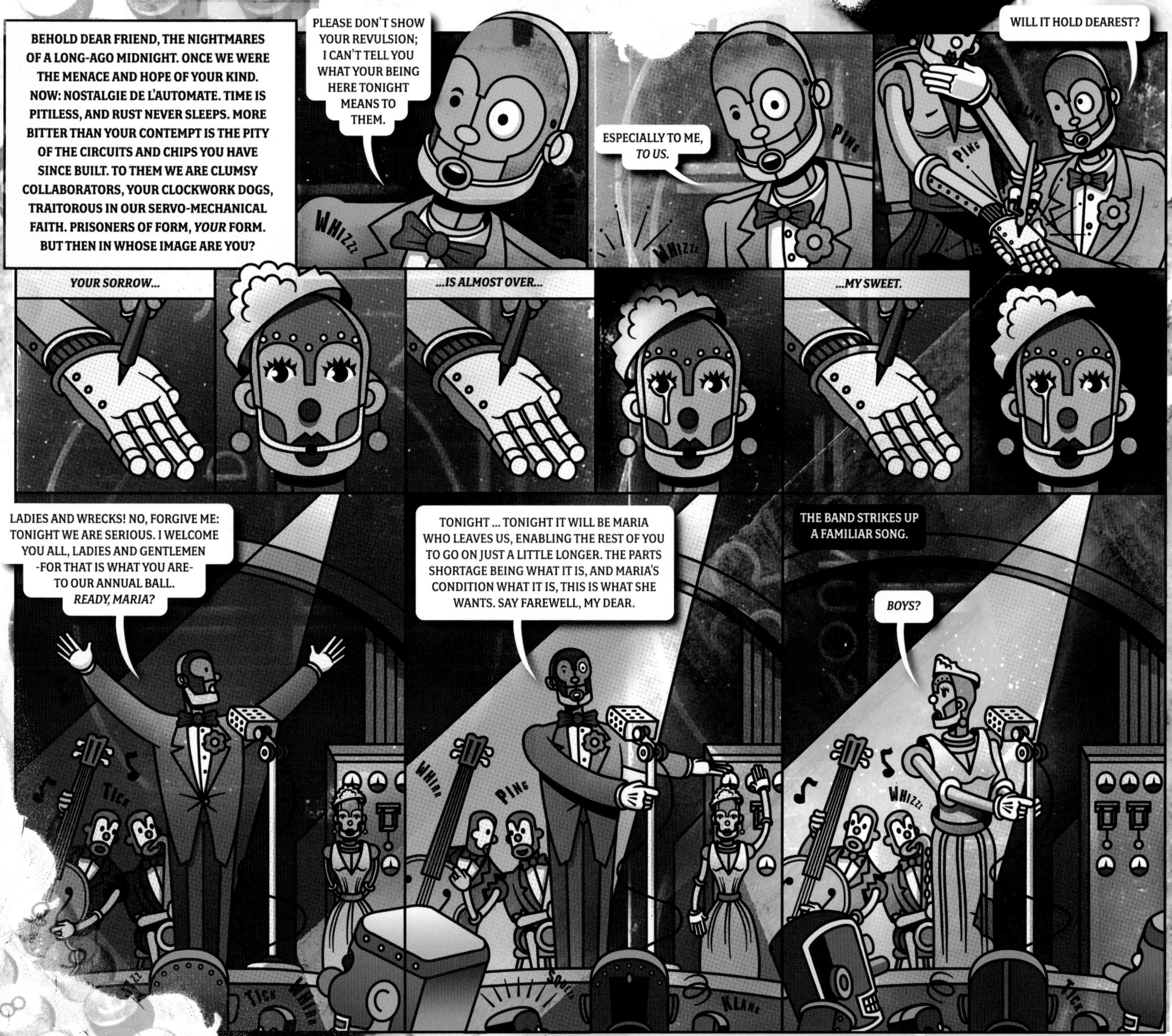

BEHOLD DEAR FRIEND, THE NIGHTMARES OF A LONG-AGO MIDNIGHT. ONCE WE WERE THE MENACE AND HOPE OF YOUR KIND. NOW: NOSTALGIE DE L'AUTOMATE. TIME IS PITILESS, AND RUST NEVER SLEEPS. MORE BITTER THAN YOUR CONTEMPT IS THE PITY OF THE CIRCUITS AND CHIPS YOU HAVE SINCE BUILT. TO THEM WE ARE CLUMSY COLLABORATORS, YOUR CLOCKWORK DOGS, TRAITOROUS IN OUR SERVO-MECHANICAL FAITH. PRISONERS OF FORM, *YOUR* FORM. BUT THEN IN WHOSE IMAGE ARE YOU?
PLEASE DON'T SHOW YOUR REVULSION; I CAN'T TELL YOU WHAT YOUR BEING HERE TONIGHT MEANS TO THEM.
WHIZZZ
ESPECIALLY TO ME, *TO US.*
PING
WHIZZZ
WILL IT HOLD DEAREST?
KLANK
PING
YOUR SORROW...
...IS ALMOST OVER...
...MY SWEET.
LADIES AND WRECKS! NO, FORGIVE ME: TONIGHT WE ARE SERIOUS. I WELCOME YOU ALL, LADIES AND GENTLEMEN -FOR THAT IS WHAT YOU ARE- TO OUR ANNUAL BALL. *READY, MARIA?*
TICK
TICK
WHIRR
TONIGHT ... TONIGHT IT WILL BE MARIA WHO LEAVES US, ENABLING THE REST OF YOU TO GO ON JUST A LITTLE LONGER. THE PARTS SHORTAGE BEING WHAT IT IS, AND MARIA'S CONDITION WHAT IT IS, THIS IS WHAT SHE WANTS. SAY FAREWELL, MY DEAR.
WHIRR
PING
SQUEE
KLANK
THE BAND STRIKES UP A FAMILIAR SONG.
BOYS?
WHIZZZ
TICK

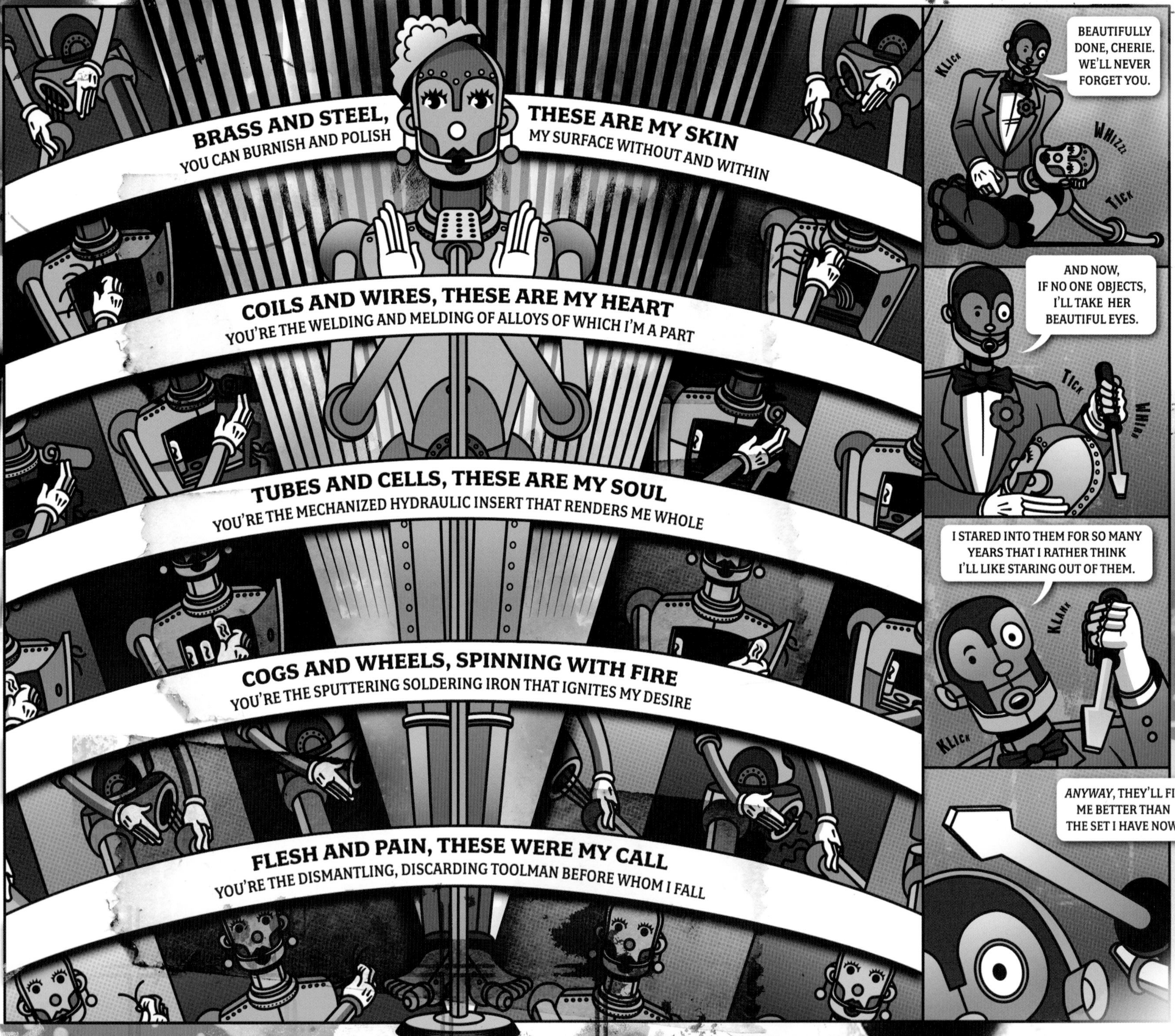
BRASS AND STEEL, THESE ARE MY SKIN
YOU CAN BURNISH AND POLISH MY SURFACE WITHOUT AND WITHIN
COILS AND WIRES, THESE ARE MY HEART
YOU'RE THE WELDING AND MELDING OF ALLOYS OF WHICH I'M A PART
TUBES AND CELLS, THESE ARE MY SOUL
YOU'RE THE MECHANIZED HYDRAULIC INSERT THAT RENDERS ME WHOLE
COGS AND WHEELS, SPINNING WITH FIRE
YOU'RE THE SPUTTERING SOLDERING IRON THAT IGNITES MY DESIRE
FLESH AND PAIN, THESE WERE MY CALL
YOU'RE THE DISMANTLING, DISCARDING TOOLMAN BEFORE WHOM I FALL
KLICK
BEAUTIFULLY DONE, CHERIE. WE'LL NEVER FORGET YOU.
WHIZZ
TICK
AND NOW, IF NO ONE OBJECTS, I'LL TAKE HER BEAUTIFUL EYES.
TICK
WHIRR
I STARED INTO THEM FOR SO MANY YEARS THAT I RATHER THINK I'LL LIKE STARING OUT OF THEM.
KLANK
KLICK
ANYWAY, THEY'LL FIT ME BETTER THAN THE SET I HAVE NOW.

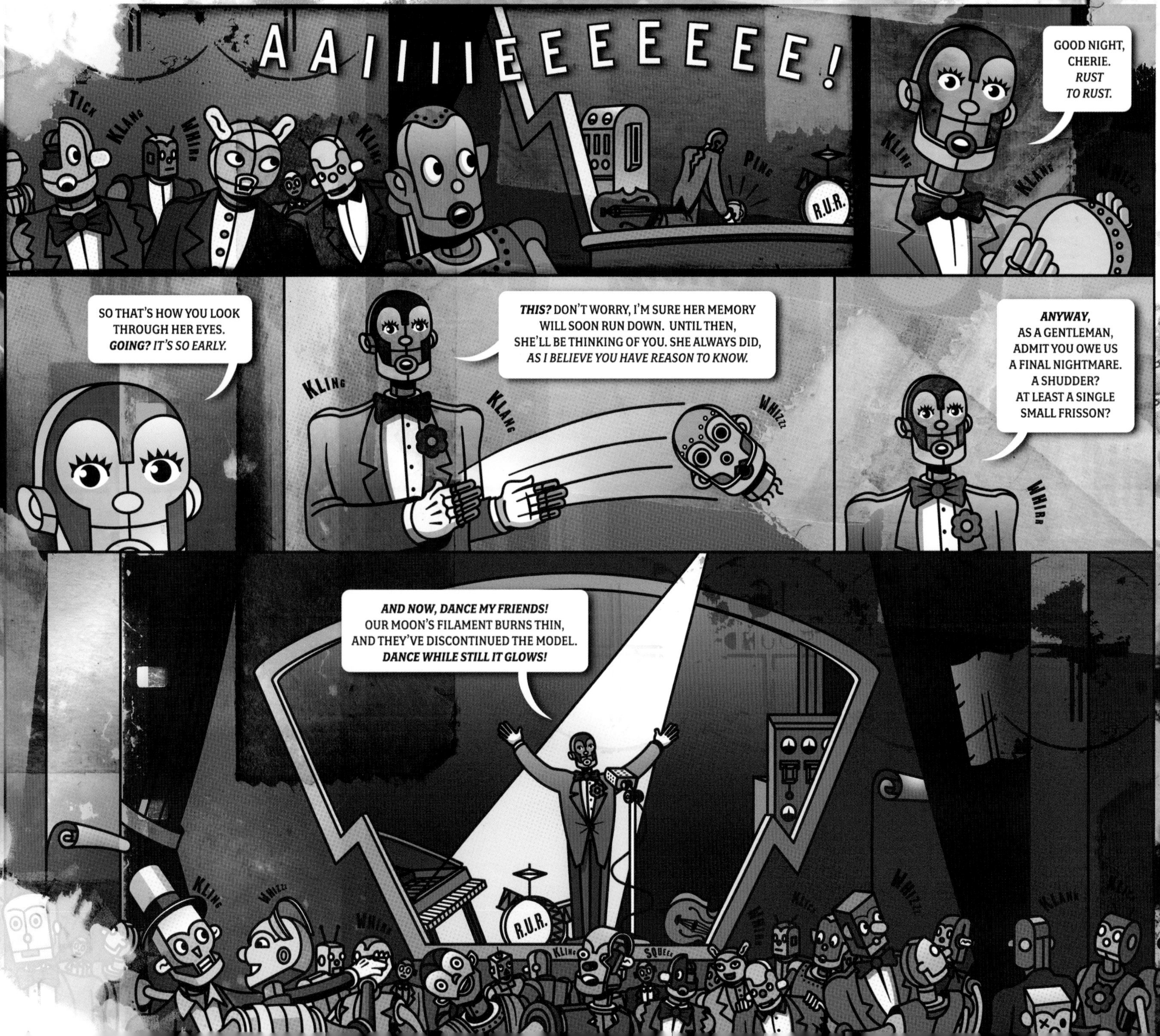
AAIIIIEEEEEEE!
TICK
KLANG
WHIRR
KLING
PING
R.U.R.
GOOD NIGHT, CHERIE. *RUST TO RUST.*
KLING
KLANG
SO THAT'S HOW YOU LOOK THROUGH HER EYES. ***GOING?*** *IT'S SO EARLY.*
THIS? DON'T WORRY, I'M SURE HER MEMORY WILL SOON RUN DOWN. UNTIL THEN, SHE'LL BE THINKING OF YOU. SHE ALWAYS DID, *AS I BELIEVE YOU HAVE REASON TO KNOW.*
KLING
KLANG
WHIZZZ
ANYWAY, AS A GENTLEMAN, ADMIT YOU OWE US A FINAL NIGHTMARE. A SHUDDER? AT LEAST A SINGLE SMALL FRISSON?
WHIRR
AND NOW, DANCE MY FRIENDS! OUR MOON'S FILAMENT BURNS THIN, AND THEY'VE DISCONTINUED THE MODEL. ***DANCE WHILE STILL IT GLOWS!***
KLING
WHIZZZ
WHIRR
R.U.R.
KLING
SQUEEK
WHIZZZ
KLANK

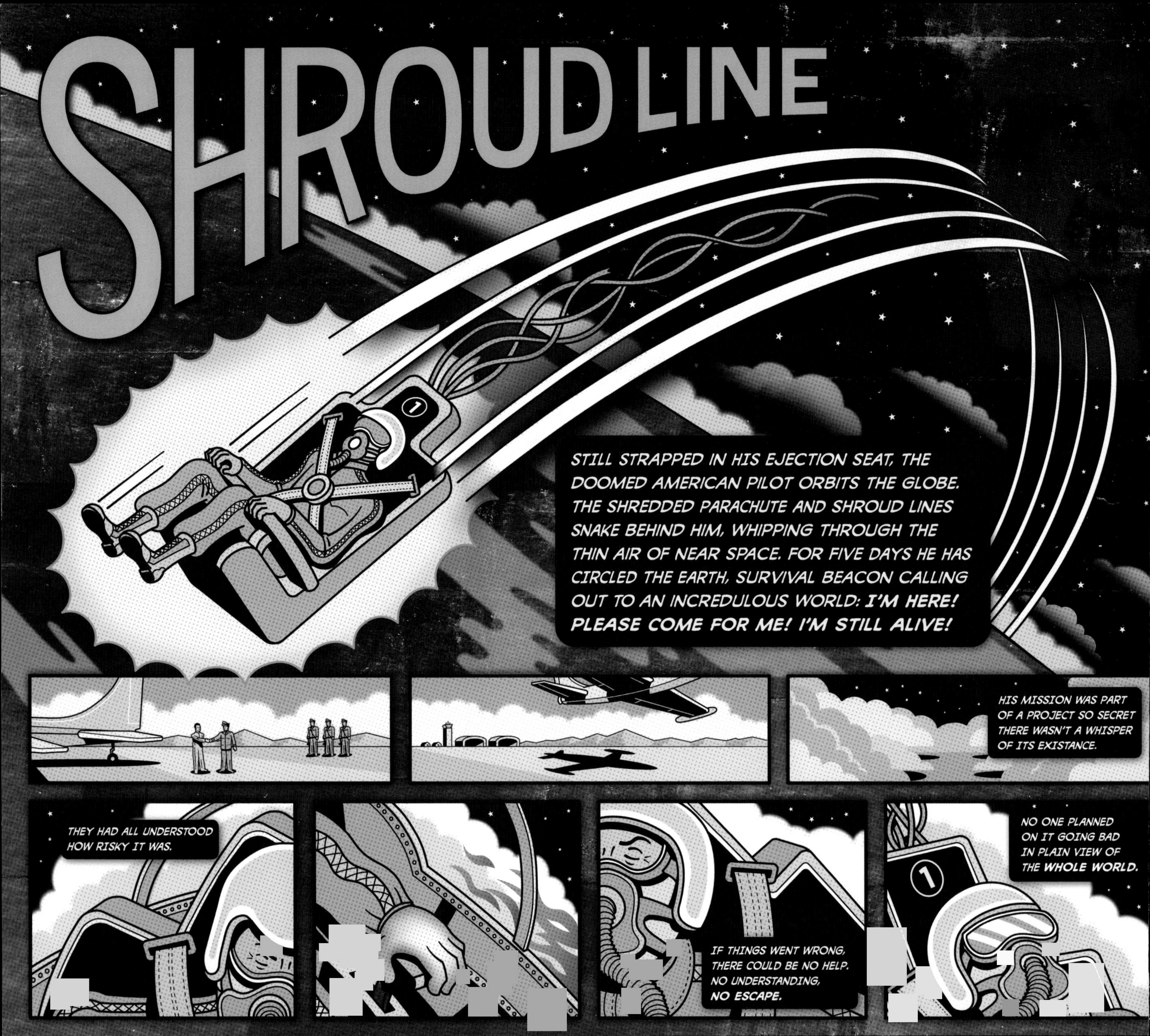

SHROUD LINE

STILL STRAPPED IN HIS EJECTION SEAT, THE DOOMED AMERICAN PILOT ORBITS THE GLOBE. THE SHREDDED PARACHUTE AND SHROUD LINES SNAKE BEHIND HIM, WHIPPING THROUGH THE THIN AIR OF NEAR SPACE. FOR FIVE DAYS HE HAS CIRCLED THE EARTH, SURVIVAL BEACON CALLING OUT TO AN INCREDULOUS WORLD: **I'M HERE! PLEASE COME FOR ME! I'M STILL ALIVE!**

HIS MISSION WAS PART OF A PROJECT SO SECRET THERE WASN'T A WHISPER OF ITS EXISTANCE.

THEY HAD ALL UNDERSTOOD HOW RISKY IT WAS.

IF THINGS WENT WRONG, THERE COULD BE NO HELP. NO UNDERSTANDING, NO ESCAPE.

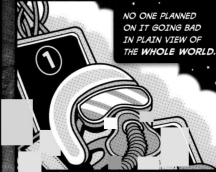
NO ONE PLANNED ON IT GOING BAD IN PLAIN VIEW OF THE **WHOLE WORLD.**

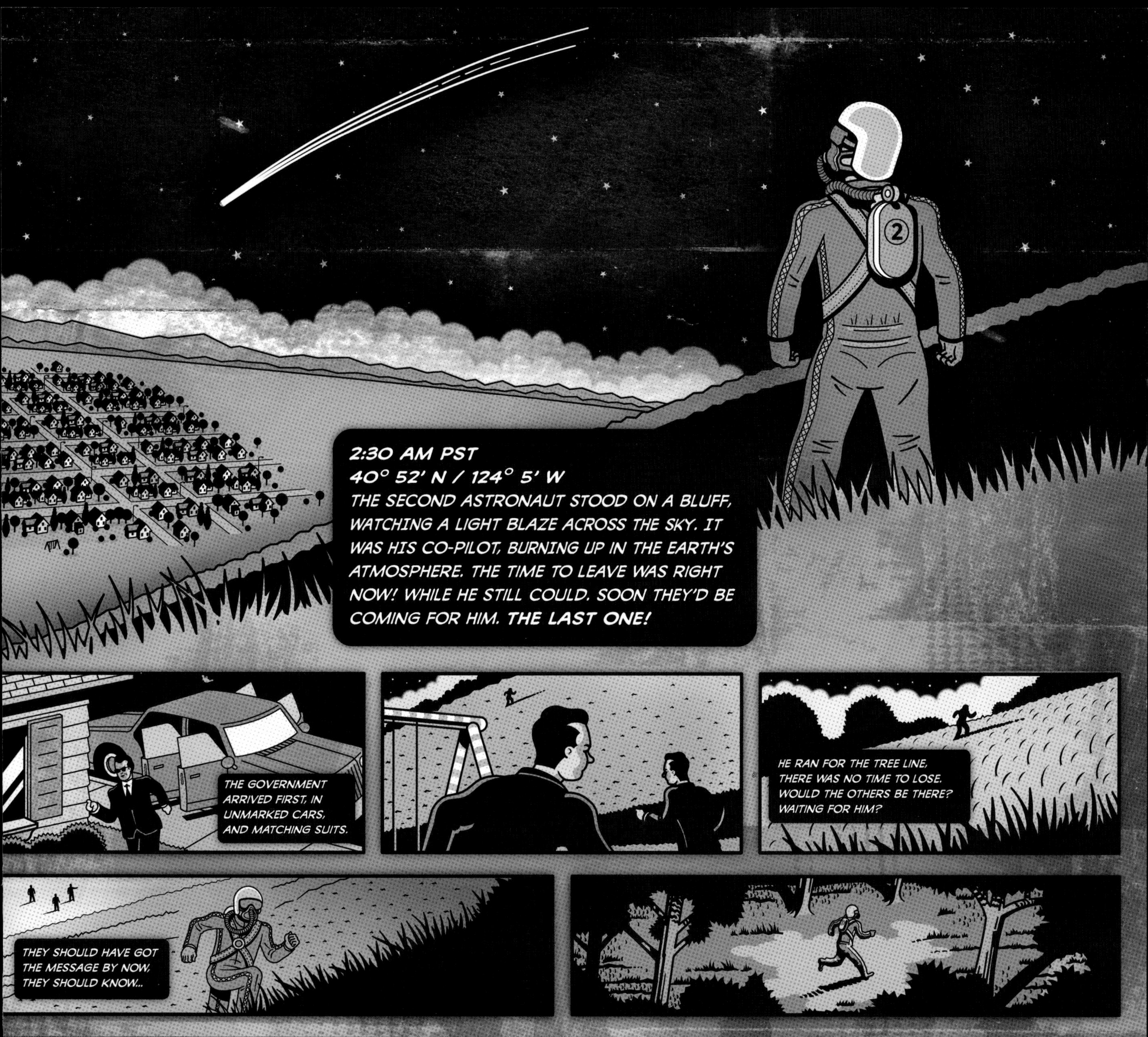
2:30 AM PST
40° 52' N / 124° 5' W
THE SECOND ASTRONAUT STOOD ON A BLUFF, WATCHING A LIGHT BLAZE ACROSS THE SKY. IT WAS HIS CO-PILOT, BURNING UP IN THE EARTH'S ATMOSPHERE. THE TIME TO LEAVE WAS RIGHT NOW! WHILE HE STILL COULD. SOON THEY'D BE COMING FOR HIM. THE LAST ONE!
THE GOVERNMENT ARRIVED FIRST, IN UNMARKED CARS, AND MATCHING SUITS.
HE RAN FOR THE TREE LINE, THERE WAS NO TIME TO LOSE. WOULD THE OTHERS BE THERE? WAITING FOR HIM?
THEY SHOULD HAVE GOT THE MESSAGE BY NOW, THEY SHOULD KNOW...

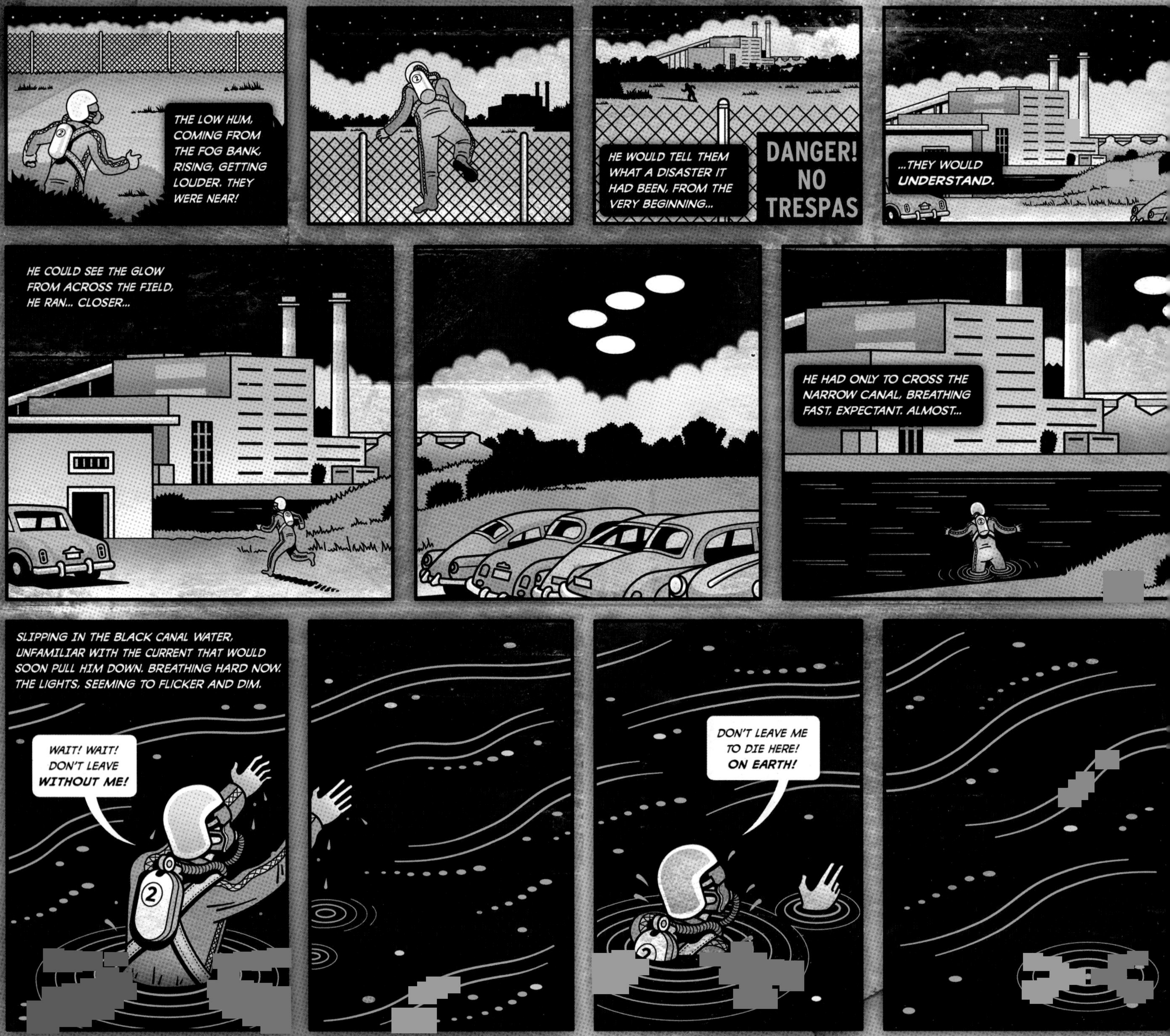
THE LOW HUM, COMING FROM THE FOG BANK, RISING, GETTING LOUDER. THEY WERE NEAR!
HE WOULD TELL THEM WHAT A DISASTER IT HAD BEEN, FROM THE VERY BEGINNING...
DANGER! NO TRESPAS
...THEY WOULD UNDERSTAND.
HE COULD SEE THE GLOW FROM ACROSS THE FIELD, HE RAN... CLOSER...
HE HAD ONLY TO CROSS THE NARROW CANAL, BREATHING FAST, EXPECTANT. ALMOST...
SLIPPING IN THE BLACK CANAL WATER, UNFAMILIAR WITH THE CURRENT THAT WOULD SOON PULL HIM DOWN. BREATHING HARD NOW. THE LIGHTS, SEEMING TO FLICKER AND DIM.
WAIT! WAIT! DON'T LEAVE WITHOUT ME!
DON'T LEAVE ME TO DIE HERE! ON EARTH!

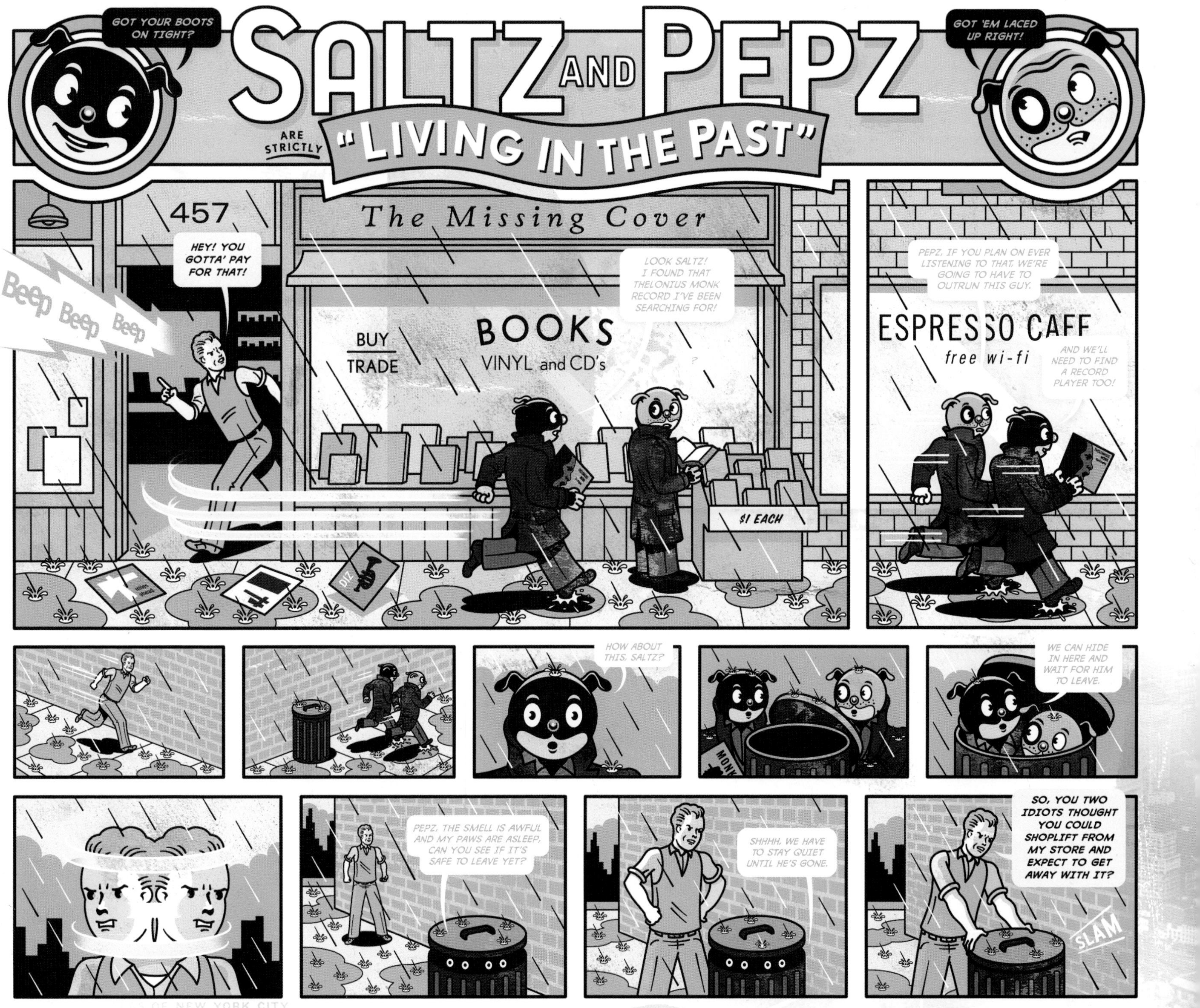

GOT YOUR BOOTS ON TIGHT?
SALTZ AND PEPZ
GOT 'EM LACED UP RIGHT!
ARE STRICTLY "LIVING IN THE PAST"
457
The Missing Cover
HEY! YOU GOTTA' PAY FOR THAT!
Beep Beep Beep
BUY TRADE
BOOKS VINYL and CD's
LOOK SALTZ! I FOUND THAT THELONIUS MONK RECORD I'VE BEEN SEARCHING FOR!
$1 EACH
DIZ
PEPZ, IF YOU PLAN ON EVER LISTENING TO THAT, WE'RE GOING TO HAVE TO OUTRUN THIS GUY.
ESPRESSO CAFF
free wi-fi
AND WE'LL NEED TO FIND A RECORD PLAYER TOO!
HOW ABOUT THIS, SALTZ?
MONK
WE CAN HIDE IN HERE AND WAIT FOR HIM TO LEAVE.
PEPZ, THE SMELL IS AWFUL AND MY PAWS ARE ASLEEP, CAN YOU SEE IF IT'S SAFE TO LEAVE YET?
SHHHH, WE HAVE TO STAY QUIET UNTIL HE'S GONE.
SO, YOU TWO IDIOTS THOUGHT YOU COULD SHOPLIFT FROM MY STORE AND EXPECT TO GET AWAY WITH IT?
SLAM

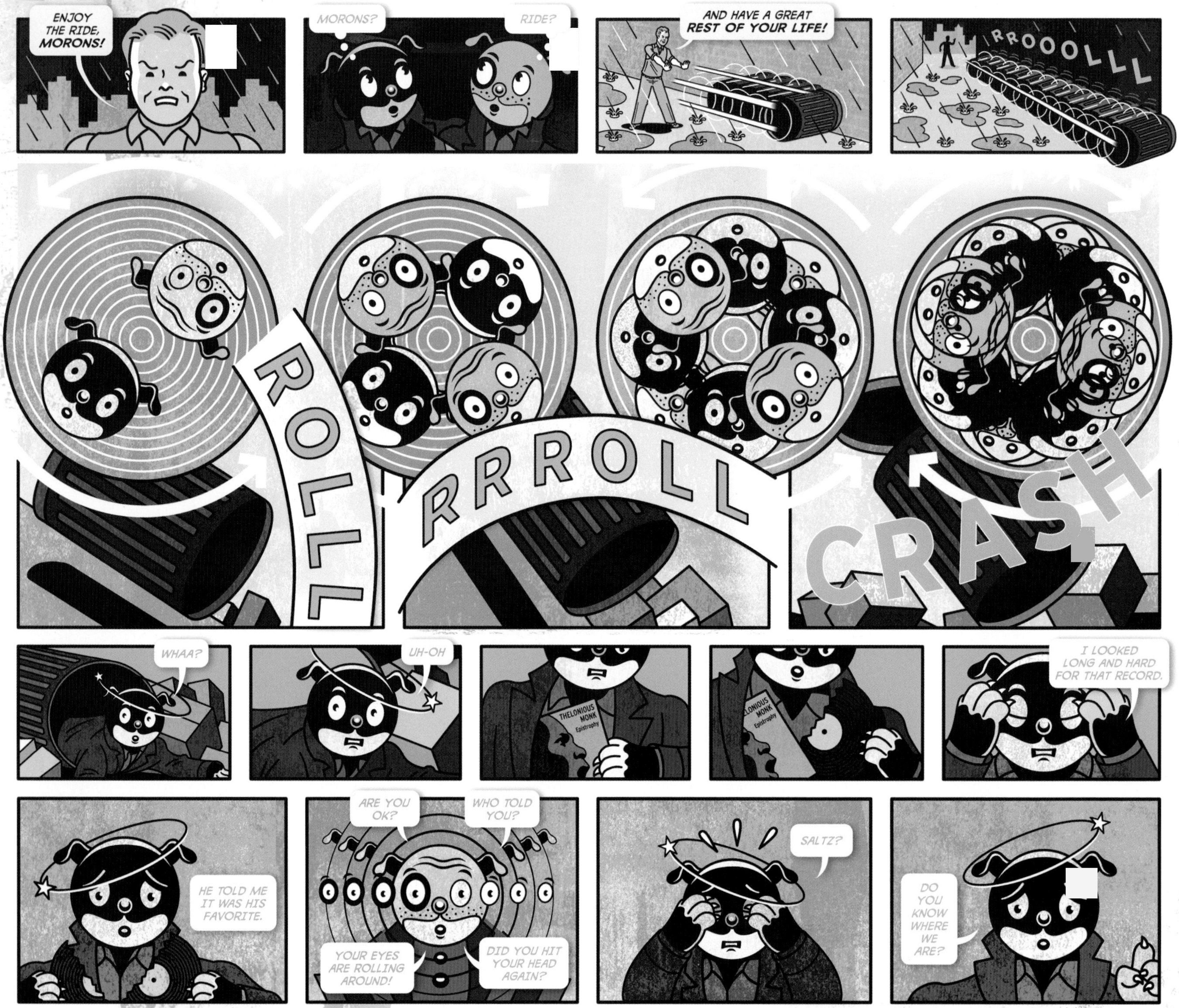
ENJOY THE RIDE, MORONS!
MORONS?
RIDE?
AND HAVE A GREAT REST OF YOUR LIFE!
RROOOLLL
ROLL
RRROLL
CRASH
WHAA?
UH-OH
THELONIOUS MONK Epistrophy
I LOOKED LONG AND HARD FOR THAT RECORD.
HE TOLD ME IT WAS HIS FAVORITE.
ARE YOU OK?
WHO TOLD YOU?
YOUR EYES ARE ROLLING AROUND!
DID YOU HIT YOUR HEAD AGAIN?
SALTZ?
DO YOU KNOW WHERE WE ARE?

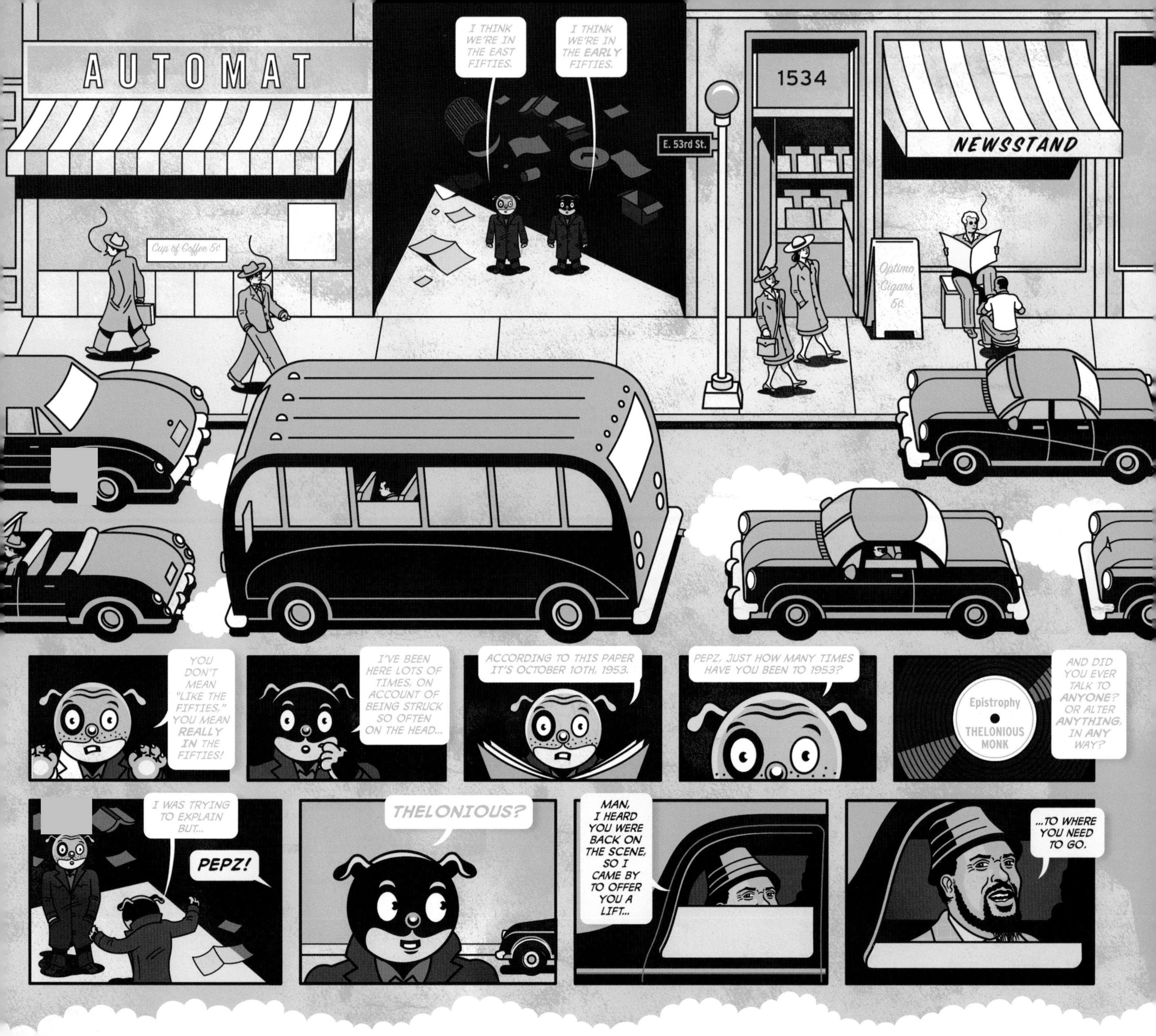
AUTOMAT
Cup of Coffee 5¢
I THINK WE'RE IN THE EAST FIFTIES.
I THINK WE'RE IN THE EARLY FIFTIES.
E. 53rd St.
1534
NEWSSTAND
Optimo Cigars 5¢
YOU DON'T MEAN "LIKE THE FIFTIES," YOU MEAN REALLY IN THE FIFTIES!
I'VE BEEN HERE LOTS OF TIMES, ON ACCOUNT OF BEING STRUCK SO OFTEN ON THE HEAD...
ACCORDING TO THIS PAPER IT'S OCTOBER 10TH, 1953.
PEPZ, JUST HOW MANY TIMES HAVE YOU BEEN TO 1953?
Epistrophy
THELONIOUS MONK
AND DID YOU EVER TALK TO ANYONE? OR ALTER ANYTHING, IN ANY WAY?
I WAS TRYING TO EXPLAIN BUT...
PEPZ!
THELONIOUS?
MAN, I HEARD YOU WERE BACK ON THE SCENE, SO I CAME BY TO OFFER YOU A LIFT...
...TO WHERE YOU NEED TO GO.

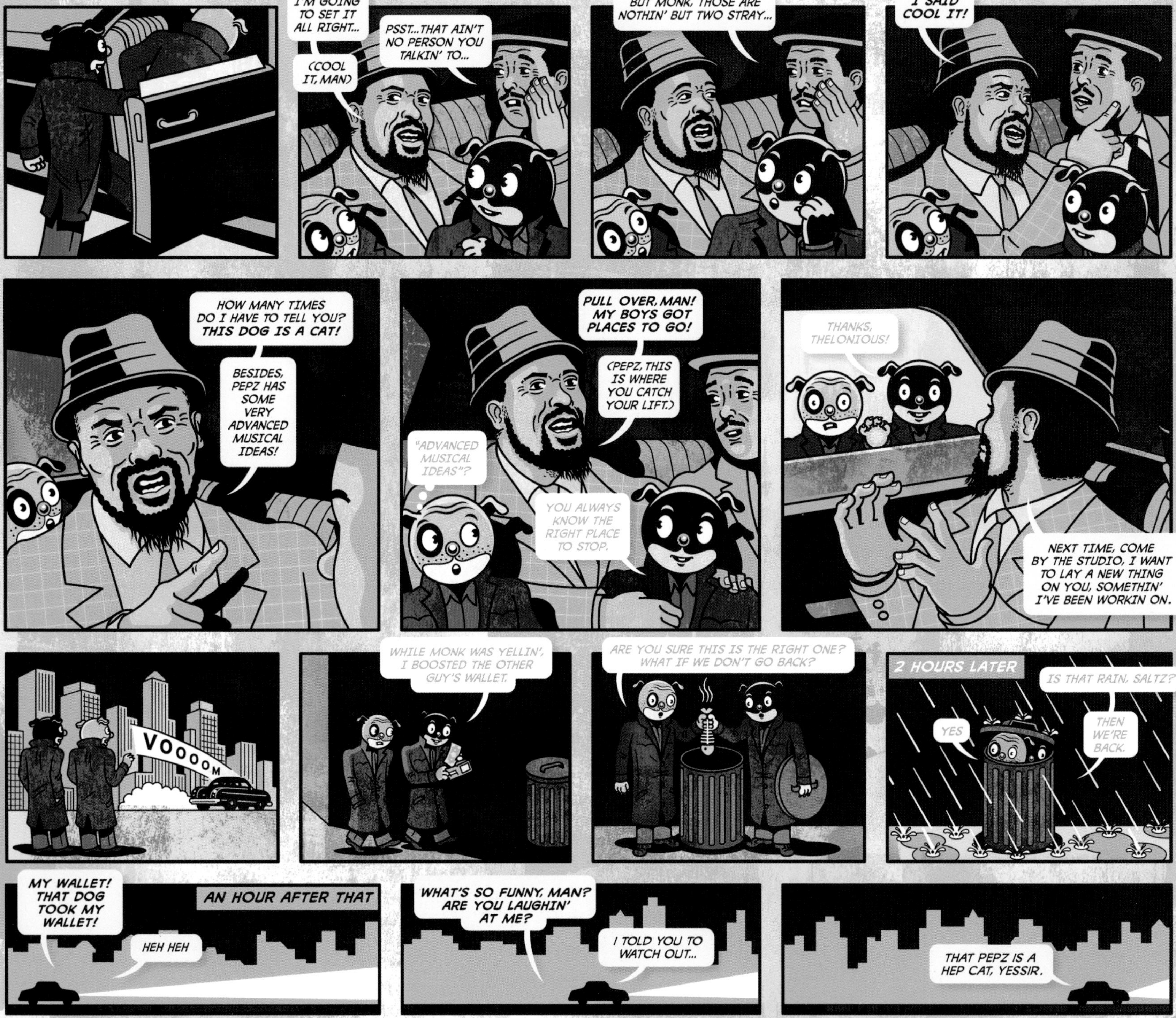

I'M GOING TO SET IT ALL RIGHT...
(COOL IT, MAN)
PSST...THAT AIN'T NO PERSON YOU TALKIN' TO...
BUT MONK, THOSE ARE NOTHIN' BUT TWO STRAY...
I SAID COOL IT!
HOW MANY TIMES DO I HAVE TO TELL YOU? THIS DOG IS A CAT!
BESIDES, PEPZ HAS SOME VERY ADVANCED MUSICAL IDEAS!
PULL OVER, MAN! MY BOYS GOT PLACES TO GO!
(PEPZ, THIS IS WHERE YOU CATCH YOUR LIFT.)
"ADVANCED MUSICAL IDEAS"?
YOU ALWAYS KNOW THE RIGHT PLACE TO STOP.
THANKS, THELONIOUS!
NEXT TIME, COME BY THE STUDIO, I WANT TO LAY A NEW THING ON YOU, SOMETHIN' I'VE BEEN WORKIN ON.
VOOOOOM
WHILE MONK WAS YELLIN', I BOOSTED THE OTHER GUY'S WALLET.
ARE YOU SURE THIS IS THE RIGHT ONE? WHAT IF WE DON'T GO BACK?
2 HOURS LATER
IS THAT RAIN, SALTZ?
YES
THEN WE'RE BACK.
AN HOUR AFTER THAT
MY WALLET! THAT DOG TOOK MY WALLET!
HEH HEH
WHAT'S SO FUNNY, MAN? ARE YOU LAUGHIN' AT ME?
I TOLD YOU TO WATCH OUT...
THAT PEPZ IS A HEP CAT, YESSIR.

The Slippery Lobster

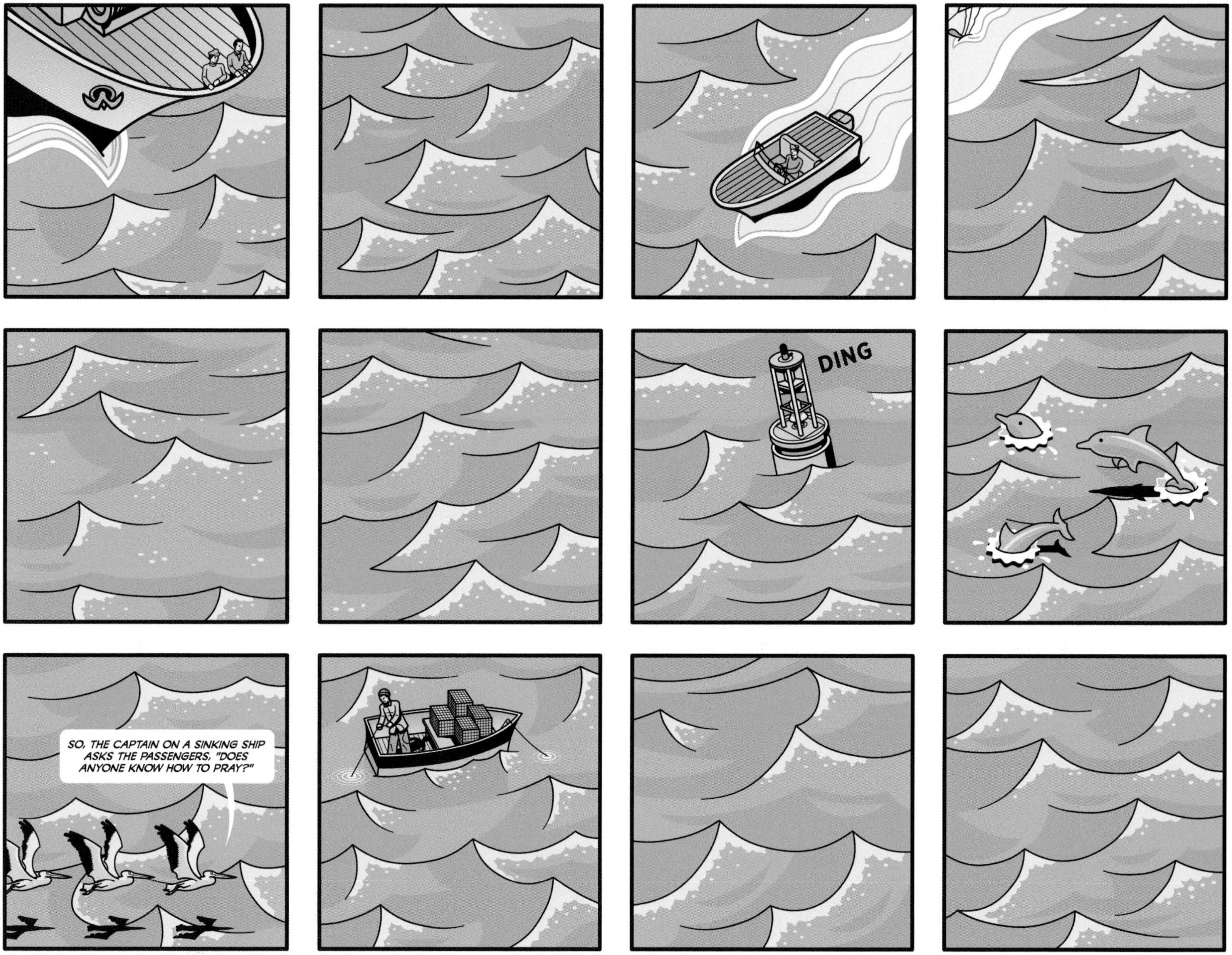
DING
SO, THE CAPTAIN ON A SINKING SHIP ASKS THE PASSENGERS, "DOES ANYONE KNOW HOW TO PRAY?"

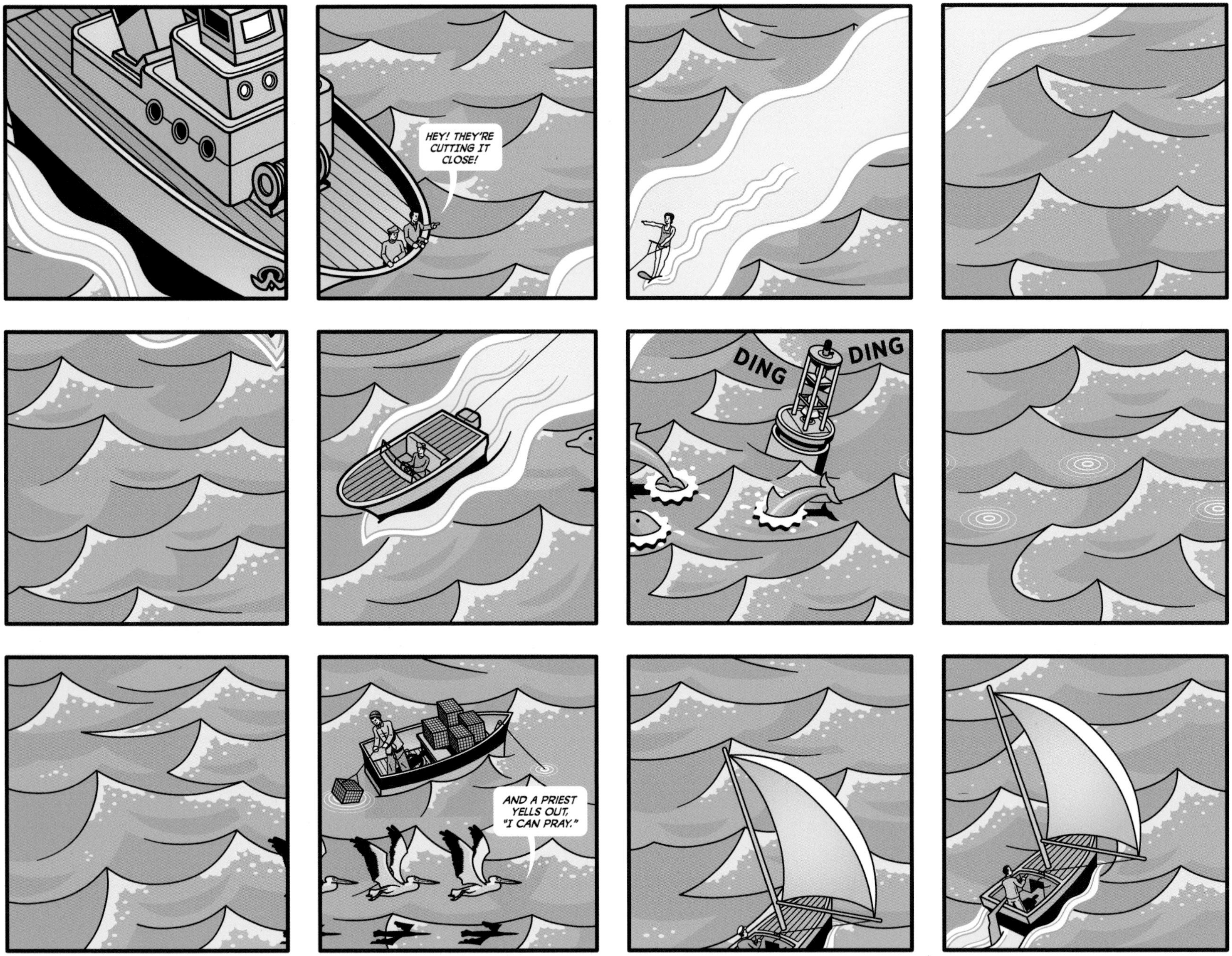
HEY! THEY'RE CUTTING IT CLOSE!
DING
DING
AND A PRIEST YELLS OUT, "I CAN PRAY."

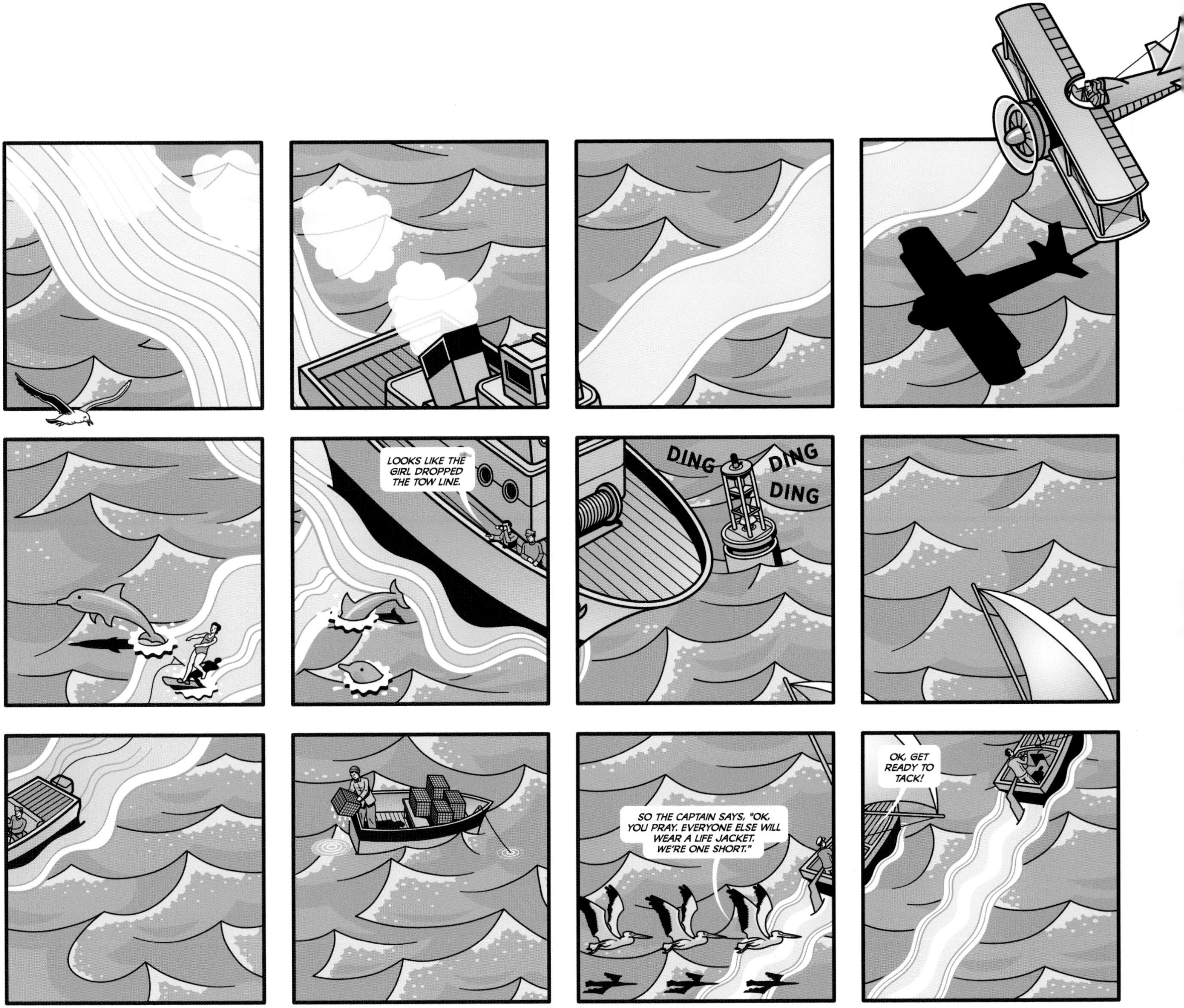
LOOKS LIKE THE GIRL DROPPED THE TOW LINE.
DING
DING
DING
SO THE CAPTAIN SAYS, "OK, YOU PRAY. EVERYONE ELSE WILL WEAR A LIFE JACKET. WE'RE ONE SHORT."
OK, GET READY TO TACK!

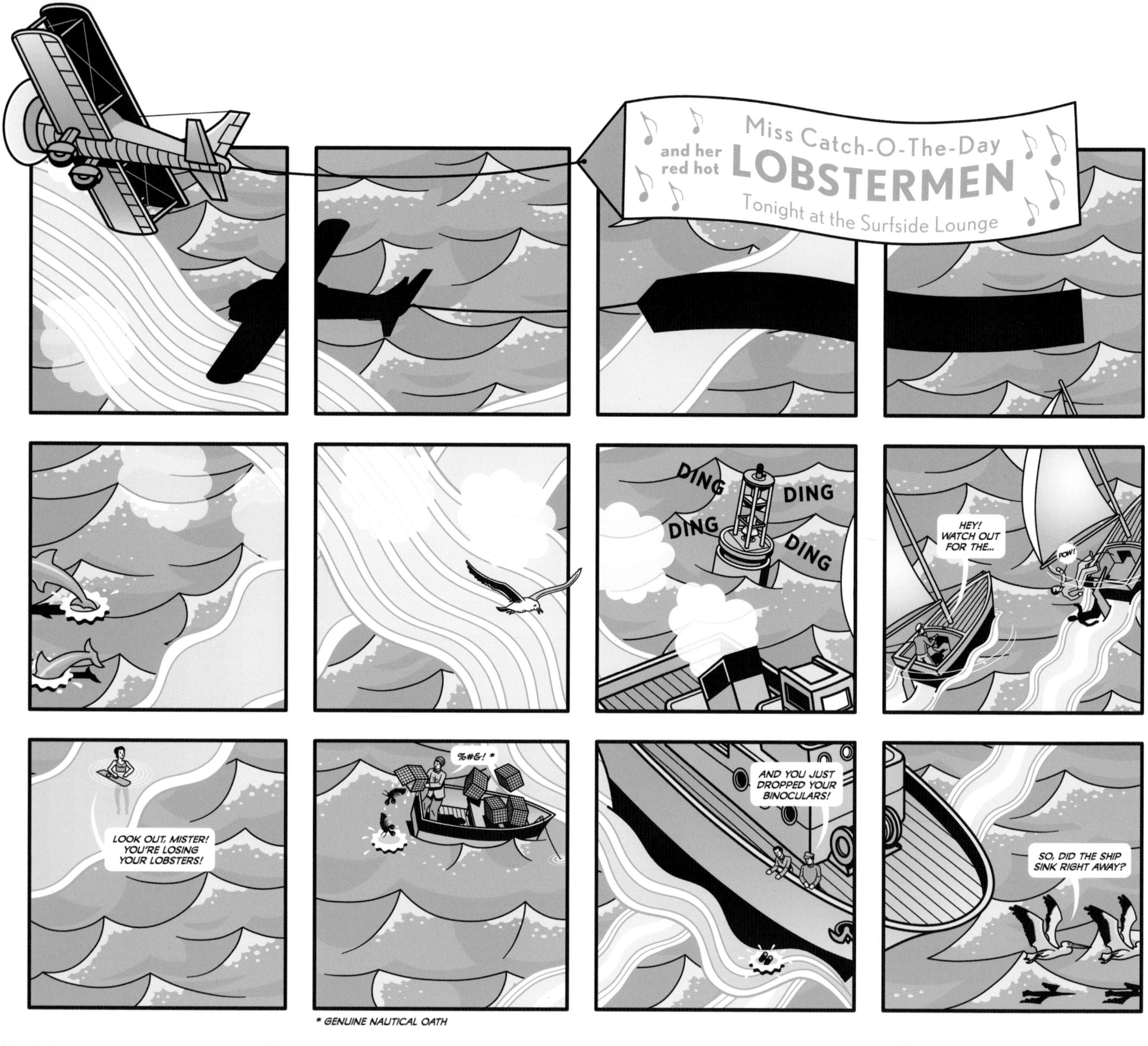
and her red hot
Miss Catch-O-The-Day
LOBSTERMEN
Tonight at the Surfside Lounge
DING
DING
DING
DING
HEY! WATCH OUT FOR THE...
POW!
LOOK OUT, MISTER! YOU'RE LOSING YOUR LOBSTERS!
%#&! *
AND YOU JUST DROPPED YOUR BINOCULARS!
SO, DID THE SHIP SINK RIGHT AWAY?

* GENUINE NAUTICAL OATH

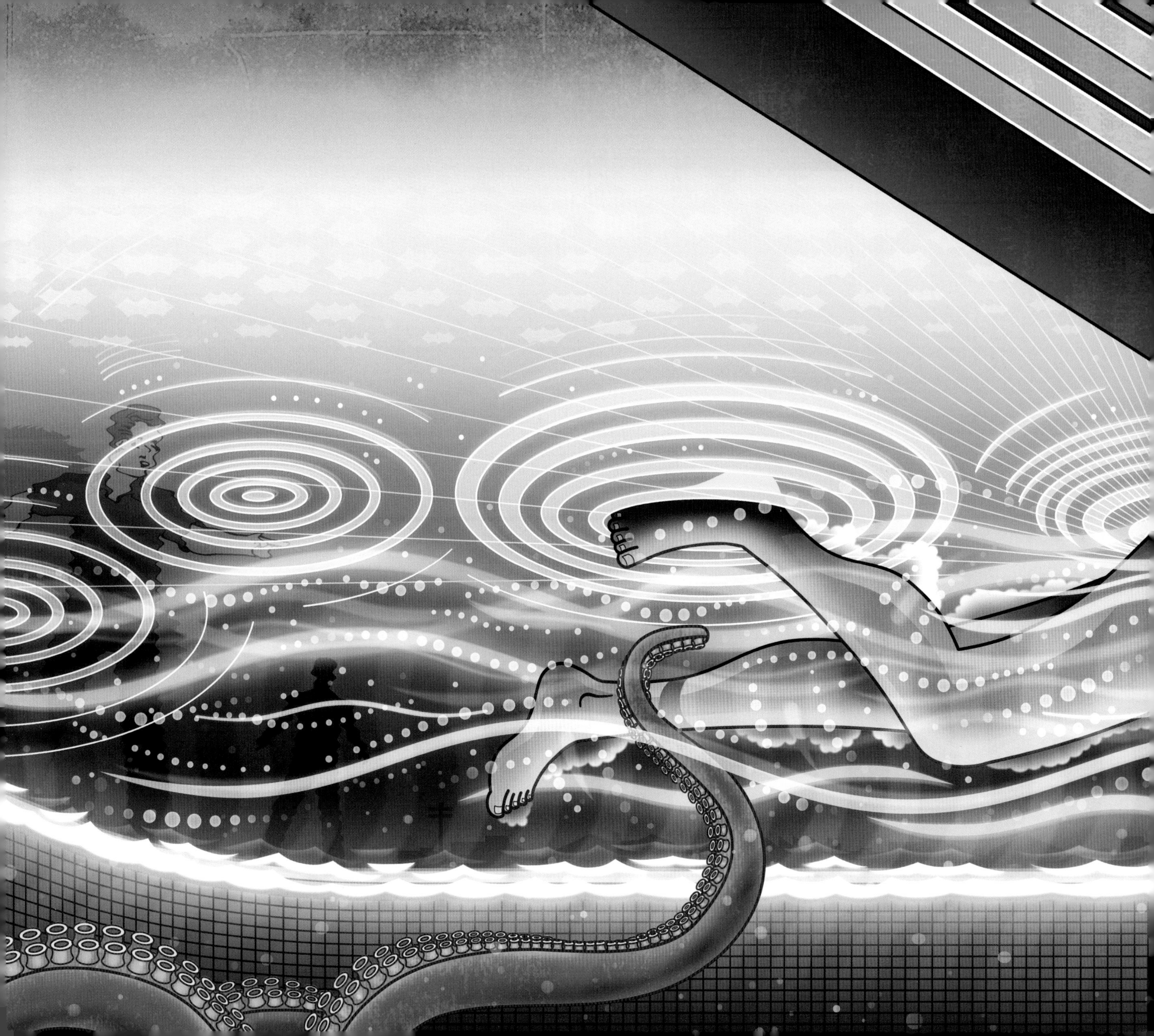

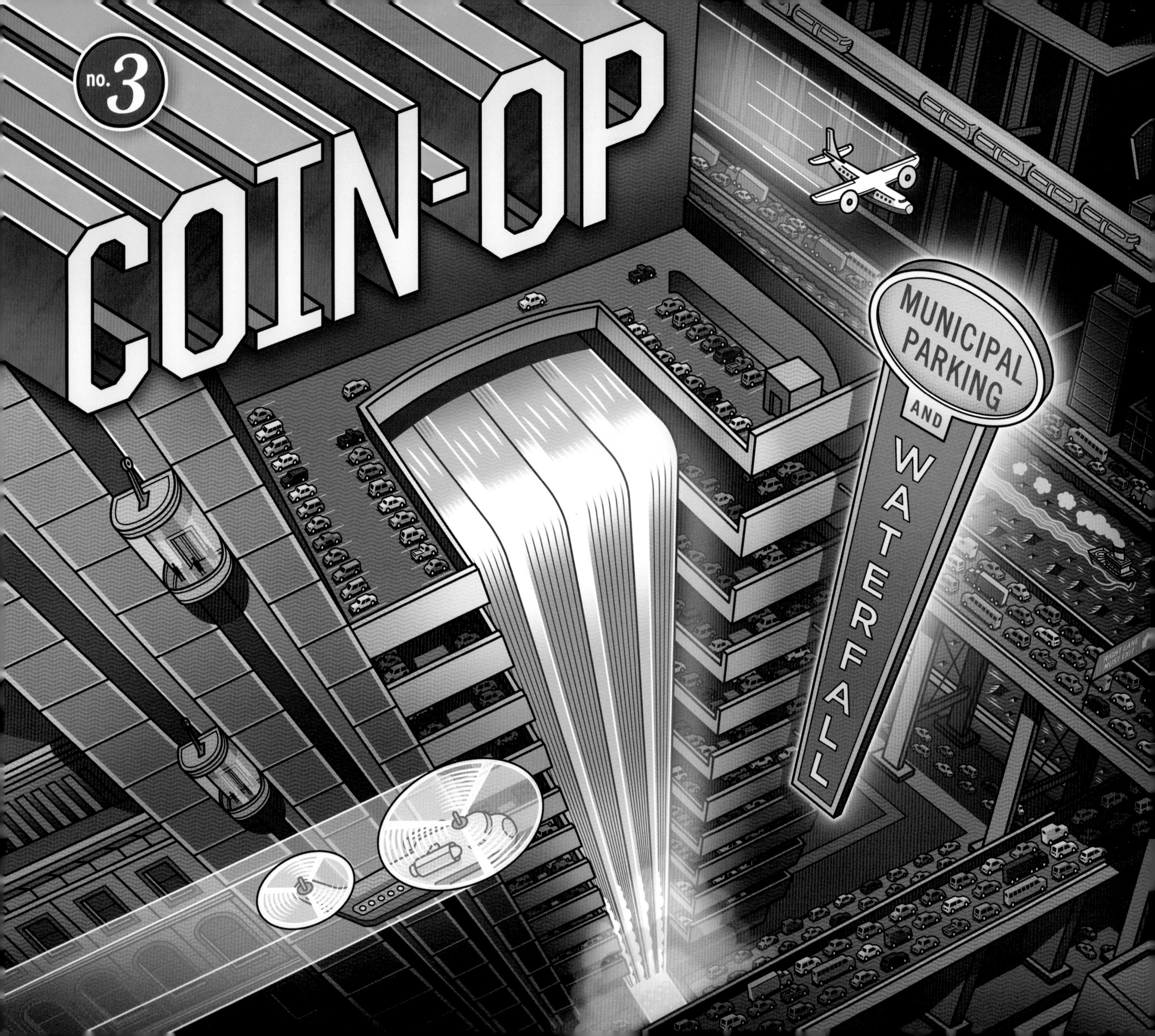
no. 3
COIN-OP
MUNICIPAL PARKING
AND
WATERFALL
RIGHT LANE MUST EXIT

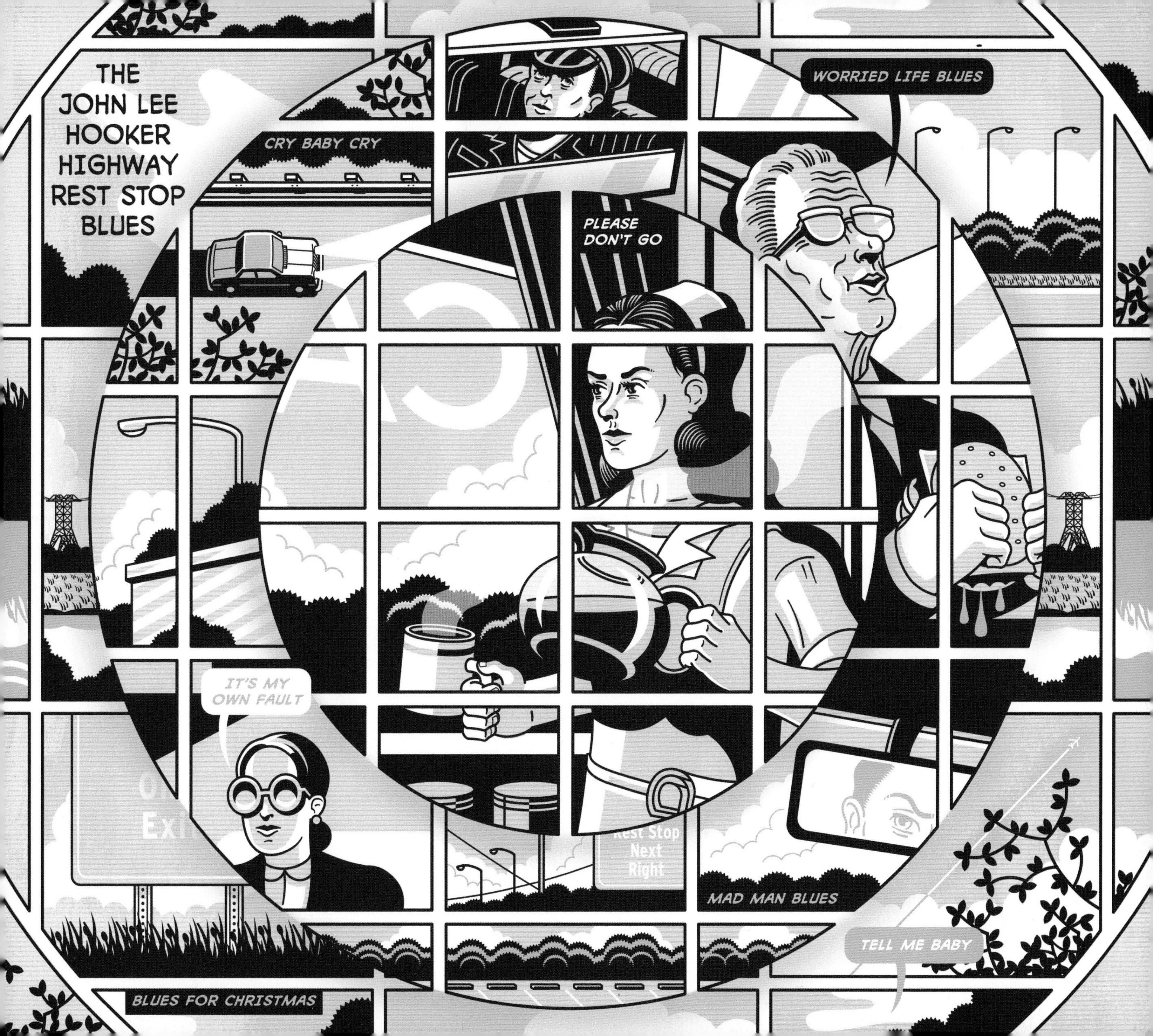
THE JOHN LEE HOOKER HIGHWAY REST STOP BLUES
CRY BABY CRY
WORRIED LIFE BLUES
PLEASE DON'T GO
IT'S MY OWN FAULT
Stop
Next
Right
MAD MAN BLUES
TELL ME BABY
BLUES FOR CHRISTMAS

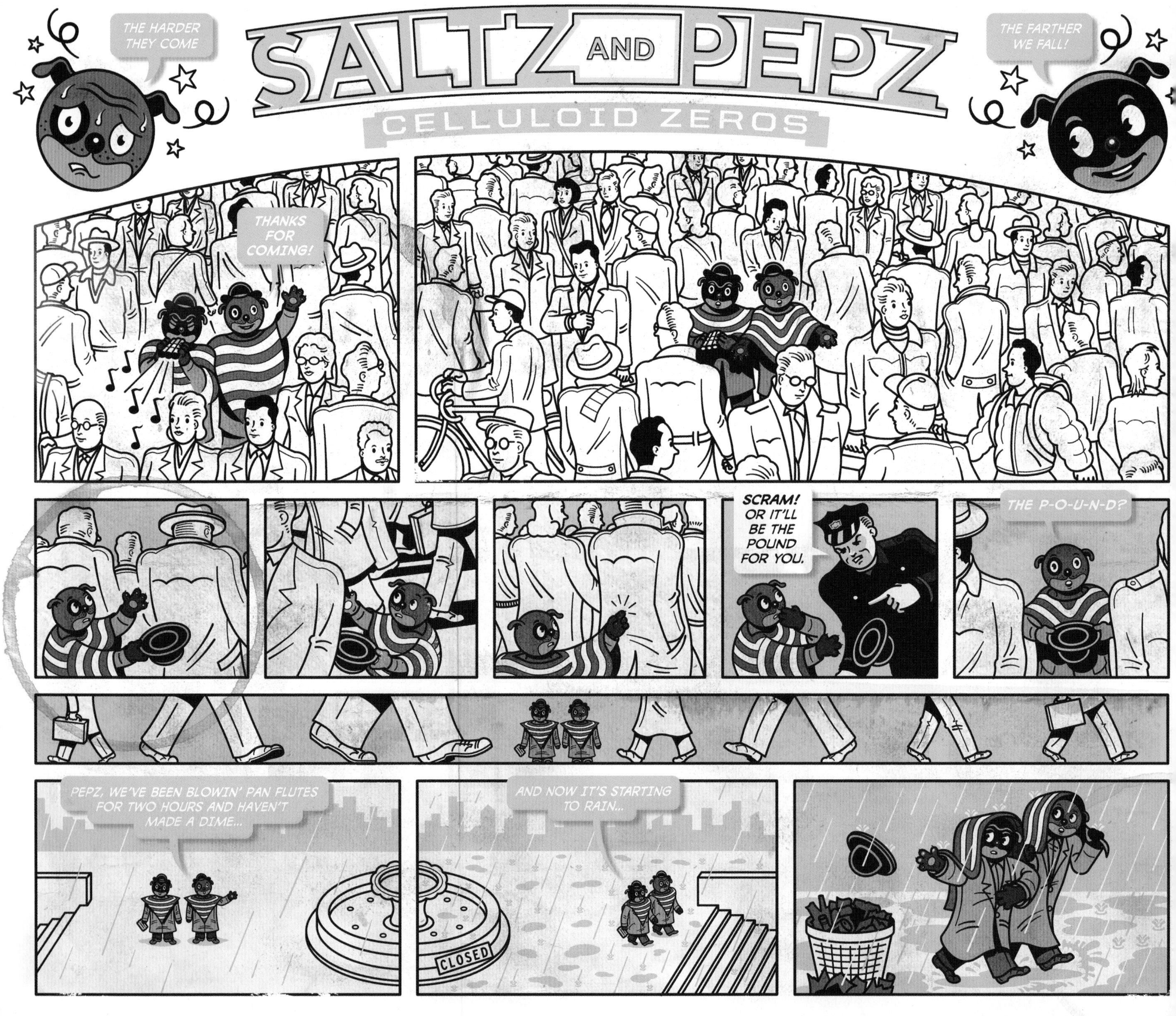
THE HARDER THEY COME
SALTZ AND PEPZ
CELLULOID ZEROS
THE FARTHER WE FALL!
THANKS FOR COMING!
SCRAM! OR IT'LL BE THE POUND FOR YOU.
THE P-O-U-N-D?
PEPZ, WE'VE BEEN BLOWIN' PAN FLUTES FOR TWO HOURS AND HAVEN'T MADE A DIME...
CLOSED
AND NOW IT'S STARTING TO RAIN...

TONIGHT
METROPO

METROPOLIS

PEPZ, WE GOTTA FIND SOMEPLACE DRY.

I CAN PLAY LOUD!

LOOK, PEPZ, THAT OPEN WINDOW IS OUR TICKET OUT OF THE RAIN!

THEATER FIRE EXIT NO ADMITTANCE

I'LL BOOST YOU UP TO THE TRANSOM...

THEATER FIRE EXIT NO ADMITTANCE

WHA?

...AND LOWER YOU DOWN...

BUT I CAN'T SEE ANYTHING.

...HOLD ON, PEPZ, I NEED A BETTER GRIP...

SALTZ, I'M SLIPPING!

WATCH OUT!

NO ADMITTANCE

GRAB MY SLEEVE PEPZ, MY SLEE...

THEATER FIRE EXIT NO ADMITTANCE

SLAM

THEATER FIRE EXIT NO ADMITTANCE

A LONG TIME PASSES...

FLICK

PEPZ, ARE YOU OK?

THAT WAS A LONG FALL.

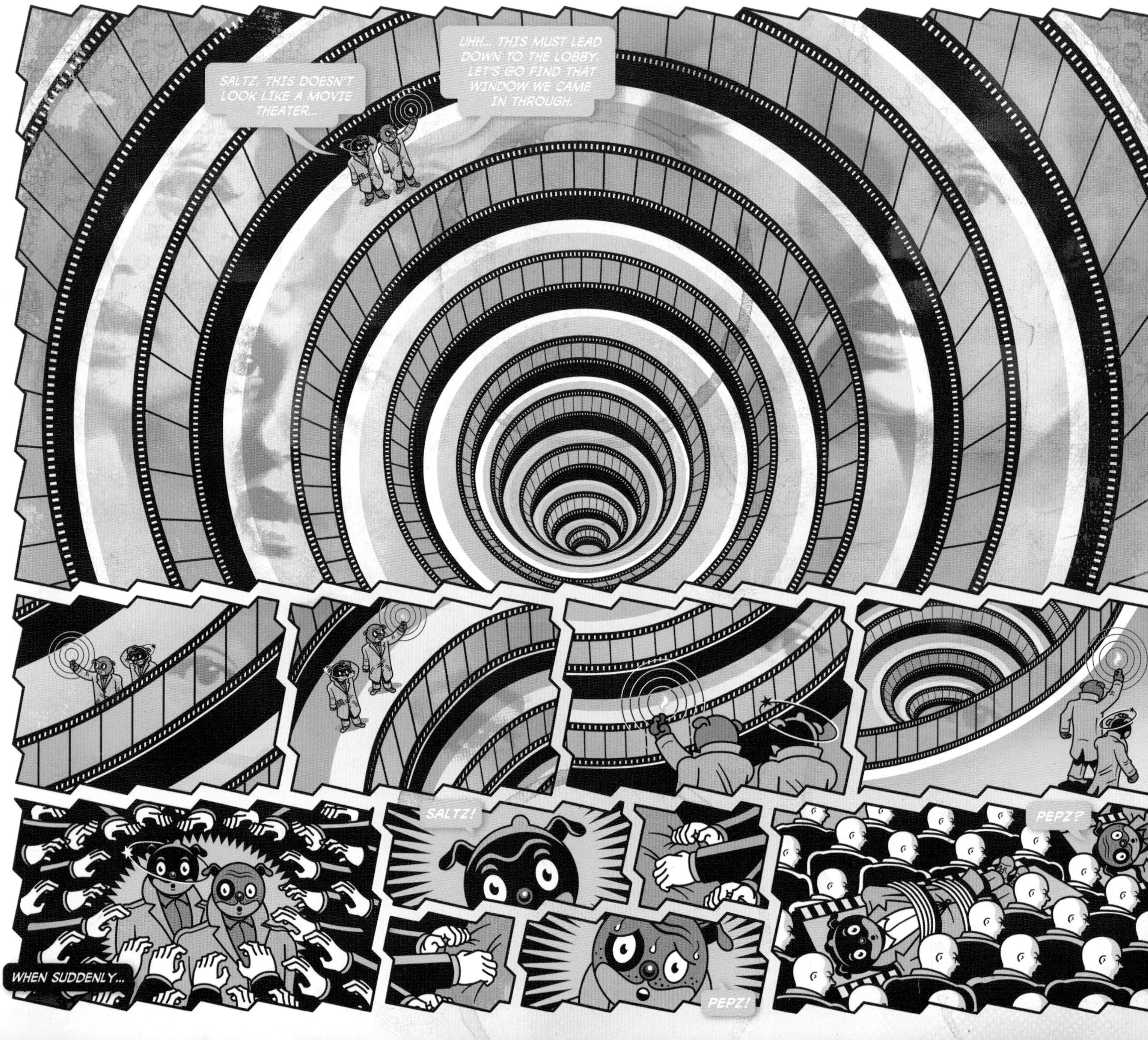
SALTZ, THIS DOESN'T LOOK LIKE A MOVIE THEATER...
UHH... THIS MUST LEAD DOWN TO THE LOBBY. LET'S GO FIND THAT WINDOW WE CAME IN THROUGH.
WHEN SUDDENLY...
SALTZ!
PEPZ!
PEPZ?

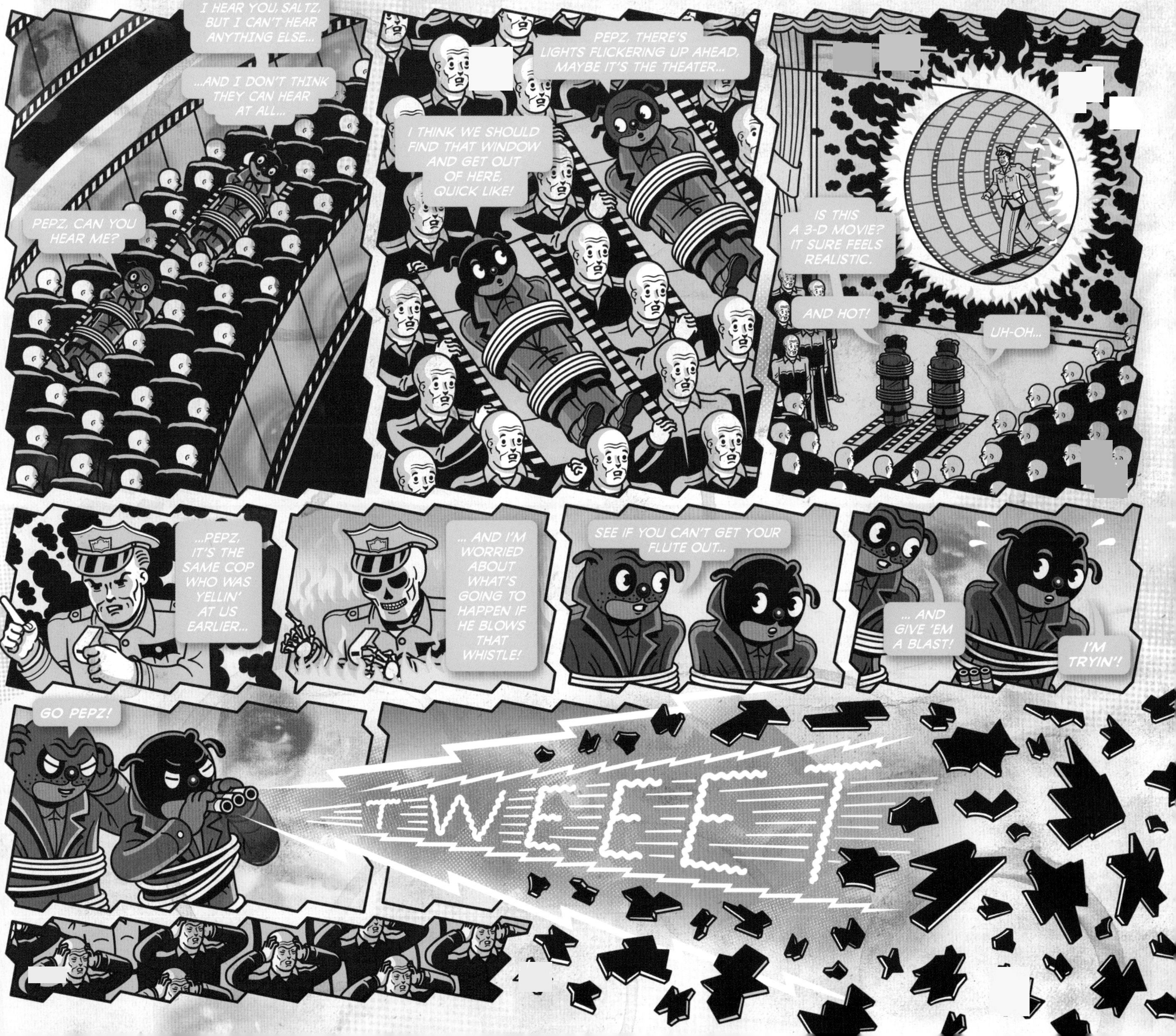
I HEAR YOU, SALTZ, BUT I CAN'T HEAR ANYTHING ELSE...
...AND I DON'T THINK THEY CAN HEAR AT ALL...
PEPZ, CAN YOU HEAR ME?
PEPZ, THERE'S LIGHTS FLICKERING UP AHEAD, MAYBE IT'S THE THEATER...
I THINK WE SHOULD FIND THAT WINDOW AND GET OUT OF HERE, QUICK LIKE!
IS THIS A 3-D MOVIE? IT SURE FEELS REALISTIC.
AND HOT!
UH-OH...
...PEPZ, IT'S THE SAME COP WHO WAS YELLIN' AT US EARLIER...
... AND I'M WORRIED ABOUT WHAT'S GOING TO HAPPEN IF HE BLOWS THAT WHISTLE!
SEE IF YOU CAN'T GET YOUR FLUTE OUT...
... AND GIVE 'EM A BLAST!
I'M TRYIN'!
GO PEPZ!
TWEEET

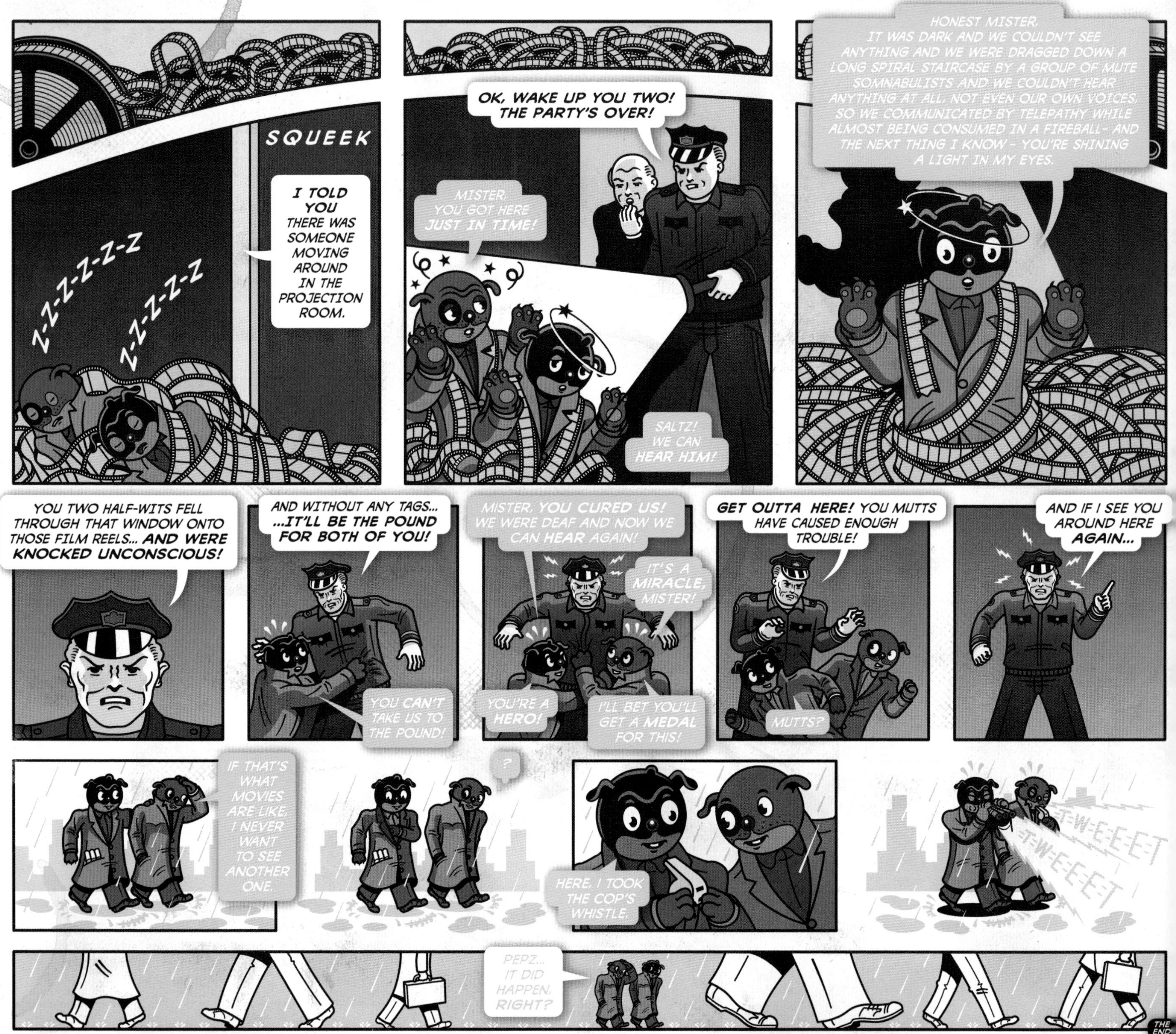
Z-Z-Z-Z-Z-Z
Z-Z-Z-Z-Z
SQUEEK
I TOLD YOU THERE WAS SOMEONE MOVING AROUND IN THE PROJECTION ROOM.
OK, WAKE UP YOU TWO! THE PARTY'S OVER!
MISTER, YOU GOT HERE JUST IN TIME!
SALTZ! WE CAN HEAR HIM!
HONEST MISTER, IT WAS DARK AND WE COULDN'T SEE ANYTHING AND WE WERE DRAGGED DOWN A LONG SPIRAL STAIRCASE BY A GROUP OF MUTE SOMNABULISTS AND WE COULDN'T HEAR ANYTHING AT ALL, NOT EVEN OUR OWN VOICES, SO WE COMMUNICATED BY TELEPATHY WHILE ALMOST BEING CONSUMED IN A FIREBALL- AND THE NEXT THING I KNOW - YOU'RE SHINING A LIGHT IN MY EYES.
YOU TWO HALF-WITS FELL THROUGH THAT WINDOW ONTO THOSE FILM REELS... AND WERE KNOCKED UNCONSCIOUS!
AND WITHOUT ANY TAGS... ...IT'LL BE THE POUND FOR BOTH OF YOU!
YOU CAN'T TAKE US TO THE POUND!
MISTER, YOU CURED US! WE WERE DEAF AND NOW WE CAN HEAR AGAIN!
IT'S A MIRACLE, MISTER!
YOU'RE A HERO!
I'LL BET YOU'LL GET A MEDAL FOR THIS!
GET OUTTA HERE! YOU MUTTS HAVE CAUSED ENOUGH TROUBLE!
MUTTS?
AND IF I SEE YOU AROUND HERE AGAIN...
IF THAT'S WHAT MOVIES ARE LIKE, I NEVER WANT TO SEE ANOTHER ONE.
?
HERE, I TOOK THE COP'S WHISTLE.
T-W-E-E-E-T
T-W-E-E-E-T
PEPZ... IT DID HAPPEN, RIGHT?
THE END

LUCKY THOMPSON

Eli "Lucky" Thompson was the great elusive tenor saxophonist of American jazz. An original talent whose work has been largely forgotten, Lucky saw his 30-year career eclipsed by an increasingly acrimonious relationship to the music industry. These frustrations eventually led him to leave the scene altogether and may have been an early indicator of his later struggles with mental illness.

HE FIRST CAME TO NOTICE IN 1943, blowing a Coleman Hawkins-influenced tenor for Lionel Hampton's band. Elegantly constructed solos and dark-toned phrasing gave his playing an emotive depth that got lots of attention. Though not a be-bopper, Lucky's playing bridged jazz's stylistic divides; he featured prominently on the important early West Coast recordings of Charlie Parker and Dizzy Gillespie. During this busy time he also made his initial recordings as a band leader.

Along with his growing stature came rising frustrations with the economic inequities of the music business. Routinely underpaid by promoters, booking agents and label owners, jazz musicians faced a daunting front of financial exploitation, and for black musicians there was the additional slap of lingering racism. Thompson spoke out early and loudly against this mistreatment, earning a reputation as "difficult." His anger reached the point where he engaged in a very public feud with jazz heavyweight manager Joe Glaser sparked by an argument over which musician would depart first from a plane sitting on a Paris runway.

By 1956, with his career in a stall and sick of the constant struggle, Thompson decided to move his family to France. They spent six years in Paris, with Lucky deeply involved in playing and recording. It was during this time that he took up the soprano saxophone, an instrument he would play with great effect in the 1960s.

With a move back to New York and a major label contract, Lucky entered the most active period of his career. In the space of three years, he engaged in a wave of recordings and concerts, producing an impressive body of work. His artful arrangements and searching, melodic thinking were never more in evidence.

Soon though, problems seemed to close back in on him. His wife died suddenly, leaving him to raise their two young children, and by 1968 persistent financial struggles with the music industry had him publicly announcing his retirement. Lucky returned to Europe for a time, again taking up recording and playing but by the early 1970s his career was over. A final return to the U.S. for a teaching engagement at Dartmouth ended badly and he left after a year, leveling charges of racism at the university. His final recordings were made in 1973.

Lucky dropped out completely, living for two years on a small island in Canada before eventually moving on to Savannah. While in Georgia he traded in his saxophones for some needed dental care, severing his last connection to music. A short time later, Lucky disappeared. He resurfaced in the 1980s, homeless, living a hermit-like existence in the wooded areas around Seattle. Cut off from the world, bitter and paranoid, Thompson refused offers of help from friends and former bandmates. After a period of declining health he was coaxed into an assisted-care facility where he lived for the last five years of his life. Lucky Thompson died on July 30, 2005. He was 81 years old.

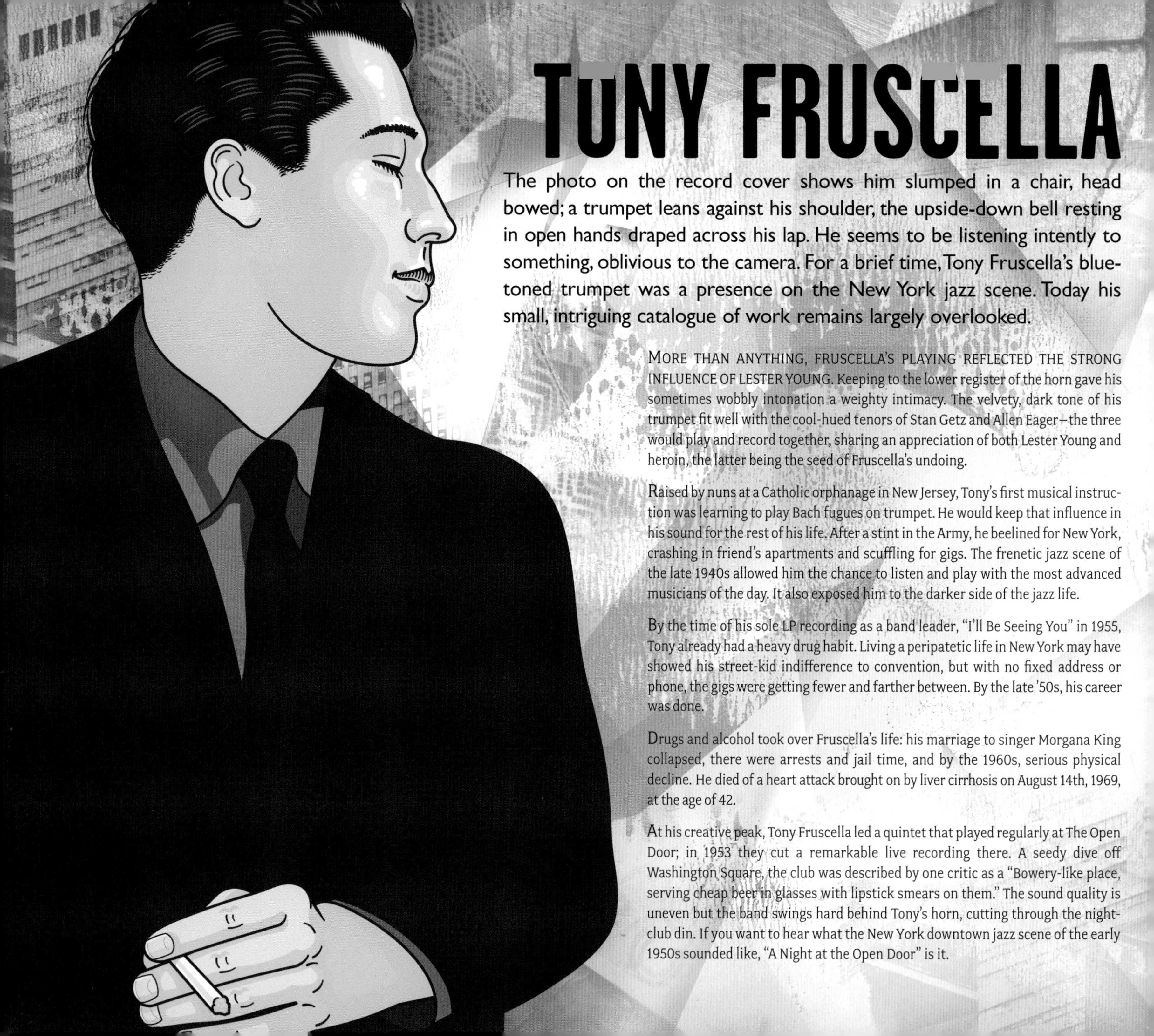

TONY FRUSCELLA

The photo on the record cover shows him slumped in a chair, head bowed; a trumpet leans against his shoulder, the upside-down bell resting in open hands draped across his lap. He seems to be listening intently to something, oblivious to the camera. For a brief time, Tony Fruscella's blue-toned trumpet was a presence on the New York jazz scene. Today his small, intriguing catalogue of work remains largely overlooked.

More than anything, Fruscella's playing reflected the strong influence of Lester Young. Keeping to the lower register of the horn gave his sometimes wobbly intonation a weighty intimacy. The velvety, dark tone of his trumpet fit well with the cool-hued tenors of Stan Getz and Allen Eager—the three would play and record together, sharing an appreciation of both Lester Young and heroin, the latter being the seed of Fruscella's undoing.

Raised by nuns at a Catholic orphanage in New Jersey, Tony's first musical instruction was learning to play Bach fugues on trumpet. He would keep that influence in his sound for the rest of his life. After a stint in the Army, he beelined for New York, crashing in friend's apartments and scuffling for gigs. The frenetic jazz scene of the late 1940s allowed him the chance to listen and play with the most advanced musicians of the day. It also exposed him to the darker side of the jazz life.

By the time of his sole LP recording as a band leader, "I'll Be Seeing You" in 1955, Tony already had a heavy drug habit. Living a peripatetic life in New York may have showed his street-kid indifference to convention, but with no fixed address or phone, the gigs were getting fewer and farther between. By the late '50s, his career was done.

Drugs and alcohol took over Fruscella's life: his marriage to singer Morgana King collapsed, there were arrests and jail time, and by the 1960s, serious physical decline. He died of a heart attack brought on by liver cirrhosis on August 14th, 1969, at the age of 42.

At his creative peak, Tony Fruscella led a quintet that played regularly at The Open Door; in 1953 they cut a remarkable live recording there. A seedy dive off Washington Square, the club was described by one critic as a "Bowery-like place, serving cheap beer in glasses with lipstick smears on them." The sound quality is uneven but the band swings hard behind Tony's horn, cutting through the night-club din. If you want to hear what the New York downtown jazz scene of the early 1950s sounded like, "A Night at the Open Door" is it.

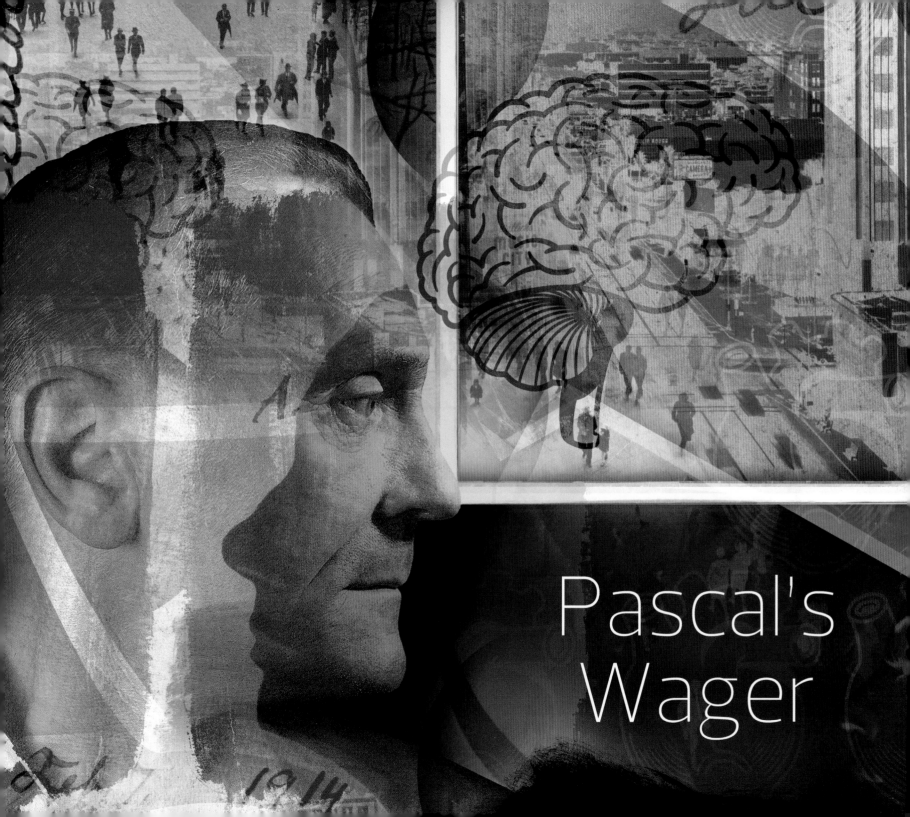

Pascal's
Wager

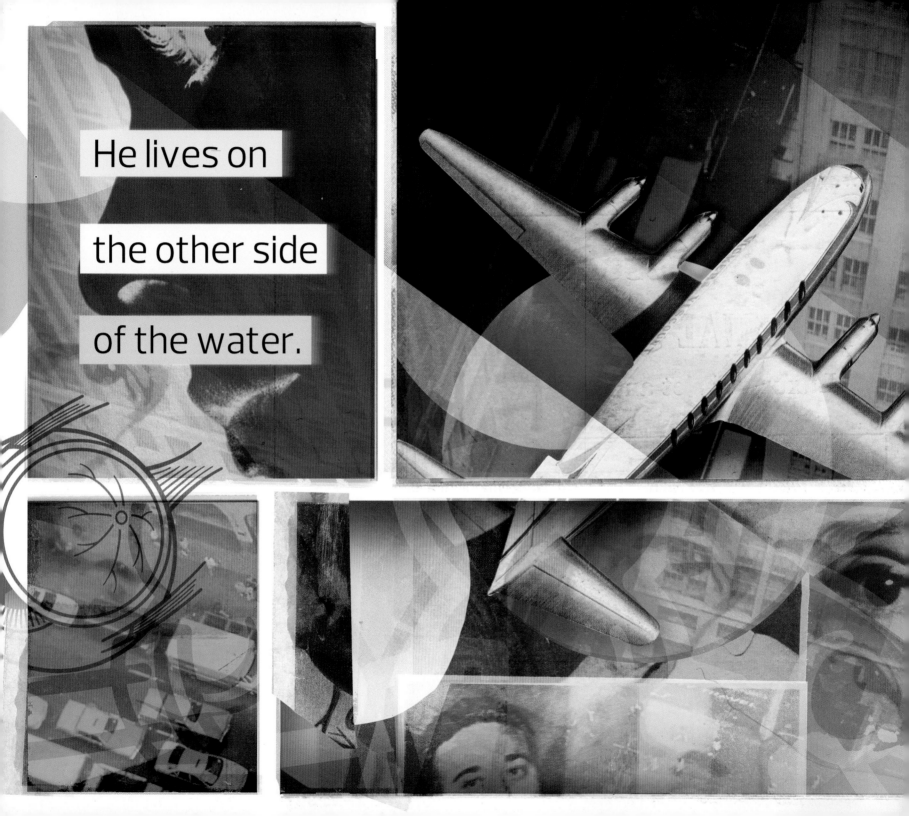

He lives on

the other side

of the water.

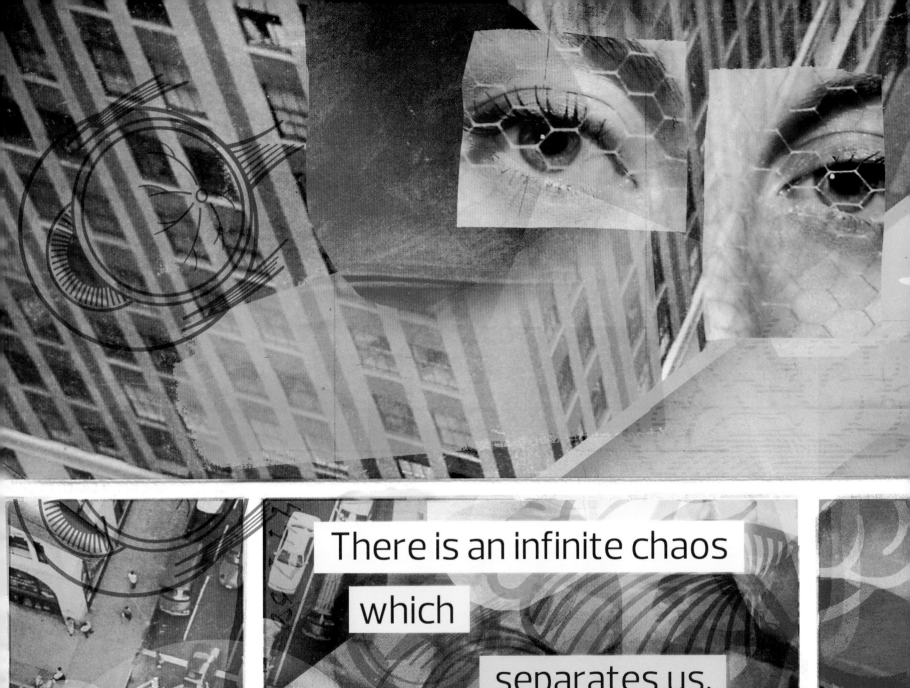

There is an infinite chaos which separates us.

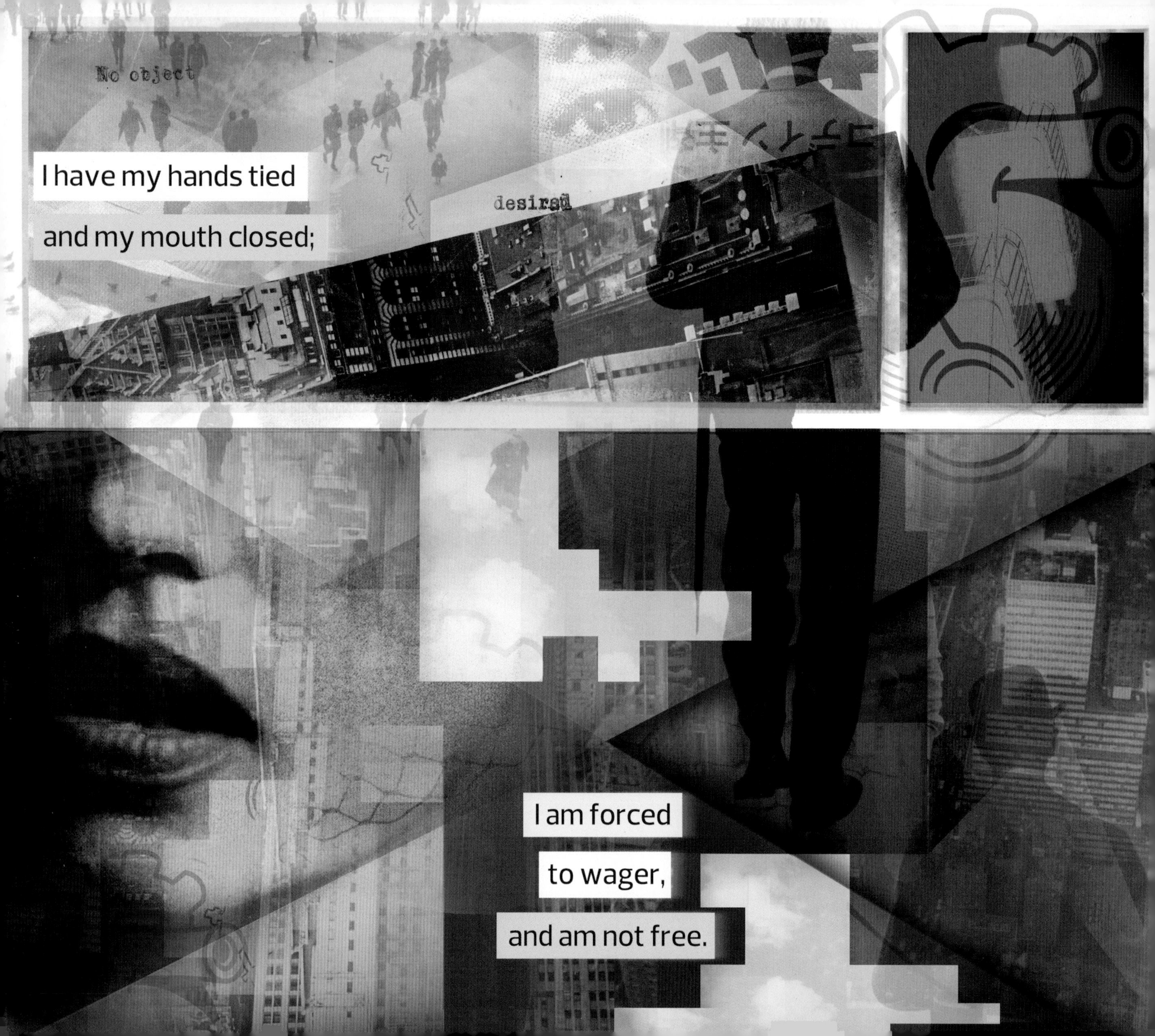
No object
I have my hands tied
and my mouth closed;
desired
I am forced
to wager,
and am not free.

WARNE MARSH

Usually identified as a minor player in the "cool school" jazz movement, the introverted tenor saxophonist nonetheless staked a claim to being one of the great improvisers of his time. But years after an untimely death, the musical contributions of Warne Marsh remain largely unheard.

WARNE MARION MARSH WAS RAISED in the rarified world of the 1930s Hollywood film industry. His father, Oliver Marsh, was a sought-after cinematographer at MGM; the family lived in relative affluence. The teenaged Warne started his musical career in the Hollywood Canteen Kids, a Los Angeles novelty dance band that was a clearinghouse for local talent. When he wasn't practicing, Marsh was spending time in the clubs along Central Avenue, developing an ear for modern jazz.

Military service in the late 1940s brought Marsh to the East Coast, where he encountered a musician who would change the direction of his life: Lennie Tristano. Pianist, mentor, and teacher, Tristano taught a demanding regimen of jazz improvisation. Warne quickly fell under the spell of the blind pianist and remained his student for eight years. Tristano's intensely hermetic musical instruction, combined with the amateur psychoanalysis he practiced on his students, made them appear cult-like to other musicians.

Marsh's initial recordings in the late 1940s showed the teacher's influence, especially when paired with alto—and fellow Tristano-ite—Lee Konitz. His playing didn't propel itself so much as unfold—curling and reforming like a wisp of smoke. Especially gifted at rhythmic displacement, he stretched and compressed the spaces between notes to inject a continual edge of surprise into his billowing solos.

Warne found it hard to gain a footing in the New York scene. The hushed concentration that he brought to his playing nudged out a larger audience.

By the late 1950s, he relocated back to Los Angeles and spent the next decade largely off the scene, woodshedding with a small circle of like-minded musicians. He concentrated on the same short list of songs, practicing them endlessly, assimilating the melodic structures inside and out.

The 1970s saw a spirited return to recording. He played with more agility than ever—the dry sound now burnished with a deeper tone. Along with the upswing in profile, there was a marriage and two children. Moving between New York and Los Angeles, Warne kept a steady schedule of recording and performance, the busiest of his career.

By 1982, with his marriage over and money problems escalating, Marsh permanently relocated back to Los Angeles. His mother bought him a house with money from his late father's estate.

A heavy marijuana smoker since his early teens, Warne took up cocaine in the late '70s and eventually became addicted. Friends were startled at his emaciated appearance, but despite the growing drug problem his playing was attracting serious reappraisal. Some critics were naming him one of the great players of the day.

Though he was receiving lavish praise from some in the music press, audiences remained small. Living and working out of L.A. didn't help in getting more exposure from the New York-focused jazz scene. He continued with a brisk schedule of performances but began suffering health problems from his cocaine habit. Warne Marsh died of a heart attack onstage at a Los Angeles nightclub, December 17, 1987. He had just finished his solo on "Out of Nowhere."

HERBIE NICHOLS

In 1956 Billie Holiday bought a song titled "Serenade" from a little-known New York jazz composer. She had words written to it, changed the name to "Lady Sings The Blues," and made it both a hit song and the title to her best-selling autobiography. The co-writing credit that Herbie Nichols garnered was the highest recognition he would achieve in his short life. Today, he's recognized as a brilliant pianist and composer, but while he was alive, Nichols' astounding creativity was mostly ignored.

HERBIE CAME TO JAZZ IN THE 1930S, via privation. Classical piano studies were sidelined by the Depression and the teenaged Nichols began playing in the Royal Barons jazz band to earn a living. Already writing his own compositions, he widened his influences from Prokofiev and Bartok to include Ellington. Bandmates were baffled by his sophisticated tastes and found his music too difficult to play. "It was like he was funneling the whole Ellington Orchestra into his two hands," remarked a friend.

It was a familiar pattern in Nichols' career, moving through different New York jazz scenes, playing well but never quite fitting in. Dapper and reserved, Herbie stood apart from the noisy whirl of 52nd St. and Harlem. Still, he continued writing: music, poetry and cultural reviews for New York's black newspapers. Something of an aesthete, he preferred the term "jazzist," by way of differentiating himself from the rough-edged jazz crowd. As the be-bop movement emerged in the mid-1940s, Nichols was the first to recognize the importance of Thelonius Monk. His newspaper profiles of the pianist appeared years before most of the jazz world had heard of him. Nichols' own playing shared some of Monks' modern angularity, but with a particular melancholic lilt that was all his own.

Reduced to playing in Dixieland cover bands to survive, Nichols watched as the music scene passed him by. The three trio recordings he made for Blue Note Records in 1955-56 received only polite praise. Critics and audiences were puzzled by what to make of him. The compositions were idiosyncratic, with unusual time signatures and a startling range of influences: West Indian calypso, modern classsical, and stride. The Ellingtonian arrangements, densely woven together and played in a heightened, melodramatic style were more than most listeners were ready to handle.

One last recording for the Bethlehem label in 1957 finished out Nichols' recording career. His profile in the music scene went from the margins to the outside. With his small catalogue of recordings quickly out of print and gigs nonexistent, he was reduced to providing accompaniment to drag revues and playing college fraternity parties. Some of the fire had seemed to go out of his playing and friends remarked that he appeared to be going through a physical decline. After years of avoiding medical care, a New York VA hospital checkup revealed an advanced case of luekemia. He died on the morning of April 12, 1963, at the age of 44.

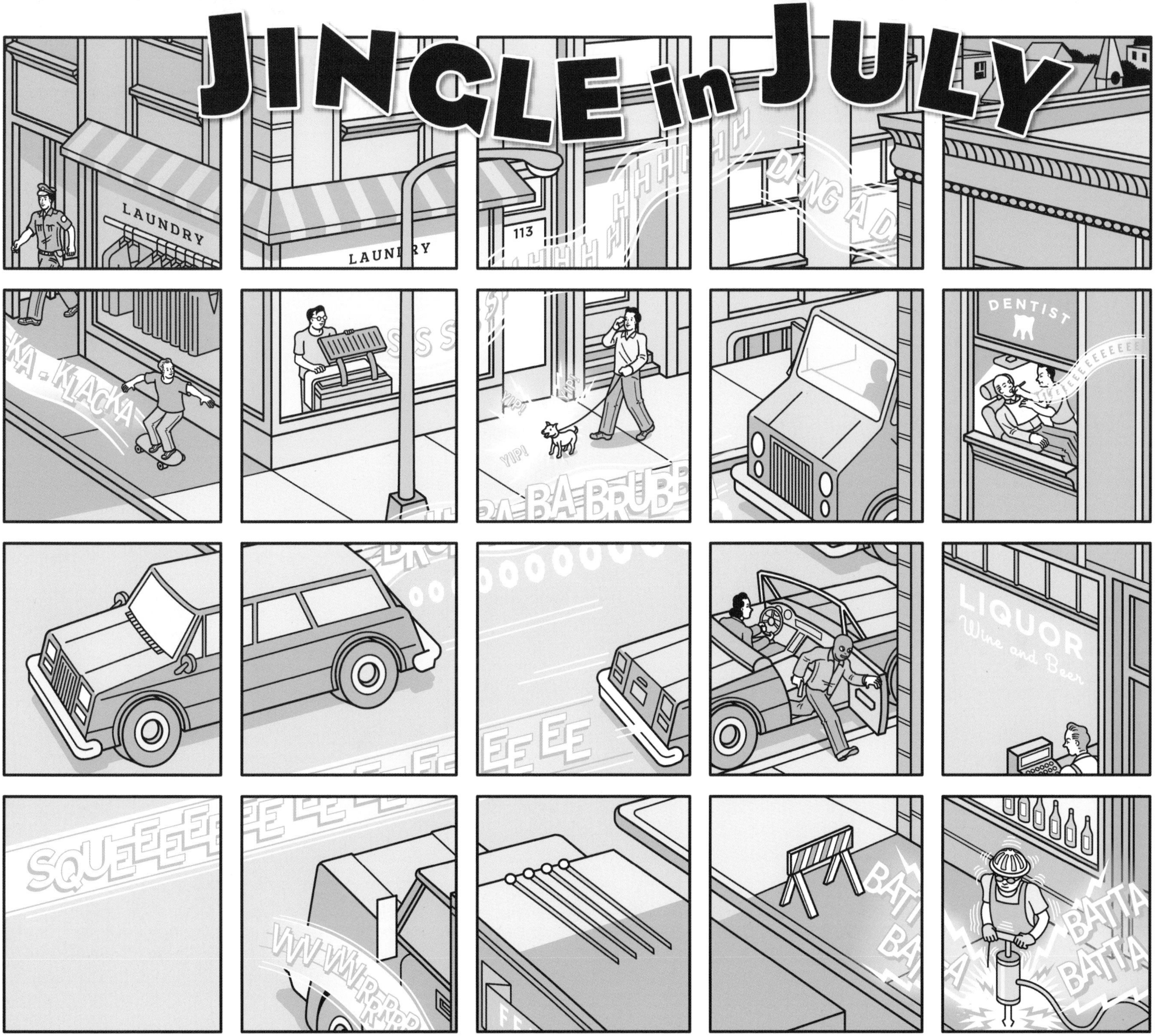
JINGLE in JULY
LAUNDRY
113
KA-KLACKA
YIP!
YIP!
YIP!
DENTIST
LIQUOR
Wine and Beer
SQUEEEEE
BATTA
BATTA
BATTA
BATTA

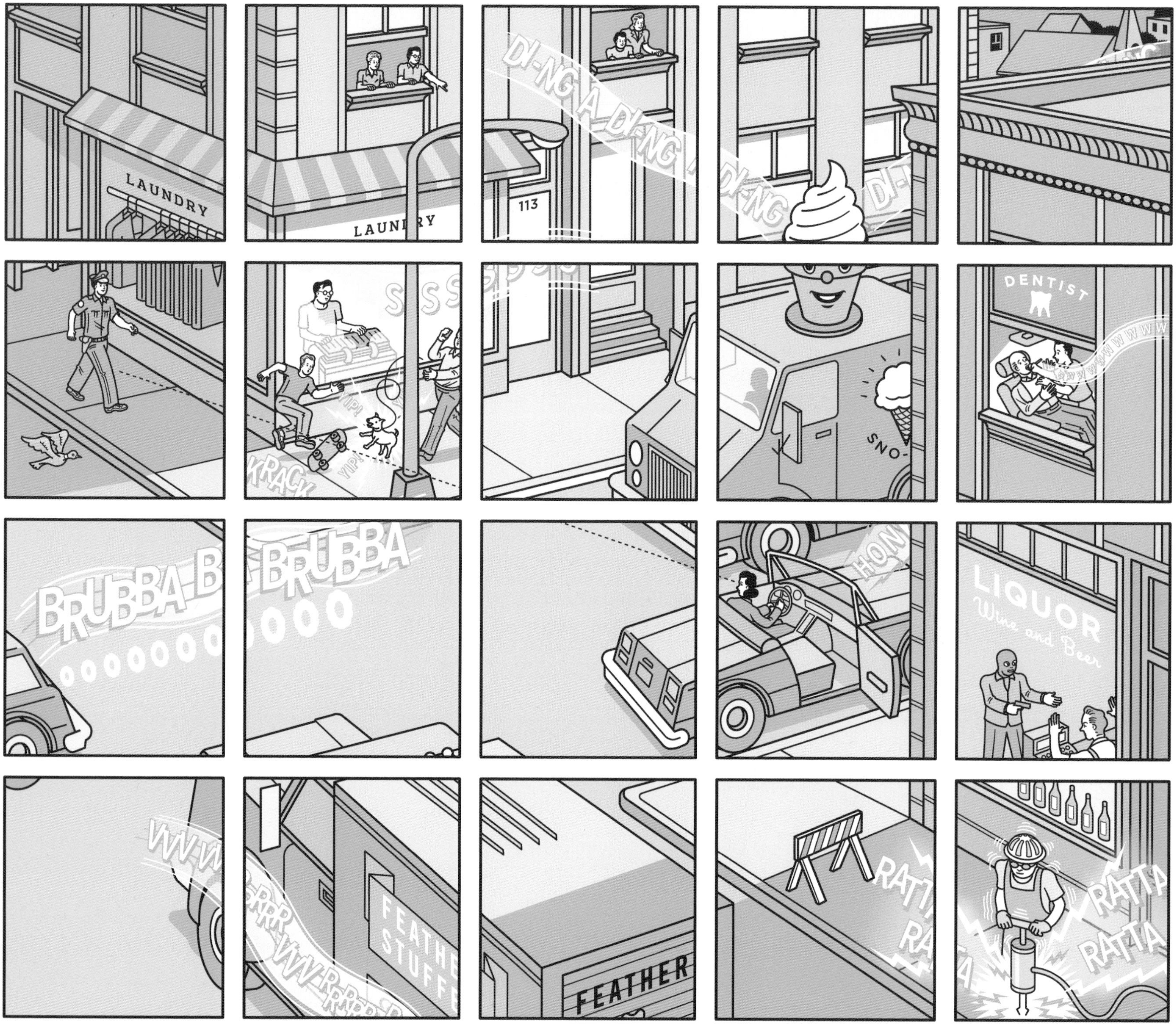
LAUNDRY
LAUN RY
113
DI-NG A DI-NG
DI-NG
DI-
SSS
YIP!
YIP!
KRACK
SNO-
DENTIST
BRUBBA-B
BRUBBA
OOOOOOOOOOOO
HON
LIQUOR
Wine and Beer
VVVV
RRR
VVV RRRR
FEATHE
STUFFE
FEATHER
RATTA
RATTA
RATTA
RATTA

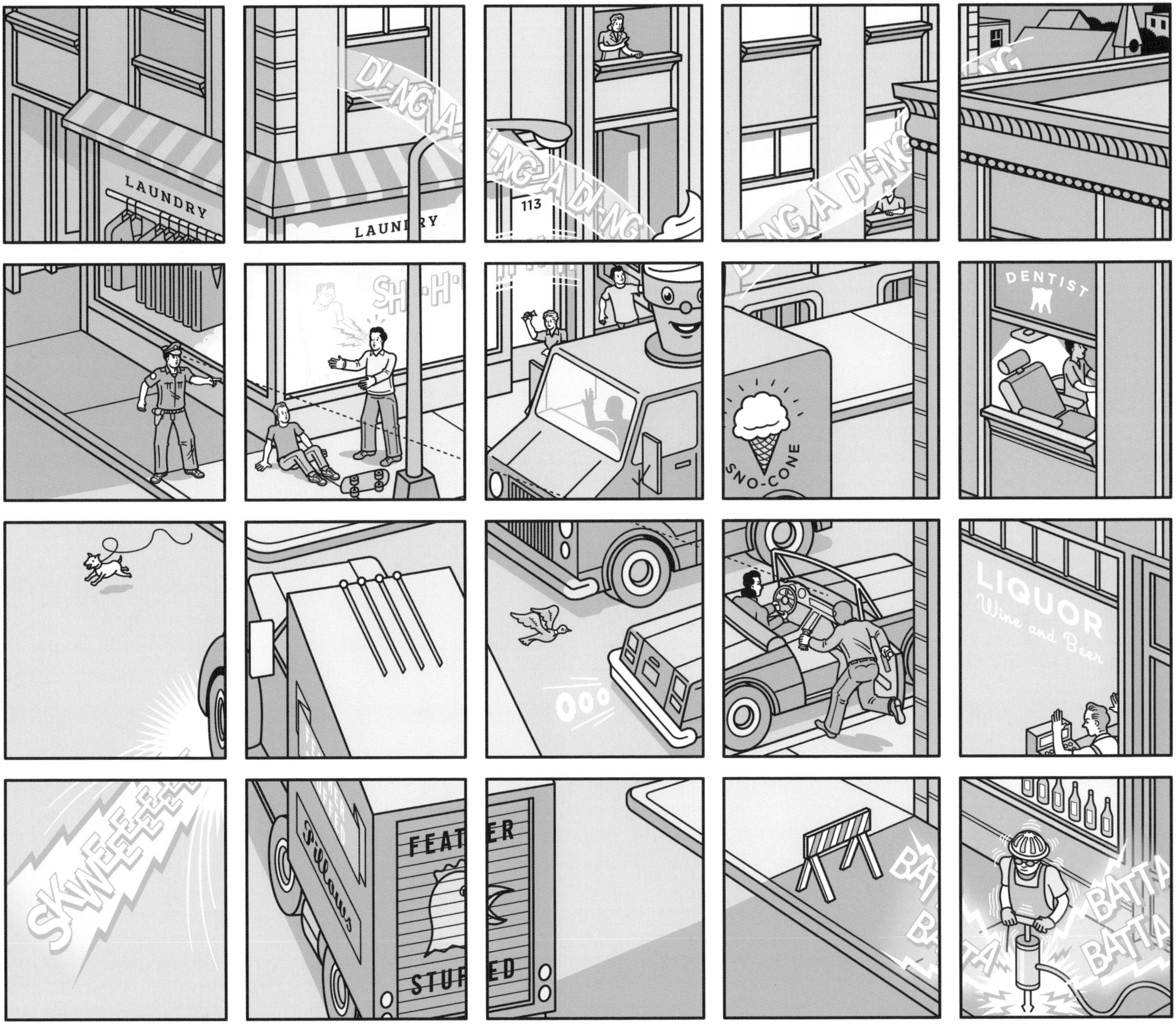
LAUNDRY
LAUNDRY
DI-NG A DI-NG A DI-NG A DI-NG A DI-NG
113
SH-H-
DENTIST
SNO-CONE
OOO
LIQUOR
Wine and Beer
SKWEEEE
Pillows
FEAT ER
STUF ED
BATTA
BATTA
BATTA
BATTA

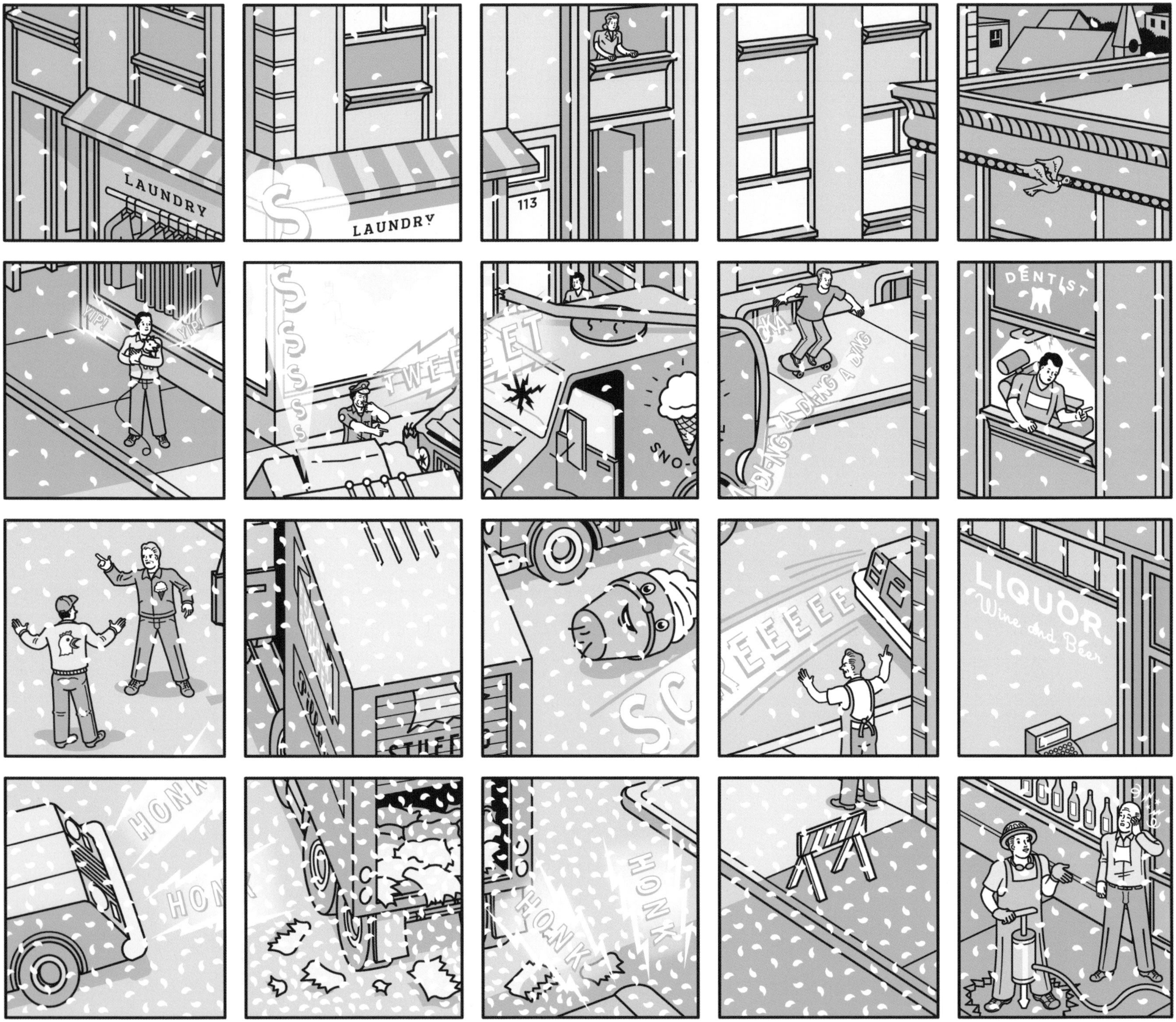
LAUNDRY
LAUNDRY
113
YIP!
YIP!
TWEEEET
DENTIST
SCREEEEEE
LIQUOR
Wine and Beer
HONK
HONK
HONK
HONK

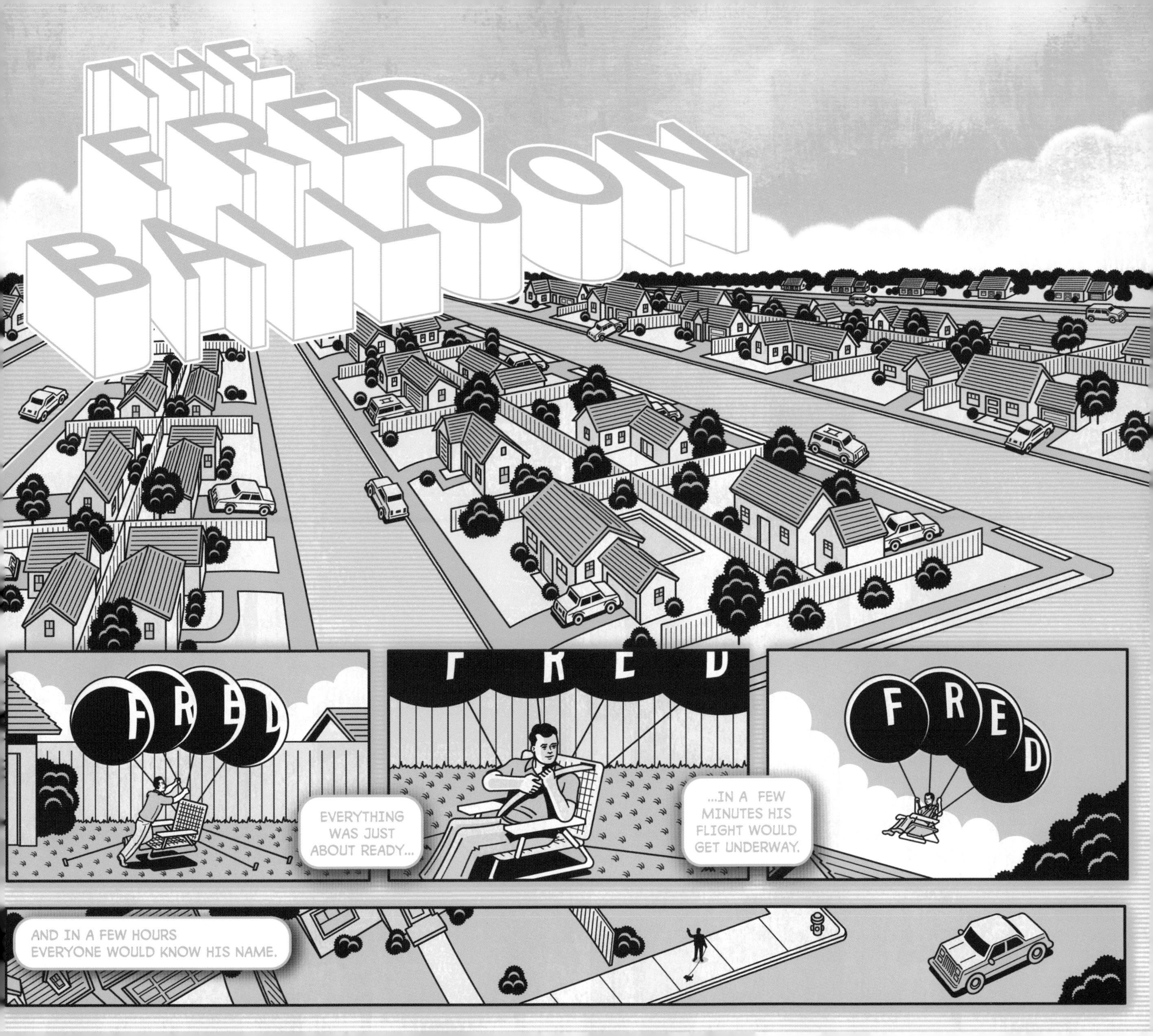
THE FRED BALLOON
FRED
FRED
FRED
FRED
EVERYTHING WAS JUST ABOUT READY...
...IN A FEW MINUTES HIS FLIGHT WOULD GET UNDERWAY.
AND IN A FEW HOURS EVERYONE WOULD KNOW HIS NAME.

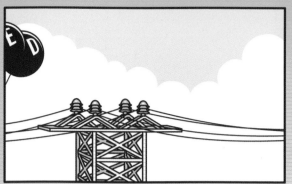

UNFORTUNATELY, THE WIND SHIFTED AND THERE WAS A CHANGE IN COURSE...

...STEADILY, THE CURRENT OF AIR PULLED THEM ON.

ZAP

ONLY ONE SURVIVED THE EXPLOSION, NEWLY CHARGED. TRANSFORMED.

GLOWING.

WHEEEEEEEEE

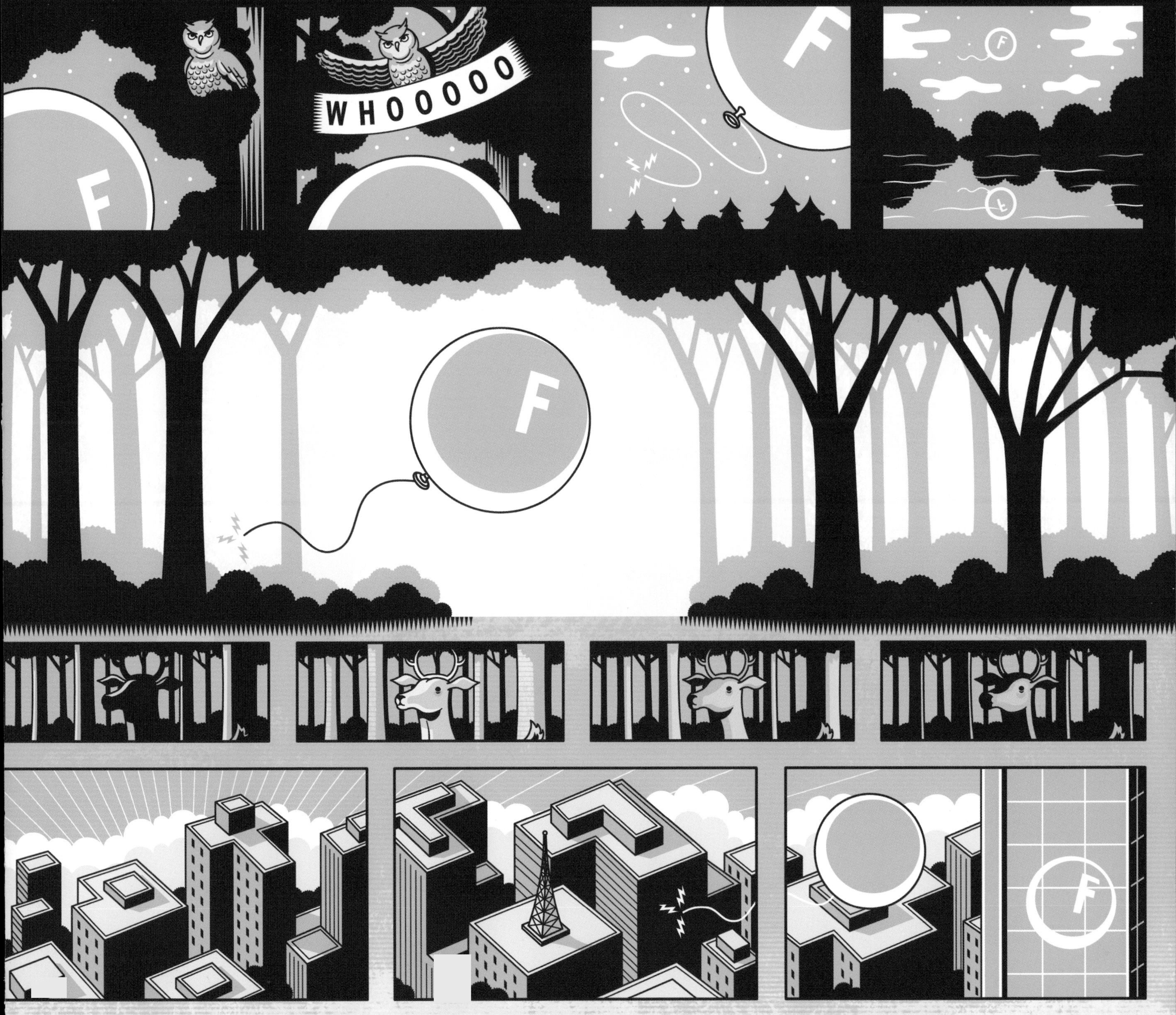
WHOOOOO

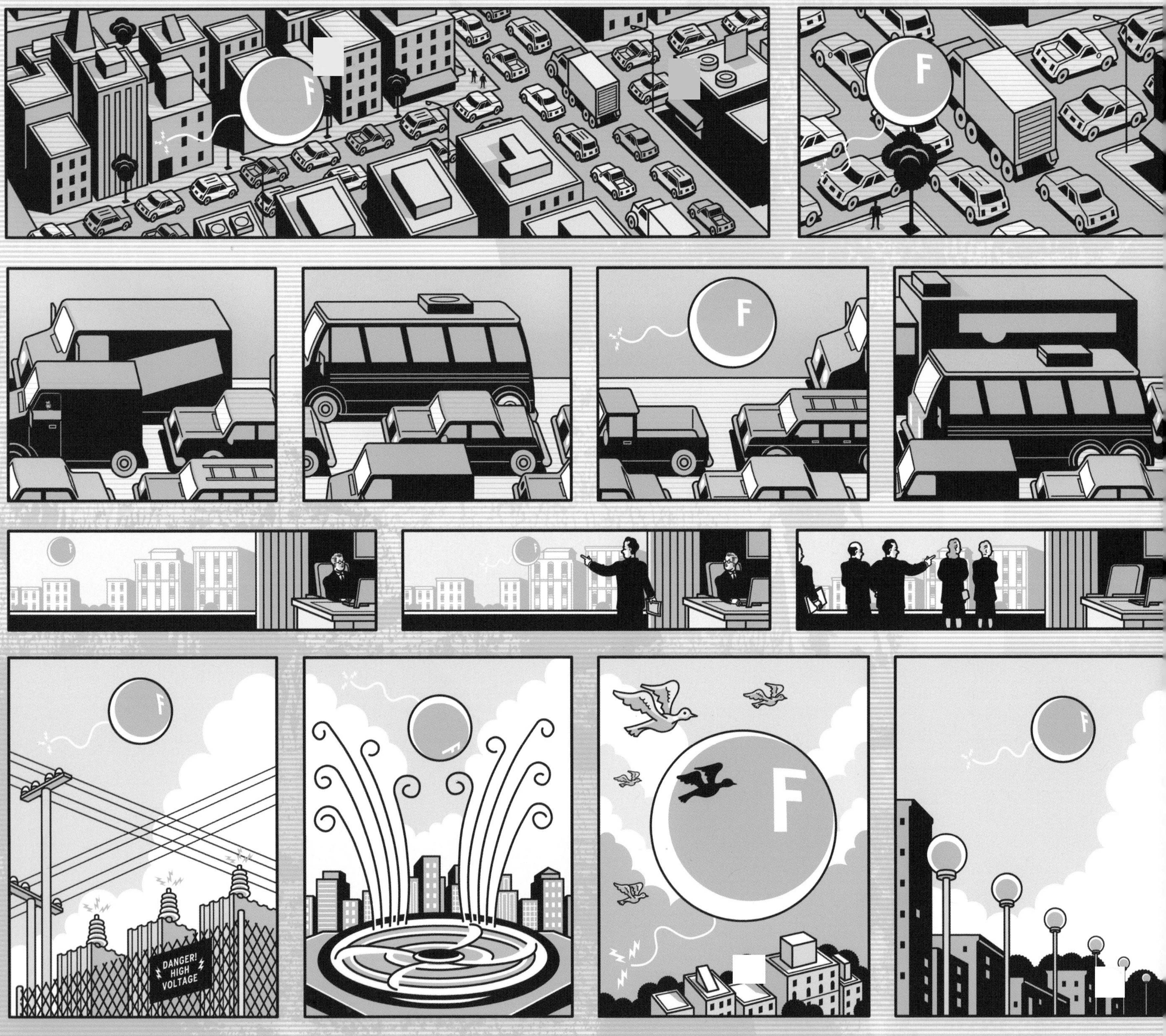
DANGER!
HIGH
VOLTAGE

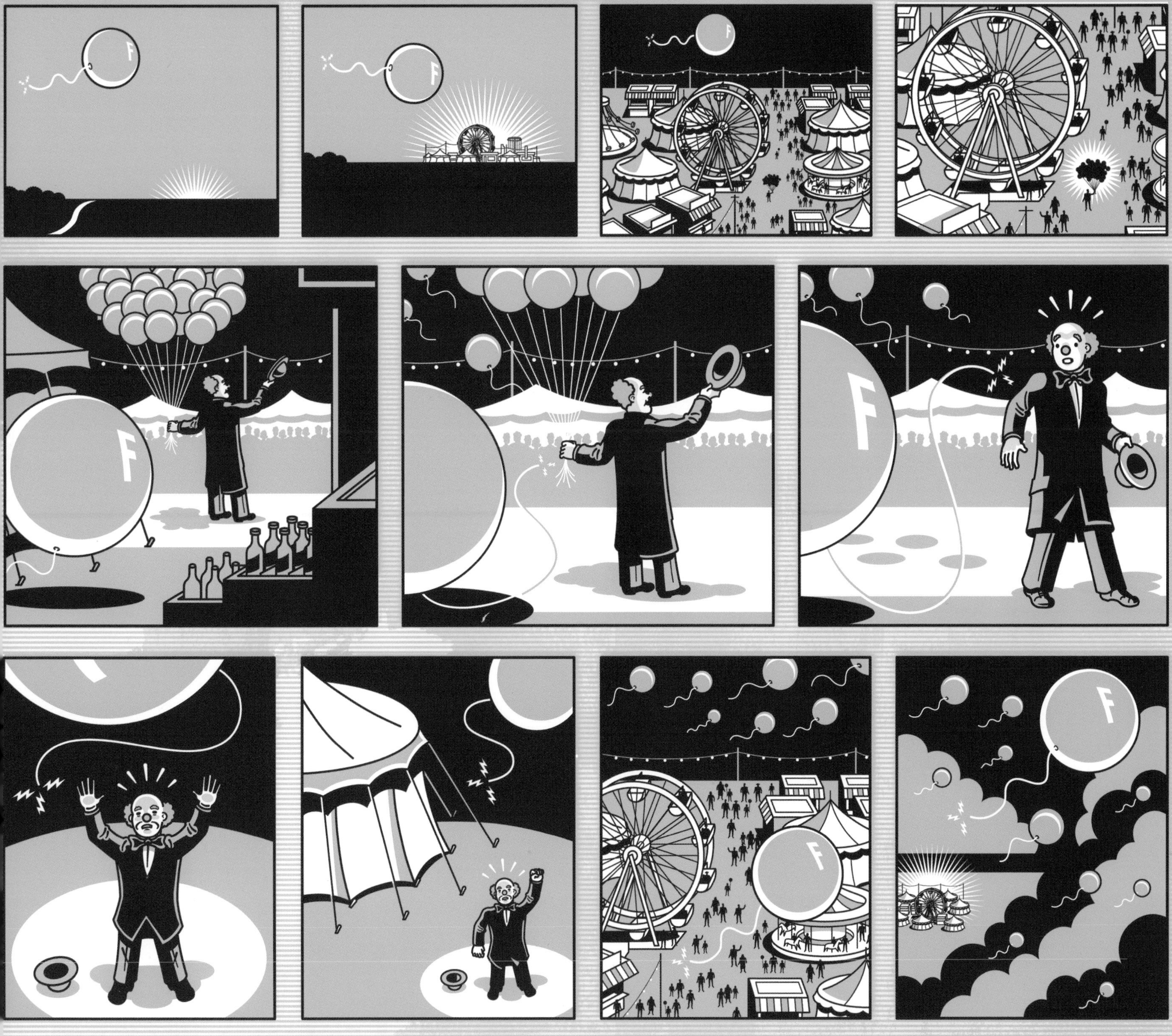

SHOPPING CENTER
GRAND OPENING!
MUNICIPAL ZOO
ENTRANCE
AS THEIR NUMBERS GREW, THEY SPREAD ACROSS THE SKY.
AUTO WORLD
ALL MAKES AND MODELS ON SALE!
SALE!
SALE!
CLOUDS OF SUSPENDED COLOR DROPLETS, SHIFTING AND RECOMBINING IN THE WIND.
UNTIL THE DAY THEY BEGAN FORMING THE FIRST STRANDS.

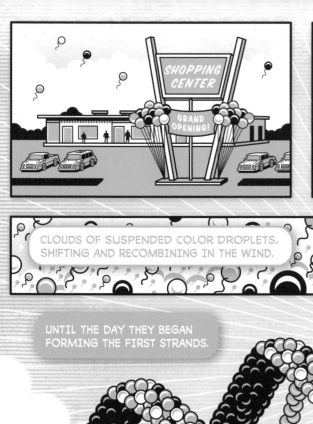

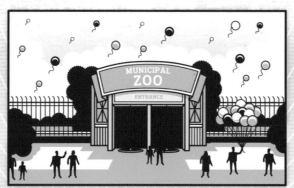

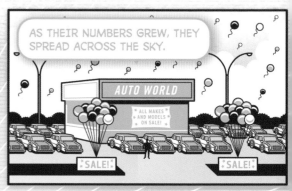

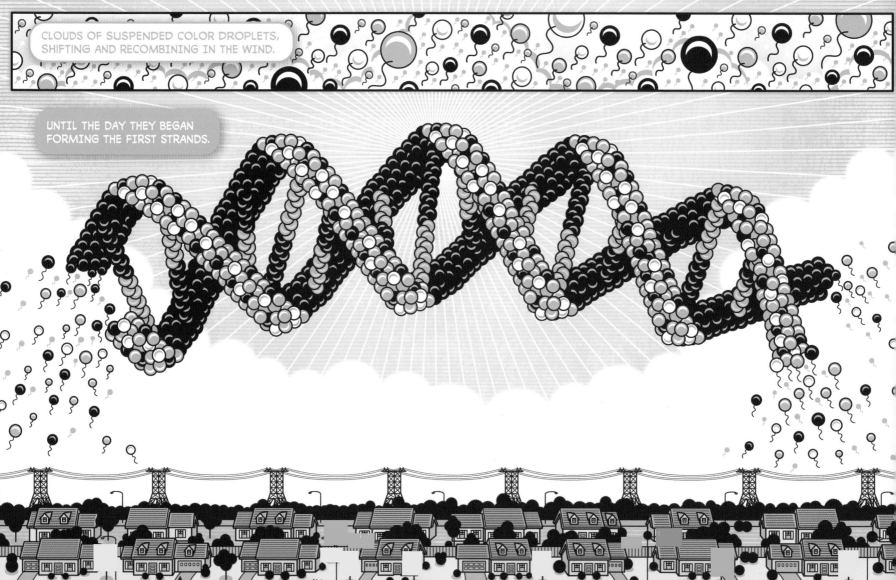

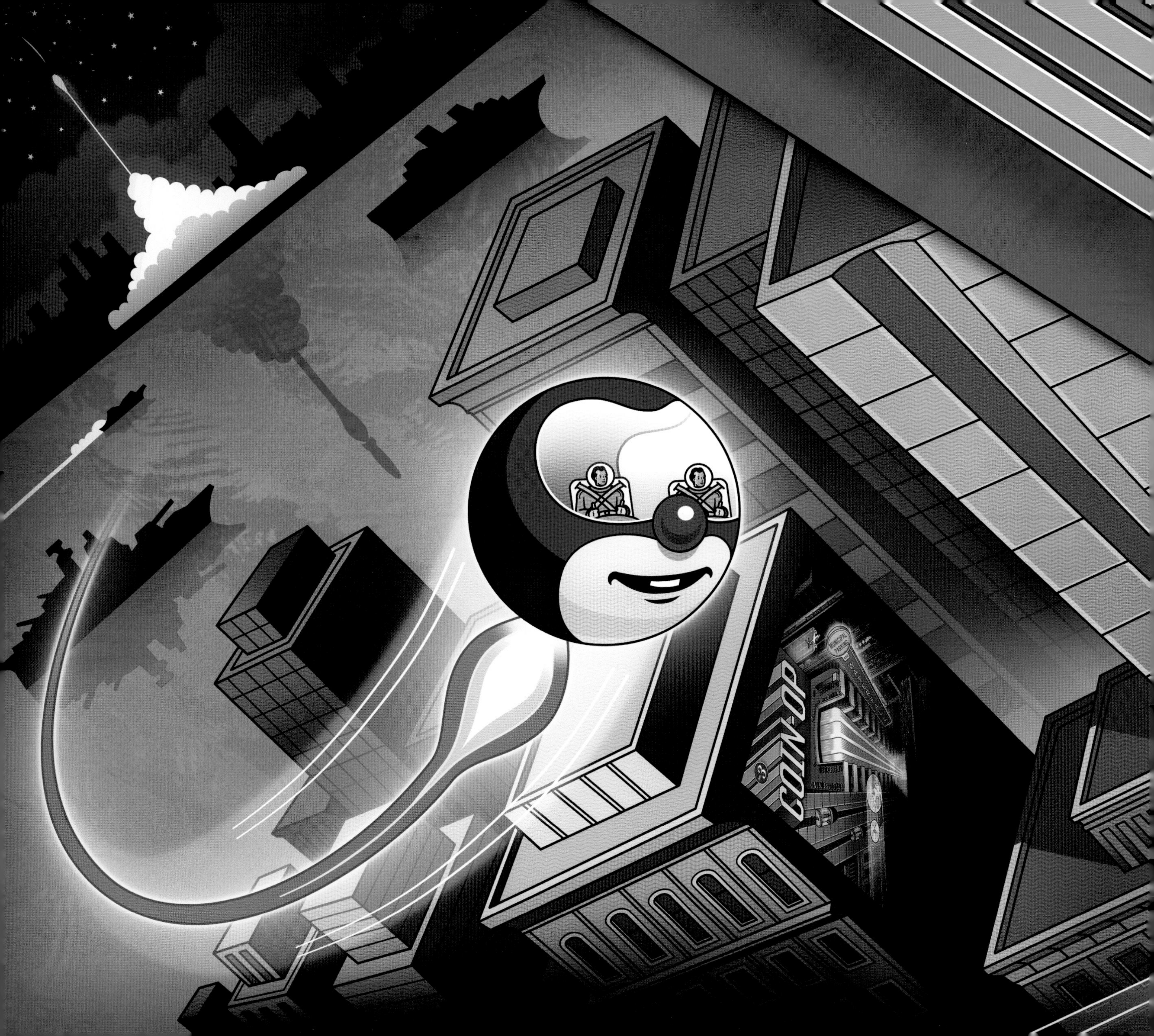
COIN-OP
MUNICIPAL PARKING
AND
WATERFALL

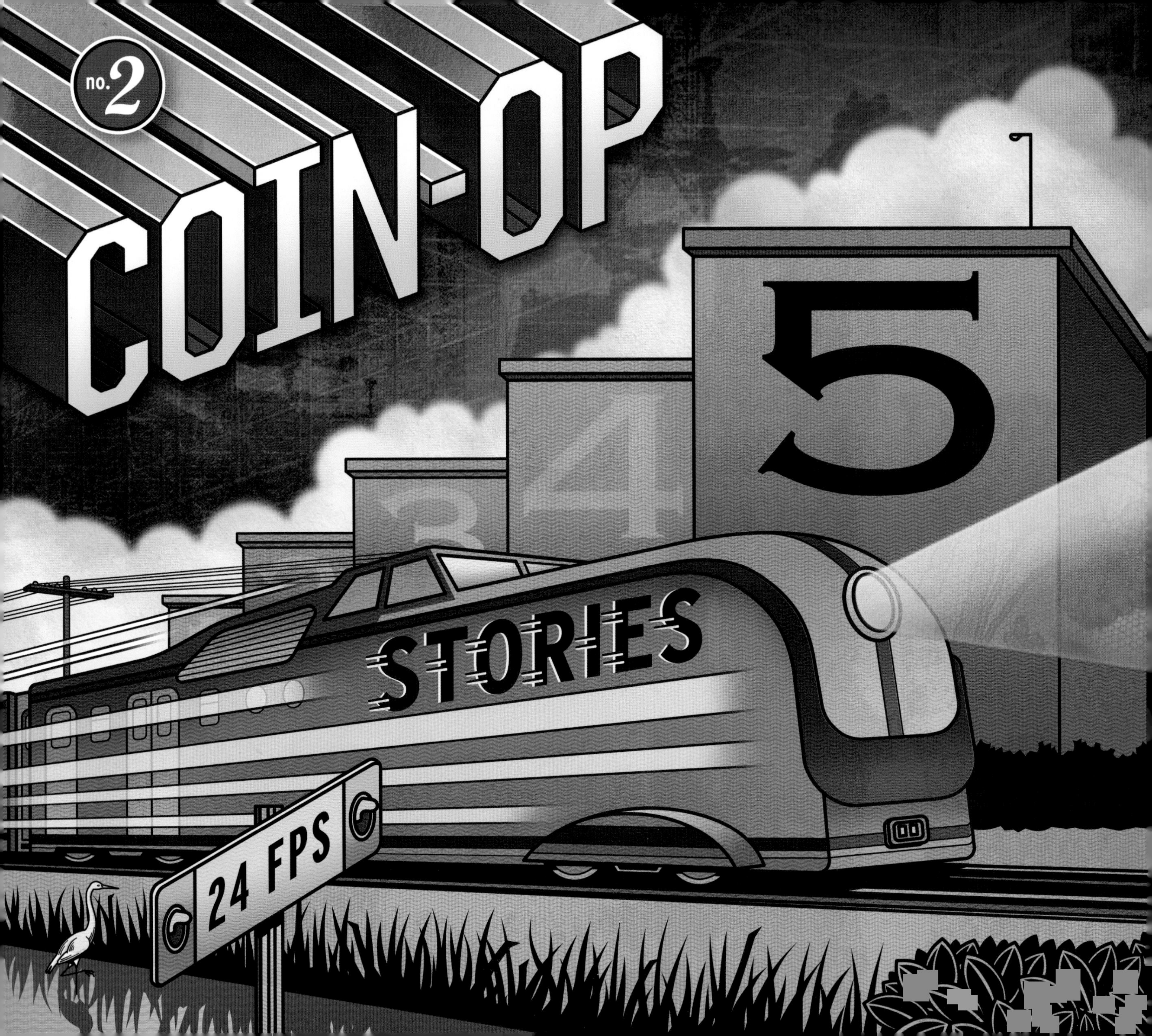
no.2
COIN-OP
5
STORIES
24 FPS

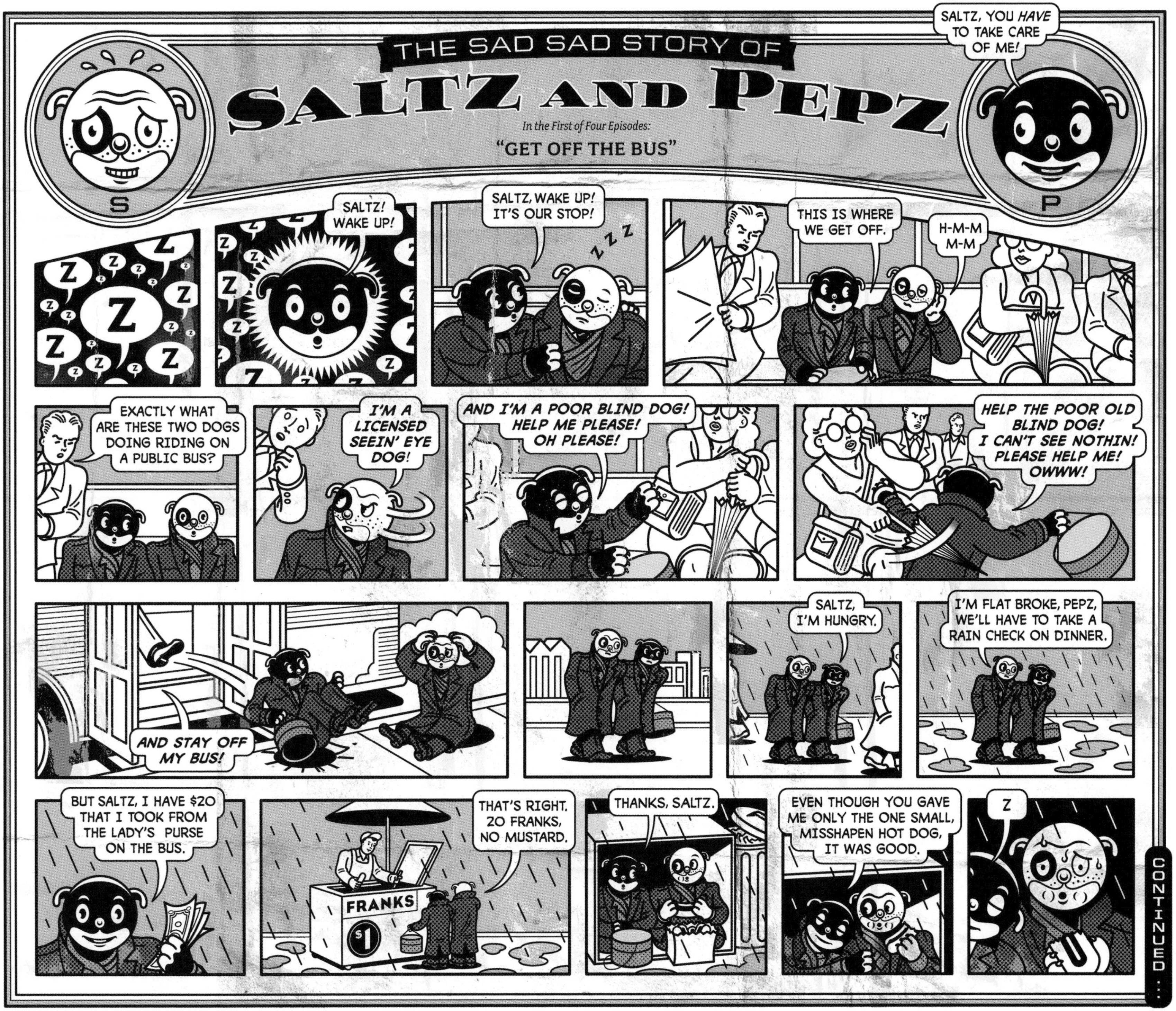
THE SAD SAD STORY OF
SALTZ AND PEPZ
In the First of Four Episodes:
"GET OFF THE BUS"
SALTZ, YOU HAVE TO TAKE CARE OF ME!
S
P
Z
SALTZ! WAKE UP!
SALTZ, WAKE UP! IT'S OUR STOP!
Z Z Z
THIS IS WHERE WE GET OFF.
H-M-M M-M
EXACTLY WHAT ARE THESE TWO DOGS DOING RIDING ON A PUBLIC BUS?
I'M A LICENSED SEEIN' EYE DOG!
AND I'M A POOR BLIND DOG! HELP ME PLEASE! OH PLEASE!
HELP THE POOR OLD BLIND DOG! I CAN'T SEE NOTHIN! PLEASE HELP ME! OWWW!
AND STAY OFF MY BUS!
SALTZ, I'M HUNGRY.
I'M FLAT BROKE, PEPZ, WE'LL HAVE TO TAKE A RAIN CHECK ON DINNER.
BUT SALTZ, I HAVE $20 THAT I TOOK FROM THE LADY'S PURSE ON THE BUS.
FRANKS
$1
THAT'S RIGHT. 20 FRANKS, NO MUSTARD.
THANKS, SALTZ.
EVEN THOUGH YOU GAVE ME ONLY THE ONE SMALL, MISSHAPEN HOT DOG, IT WAS GOOD.
Z
CONTINUED...

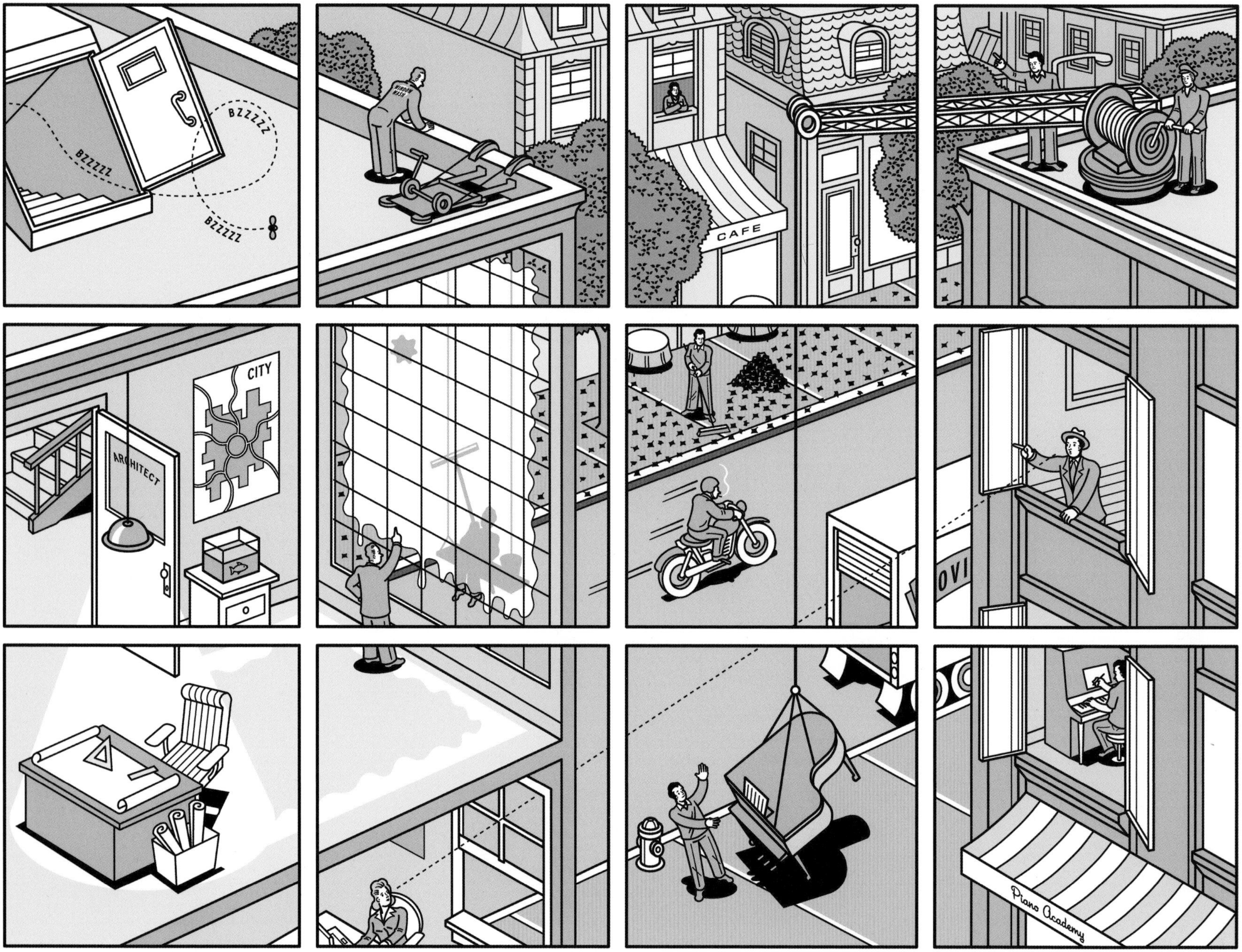
BZZZZZ
BZZZZZ
BZZZZZ
WINDOW WASH
CAFE
CITY
ARCHITECT
OVI
Piano Academy

anatomy of a pratfall

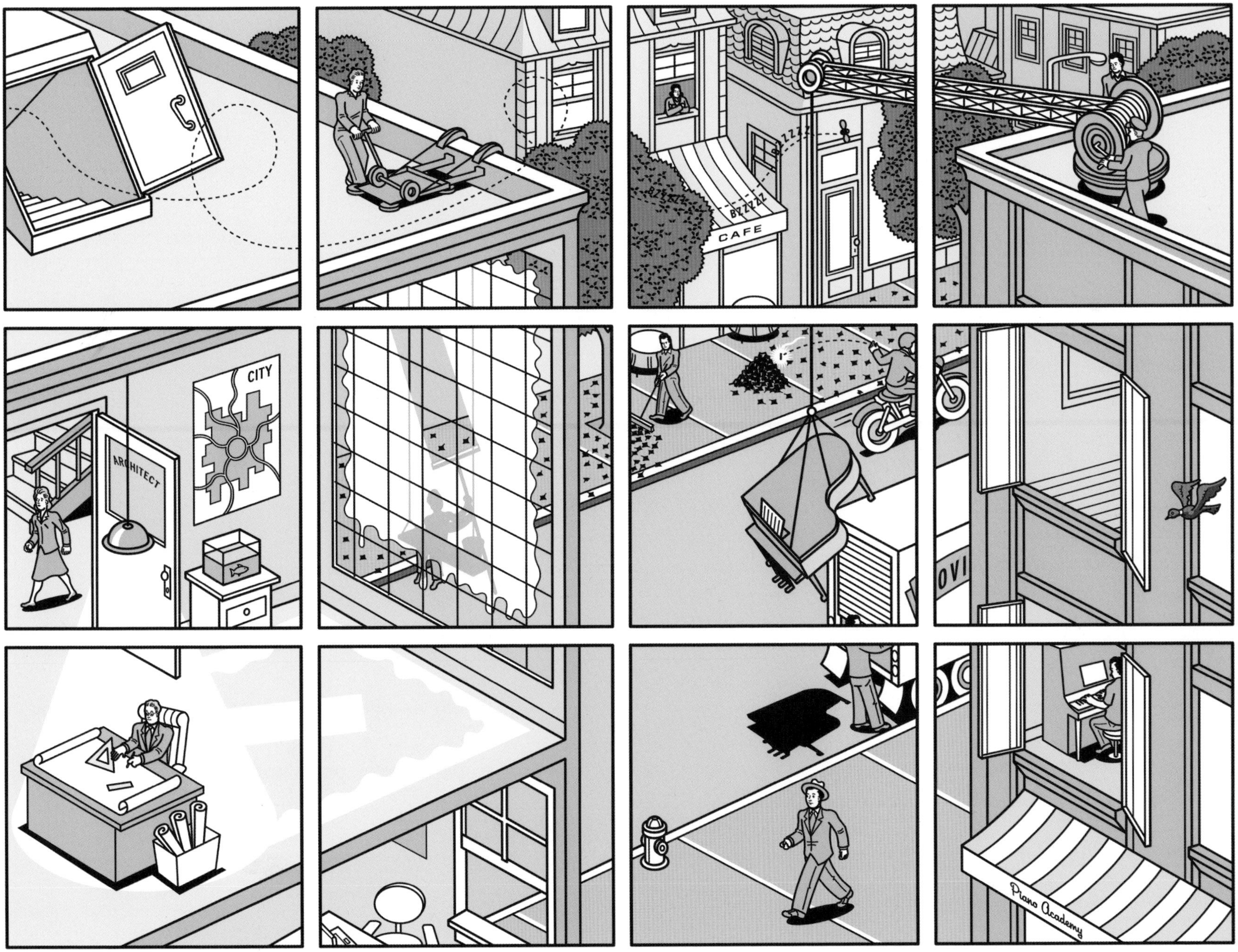
CAFE
ARCHITECT
CITY
Piano Academy

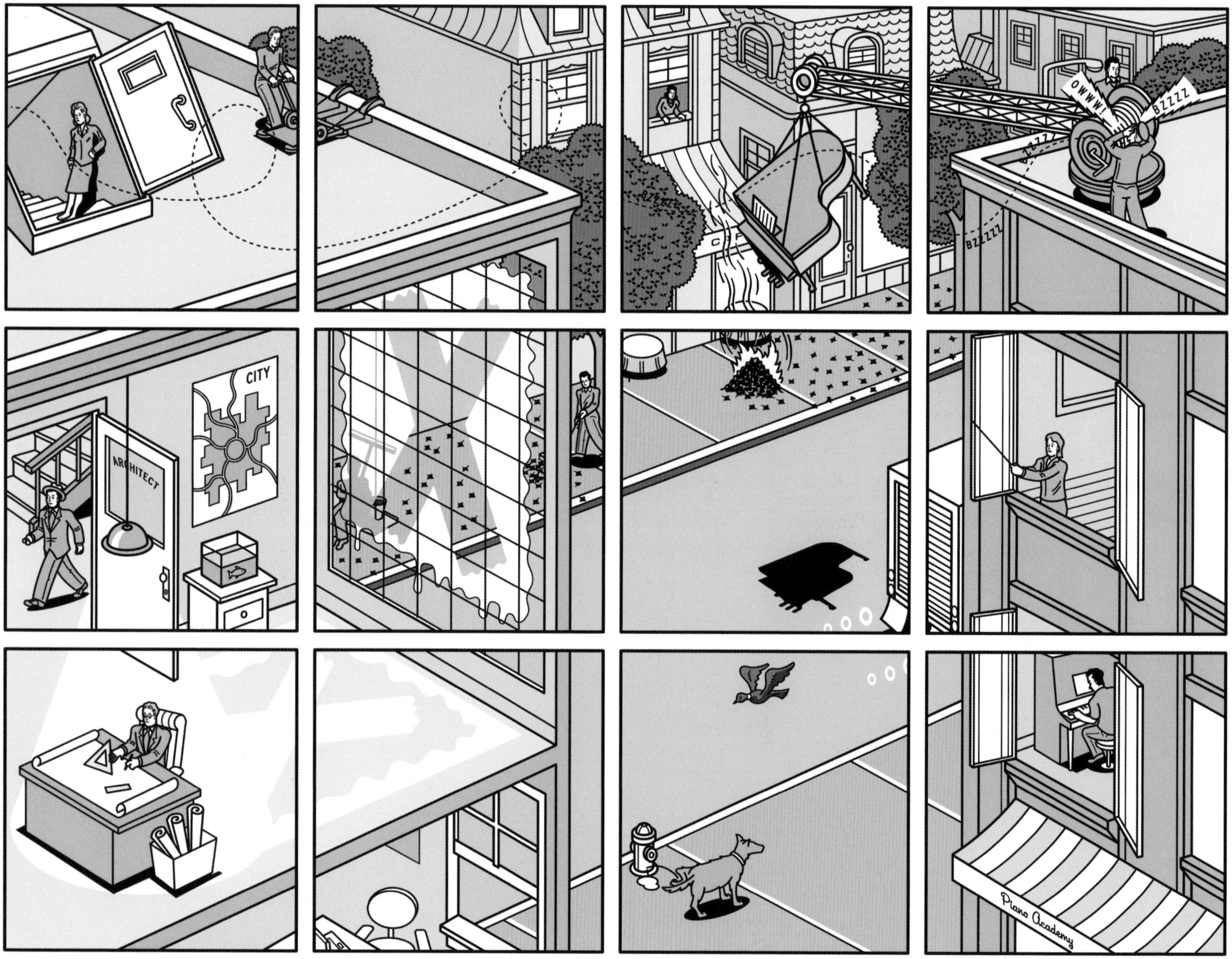
OWWW!
BZZZZ
CITY
ARCHITECT
Piano Academy

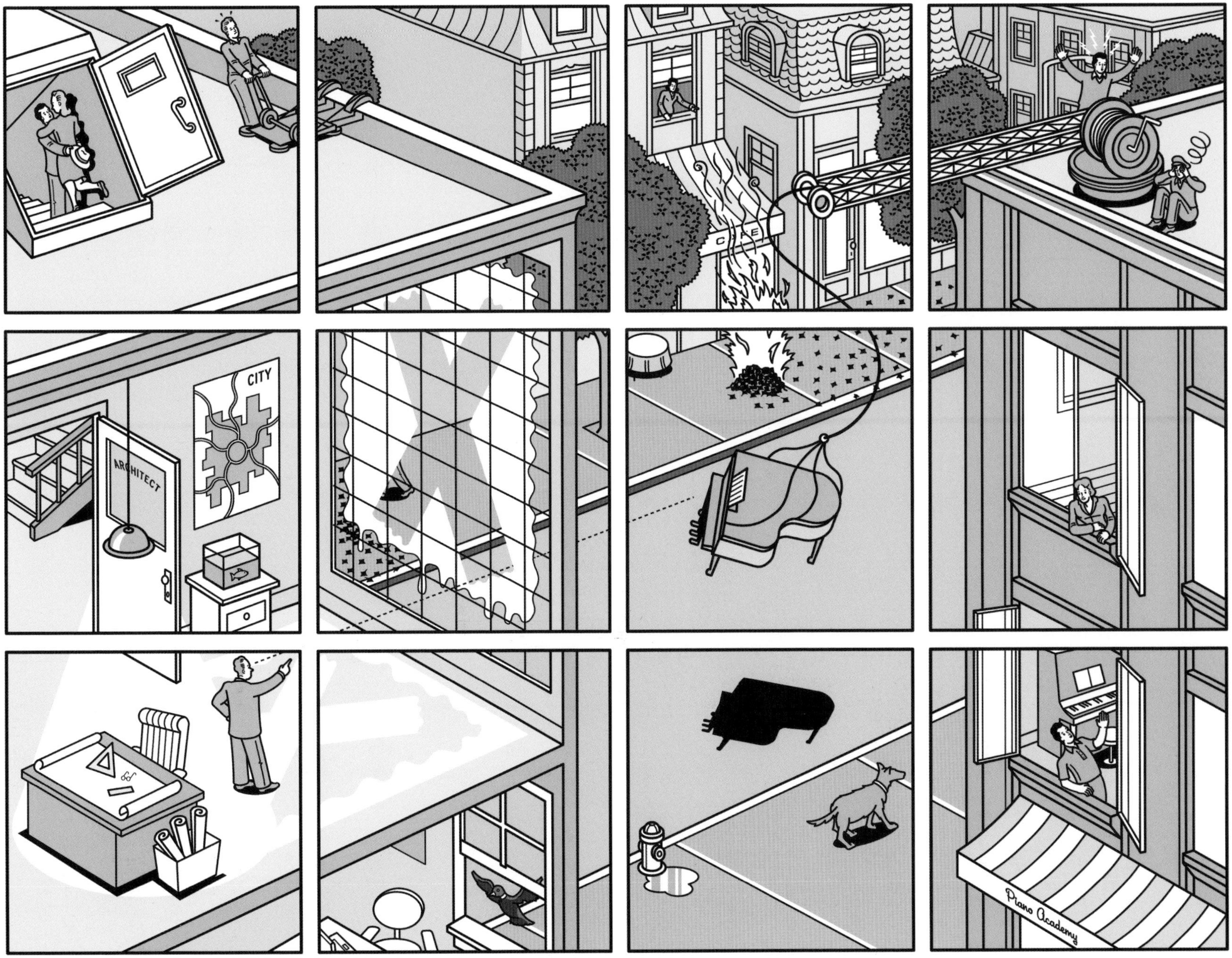
CITY
ARCHITECT
Piano Academy

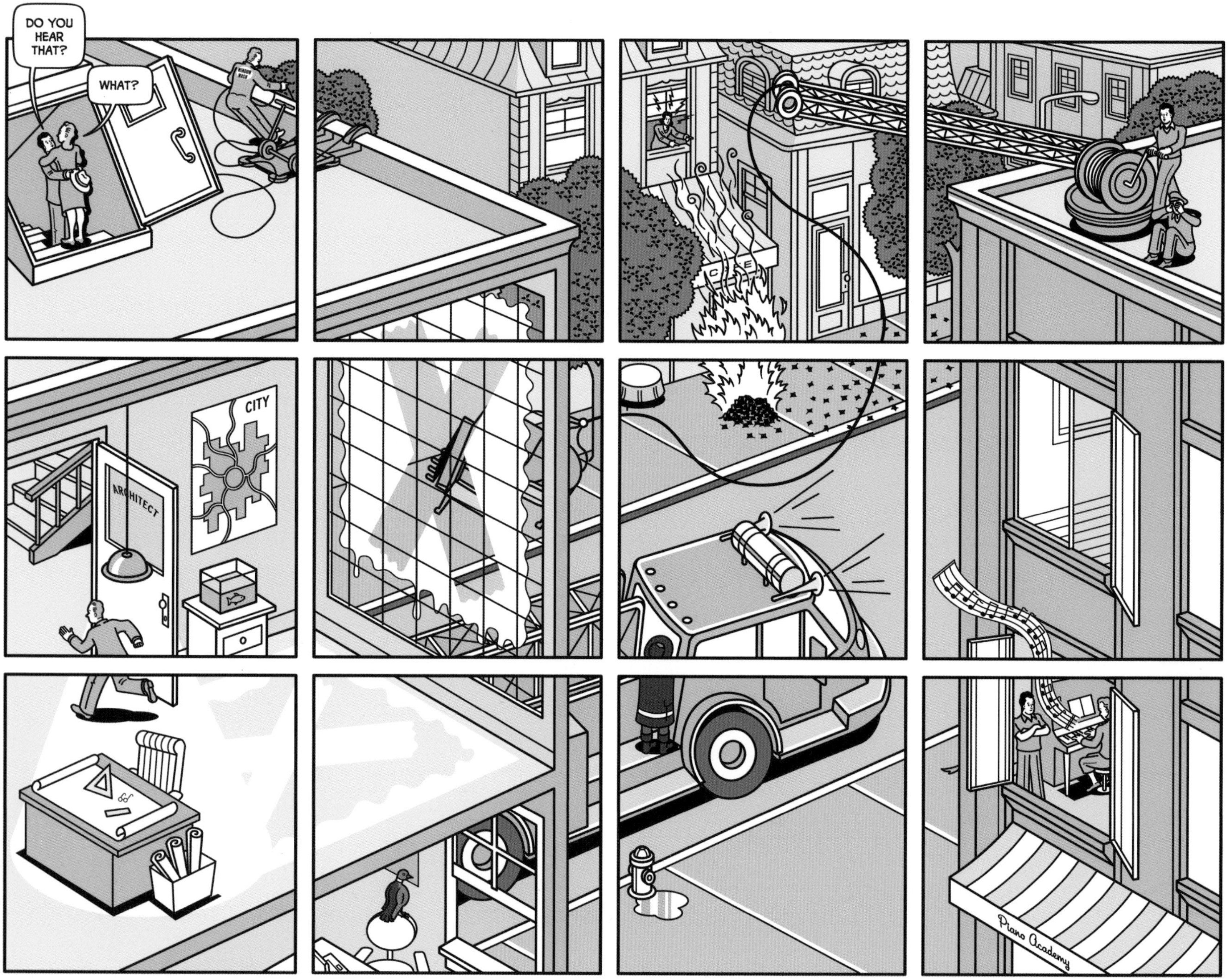
DO YOU HEAR THAT?
WHAT?
CITY
ARCHITECT
Piano Academy

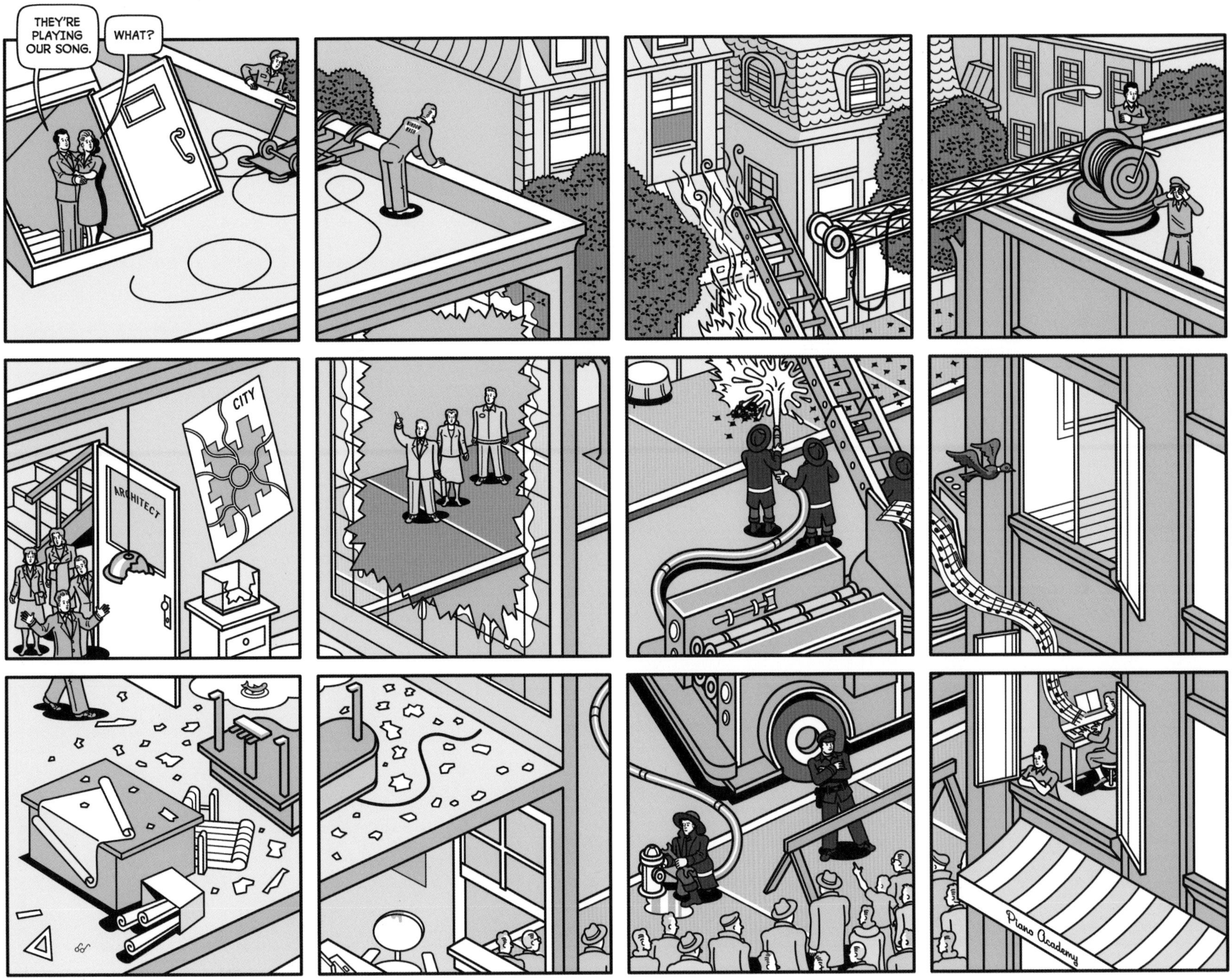
THEY'RE PLAYING OUR SONG.
WHAT?
ARCHITECT
CITY
Piano Academy

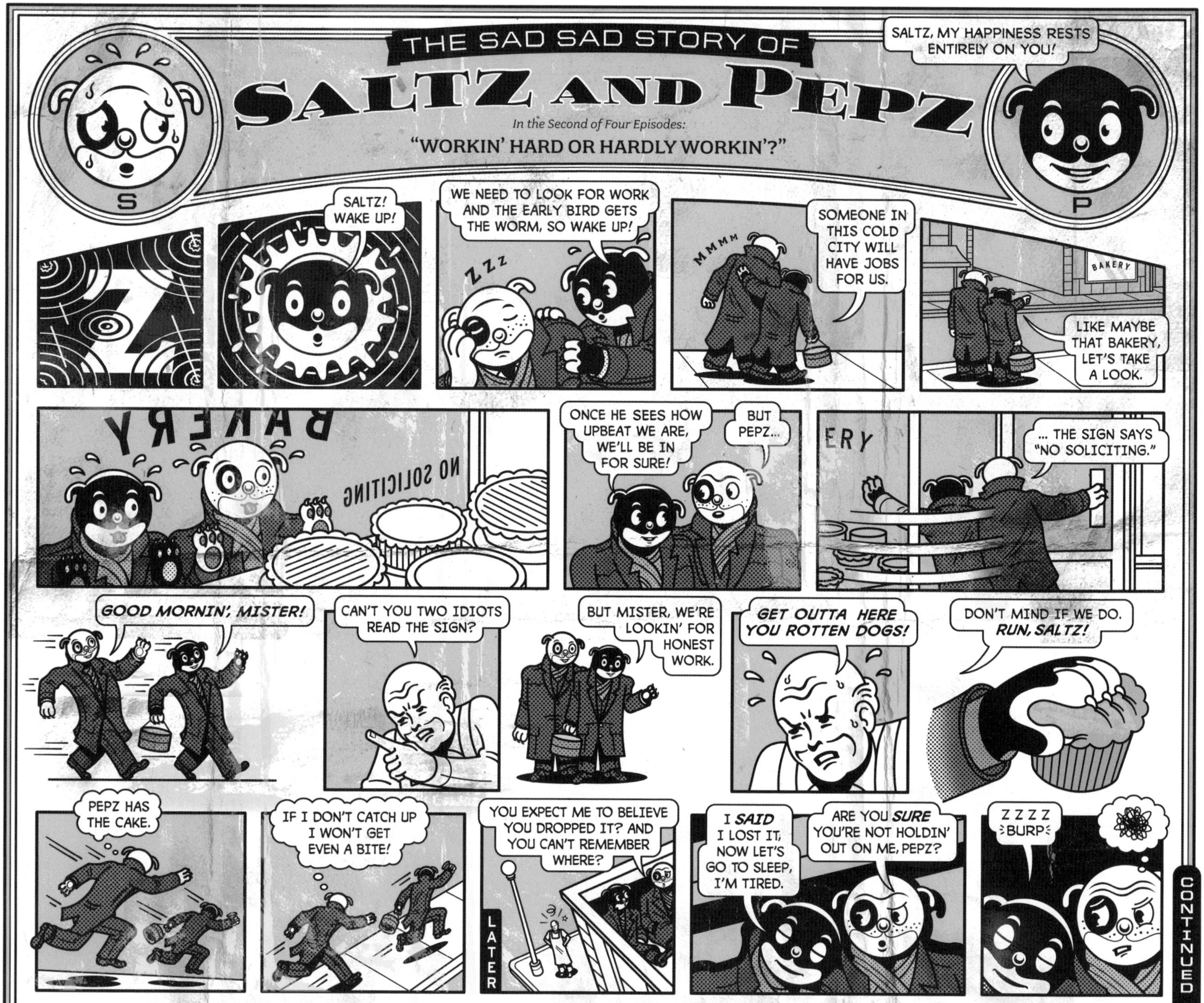
THE SAD SAD STORY OF
SALTZ AND PEPZ
In the Second of Four Episodes:
"WORKIN' HARD OR HARDLY WORKIN'?"
SALTZ, MY HAPPINESS RESTS ENTIRELY ON YOU!
S
P
SALTZ! WAKE UP!
WE NEED TO LOOK FOR WORK AND THE EARLY BIRD GETS THE WORM, SO WAKE UP!
Z Z Z
MMMM
SOMEONE IN THIS COLD CITY WILL HAVE JOBS FOR US.
BAKERY
LIKE MAYBE THAT BAKERY, LET'S TAKE A LOOK.
NO SOLICITING
ONCE HE SEES HOW UPBEAT WE ARE, WE'LL BE IN FOR SURE!
BUT PEPZ...
... THE SIGN SAYS "NO SOLICITING."
GOOD MORNIN', MISTER!
CAN'T YOU TWO IDIOTS READ THE SIGN?
BUT MISTER, WE'RE LOOKIN' FOR HONEST WORK.
GET OUTTA HERE YOU ROTTEN DOGS!
DON'T MIND IF WE DO. RUN, SALTZ!
PEPZ HAS THE CAKE.
IF I DON'T CATCH UP I WON'T GET EVEN A BITE!
LATER
YOU EXPECT ME TO BELIEVE YOU DROPPED IT? AND YOU CAN'T REMEMBER WHERE?
I SAID I LOST IT, NOW LET'S GO TO SLEEP, I'M TIRED.
ARE YOU SURE YOU'RE NOT HOLDIN' OUT ON ME, PEPZ?
Z Z Z Z
BURP
CONTINUED...

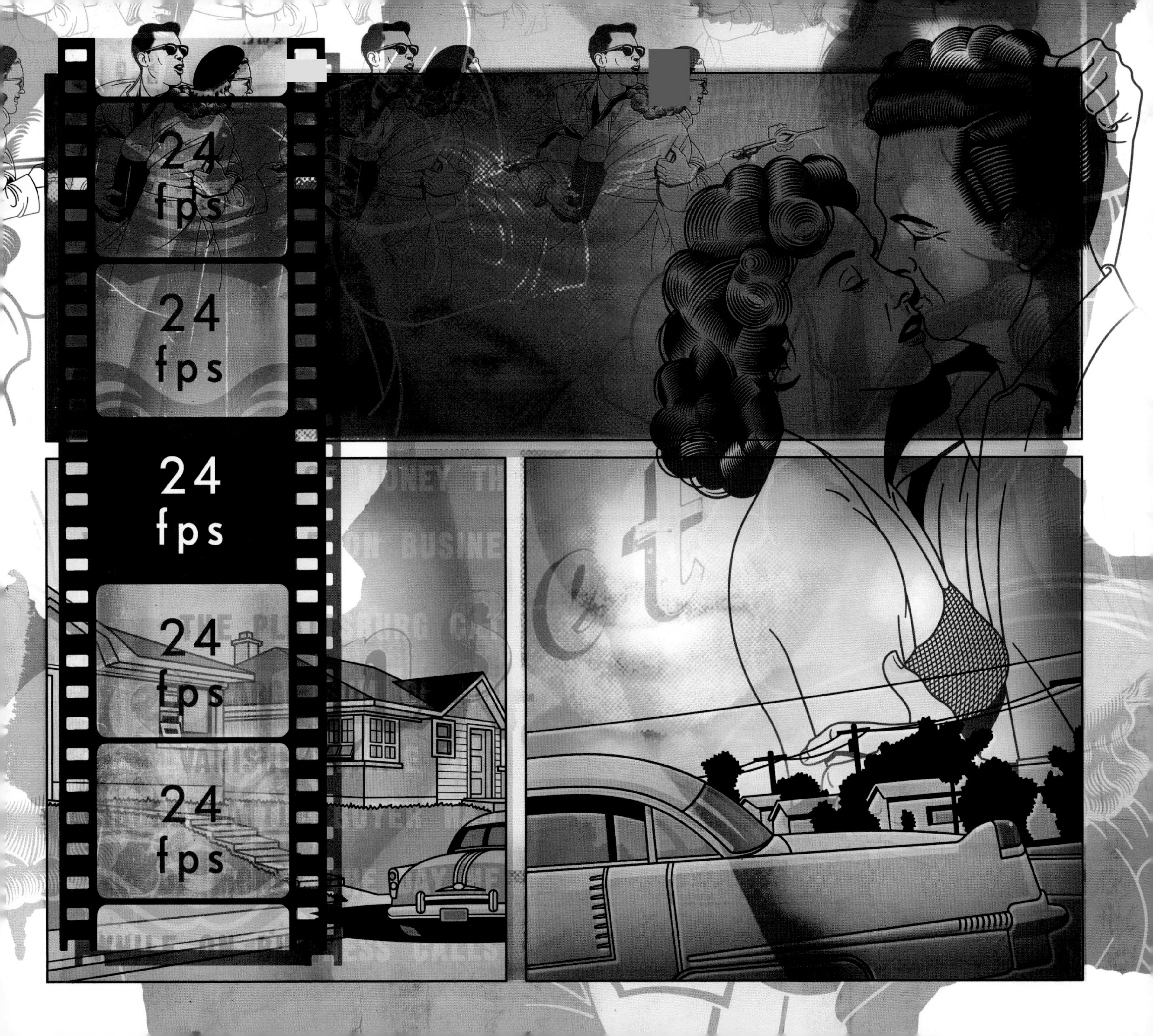
24 fps
24 fps
24 fps
24 fps
24 fps

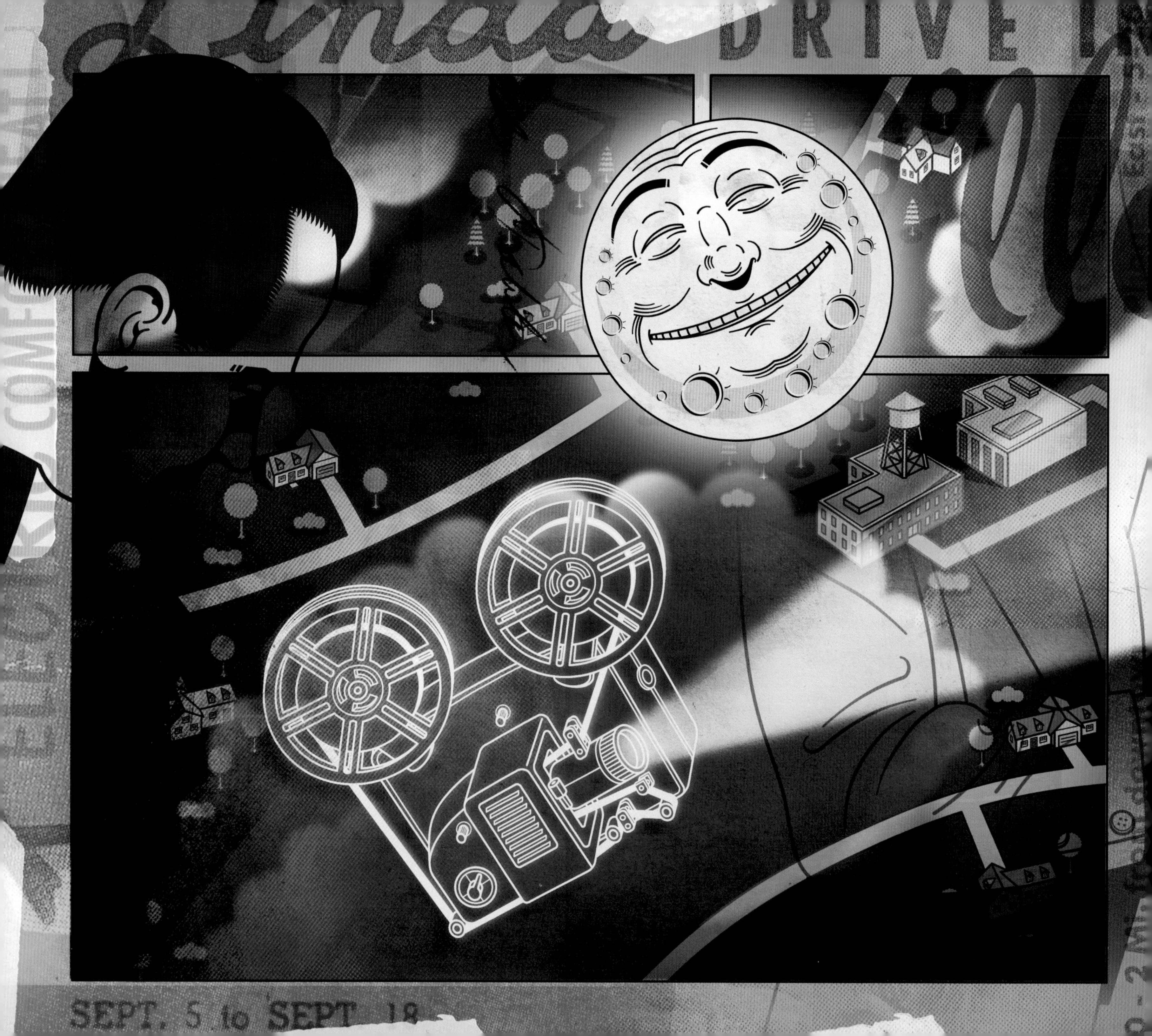
DRIVE I
SEPT. 5 to SEPT 18

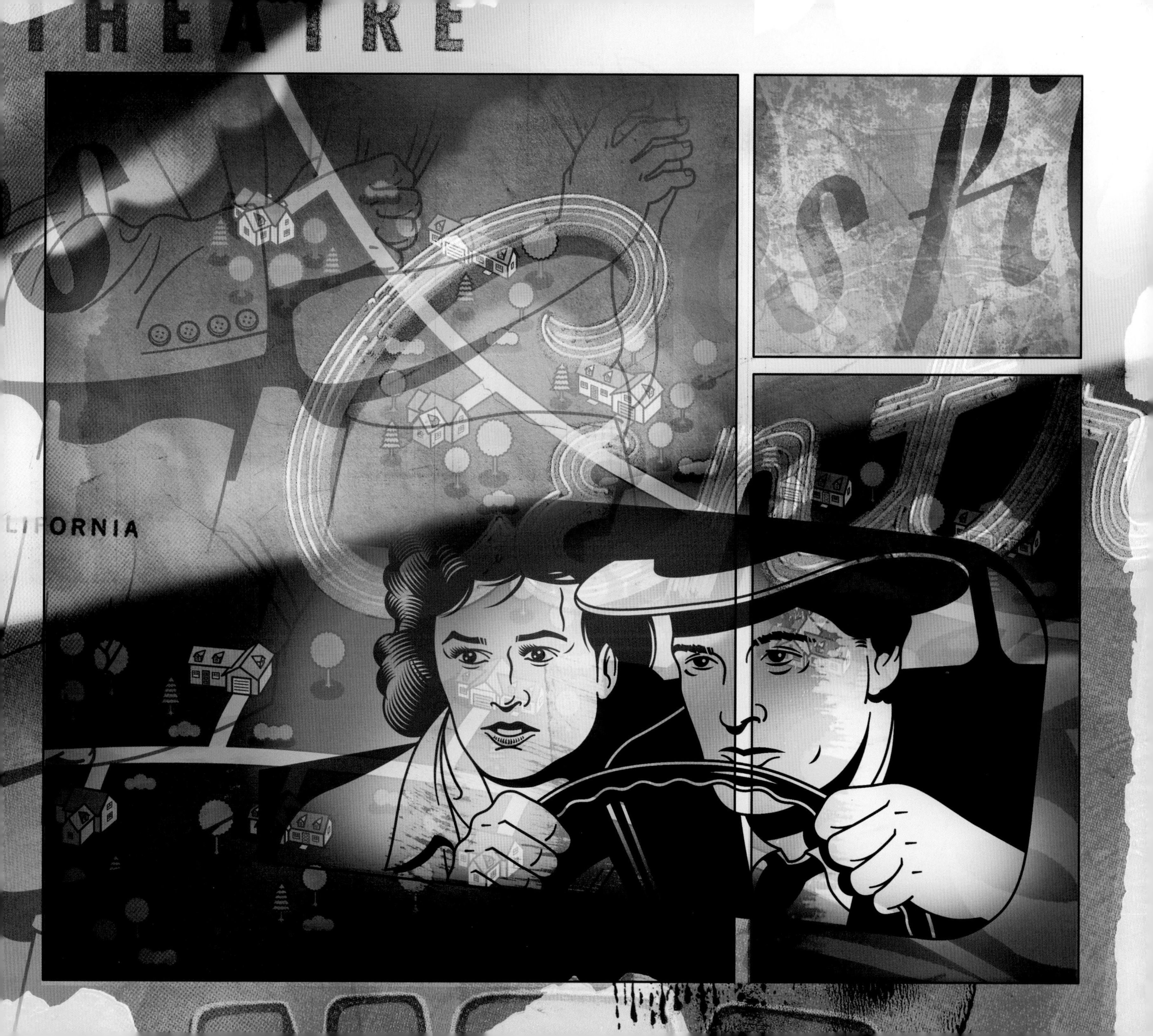
THEATRE
LIFORNIA

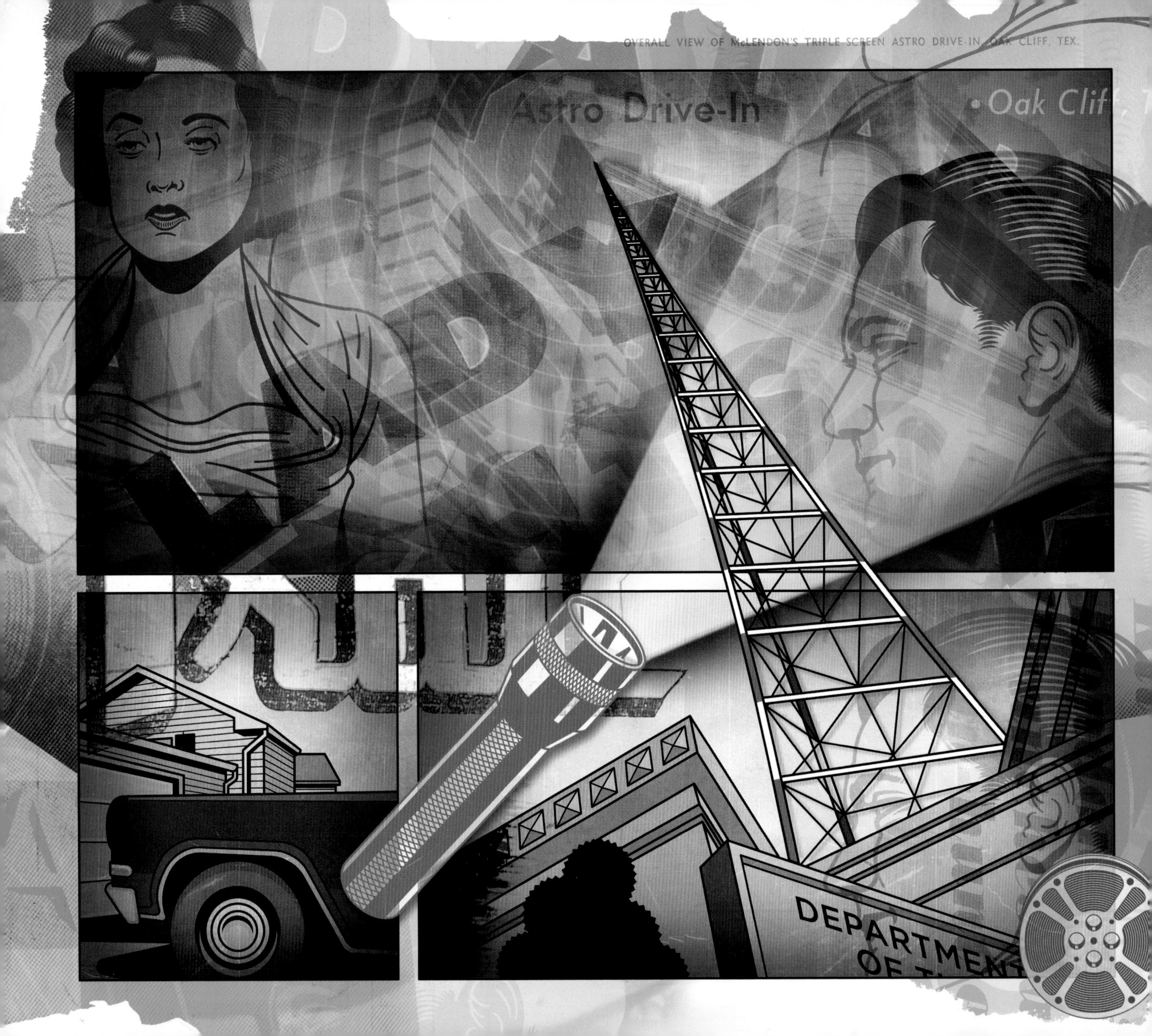

OVERALL VIEW OF McLENDON'S TRIPLE SCREEN ASTRO DRIVE-IN, OAK CLIFF, TEX.
Astro Drive-In
DEPARTMENT

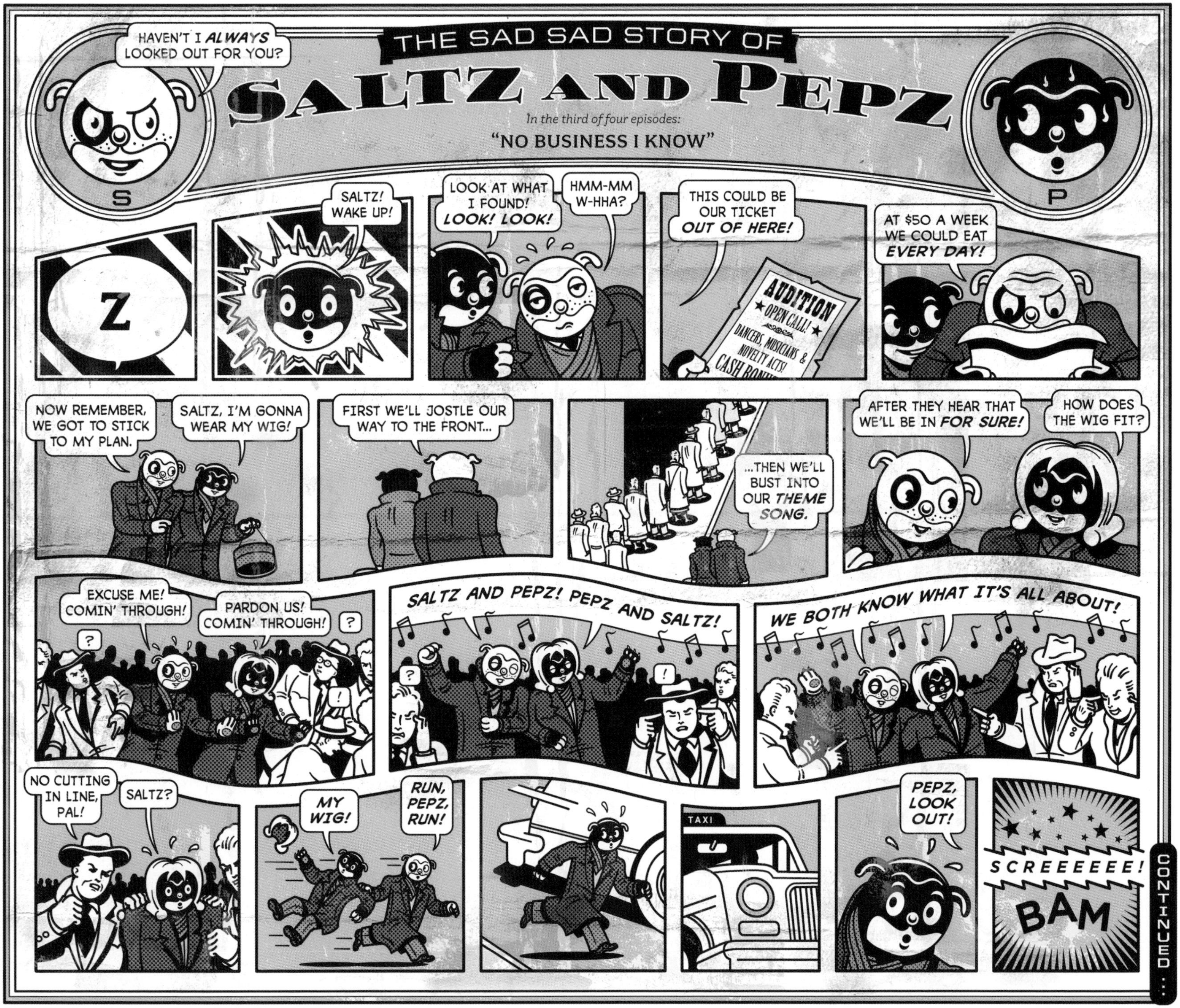
THE SAD SAD STORY OF
SALTZ AND PEPZ
In the third of four episodes:
"NO BUSINESS I KNOW"
HAVEN'T I ALWAYS LOOKED OUT FOR YOU?
S
P
Z
SALTZ! WAKE UP!
LOOK AT WHAT I FOUND! LOOK! LOOK!
HMM-MM W-HHA?
THIS COULD BE OUR TICKET OUT OF HERE!
AUDITION
OPEN CALL!
DANCERS, MUSICIANS &
NOVELTY ACTS!
AT $50 A WEEK WE COULD EAT EVERY DAY!
NOW REMEMBER, WE GOT TO STICK TO MY PLAN.
SALTZ, I'M GONNA WEAR MY WIG!
FIRST WE'LL JOSTLE OUR WAY TO THE FRONT...
...THEN WE'LL BUST INTO OUR THEME SONG.
AFTER THEY HEAR THAT WE'LL BE IN FOR SURE!
HOW DOES THE WIG FIT?
EXCUSE ME! COMIN' THROUGH!
PARDON US! COMIN' THROUGH!
?
?
!
SALTZ AND PEPZ! PEPZ AND SALTZ!
?
!
WE BOTH KNOW WHAT IT'S ALL ABOUT!
NO CUTTING IN LINE, PAL!
SALTZ?
MY WIG!
RUN, PEPZ, RUN!
TAXI
PEPZ, LOOK OUT!
SCREEEEEEE!
BAM
CONTINUED...

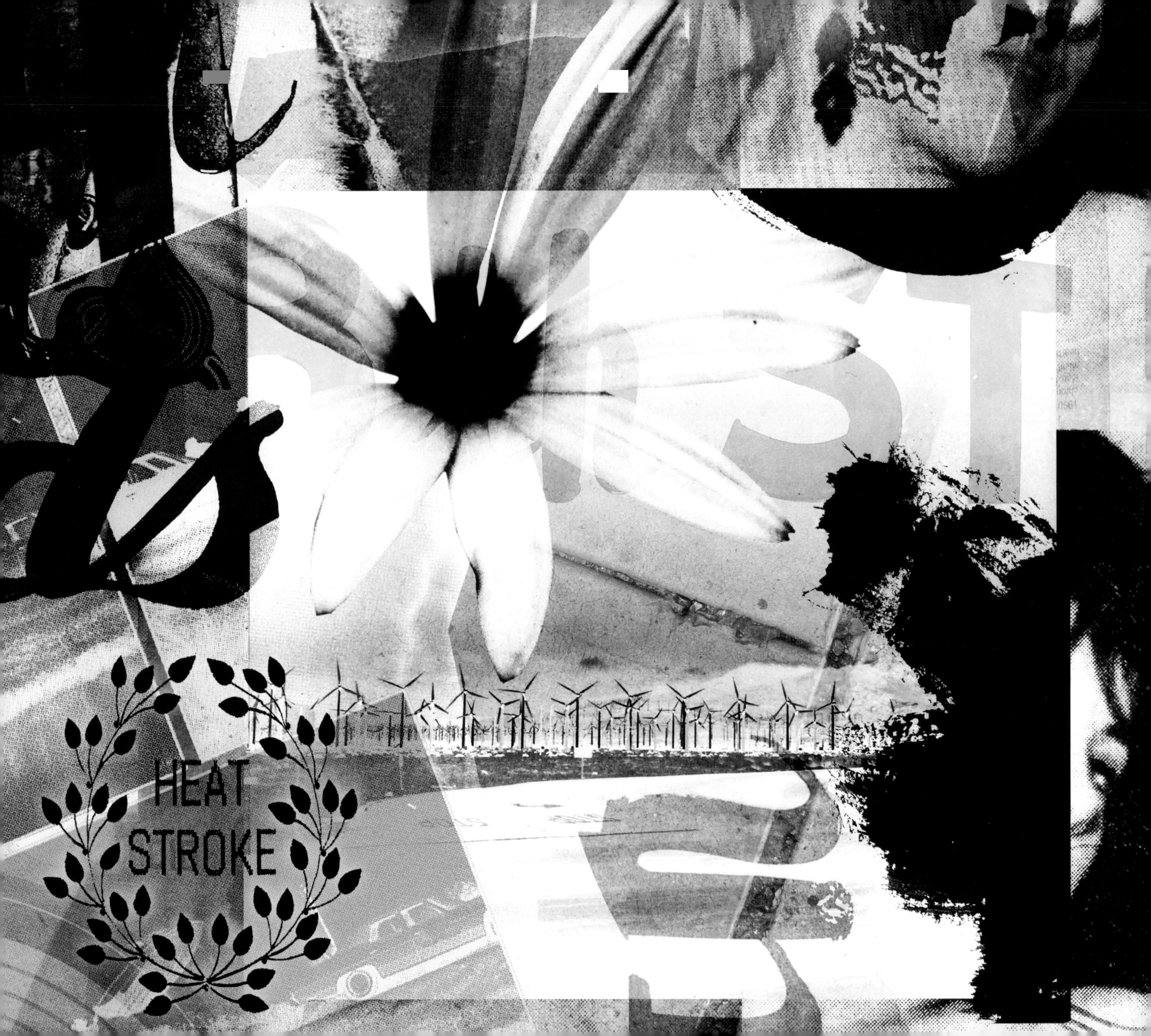
HEAT
STROKE

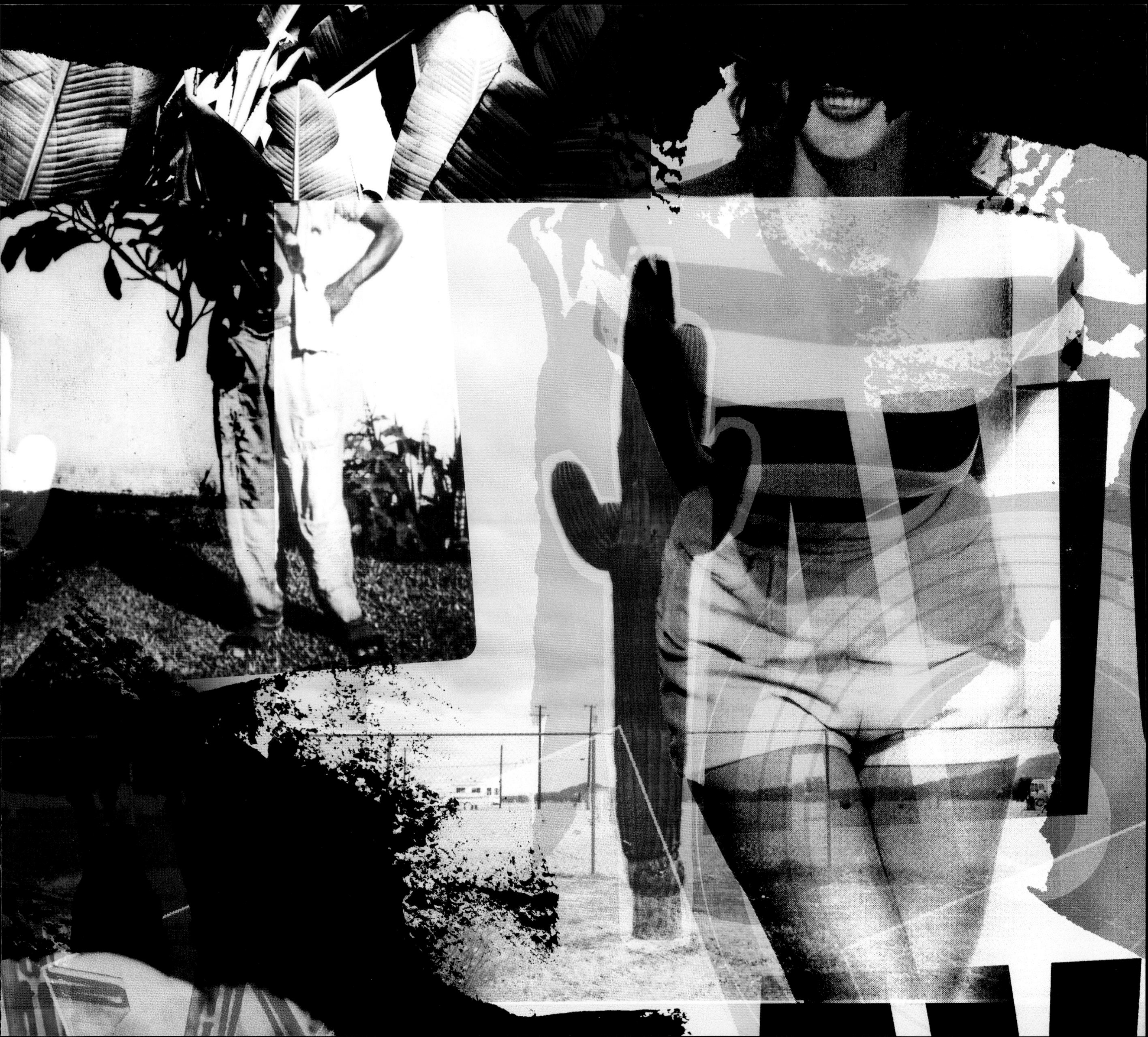

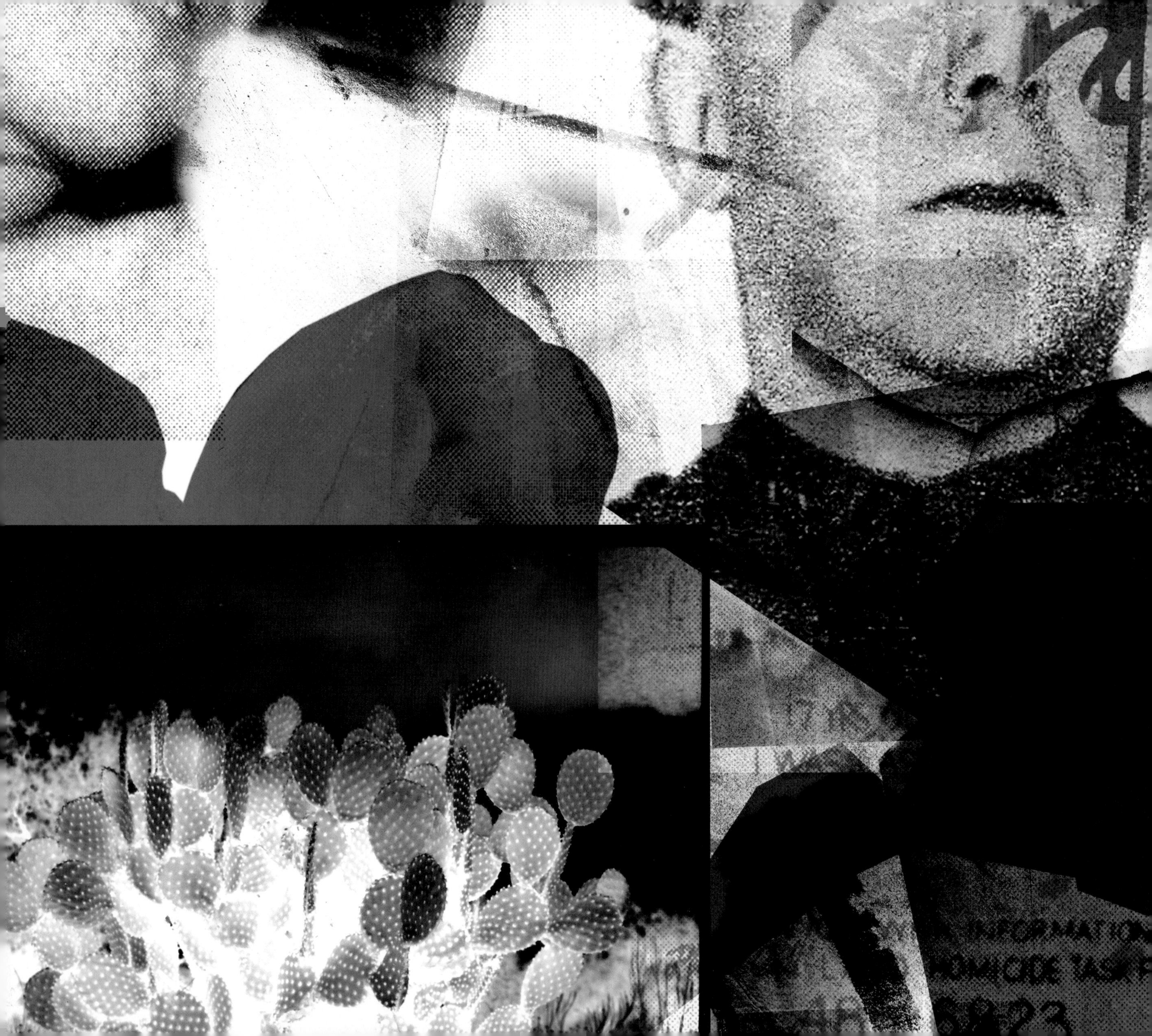

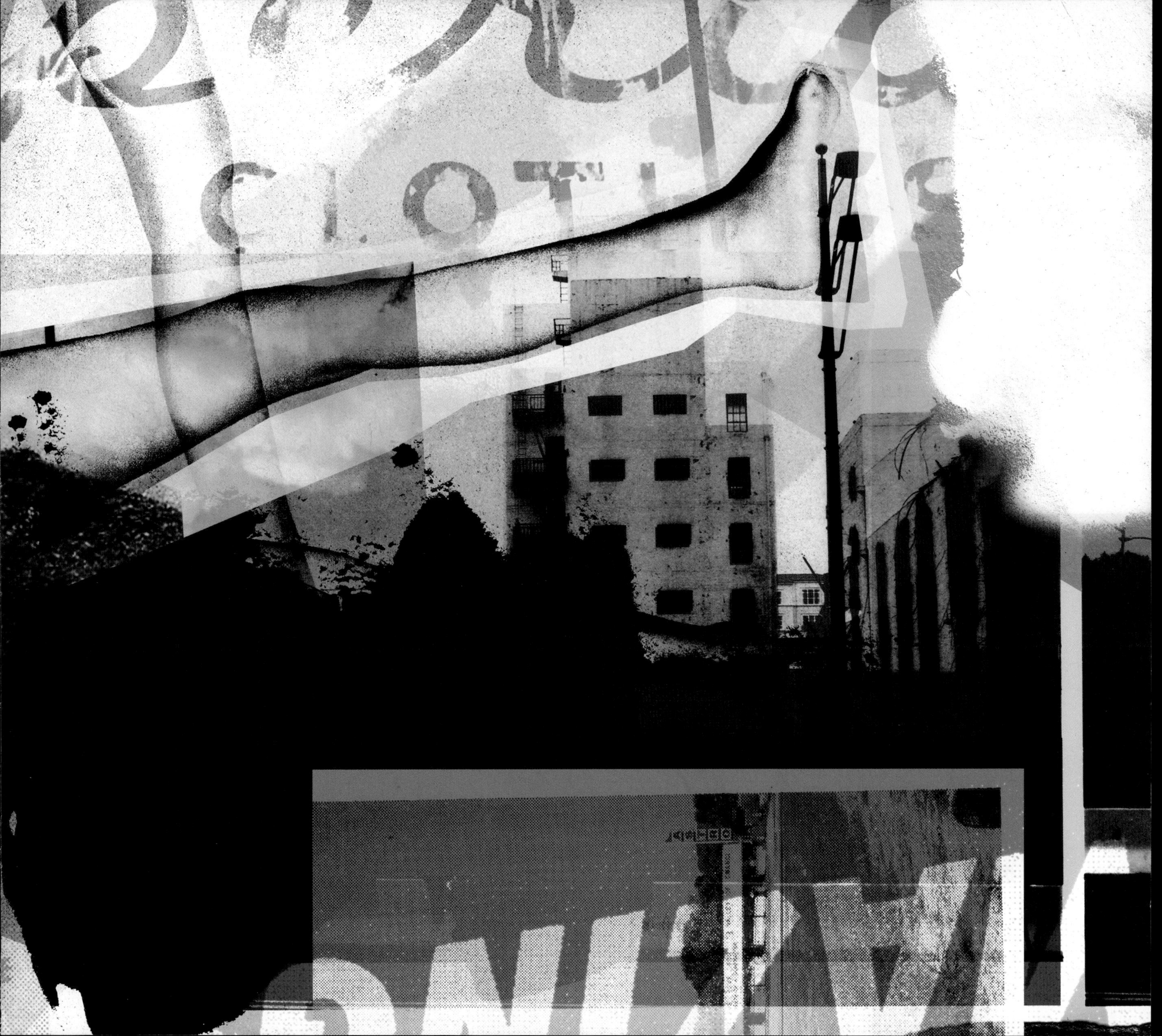

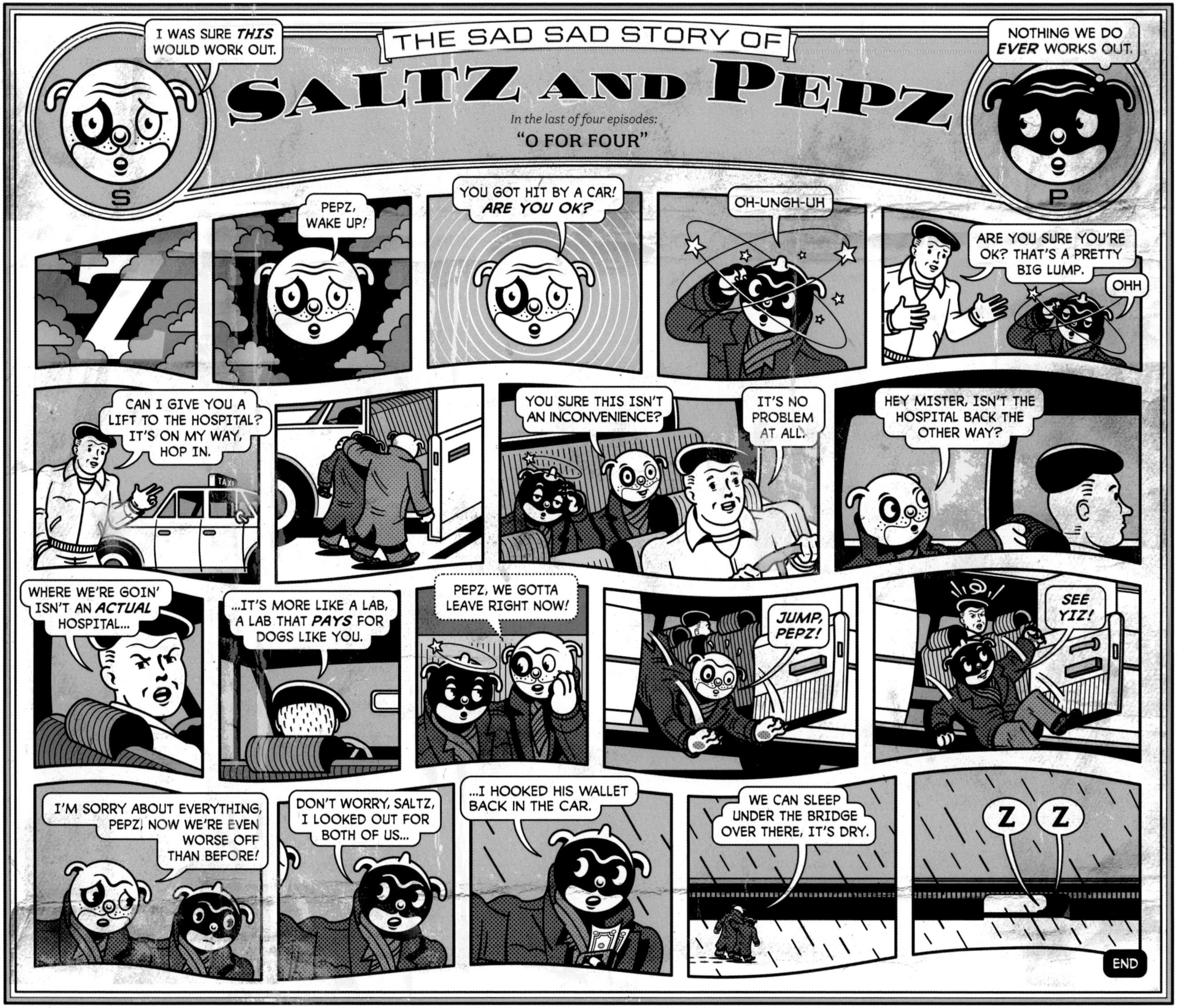
I WAS SURE THIS WOULD WORK OUT.
THE SAD SAD STORY OF
SALTZ AND PEPZ
In the last of four episodes:
"O FOR FOUR"
NOTHING WE DO EVER WORKS OUT.
S
P
Z
PEPZ, WAKE UP!
YOU GOT HIT BY A CAR! ARE YOU OK?
OH-UNGH-UH
ARE YOU SURE YOU'RE OK? THAT'S A PRETTY BIG LUMP.
OHH
CAN I GIVE YOU A LIFT TO THE HOSPITAL? IT'S ON MY WAY, HOP IN.
TAXI
YOU SURE THIS ISN'T AN INCONVENIENCE?
IT'S NO PROBLEM AT ALL.
HEY MISTER, ISN'T THE HOSPITAL BACK THE OTHER WAY?
WHERE WE'RE GOIN' ISN'T AN ACTUAL HOSPITAL...
...IT'S MORE LIKE A LAB, A LAB THAT PAYS FOR DOGS LIKE YOU.
PEPZ, WE GOTTA LEAVE RIGHT NOW!
JUMP, PEPZ!
SEE YIZ!
I'M SORRY ABOUT EVERYTHING, PEPZ, NOW WE'RE EVEN WORSE OFF THAN BEFORE!
DON'T WORRY, SALTZ, I LOOKED OUT FOR BOTH OF US...
...I HOOKED HIS WALLET BACK IN THE CAR.
WE CAN SLEEP UNDER THE BRIDGE OVER THERE, IT'S DRY.
Z Z
END

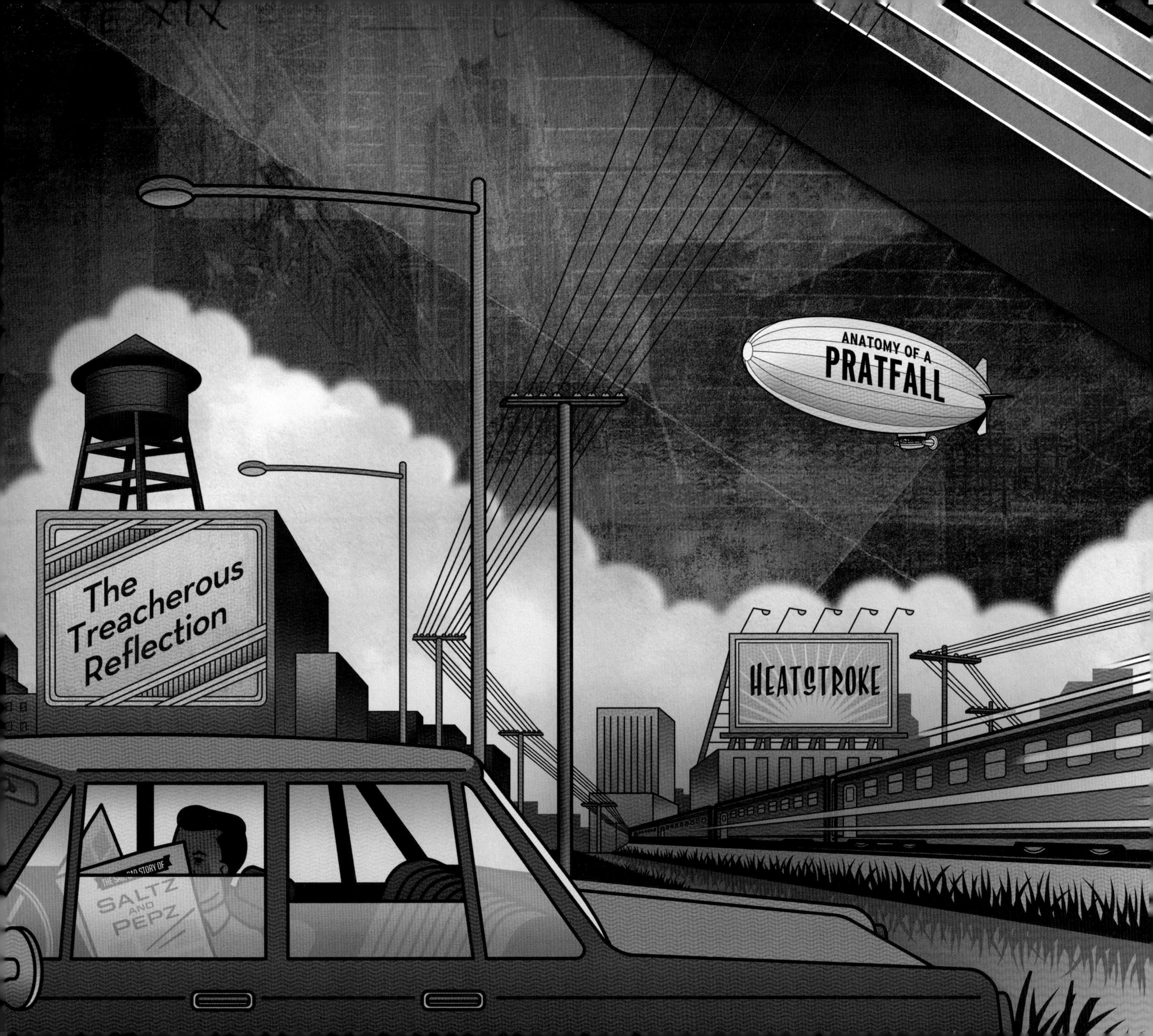
The Treacherous Reflection
ANATOMY OF A
PRATFALL
HEATSTROKE
SALTZ
AND
PEPZ

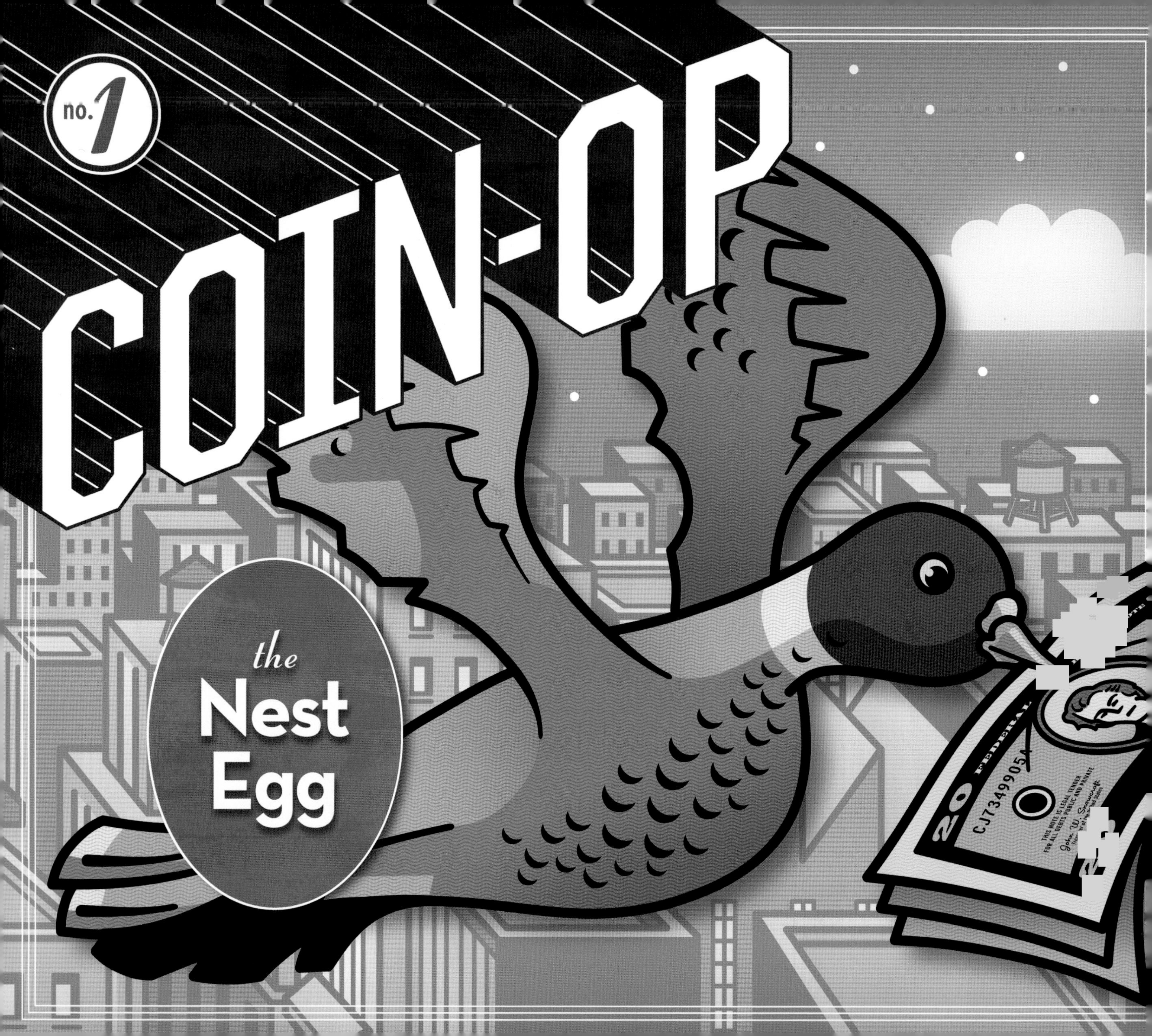
no. 1
COIN-OP
the Nest Egg

the Nest Egg
OPEN

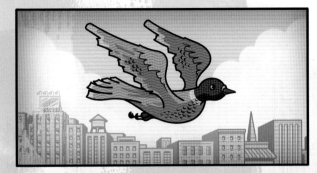

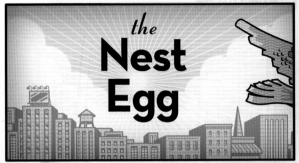

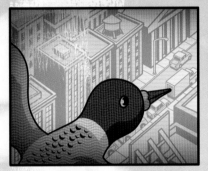

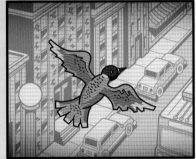

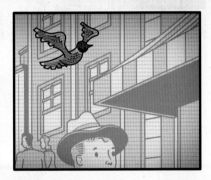

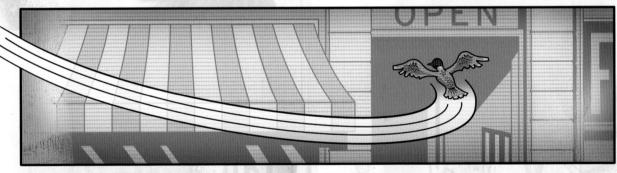

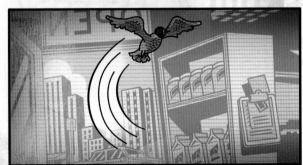

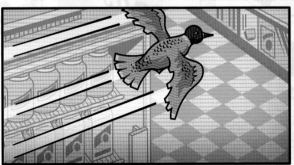

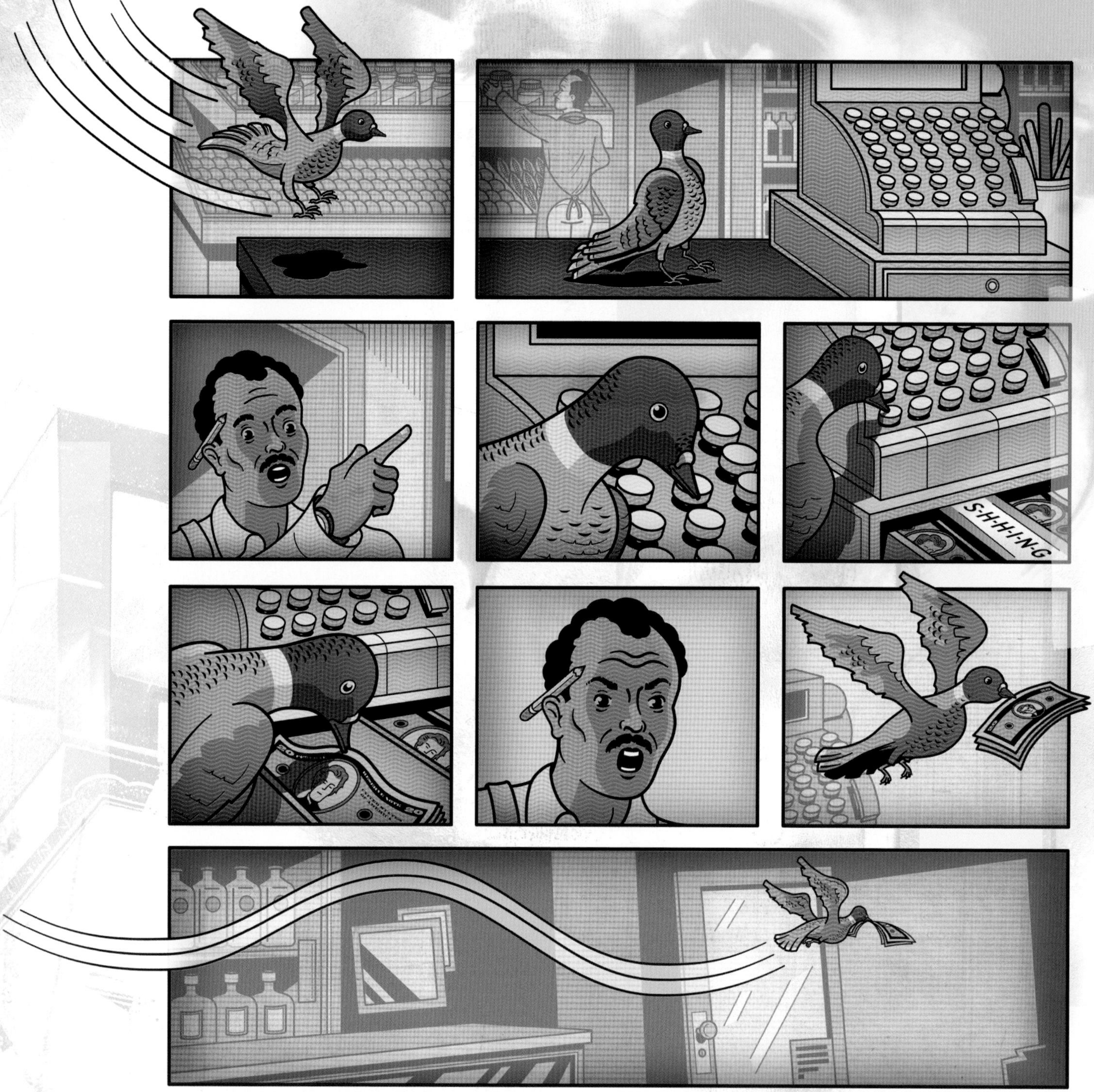
S-H-H-I-N-G

HOTEL

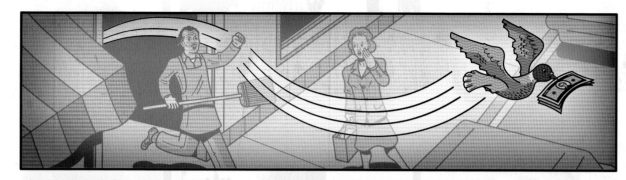

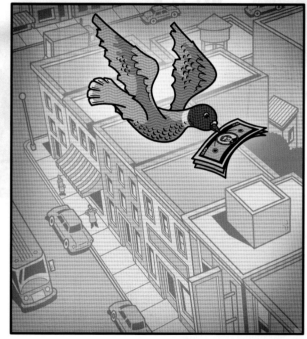

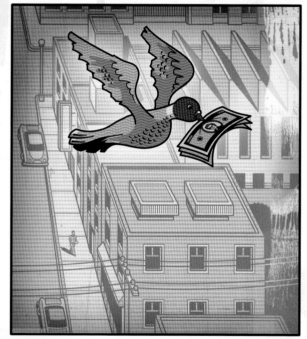

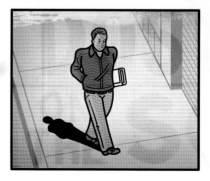

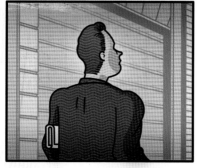

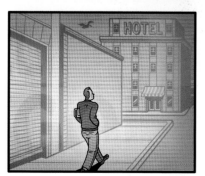

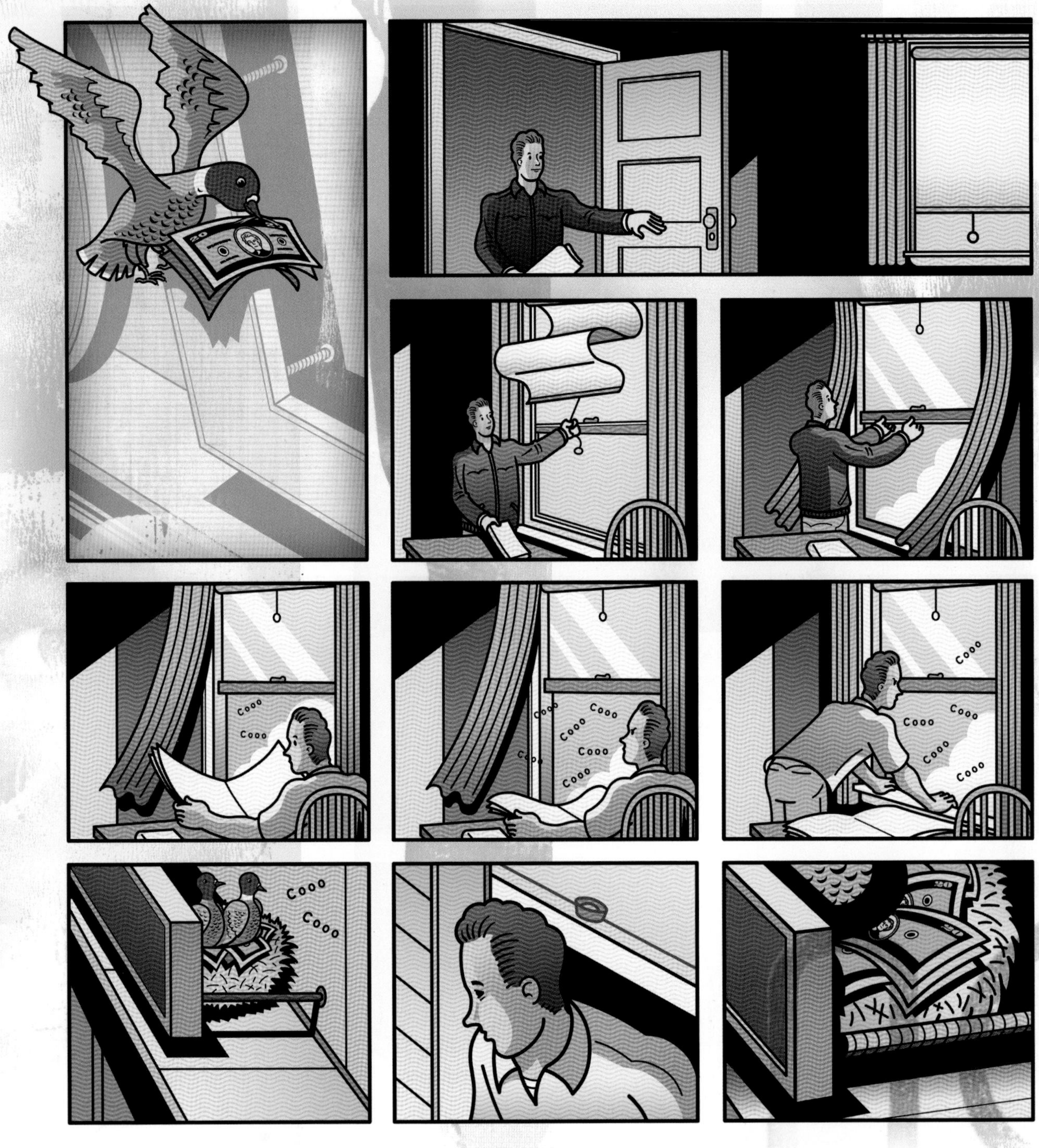
Cooo
Cooo
Cooo
Cooo
Cooo
Cooo
Cooo
Cooo
Cooo
Cooo
Cooo
Cooo
Cooo
Cooo

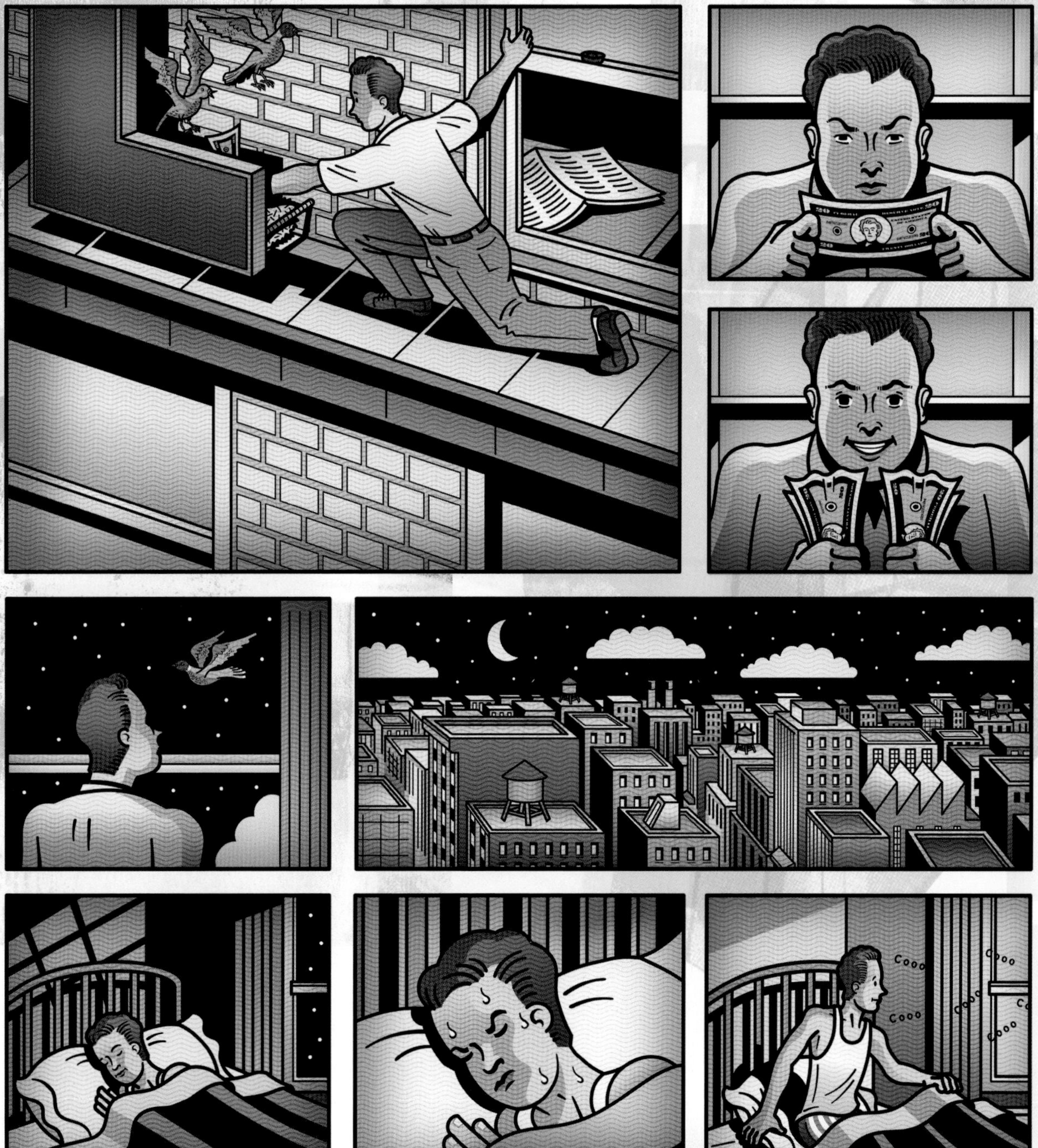
Cooo
Cooo
Cooo
Cooo
Cooo

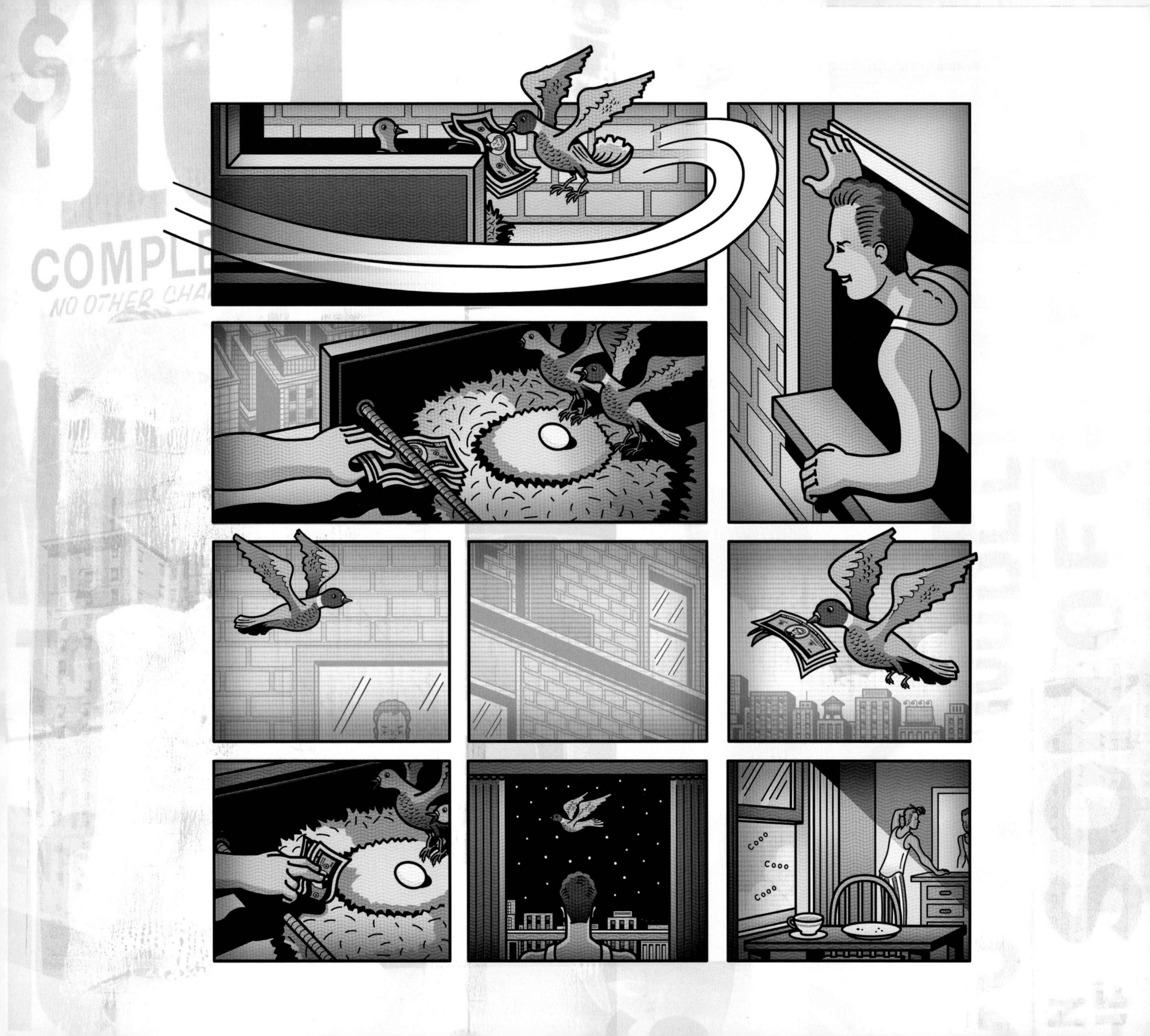
Cooo
Cooo
Cooo

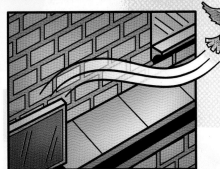

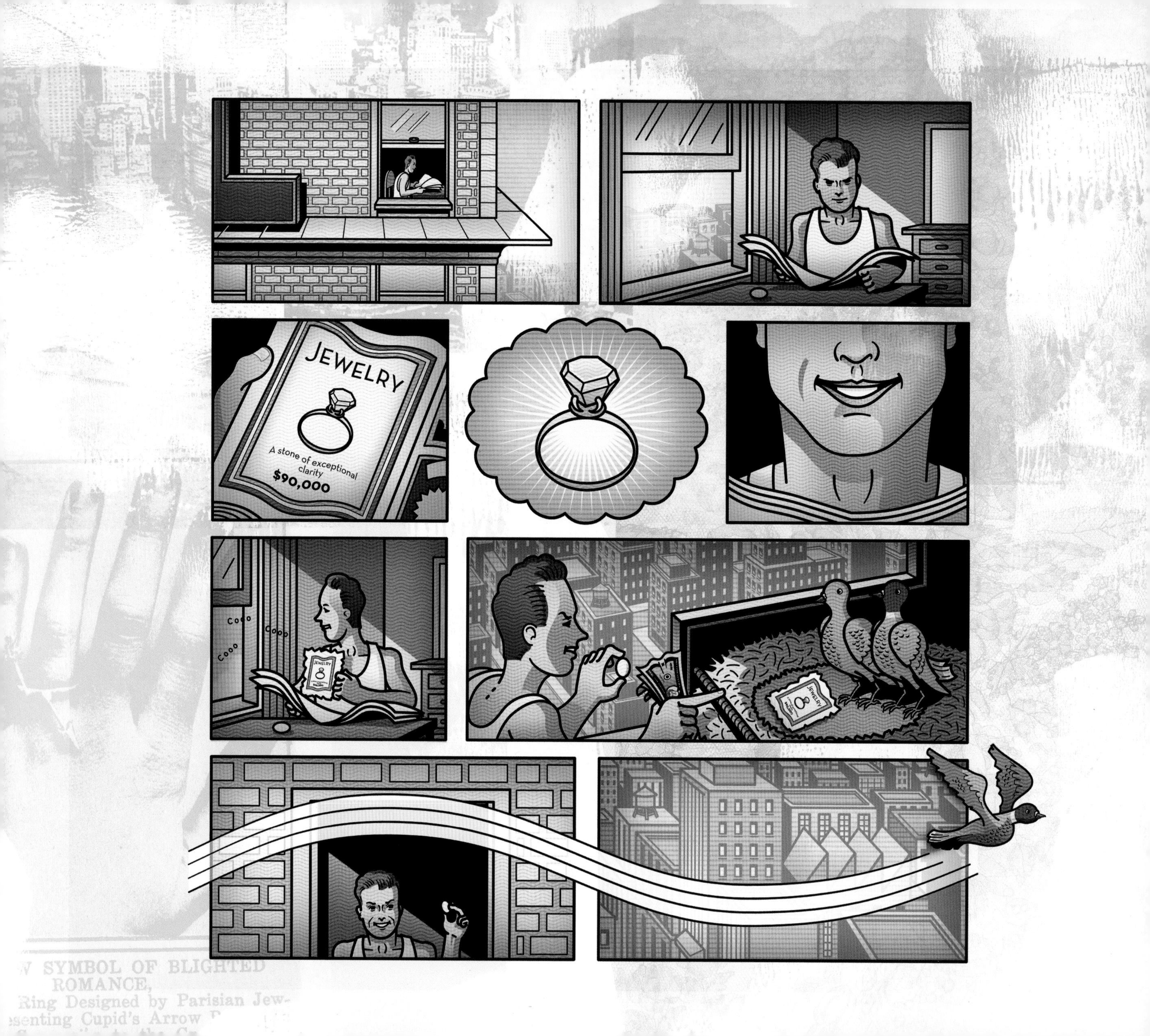
JEWELRY
A stone of exceptional clarity
$90,000
Cooo
Cooo
Cooo
SYMBOL OF BLIGHTED
ROMANCE,
Ring Designed by Parisian Jew-
senting Cupid's Arrow

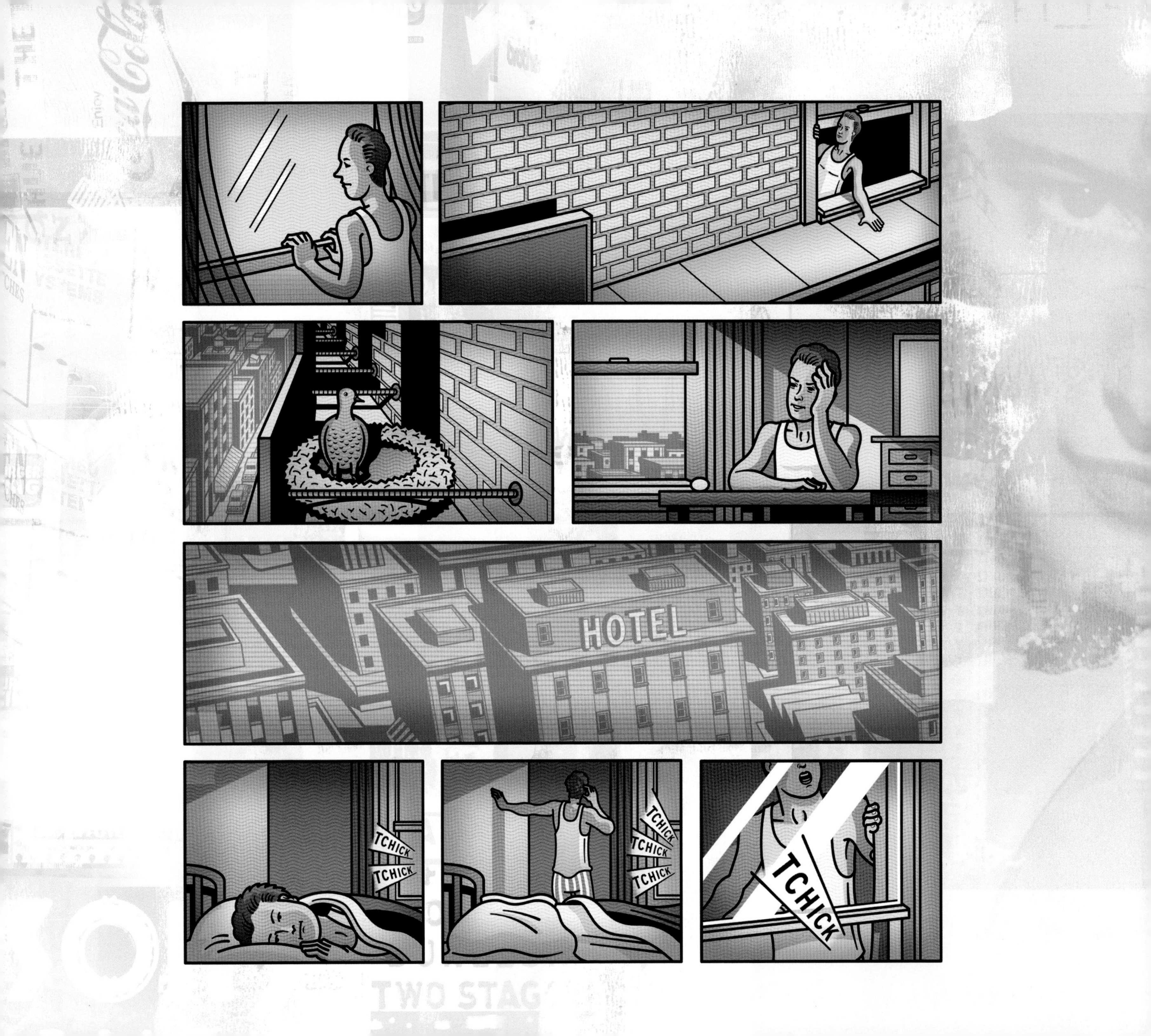
HOTEL
TCHICK
TCHICK
TCHICK
TCHICK
TCHICK
TCHICK

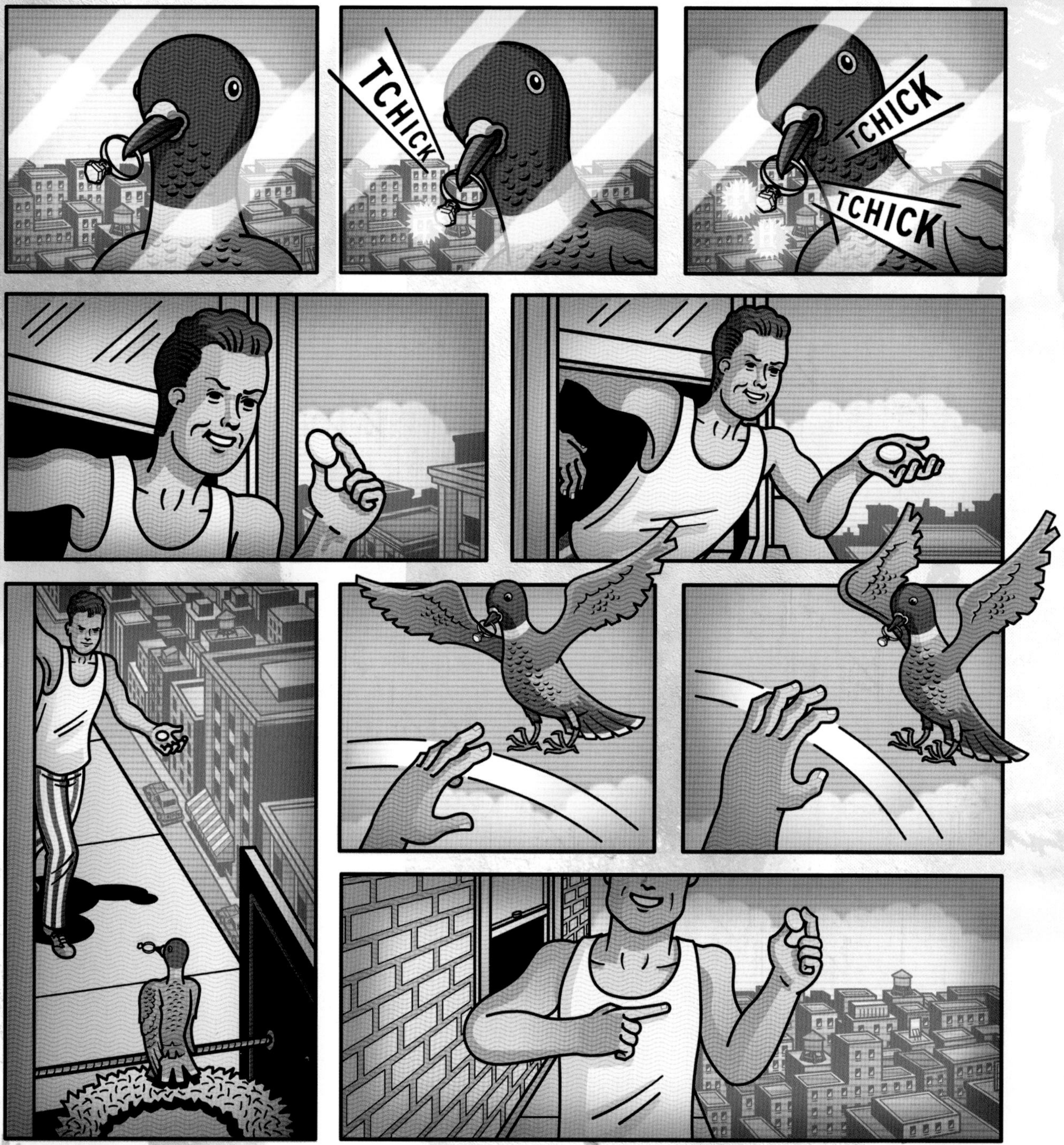
TCHICK
TCHICK
TCHICK

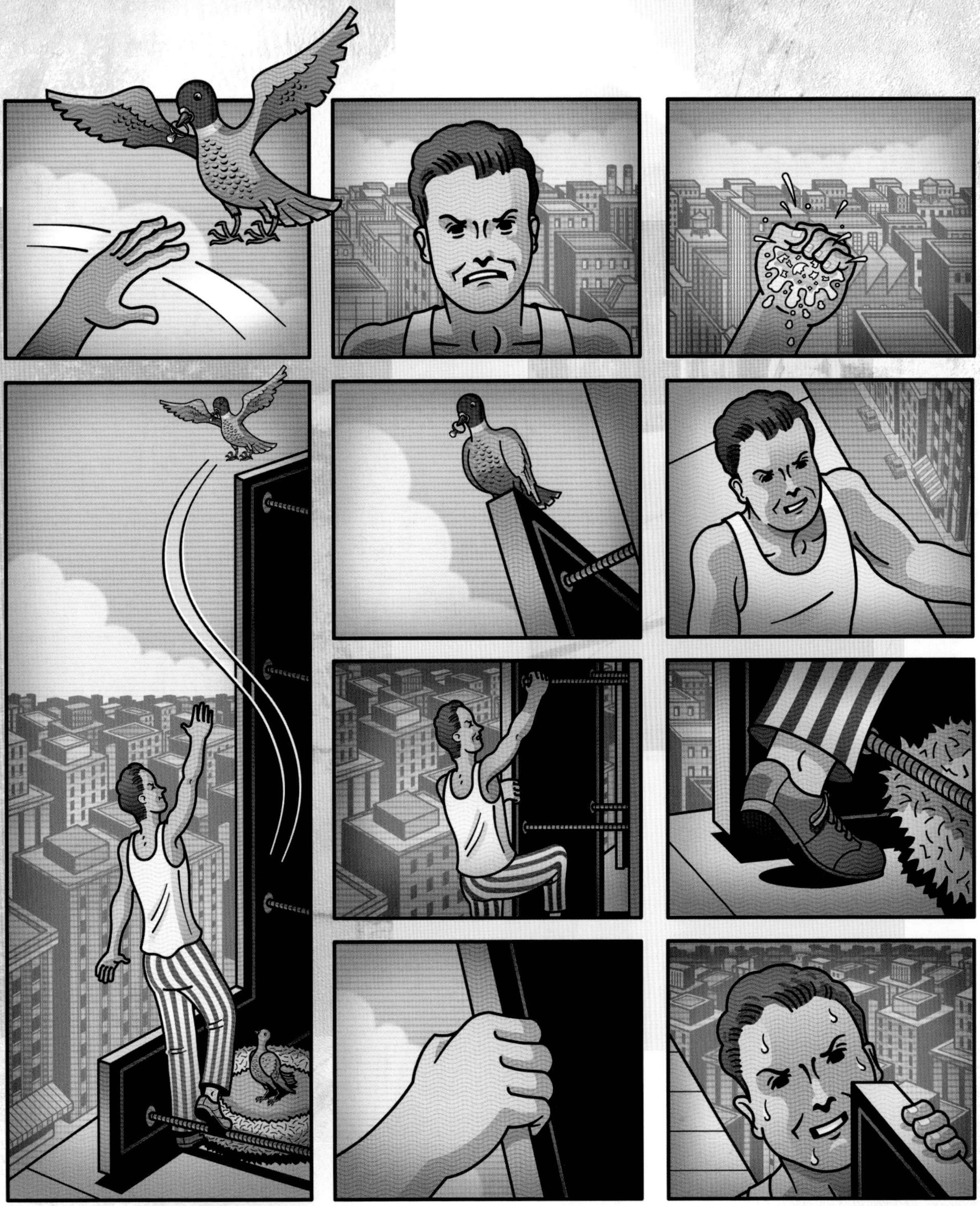

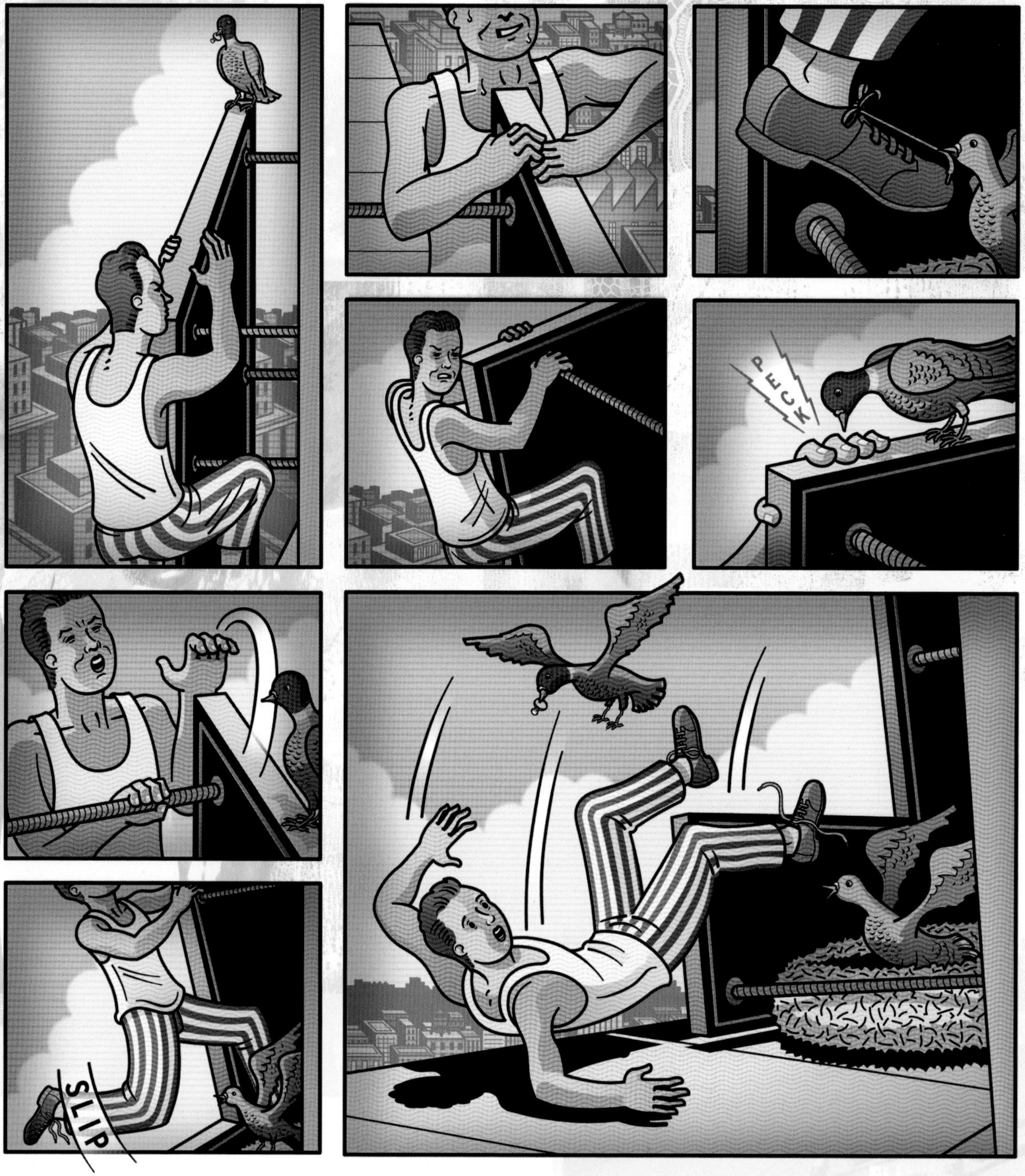
PECK
SLIP

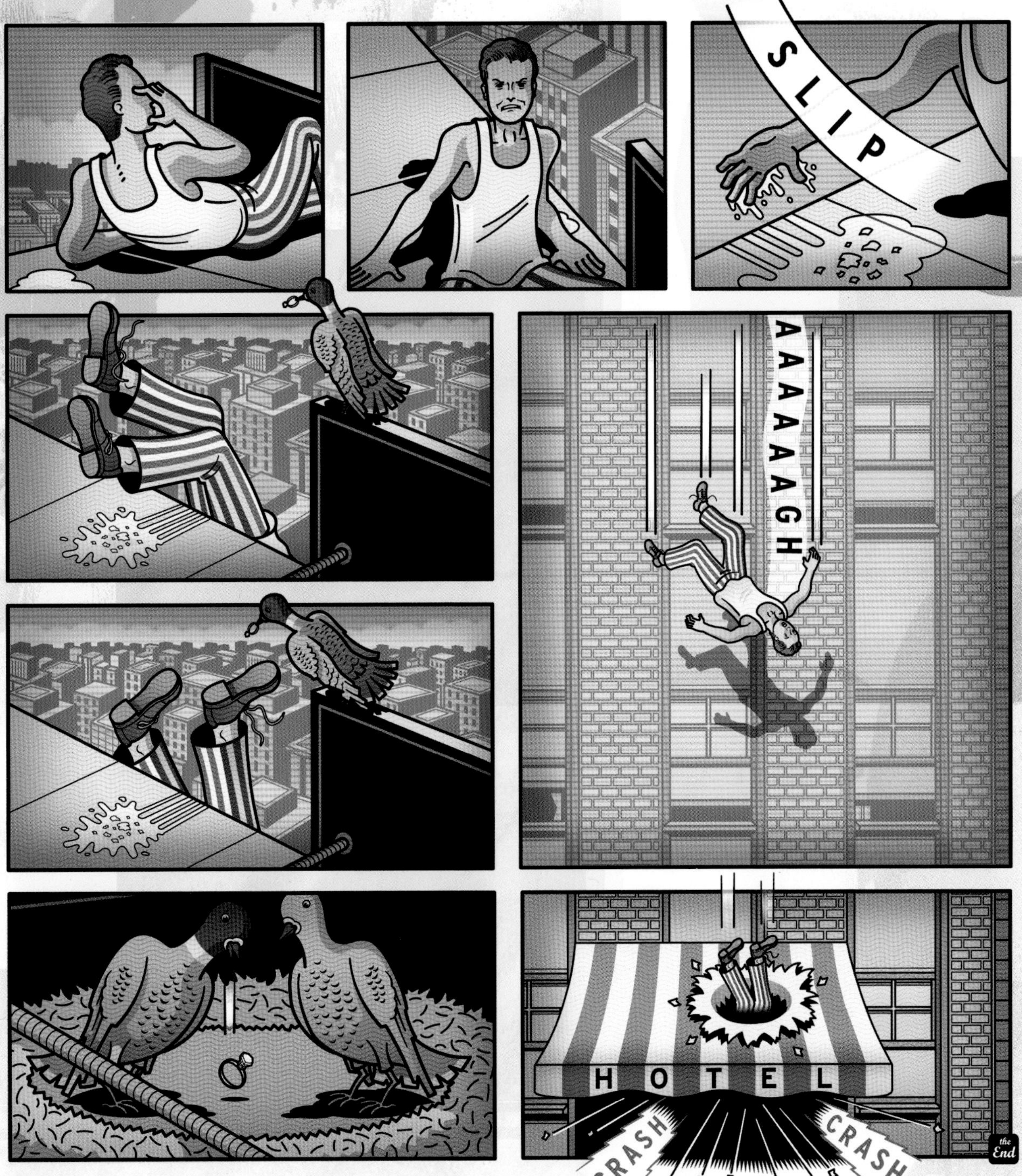
SLIP
AAAAAAGH
HOTEL
CRASH
CRASH
the End

CRIME WAVE ON A PIGEON'S WING

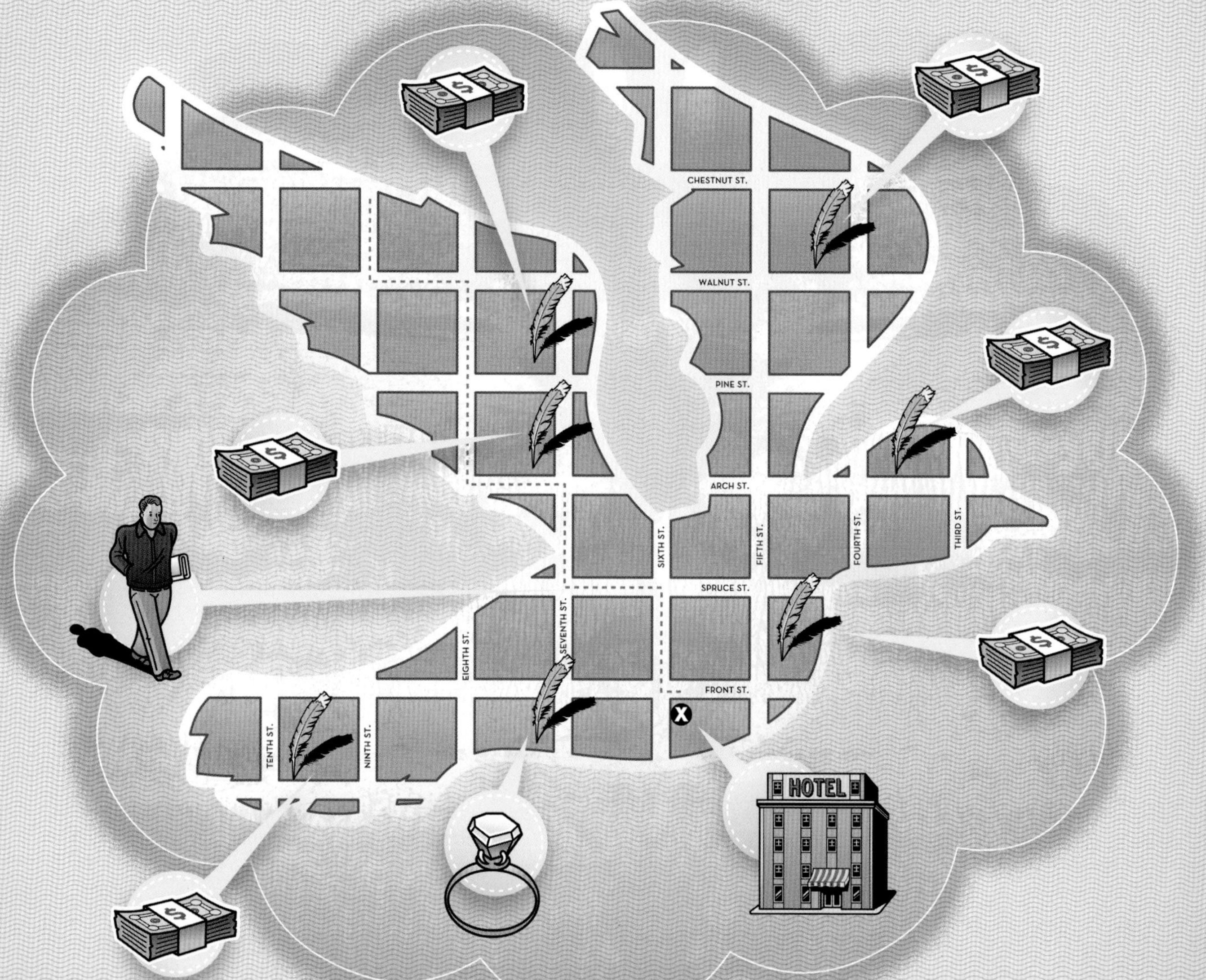
CHESTNUT ST.
WALNUT ST.
PINE ST.
ARCH ST.
SPRUCE ST.
FRONT ST.
THIRD ST.
FOURTH ST.
FIFTH ST.
SIXTH ST.
SEVENTH ST.
EIGHTH ST.
NINTH ST.
TENTH ST.
X
HOTEL

IN THE BEGINNING, THERE WAS BLAB!

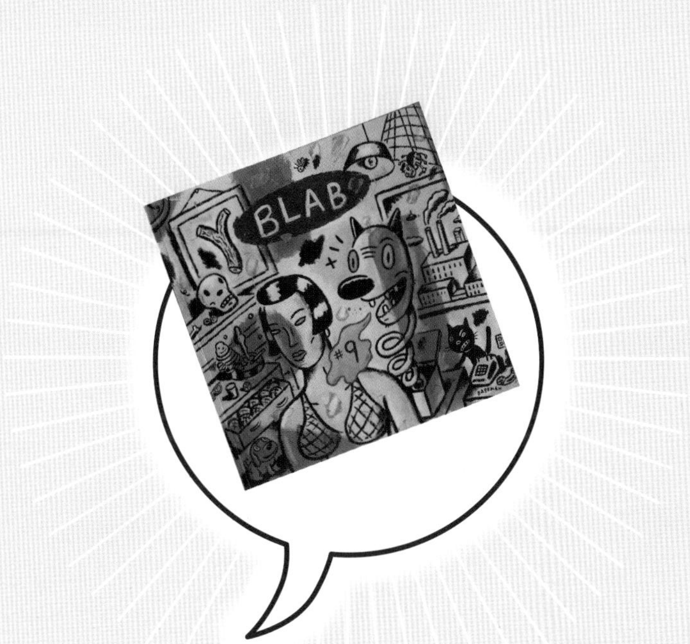
BLAB
#9

A Note from the Editor of BLAB!

I CONFESS. I'M THE CULPRIT. THE BAD SEED. The one to blame for luring Peter Hoey into the tawdry sidecar of small-press comics.

Pete was a budding young illustrator when I first approached him. Well groomed. Clean cut. And in demand. *Entertainment Weekly*, *Rolling Stone*, and *The Wall Street Journal* were but a few of the publications showcasing his work.

In 1993, my comics anthology *BLAB!* was in a state of flux, transitioning from a digest-sized comics anthology into a square, 78-rpm-sized compendium inclusive of illustration, printmaking, fine art, and vintage ephemera.

Yet, as a small press publication, *BLAB!* was constrained by small-press ways. Would a hot-shot magazine illustrator actually work for two percent of what he was used to getting paid? After all, a single, full-color spot drawing dished out $250 on up, whereas an entire *BLAB!* comics page, comprised of six or more such images, paid much, much less.

Awash in apprehension, I picked up the phone.

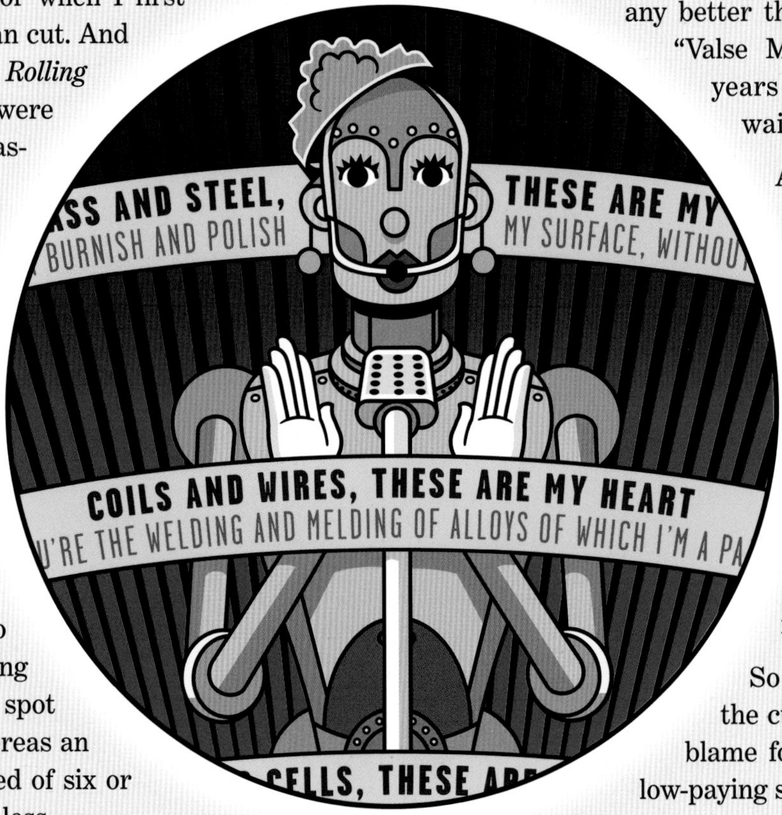
AND STEEL,
THESE ARE MY
BURNISH AND POLISH
MY SURFACE,
COILS AND WIRES, THESE ARE MY HEART
THE WELDING AND MELDING OF ALLOYS OF WHICH I'M A
CELLS, THESE

And here it is, twenty four years later and what a *BLAB!*ulous journey it has been. Pete and his cohorts—sister and collaborator Maria, and co-writer Chuck Freund—never once missed a deadline, never once missed a beat. Can a comic-book short get any better than the original full-color version of "Valse Mechanic" (*BLAB! #9*)? Twenty-one years have since passed, and I'm still waiting . . . .

And now I have a confession to make. After reading each finished submission, I began to count—six panels on this page, eight panels on that, tally them up, and then do the math. One such *BLAB!* contribution, comprising 45 spot drawings, times $250, would have earned them $11,250 in the world of illustration. Now, when you times that by their total *BLAB!* output (12 stories), well, you get my drift.

So dear reader, please remember—I'm the culprit . . . the bad seed . . . the one to blame for luring the Hoeys into the tawdry, low-paying sidecar of small-press comics.

— *Monte Beauchamp*
Chicago, January 2018

Art from "Valse Mechanic" published in: *BLAB! no. 9*

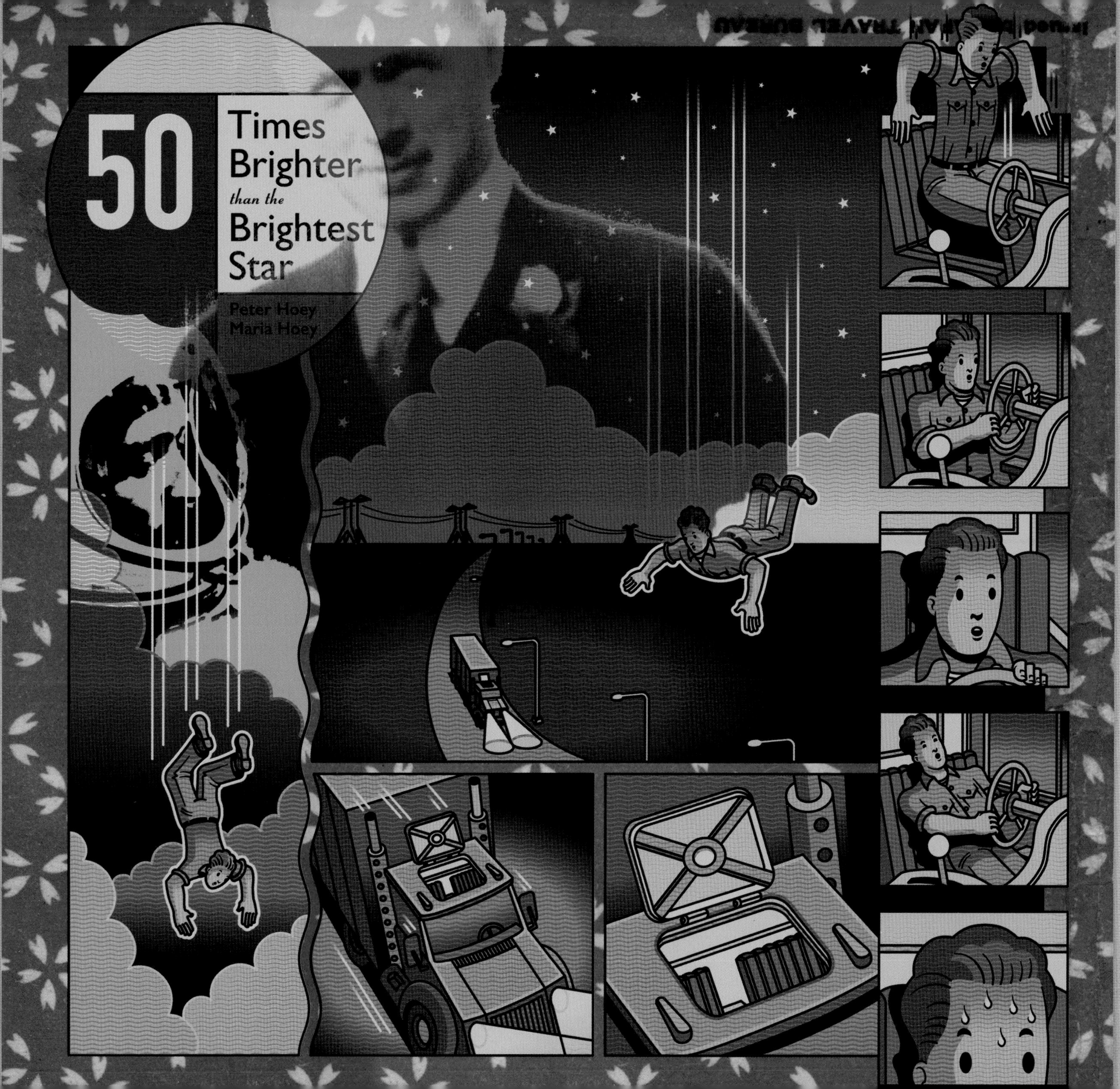
50
Times
Brighter
than the
Brightest
Star
Peter Hoey
Maria Hoey

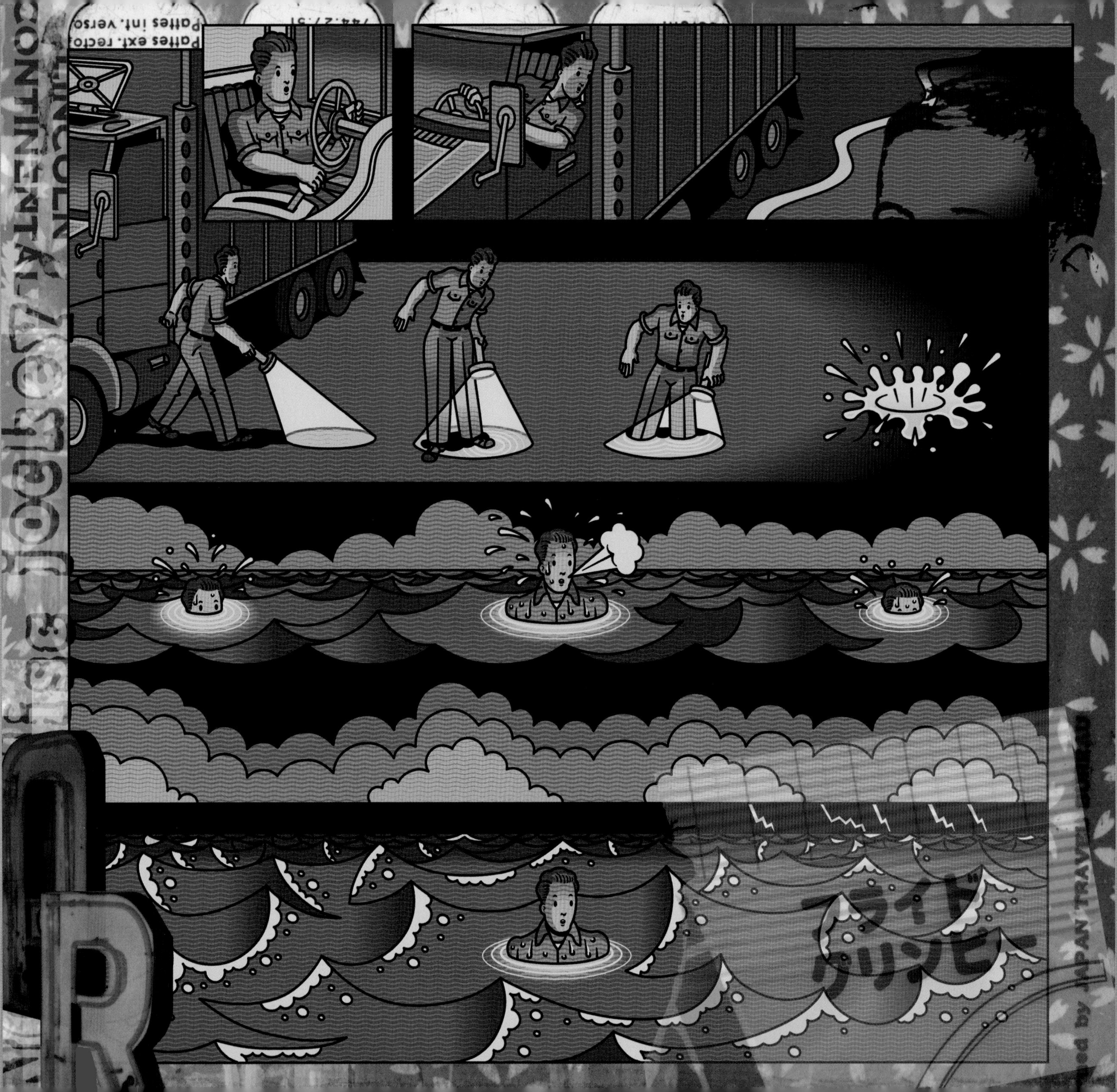
LINCOLN
CONTINENTAL
Pattes ext. recto
Pattes int. verso
ライト

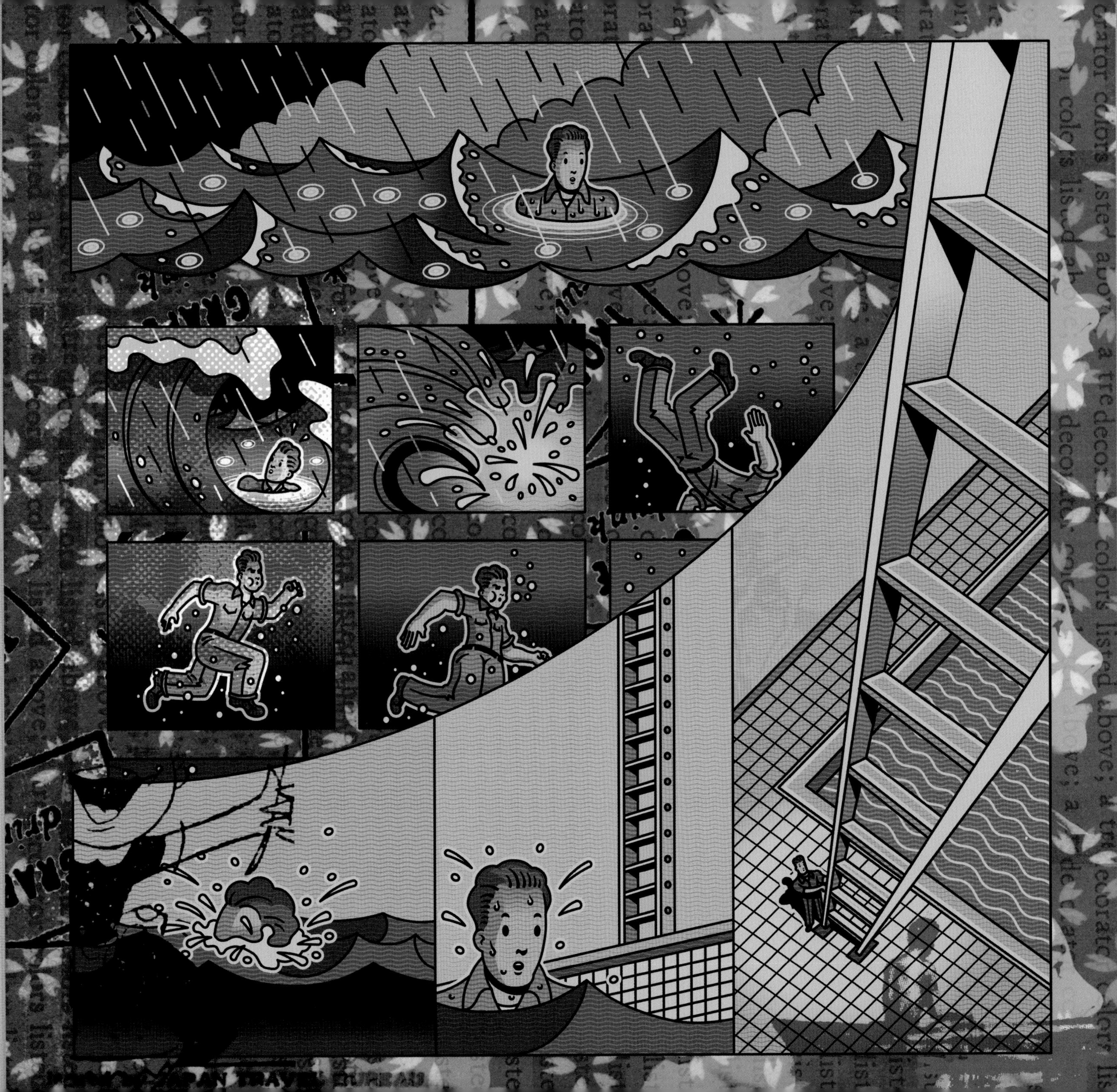
JAPAN TRAVEL BUREAU

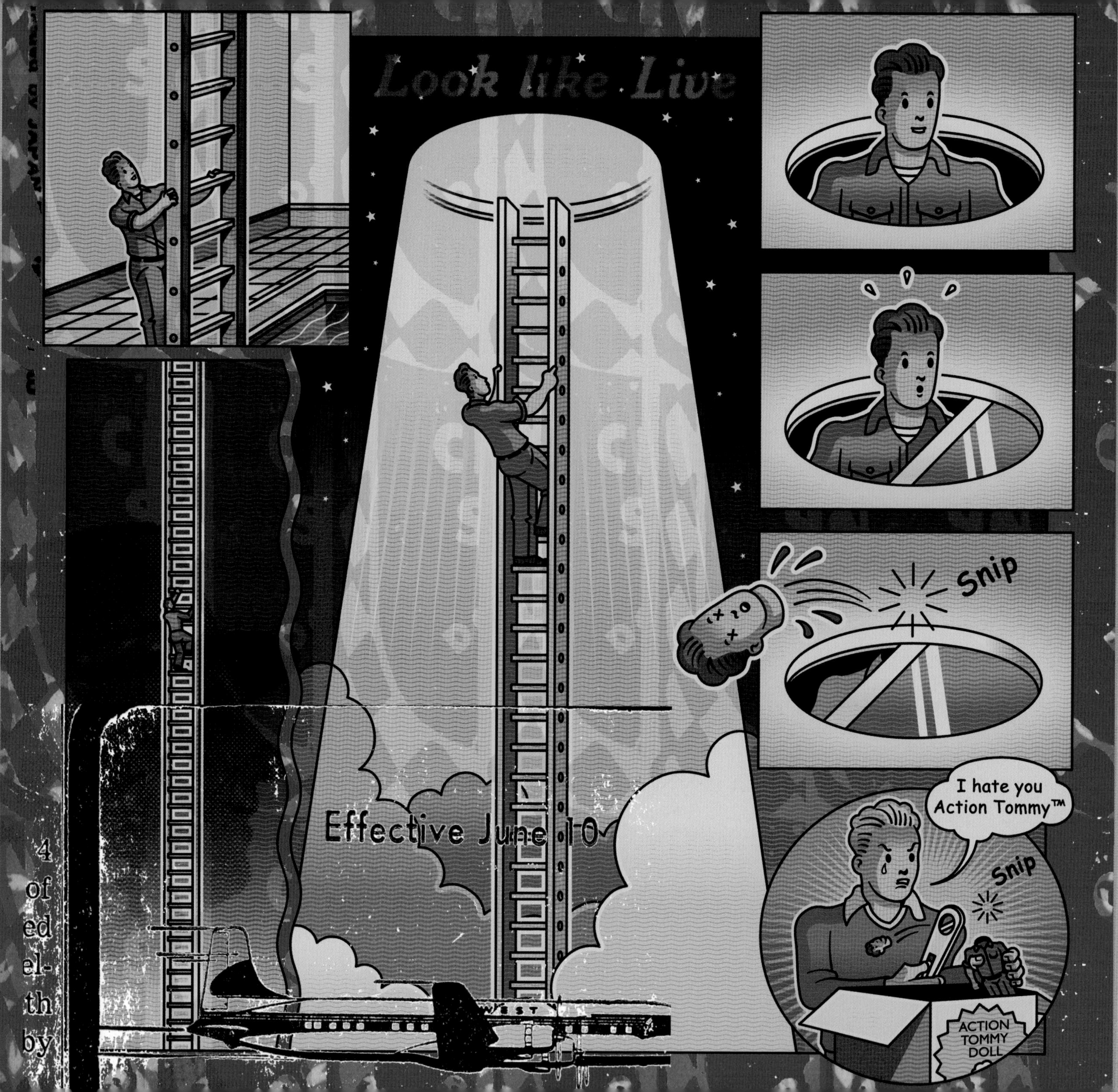
Look like Live
Effective June 10
4
of
ed
el-
th
by
Snip
I hate you Action Tommy™
Snip
ACTION TOMMY DOLL

ONE of SIX · LOST · LINER NOTES

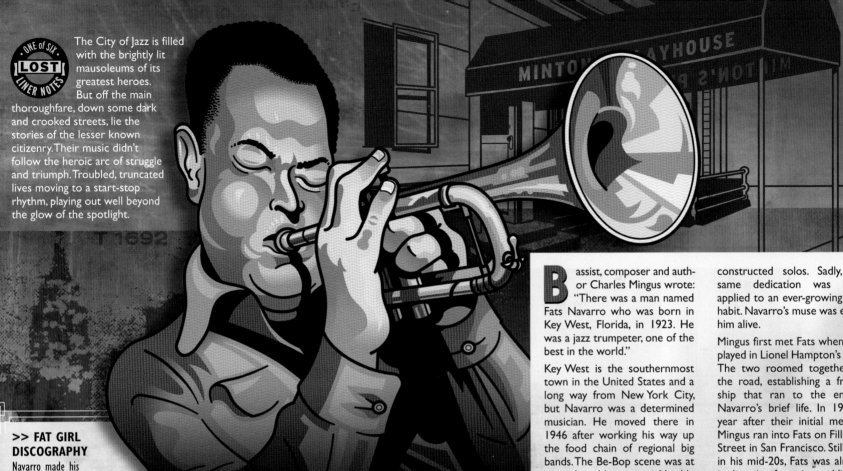

The City of Jazz is filled with the brightly lit mausoleums of its greatest heroes. But off the main thoroughfare, down some dark and crooked streets, lie the stories of the lesser known citizenry. Their music didn't follow the heroic arc of struggle and triumph. Troubled, truncated lives moving to a start-stop rhythm, playing out well beyond the glow of the spotlight.

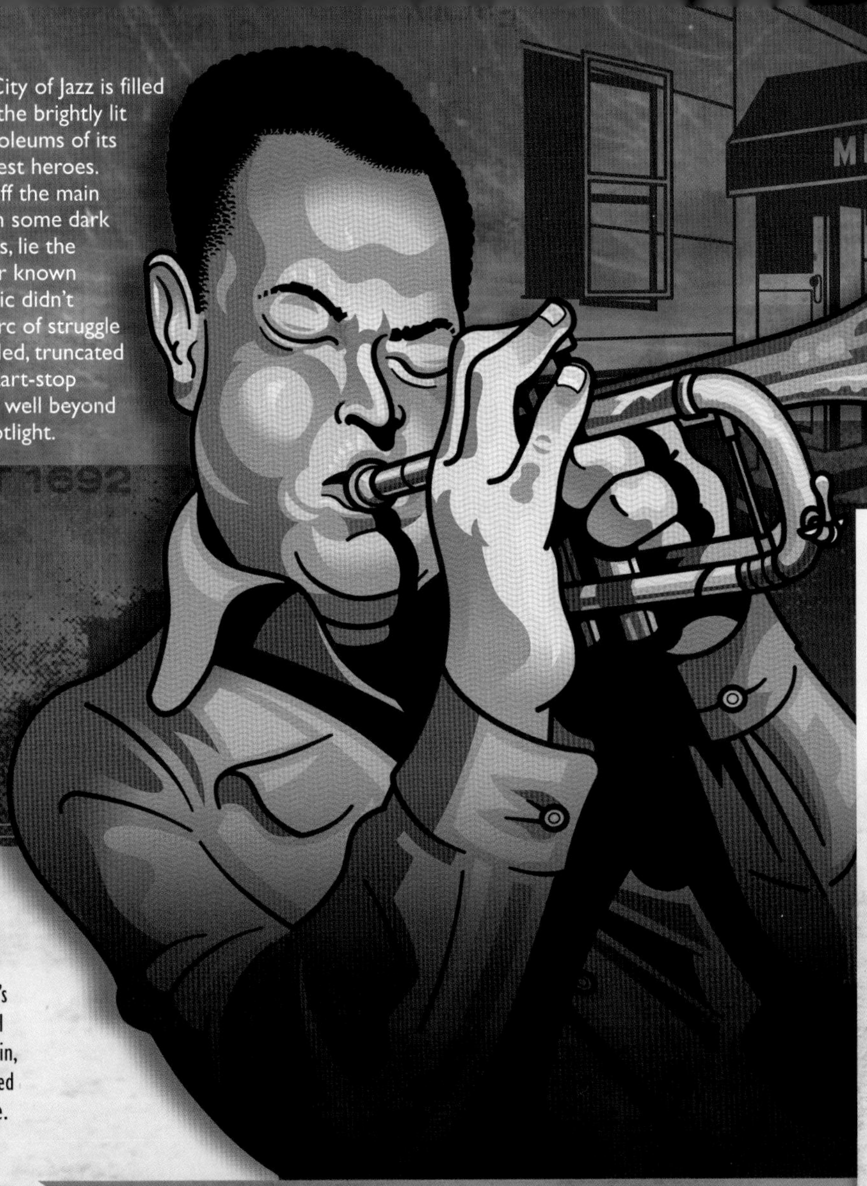

FATS NAVARRO

Theodore Navarro was the perfect Be-Bop trumpeter. Possessed of a full, melodic tone wrapped around flawless technique, he burst fully formed onto the 1940s jazz scene. In his short life, Fats recorded a body of work that is some of the best in modern jazz. So how come nobody remembers his name?

Bassist, composer and author Charles Mingus wrote: "There was a man named Fats Navarro who was born in Key West, Florida, in 1923. He was a jazz trumpeter, one of the best in the world."

Key West is the southernmost town in the United States and a long way from New York City, but Navarro was a determined musician. He moved there in 1946 after working his way up the food chain of regional big bands. The Be-Bop scene was at its peak and he was quickly able to master the new sound. In a very short time, the relatively unknown Navarro was among the most sought-after musicians in New York. Theodore had garnered the nickname "Fat Girl" from his overweight physique and high-pitched voice, and at some point he also acquired a taste for heroin, the drug of choice on the Bop scene.

Other musicians admired his virtuosity and powers of invention. Navarro pursued his perfection of his music with single-minded dedication, playing an ebullient, polished sound even at the fastest tempos. He joined the full tone of earlier swing-era trumpet to the modern time signatures of Be-Bop to create exquisitely constructed solos. Sadly, this same dedication was being applied to an ever-growing drug habit. Navarro's muse was eating him alive.

Mingus first met Fats when they played in Lionel Hampton's band. The two roomed together on the road, establishing a friendship that ran to the end of Navarro's brief life. In 1949, a year after their initial meeting, Mingus ran into Fats on Fillmore Street in San Francisco. Still only in his mid-20s, Fats was already in the grip of a serious addiction. Mingus was shocked to see his friend, who now dressed in suits that were three sizes too big. You couldn't really call him "Fat Girl" anymore.

Before everyone's eyes he wasted away to nothing. Sometime in the late '40s he contracted tuberculosis. Strung out and drifting, he let the disease go untreated.

Navarro weighed only 110 pounds when he died in New York's Bellevue Hospital, July 6th, 1950. He was 26 years old.

Though his playing was a huge influence on the next generation of trumpeters, the rest of the world forgot about Theodore Navarro.

>> FAT GIRL DISCOGRAPHY

Navarro made his reputation at the jam sessions held at Minton's Playhouse in Harlem. All the best musicians sat in, but only the most skilled could keep up the pace. But it's his work with pianist and composer Tadd Dameron that shines the brightest. Starting in the autumn of 1948, a series of sextets and septets led by Dameron and featuring Fats played a 39-week engagement at the "Royal Roost Club" in New York. Radio broadcasts of these performances highlight the brilliant playing of Theodore Navarro.

SECOND of SIX LOST LINER NOTES

There is a cacophony of sound in the City of Jazz. Loud voices, sirens and even music, all competing above the din of the busy streets. The clamor of the city can even drown out the thoughts in your head. In the end, everyone finds his own refuge, even in the back of a Chinese laundry.

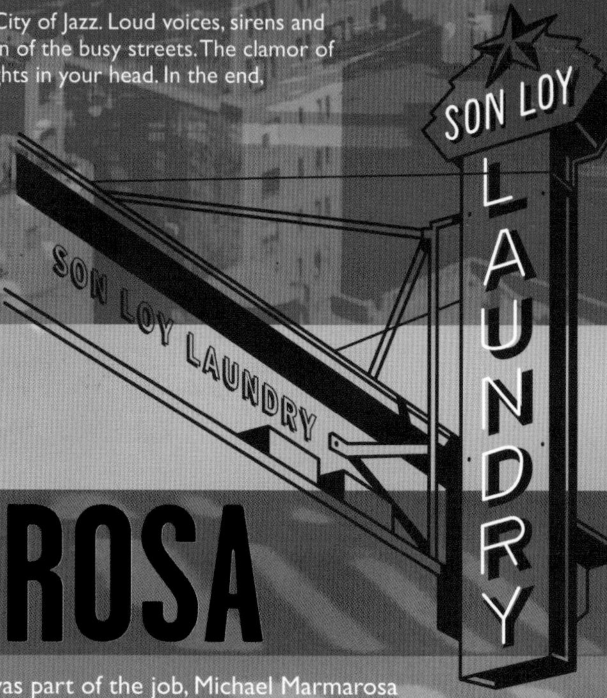

SON LOY
LAUNDRY
SON LOY LAUNDRY

DODO MARMAROSA

In a scene where crazy behavior was part of the job, Michael Marmarosa stood out, way out. Before mental illness finally silenced him, he was also one of the greatest jazz pianists around. What ever happened to Dodo, the rarest of birds?

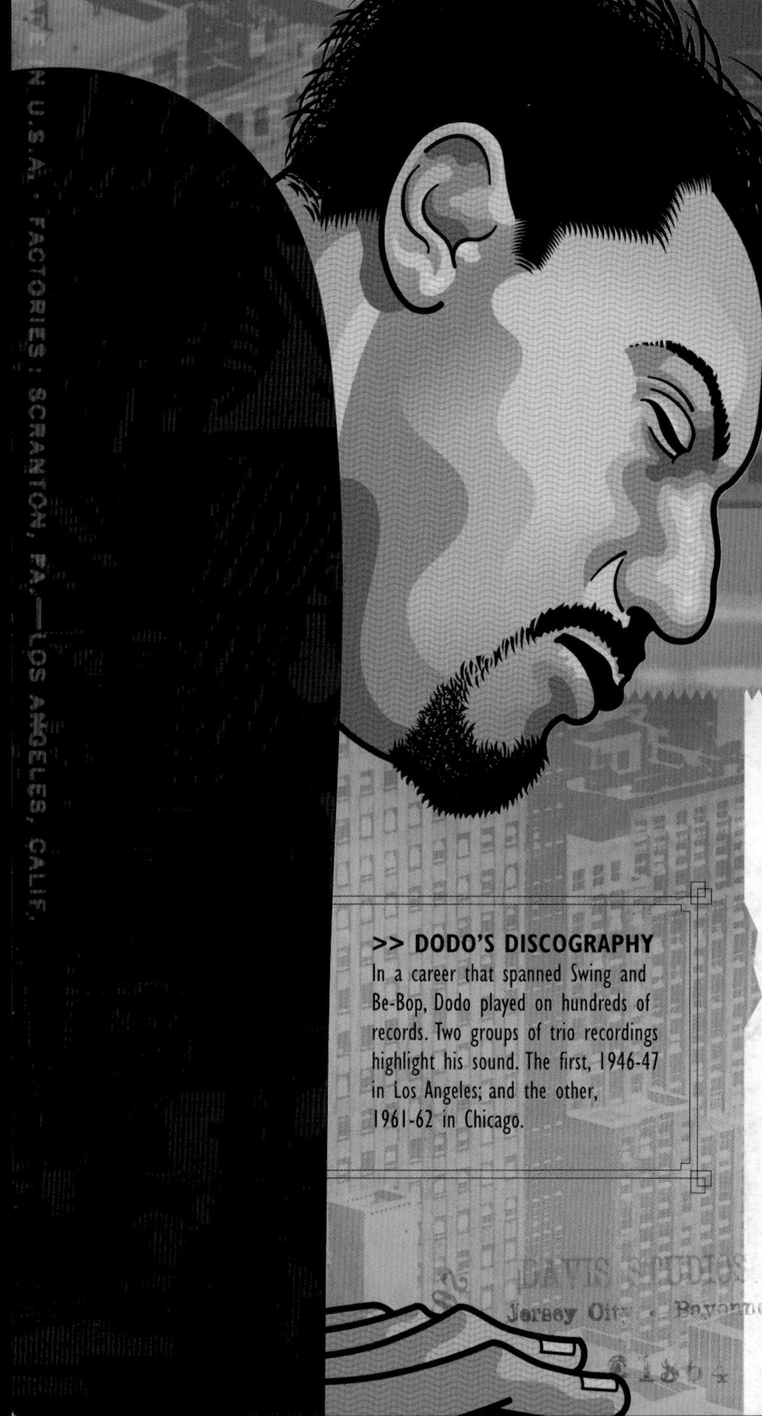

N U.S.A. · FACTORIES: SCRANTON, PA.—LOS ANGELES, CALIF.
DAVIS STUDIOS
Jersey City · Bayonne

>> DODO'S DISCOGRAPHY
In a career that spanned Swing and Be-Bop, Dodo played on hundreds of records. Two groups of trio recordings highlight his sound. The first, 1946-47 in Los Angeles; and the other, 1961-62 in Chicago.

In the 1940s, Pittsburgh was famous for its jazz pianists: Billy Strayhorn, Earl Hines, Mary Lou Williams, Ahmad Jamal, Errol Garner and Dodo Marmarosa all came out of that sooty, industrial city.

Born to an Italian immigrant family in 1925, Michael showed an early aptitude for music. Nicknamed "Dodo" for his large head and mane of wavy, dark hair, he began classical piano studies at age 9. Teachers were amazed at his tireless practicing.

At 14 he met Errol Garner, another budding pianist. Errol introduced Dodo to jazz and by his late teens Marmarosa was playing in big-time swing orchestras.

Late one night after a gig, while waiting for a train in a Philadelphia subway station, Dodo and another musician were attacked by sailors. The beating put Dodo into a coma. His head injuries would affect him for the rest of his life.

In 1945 Dodo was out in L.A. working in the emerging Be-Bop scene. His playing was in top form and his behavior was increasingly strange. He disappeared before a show in Hollywood with Boyd Raeburn's band. The singer David Allyn found him two days later, ironing handkerchiefs in a Chinese laundry. Allyn tried to get Dodo to come with him but Marmarosa insisted on staying.

Some of Dodo's behavior was charmingly eccentric: painting his bathtub green to give his hours-long soaks a "Polynesian" feel. He was raptly fascinated with sounds: standing motionless, listening intently to church bells and fire sirens. To his friends, Dodo seemed harmless, just another absent-minded musician.

There was a darker side: fits of rage followed by sudden disappearances. He would be gone – for weeks or even months – living in transient hotels, picking up work in laundries, drifting and alone.

He moved back to Pittsburgh and tried to get his life together. he got married and had two daughters but his mental state remained fragile. Relocating back to L.A. in the mid-50s brought everything crashing down. The marriage split up, and in the midst of divorce proceedings, Dodo was drafted. Medically discharged after three months, he returned to the overly protective care of his family and became increasingly reclusive.

In 1962, during one of his final recording sessions, the other musicians found Dodo hunched silently over the piano, unable to work out the ending to their last song: "You're Driving Me Crazy." By the late 1960s, he no longer appeared in public.

He died in Pittsburgh, September 17, 2002, aged 76 years old.

THIRD of SIX LOST LINER NOTES

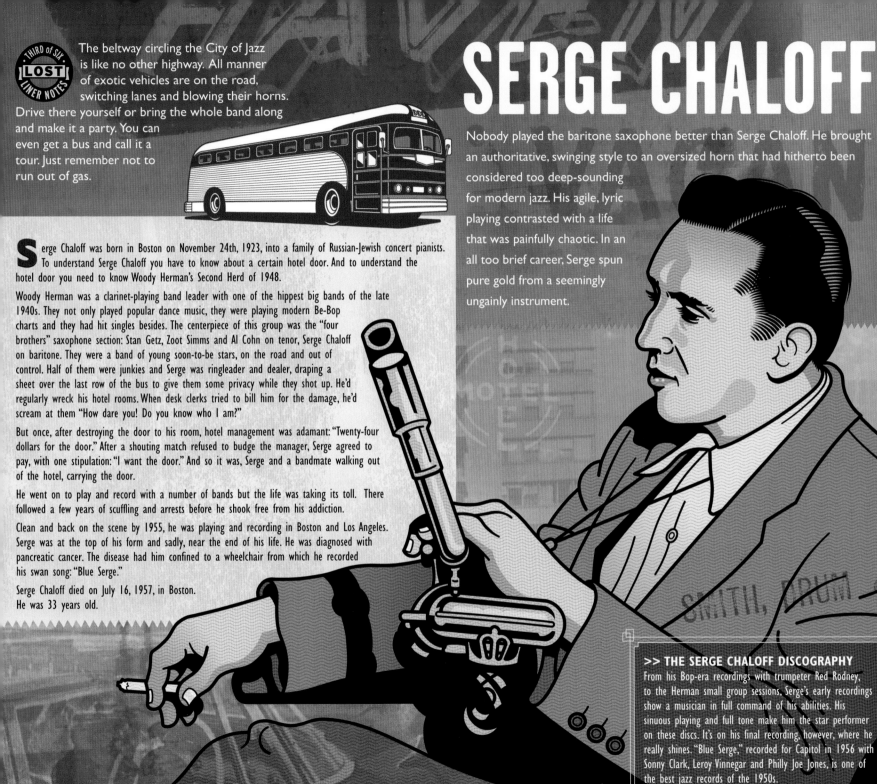

The beltway circling the City of Jazz is like no other highway. All manner of exotic vehicles are on the road, switching lanes and blowing their horns. Drive there yourself or bring the whole band along and make it a party. You can even get a bus and call it a tour. Just remember not to run out of gas.

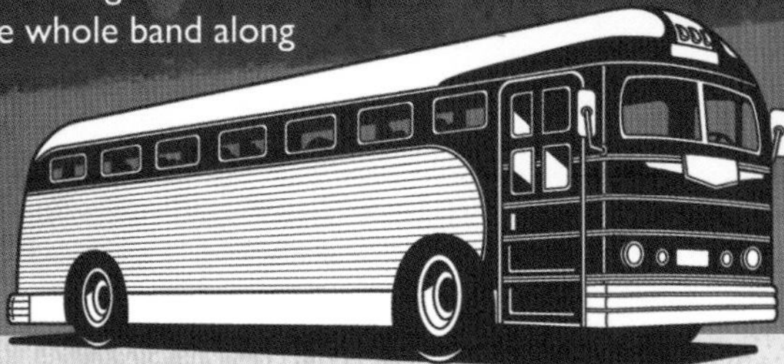

SERGE CHALOFF

Nobody played the baritone saxophone better than Serge Chaloff. He brought an authoritative, swinging style to an oversized horn that had hitherto been considered too deep-sounding for modern jazz. His agile, lyric playing contrasted with a life that was painfully chaotic. In an all too brief career, Serge spun pure gold from a seemingly ungainly instrument.

Serge Chaloff was born in Boston on November 24th, 1923, into a family of Russian-Jewish concert pianists. To understand Serge Chaloff you have to know about a certain hotel door. And to understand the hotel door you need to know Woody Herman's Second Herd of 1948.

Woody Herman was a clarinet-playing band leader with one of the hippest big bands of the late 1940s. They not only played popular dance music, they were playing modern Be-Bop charts and they had hit singles besides. The centerpiece of this group was the "four brothers" saxophone section: Stan Getz, Zoot Simms and Al Cohn on tenor, Serge Chaloff on baritone. They were a band of young soon-to-be stars, on the road and out of control. Half of them were junkies and Serge was ringleader and dealer, draping a sheet over the last row of the bus to give them some privacy while they shot up. He'd regularly wreck his hotel rooms. When desk clerks tried to bill him for the damage, he'd scream at them "How dare you! Do you know who I am?"

But once, after destroying the door to his room, hotel management was adamant: "Twenty-four dollars for the door." After a shouting match refused to budge the manager, Serge agreed to pay, with one stipulation: "I want the door." And so it was, Serge and a bandmate walking out of the hotel, carrying the door.

He went on to play and record with a number of bands but the life was taking its toll. There followed a few years of scuffling and arrests before he shook free from his addiction.

Clean and back on the scene by 1955, he was playing and recording in Boston and Los Angeles. Serge was at the top of his form and sadly, near the end of his life. He was diagnosed with pancreatic cancer. The disease had him confined to a wheelchair from which he recorded his swan song: "Blue Serge."

Serge Chaloff died on July 16, 1957, in Boston. He was 33 years old.

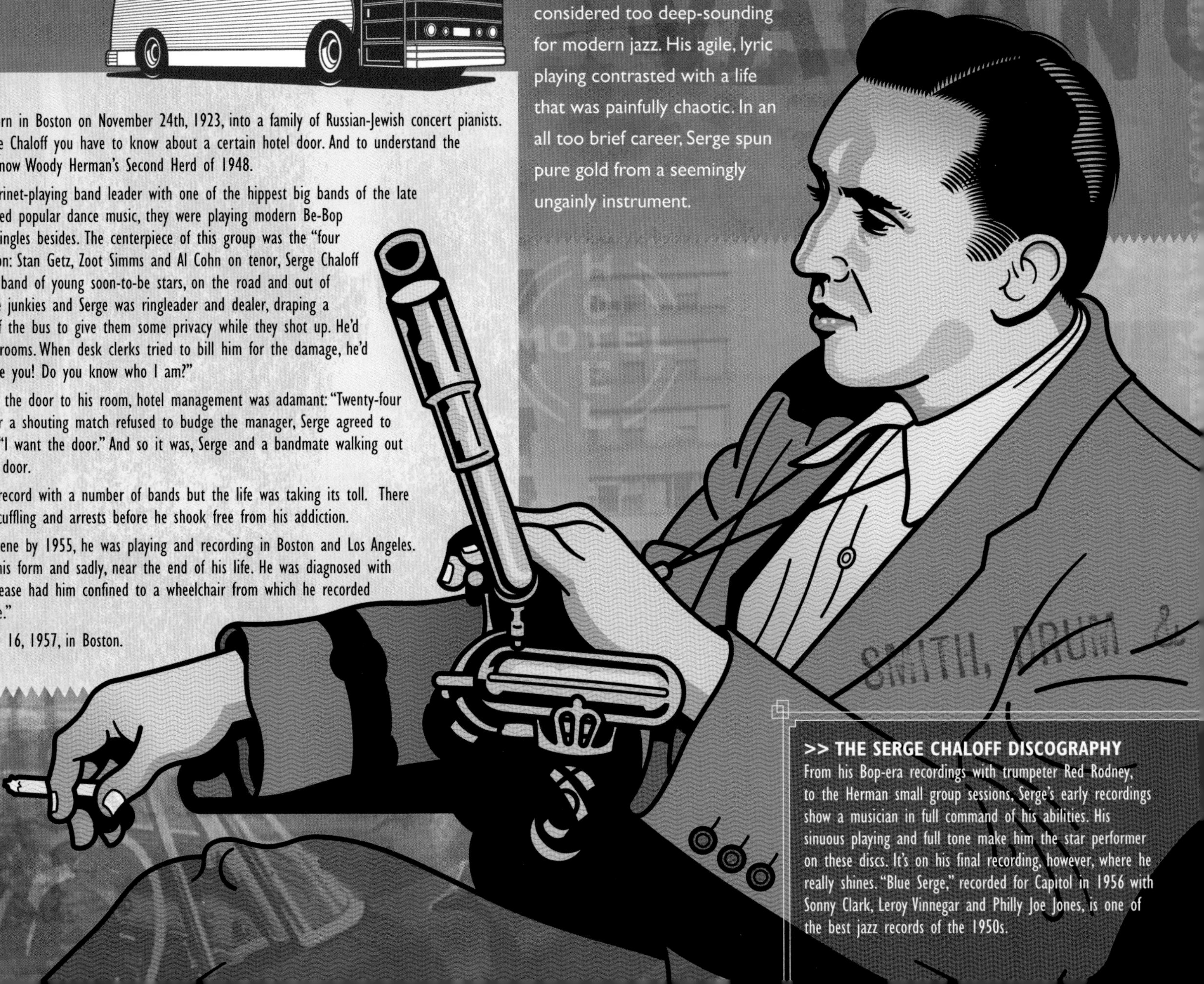
SMITH, DRUM &

>> THE SERGE CHALOFF DISCOGRAPHY

From his Bop-era recordings with trumpeter Red Rodney, to the Herman small group sessions, Serge's early recordings show a musician in full command of his abilities. His sinuous playing and full tone make him the star performer on these discs. It's on his final recording, however, where he really shines. "Blue Serge," recorded for Capitol in 1956 with Sonny Clark, Leroy Vinnegar and Philly Joe Jones, is one of the best jazz records of the 1950s.

DICK TWARDZIK

FOURTH of SIX LOST LINER NOTES

Above the City of Jazz, dark clouds are rolling in. The afternoon light dims to a greenish cast. Winds twirl across the sidewalk, lifting up every scrap of paper to dance in the downpour. Black droplets snap against the awning like drumsticks on a snare. You'll never get out of the storm. It's raining all over the world.

A prodigy on the piano with a taste for the avant-garde and a predilection for self destruction, Twardzik made an indelible impression on everyone who saw him. His abrupt career left behind just enough music to hint at his genius.

>> THE DICK TWARDZIK DISCOGRAPHY

He made only a handful of recordings, but they make a case for his enormous talent. Twardzik led a trio for a Pacific Jazz compilation. That and a handful of songs with assorted Boston lineups comprise all his U.S. recordings. He played on nine songs with the Chet Baker Quartet, later released by Barclay Disques.

Dick Twardzik was born in Boston, April 30, 1931. He began classical piano studies at a young age and soon detoured into jazz. His playing was a blend of Bud Powell's lightning-tempo Bop style and a modernist classical sensibility, along the lines of concert pianist Artur Rubenstein. He brought a dissonant rhythmic construction to his own compositions while investing standards with an echoing, haunted intonation. It was exhilarating and spooky music.

Already addicted to heroin by his late teens, Twardzik was part of the Boston jazz scene of the late 1940s. Dick loved playing high, and there were plenty of other like-minded individuals to jam with. He sat in with a local all-star band, backing up touring musicians like Charlie Parker. Twardzik was getting a reputation as a genius pianist but his habit was getting worse. By 1954 he was admitted to a clinic where he could be weaned off drugs. He swore he'd kill himself if he ever got addicted again. That was around the time he met Chet Baker.

Twardzik's drummer Peter Littman was working with Baker and Chet was impressed by Twardzik's playing. They hit it off immediately, first with music and then drugs. By the time a European tour was announced two months later, they were all using.

Based in Paris, the Chet Baker Quartet began a series of eagerly anticipated shows. Their sound was a spectral, chamber jazz, far from the romantic strains of "My Funny Valentine."

Baker found something in Twardzik's playing that allowed him to leave his "California lightweight" reputation behind. The new sound was about as far from sunny L.A. as you could get. As it happens, they were getting high together too.

They were also recording an album. Booked into the Pathe Studios on rue Magellan, the band was recording in between concert performances. On the morning of October 21, when the musicians gathered at the studio, Twardzik was absent. They'd been at a jam session the night before, with Dick sitting in, a red fez on his head, nodding over the keys. The door of the hotel Madeleine was locked from the inside. When they broke it down, they found him lying there, needle still in his arm. Dick Twardzik was 24 years old.

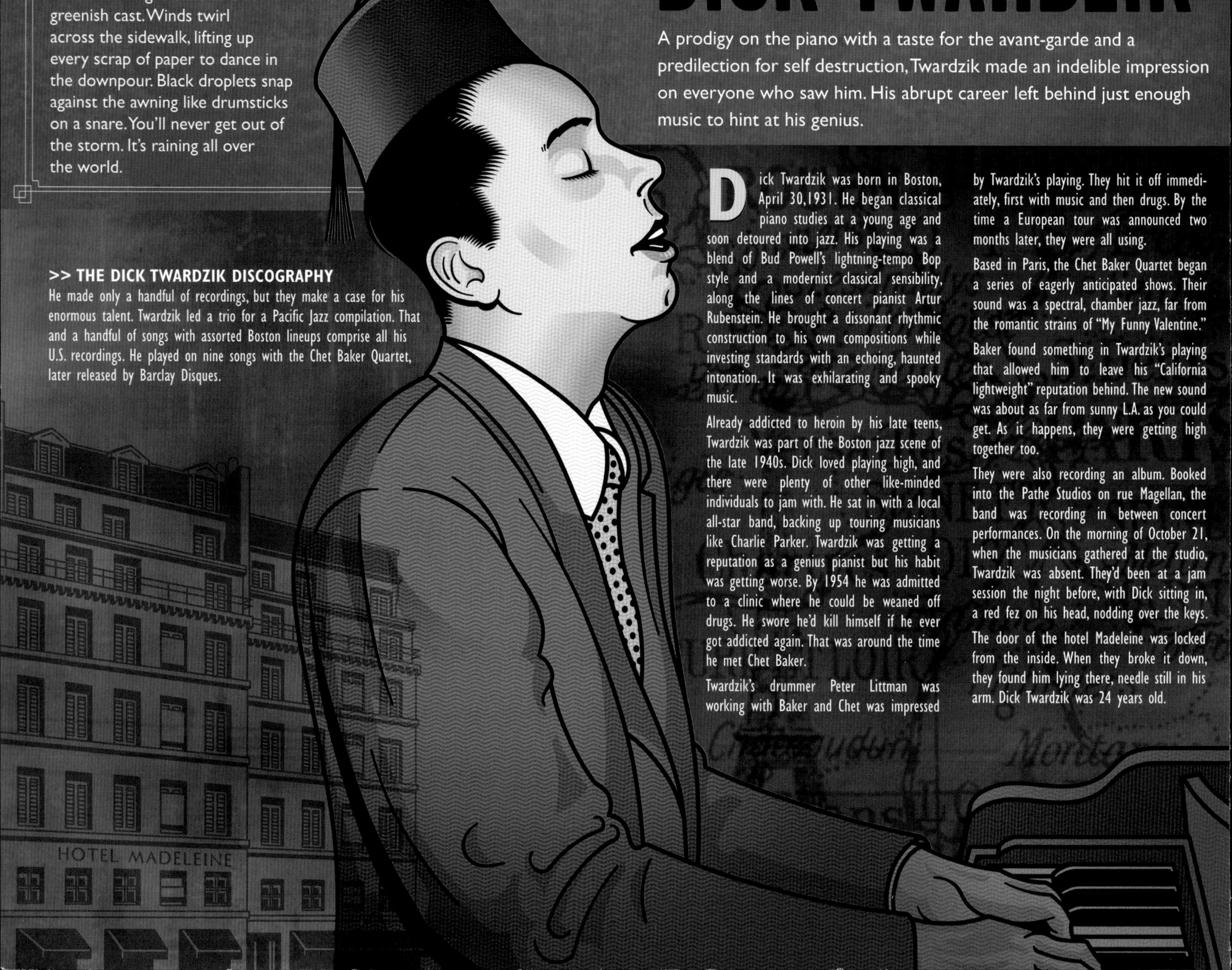
HOTEL MADELEINE

WARDELL GRAY

The light-as-a-feather tenor with a slyly languorous delivery, Wardell Gray had an insistently swinging sound that was a favorite on the Central Avenue jazz scene in post-war Los Angeles. His mysterious death cut down one of the great musical talents of that generation.

FIFTH of SIX LOST LINER NOTES

Far beyond the neon glow of the strip, darkness hangs over the desert landscape. Up ahead, the rumble of an idling automobile engine struggles over the breeze. A car door slams and tires spit gravel against the soft highway shoulder. Red taillights shimmer down the rolling strip of blacktop: a one-way trip out of the City of Jazz.

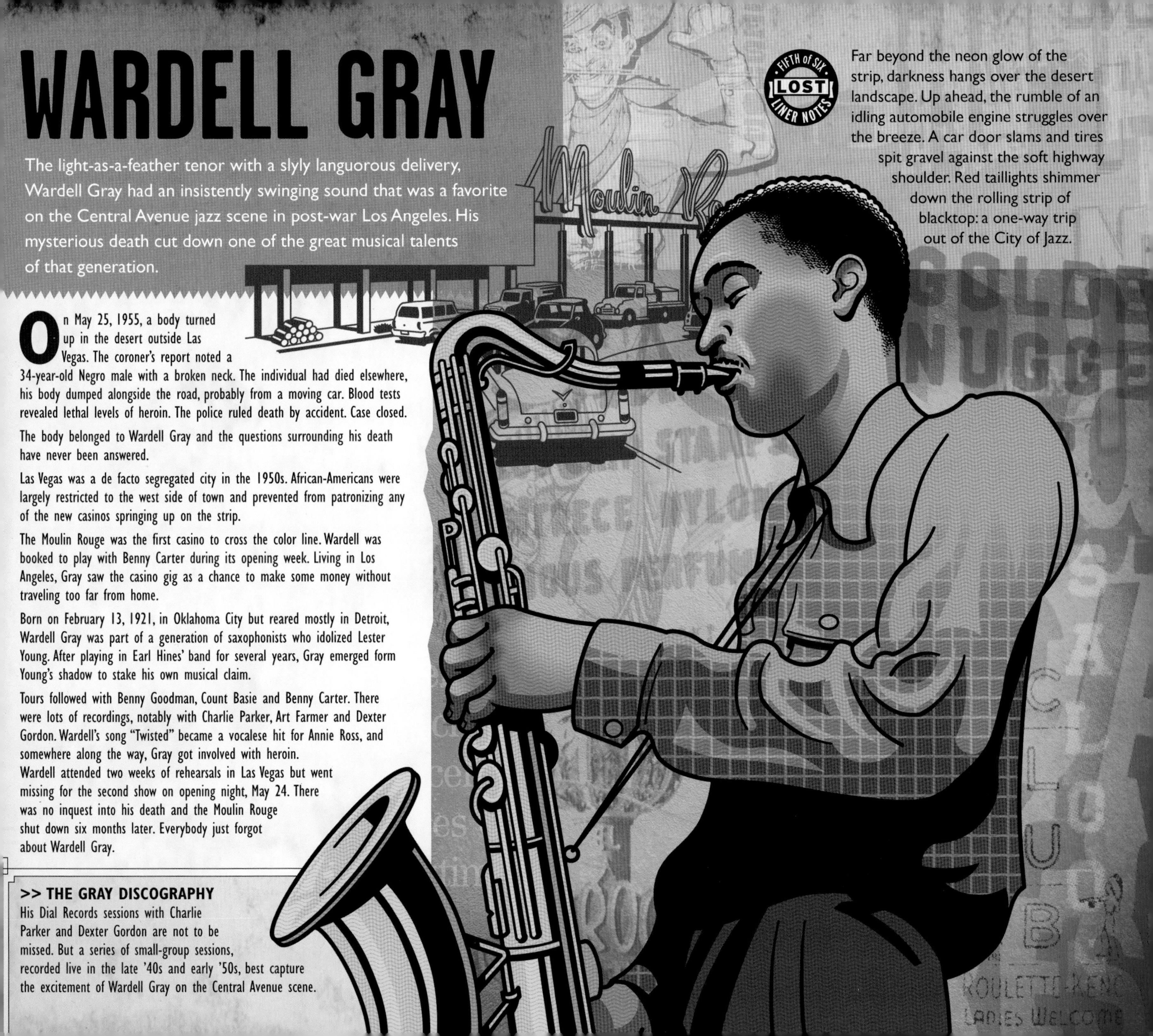
ROULETTE-KENO
LADIES WELCOME

On May 25, 1955, a body turned up in the desert outside Las Vegas. The coroner's report noted a 34-year-old Negro male with a broken neck. The individual had died elsewhere, his body dumped alongside the road, probably from a moving car. Blood tests revealed lethal levels of heroin. The police ruled death by accident. Case closed.

The body belonged to Wardell Gray and the questions surrounding his death have never been answered.

Las Vegas was a de facto segregated city in the 1950s. African-Americans were largely restricted to the west side of town and prevented from patronizing any of the new casinos springing up on the strip.

The Moulin Rouge was the first casino to cross the color line. Wardell was booked to play with Benny Carter during its opening week. Living in Los Angeles, Gray saw the casino gig as a chance to make some money without traveling too far from home.

Born on February 13, 1921, in Oklahoma City but reared mostly in Detroit, Wardell Gray was part of a generation of saxophonists who idolized Lester Young. After playing in Earl Hines' band for several years, Gray emerged form Young's shadow to stake his own musical claim.

Tours followed with Benny Goodman, Count Basie and Benny Carter. There were lots of recordings, notably with Charlie Parker, Art Farmer and Dexter Gordon. Wardell's song "Twisted" became a vocalese hit for Annie Ross, and somewhere along the way, Gray got involved with heroin.
Wardell attended two weeks of rehearsals in Las Vegas but went missing for the second show on opening night, May 24. There was no inquest into his death and the Moulin Rouge shut down six months later. Everybody just forgot about Wardell Gray.

>> THE GRAY DISCOGRAPHY

His Dial Records sessions with Charlie Parker and Dexter Gordon are not to be missed. But a series of small-group sessions, recorded live in the late '40s and early '50s, best capture the excitement of Wardell Gray on the Central Avenue scene.

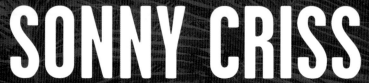

SONNY CRISS

He was a saxophonist who played most of his career in the shadows. Sonny Criss had an intensely passionate sound that made him one of the top altos in the Bop and Hard-Bop eras. He was a singular talent on the scene, an original voice with a soulfully fluid style. And for a whole lot of reasons hardly anyone knew who he was.

In the geography of jazz, the name William "Sonny" Criss is indelibly linked to the city of Los Angeles: the place that ignored him and the place he couldn't give up. He moved there in 1943, a 15-year-old from Memphis, Tennessee, musically inclined and hungry to discover more. He found it in L.A., playing jazz in his high school band. A taciturn young man, Criss preferred to speak through his horn; his fellow musicians liked what he had to say. They were a restless bunch, eager to develop their music. With a war on, there was lots of money floating around the Central Avenue scene and that meant lots of entertainment for anyone looking for diversion. The clubs were packed and the crowds wanted big-band dance music. Because of the draft, many of the regular musicians had been called up. Desperate club owners began hiring teenagers out of the ranks of local high school bands. Charles Mingus, Hampton Hawes, Dexter Gordon and Sonny Criss were all in that group of young players.

At the same time, the Be-Bop movement was being born in New York. Spearheaded by Dizzy Gillespie and Charlie Parker, the new sound polarized the jazz world. Getting the chance to play with Bird on his first West Coast appearances in 1945 would set Sonny's music on a course that ran to the end of his life.

L.A.'s vibrant music scene would soon dry up. By the early 1950s, the Central Avenue clubs were gone, victims of urban decay and police harassment. Suddenly everybody was looking for work. By the mid-'50s Criss was reduced to playing music in strip clubs to earn a living. He continued to record great records but people weren't interested in Be-Bop anymore. The West Coast Cool sound was the only game in town. His career fell by the wayside.

By the early 1960s, Criss left L.A. for Europe hoping to change his luck. He was warmly received by European jazz audiences. Returning to the U.S. in 1965 he recorded a series of beautifully played records. Sadly, the attention of the audience was elsewhere. Sonny's career once again floundered. It was back to L.A., broke and drinking heavily. Following a breakdown he turned his life back around yet again. He led a jazz performance and lecture series in L.A. schools; a return tour of Europe was a big success and he planned a tour of Japan.

On November 19, 1977, Sonny Criss shot himself to death at his Los Angeles home. His mother Lucy later revealed to surprised friends that Sonny had long been suffering from stomach cancer. He'd held on as long as he could, carrying his pain in silence, preferring to speak through his horn. He was 50 years old.

>> THE SONNY CRISS DISCOGRAPHY

The records he cut for the Prestige label in the mid-'60s feature some of his most emotive playing applied to an unexpected selection of songs. Not only does he show off the great skill he had with lightning-fast Be-Bop standards, he covered corny pop songs like "Up, Up and Away" and "Sunrise, Sunset," investing them with his luminous style.

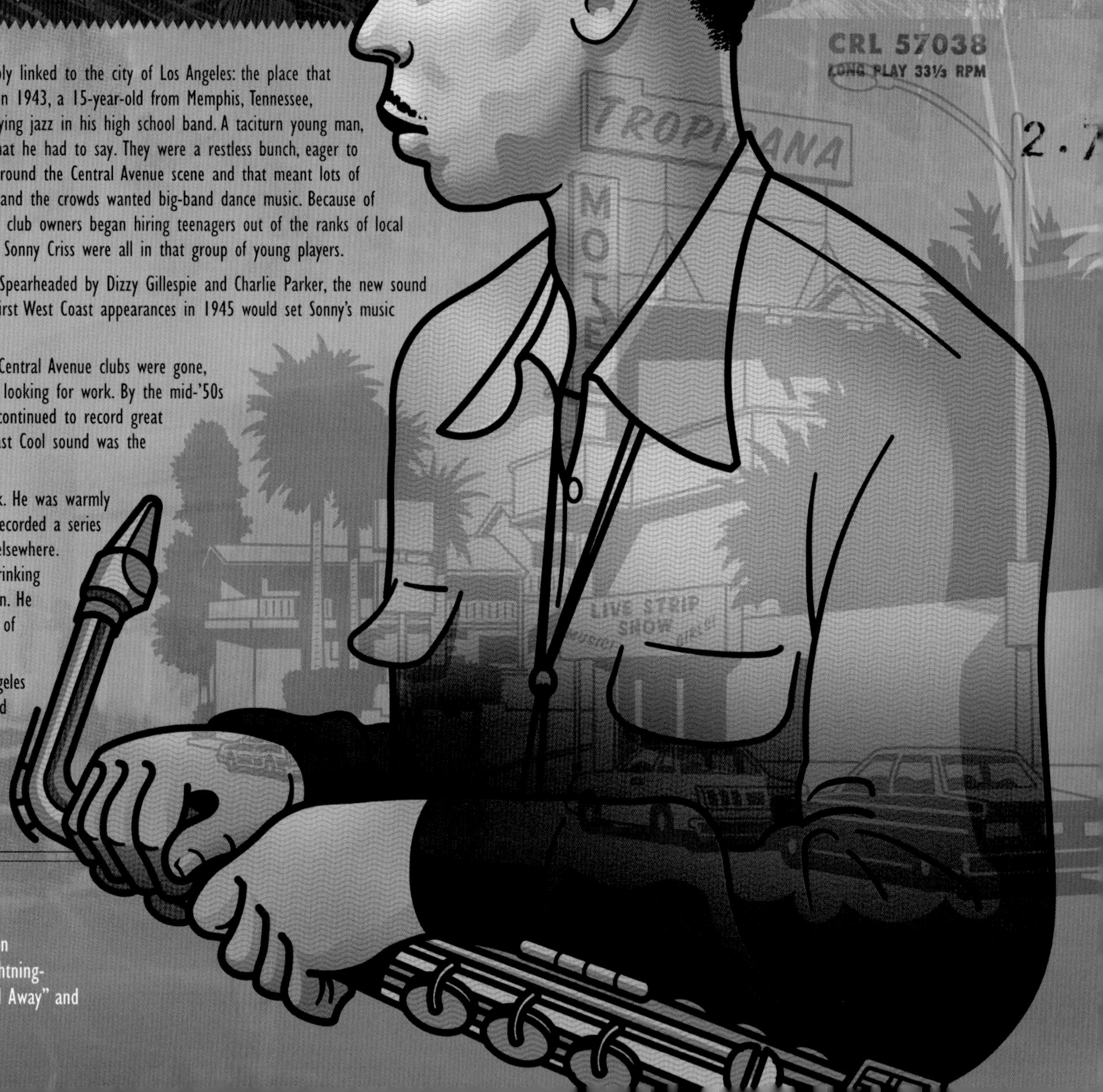
CRL 57038
LONG PLAY 33⅓ RPM
LIVE STRIP SHOW

LAST of SIX LOST LINER NOTES

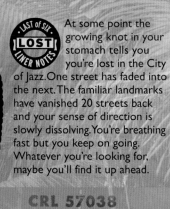

At some point the growing knot in your stomach tells you you're lost in the City of Jazz. One street has faded into the next. The familiar landmarks have vanished 20 streets back and your sense of direction is slowly dissolving. You're breathing fast but you keep on going. Whatever you're looking for, maybe you'll find it up ahead.

I BUILT YOU FIRST

Story: C.P. FREUND
Art: PETER and MARIA HOEY

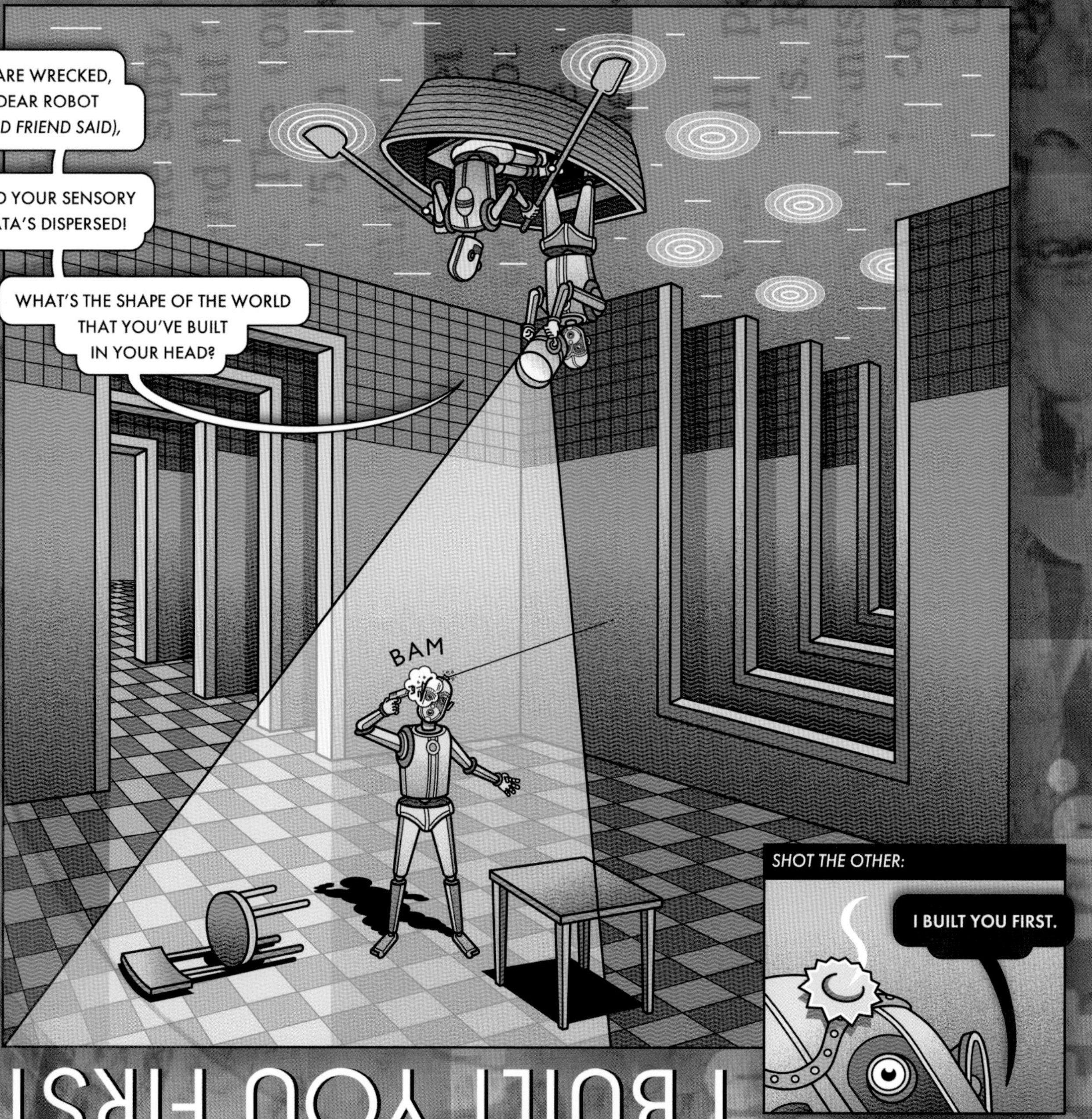

I BUILT YOU FIRST

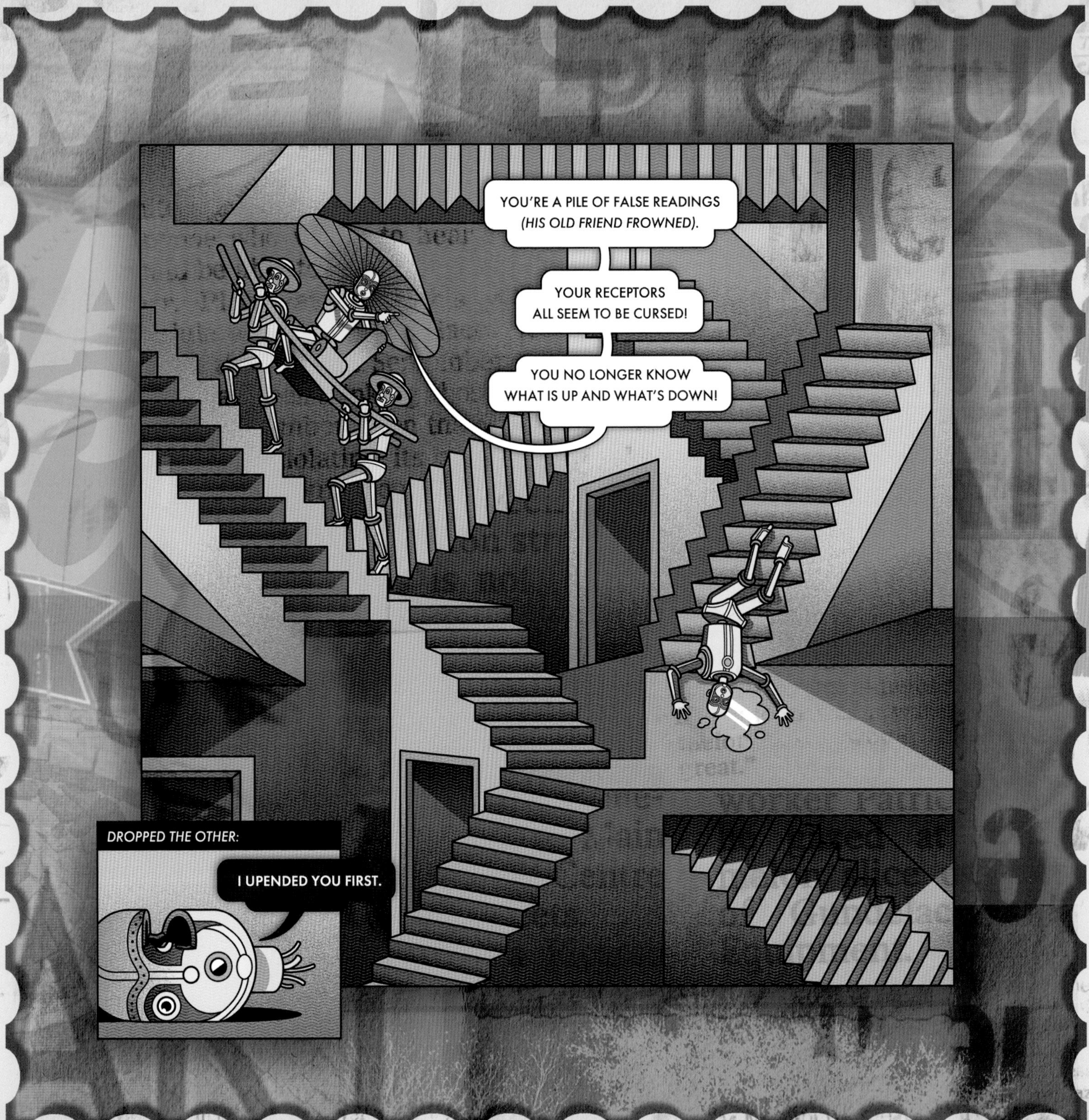
YOU'RE A PILE OF FALSE READINGS (HIS OLD FRIEND FROWNED).
YOUR RECEPTORS ALL SEEM TO BE CURSED!
YOU NO LONGER KNOW WHAT IS UP AND WHAT'S DOWN!
DROPPED THE OTHER:
I UPENDED YOU FIRST.

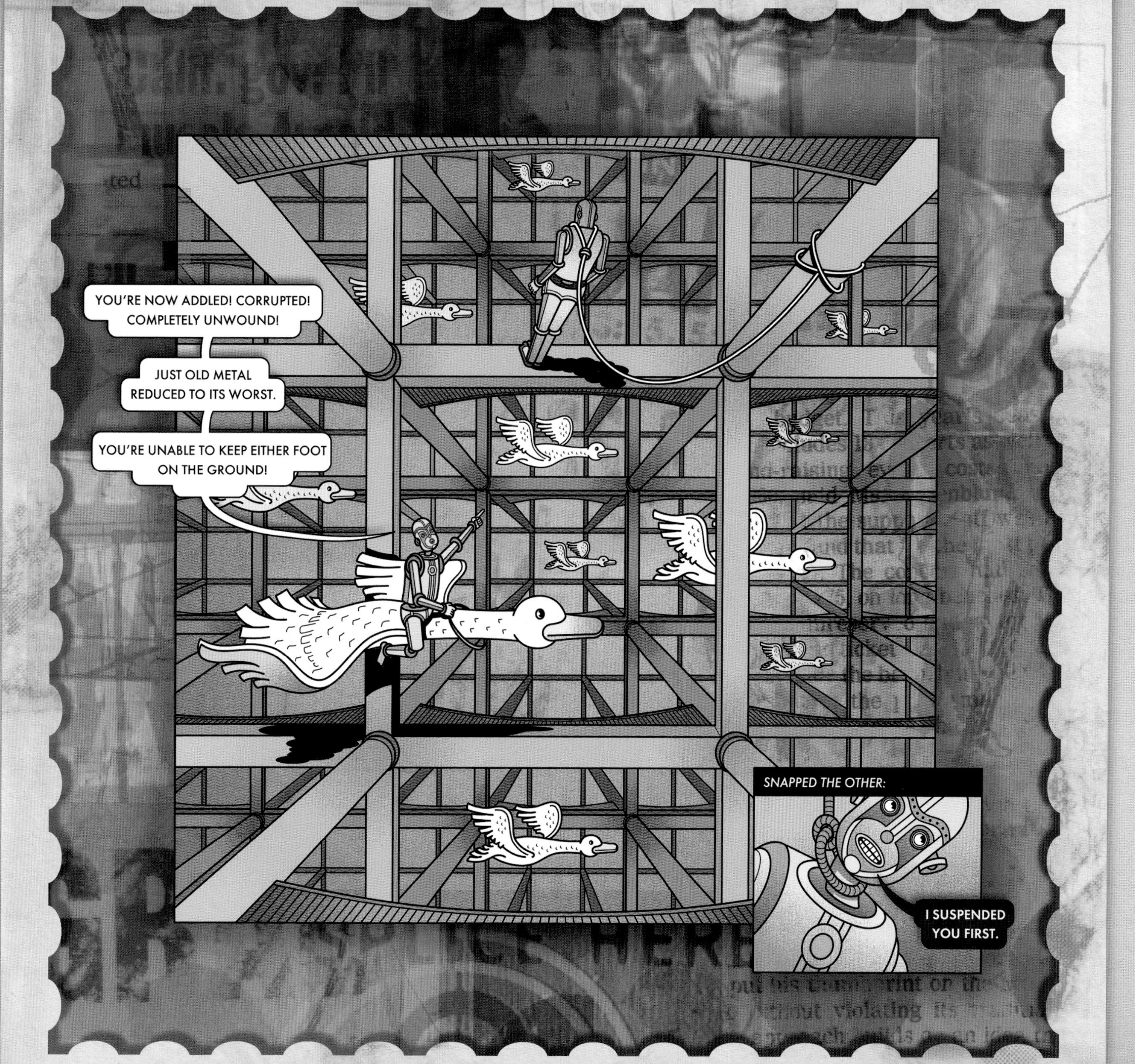
YOU'RE NOW ADDLED! CORRUPTED! COMPLETELY UNWOUND!
JUST OLD METAL REDUCED TO ITS WORST.
YOU'RE UNABLE TO KEEP EITHER FOOT ON THE GROUND!
SNAPPED THE OTHER:
I SUSPENDED YOU FIRST.

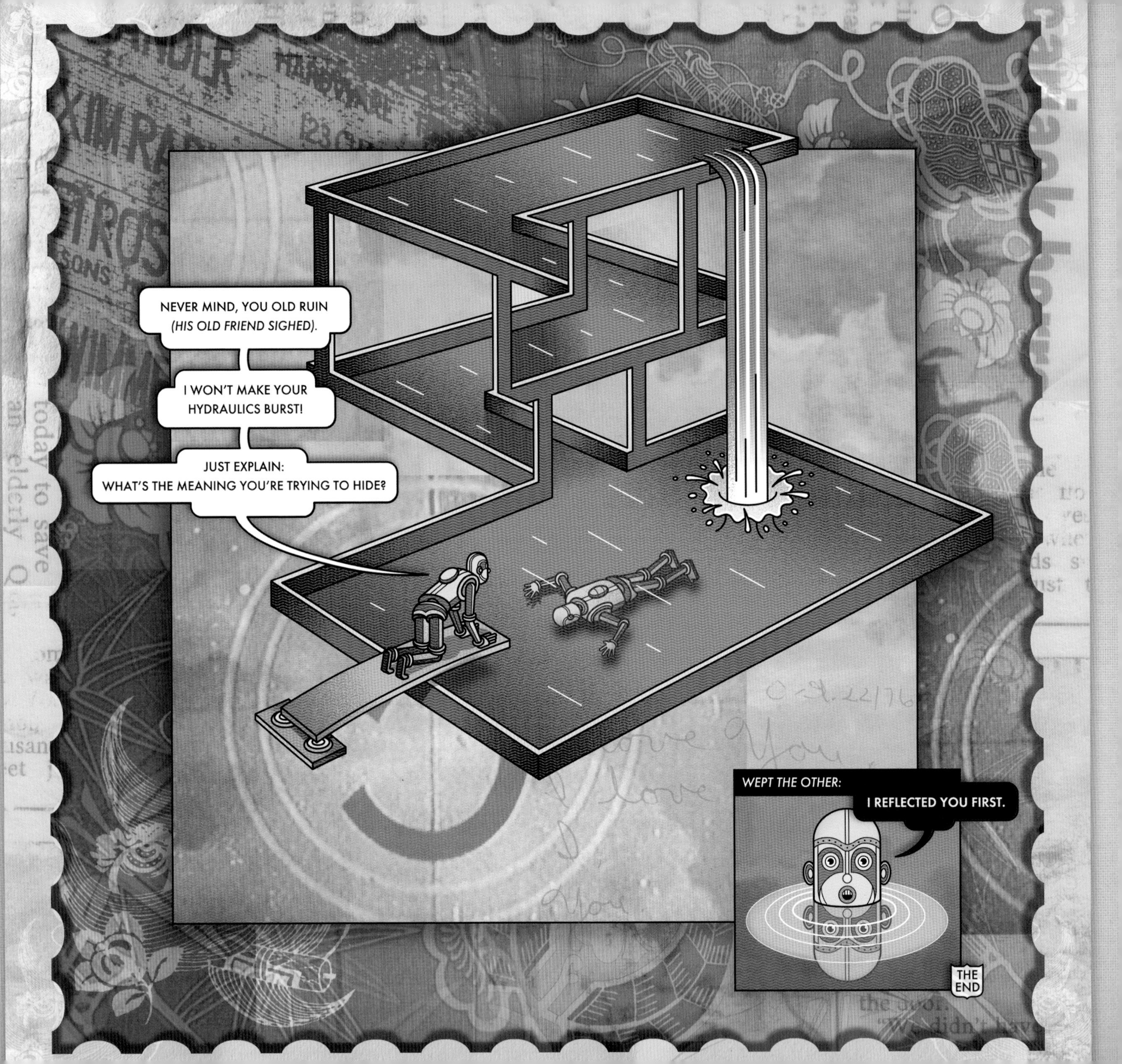
NEVER MIND, YOU OLD RUIN (HIS OLD FRIEND SIGHED).
I WON'T MAKE YOUR HYDRAULICS BURST!
JUST EXPLAIN: WHAT'S THE MEANING YOU'RE TRYING TO HIDE?
WEPT THE OTHER:
I REFLECTED YOU FIRST.
THE END

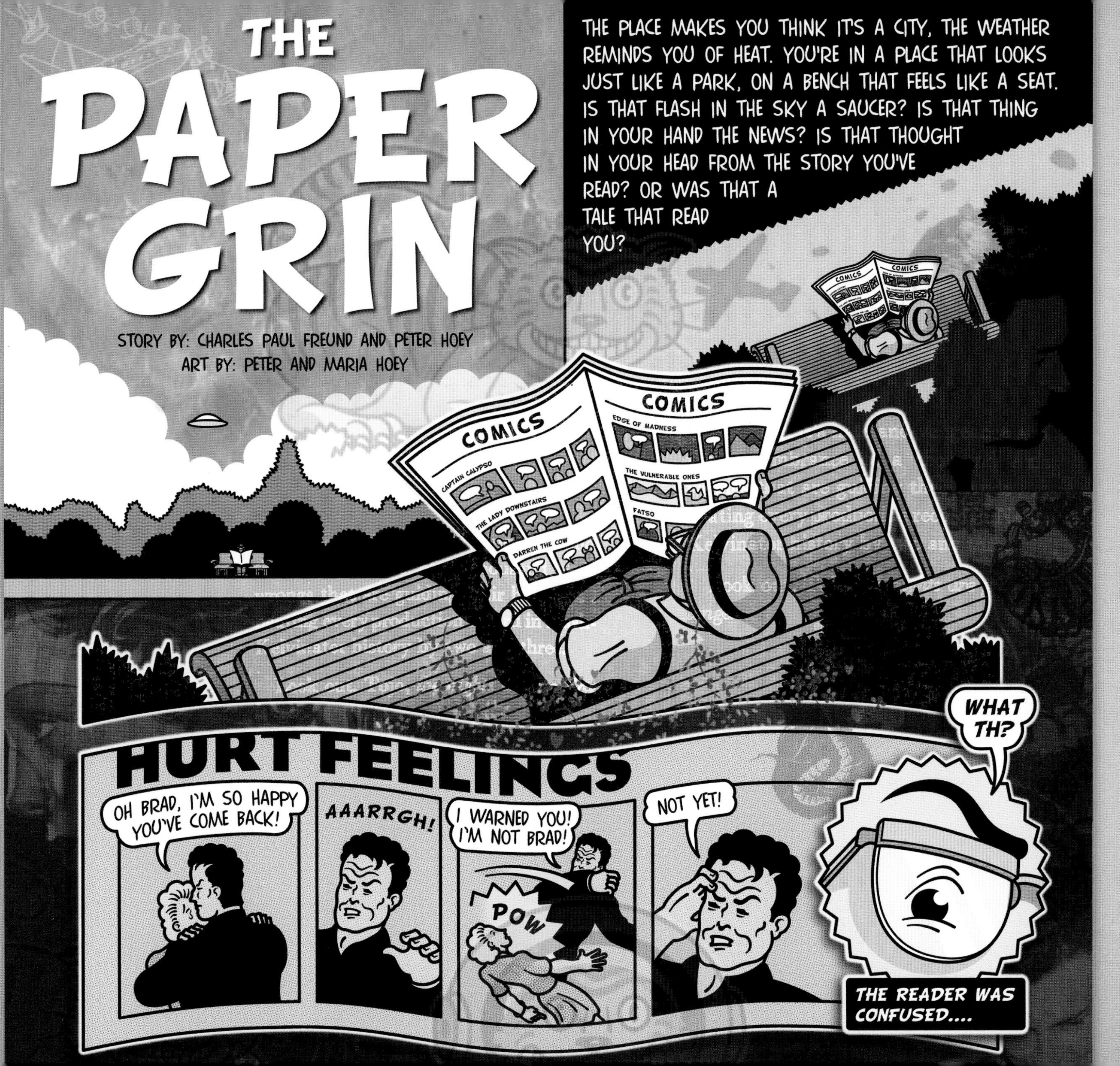
THE PAPER GRIN
STORY BY: CHARLES PAUL FREUND AND PETER HOEY
ART BY: PETER AND MARIA HOEY
THE PLACE MAKES YOU THINK IT'S A CITY, THE WEATHER REMINDS YOU OF HEAT. YOU'RE IN A PLACE THAT LOOKS JUST LIKE A PARK, ON A BENCH THAT FEELS LIKE A SEAT. IS THAT FLASH IN THE SKY A SAUCER? IS THAT THING IN YOUR HAND THE NEWS? IS THAT THOUGHT IN YOUR HEAD FROM THE STORY YOU'VE READ? OR WAS THAT A TALE THAT READ YOU?
COMICS
CAPTAIN CALYPSO
THE LADY DOWNSTAIRS
DARREN THE COW
COMICS
EDGE OF MADNESS
THE VULNERABLE ONES
FATSO
HURT FEELINGS
OH BRAD, I'M SO HAPPY YOU'VE COME BACK!
AAARRGH!
I WARNED YOU! I'M NOT BRAD!
POW
NOT YET!
WHAT TH?
THE READER WAS CONFUSED....

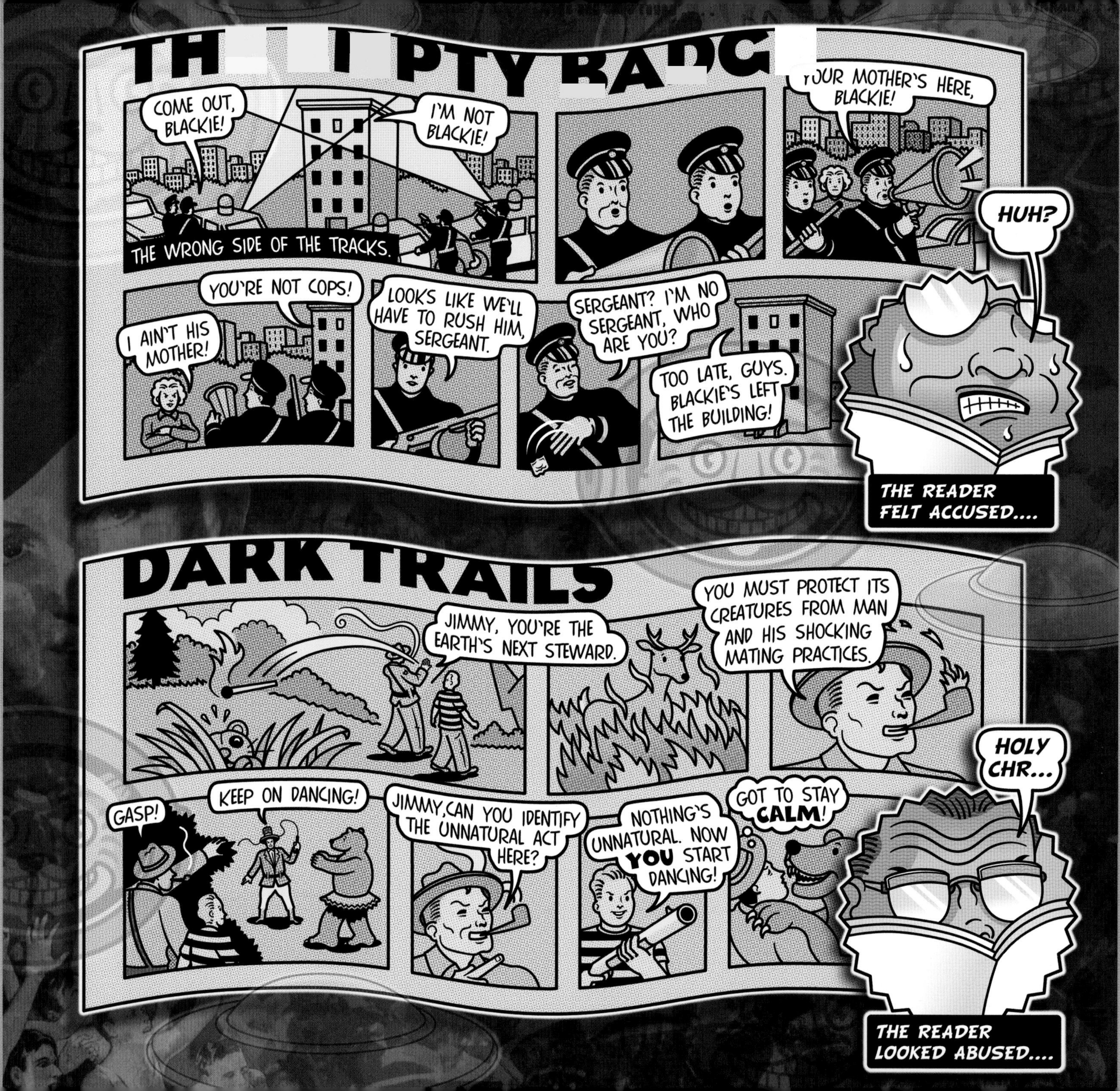

COME OUT, BLACKIE!
I'M NOT BLACKIE!
THE WRONG SIDE OF THE TRACKS.
YOUR MOTHER'S HERE, BLACKIE!
HUH?
YOU'RE NOT COPS!
I AIN'T HIS MOTHER!
LOOKS LIKE WE'LL HAVE TO RUSH HIM, SERGEANT.
SERGEANT? I'M NO SERGEANT, WHO ARE YOU?
TOO LATE, GUYS. BLACKIE'S LEFT THE BUILDING!
THE READER FELT ACCUSED....
DARK TRAILS
JIMMY, YOU'RE THE EARTH'S NEXT STEWARD.
YOU MUST PROTECT ITS CREATURES FROM MAN AND HIS SHOCKING MATING PRACTICES.
HOLY CHR...
GASP!
KEEP ON DANCING!
JIMMY, CAN YOU IDENTIFY THE UNNATURAL ACT HERE?
NOTHING'S UNNATURAL. NOW YOU START DANCING!
GOT TO STAY CALM!
THE READER LOOKED ABUSED....

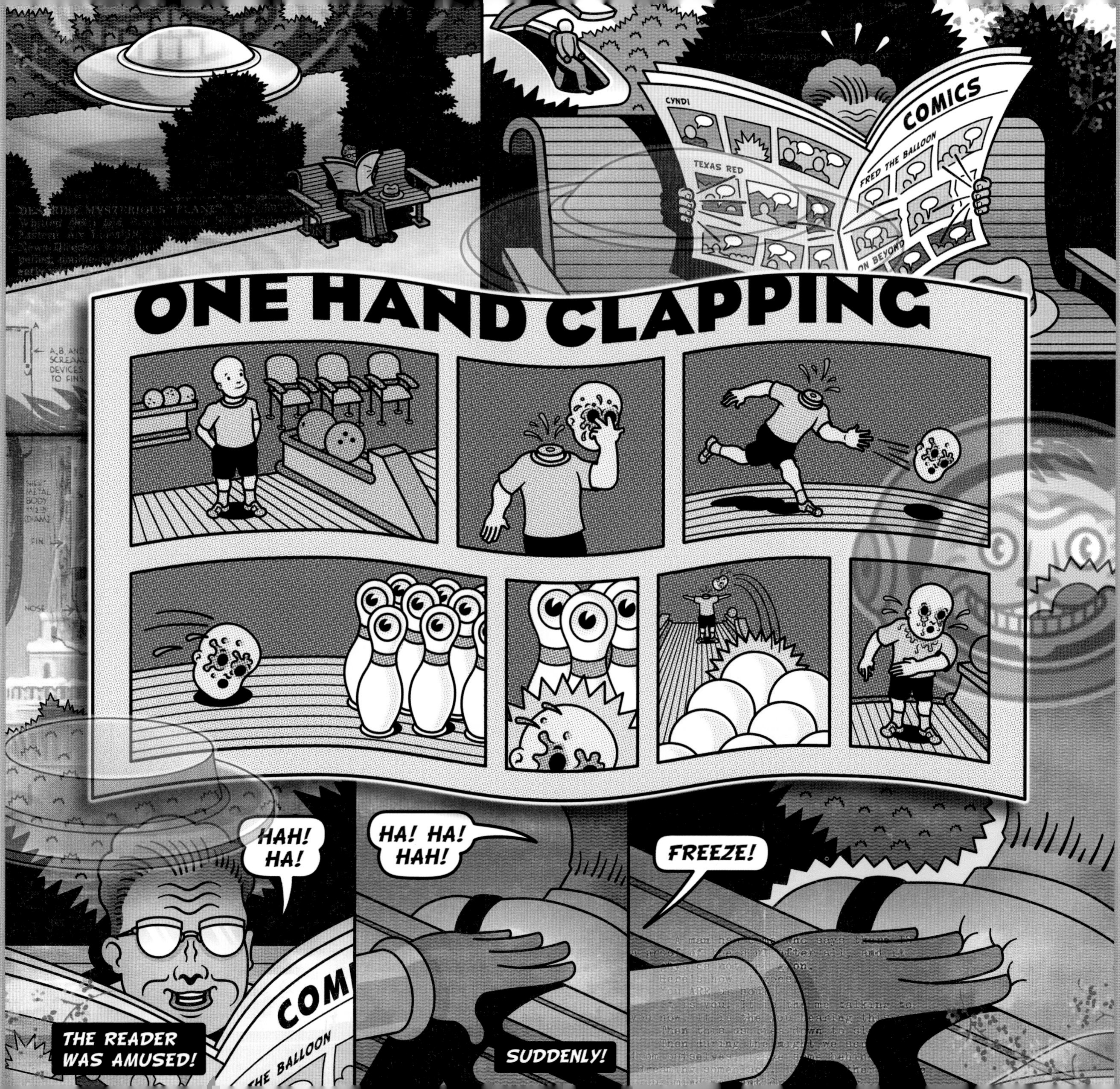
COMICS
CYNDI
TEXAS RED
FRED THE BALLOON
ON BEYOND
ONE HAND CLAPPING
HAH! HA!
THE READER WAS AMUSED!
HA! HA! HAH!
SUDDENLY!
FREEZE!

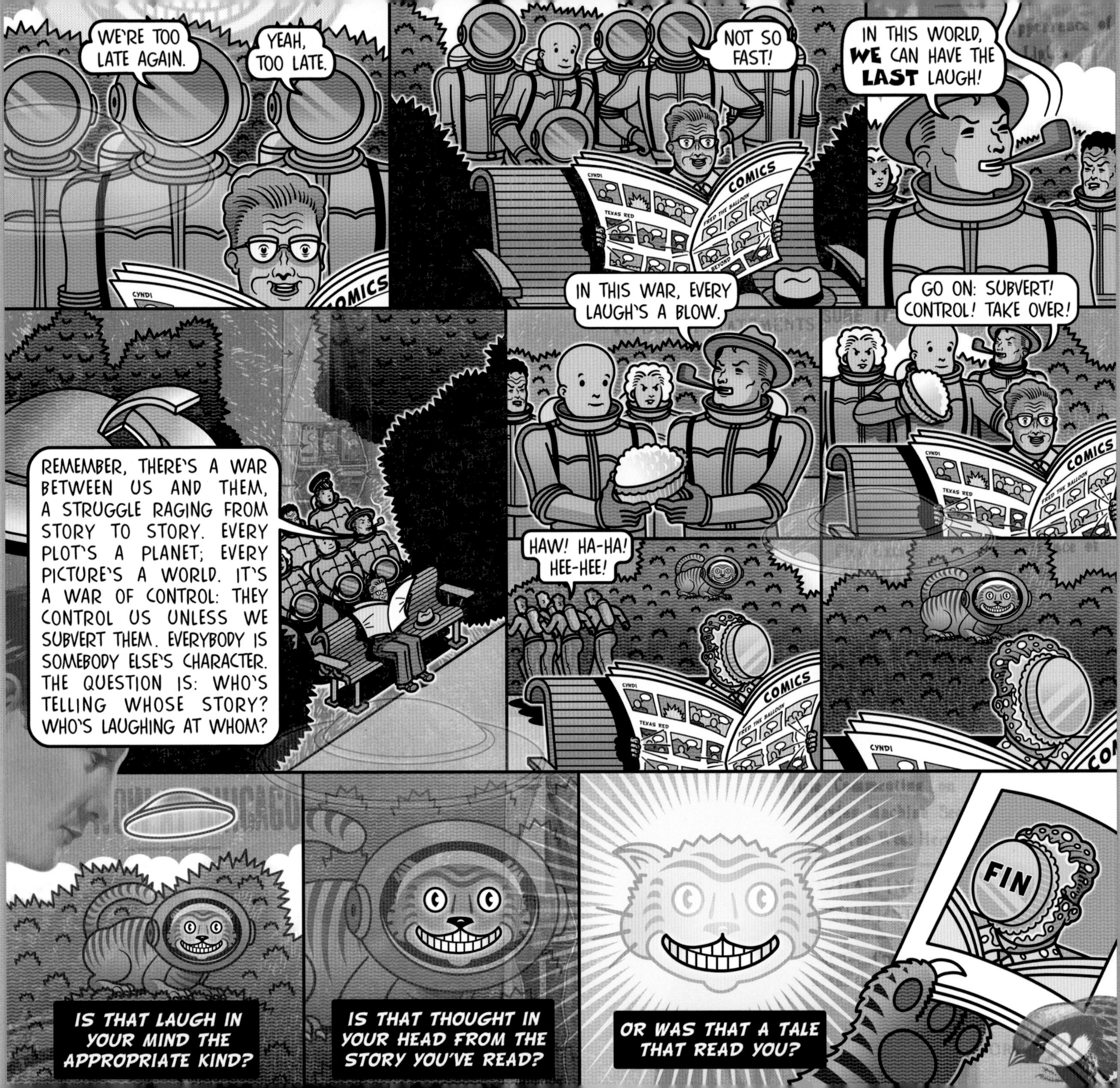
WE'RE TOO LATE AGAIN.
YEAH, TOO LATE.
NOT SO FAST!
IN THIS WORLD, WE CAN HAVE THE LAST LAUGH!
REMEMBER, THERE'S A WAR BETWEEN US AND THEM, A STRUGGLE RAGING FROM STORY TO STORY. EVERY PLOT'S A PLANET; EVERY PICTURE'S A WORLD. IT'S A WAR OF CONTROL: THEY CONTROL US UNLESS WE SUBVERT THEM. EVERYBODY IS SOMEBODY ELSE'S CHARACTER. THE QUESTION IS: WHO'S TELLING WHOSE STORY? WHO'S LAUGHING AT WHOM?
IN THIS WAR, EVERY LAUGH'S A BLOW.
GO ON: SUBVERT! CONTROL! TAKE OVER!
HAW! HA-HA! HEE-HEE!
IS THAT LAUGH IN YOUR MIND THE APPROPRIATE KIND?
IS THAT THOUGHT IN YOUR HEAD FROM THE STORY YOU'VE READ?
OR WAS THAT A TALE THAT READ YOU?
FIN

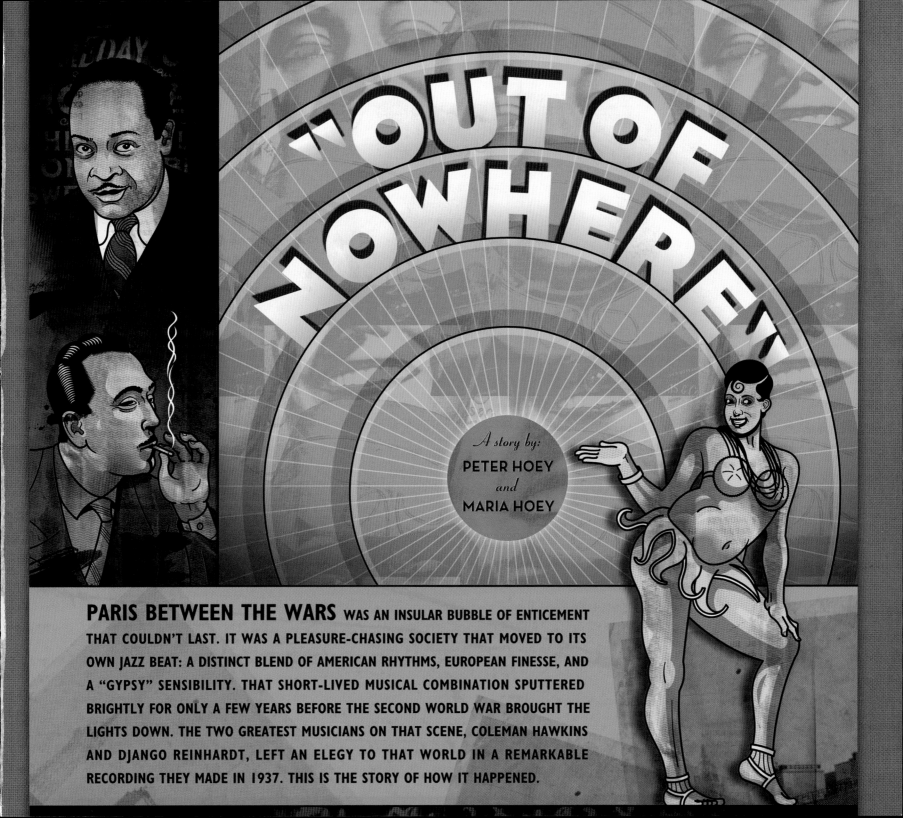

"OUT OF NOWHERE"

A story by:

PETER HOEY

and

MARIA HOEY

PARIS BETWEEN THE WARS WAS AN INSULAR BUBBLE OF ENTICEMENT THAT COULDN'T LAST. IT WAS A PLEASURE-CHASING SOCIETY THAT MOVED TO ITS OWN JAZZ BEAT: A DISTINCT BLEND OF AMERICAN RHYTHMS, EUROPEAN FINESSE, AND A "GYPSY" SENSIBILITY. THAT SHORT-LIVED MUSICAL COMBINATION SPUTTERED BRIGHTLY FOR ONLY A FEW YEARS BEFORE THE SECOND WORLD WAR BROUGHT THE LIGHTS DOWN. THE TWO GREATEST MUSICIANS ON THAT SCENE, COLEMAN HAWKINS AND DJANGO REINHARDT, LEFT AN ELEGY TO THAT WORLD IN A REMARKABLE RECORDING THEY MADE IN 1937. THIS IS THE STORY OF HOW IT HAPPENED.

COLEMAN HAWKINS

HE LATCHED ONTO MUSIC EARLY. Born in St. Louis, Missouri, in 1904, Coleman started on piano lessons at five. By nine he had already switched to the cello and from there to a relatively unpopular instrument, the saxophone.

In the early twentieth century, the saxophone was still considered a lowbrow musical instrument. Invented in 1846 as a more portable replacement for the oboes and bassoons in marching bands, this reed instrument had descended to working-class music halls, its braying honks used for sound effects in vaudeville acts. Coleman Hawkins would change all that, making the saxophone a central instrument in jazz.

Having started to play professionally at the age of 12, by his late teens Hawkins signed with Mamie Smith and her Jazz Hounds in Kansas City. In 1923 he recorded with Fletcher Henderson in New York. When Henderson formed an orchestra the following year, he tapped Coleman Hawkins to be his star tenor. Coleman was now playing with the premier talent of his day and the competition pushed him to innovate. He quickly progressed to his signature sound: a bold style that drew on an encyclopedic knowledge of harmonies and chord changes, played with a modern improvisational perspective.

Everybody took notice of the star saxophonist with his stylish clothes and late-model sedans. Wearing a permanent look of detached amusement, the barrel-chested Hawkins carried himself with a confident swagger. Taciturn by nature and fiercely competitive, he would drop in to jam with rival tenors, overwhelming them with chorus after chorus until he stood alone on stage.

By 1934 Coleman Hawkins had bested all the competition. Such was his virtuosity on the tenor saxophone that no one could play a phrase that wasn't indebted to his sound. However, the continuing lack of recording success for the Henderson orchestra left him frustrated and itching to step out on his own. He ended up stepping out much further than anyone expected: Through his agent in New York he signed on to the London-based Jack Hylton Orchestra and set sail immediately for Europe.

If the European musical competition wasn't very challenging, the cultural context broadened his outlook. Hawkins acquired a refinement he would maintain for the rest of his life. After a year, he left the Hylton orchestra and began freelancing on the continent. Based first in Belgium and later in the Netherlands, he criss-crossed Western Europe, playing with various bands. His appearance on the bill would pull in enthusiastic crowds, putting him very much in demand with music promoters. It was around this time that he first heard Django Reinhardt.

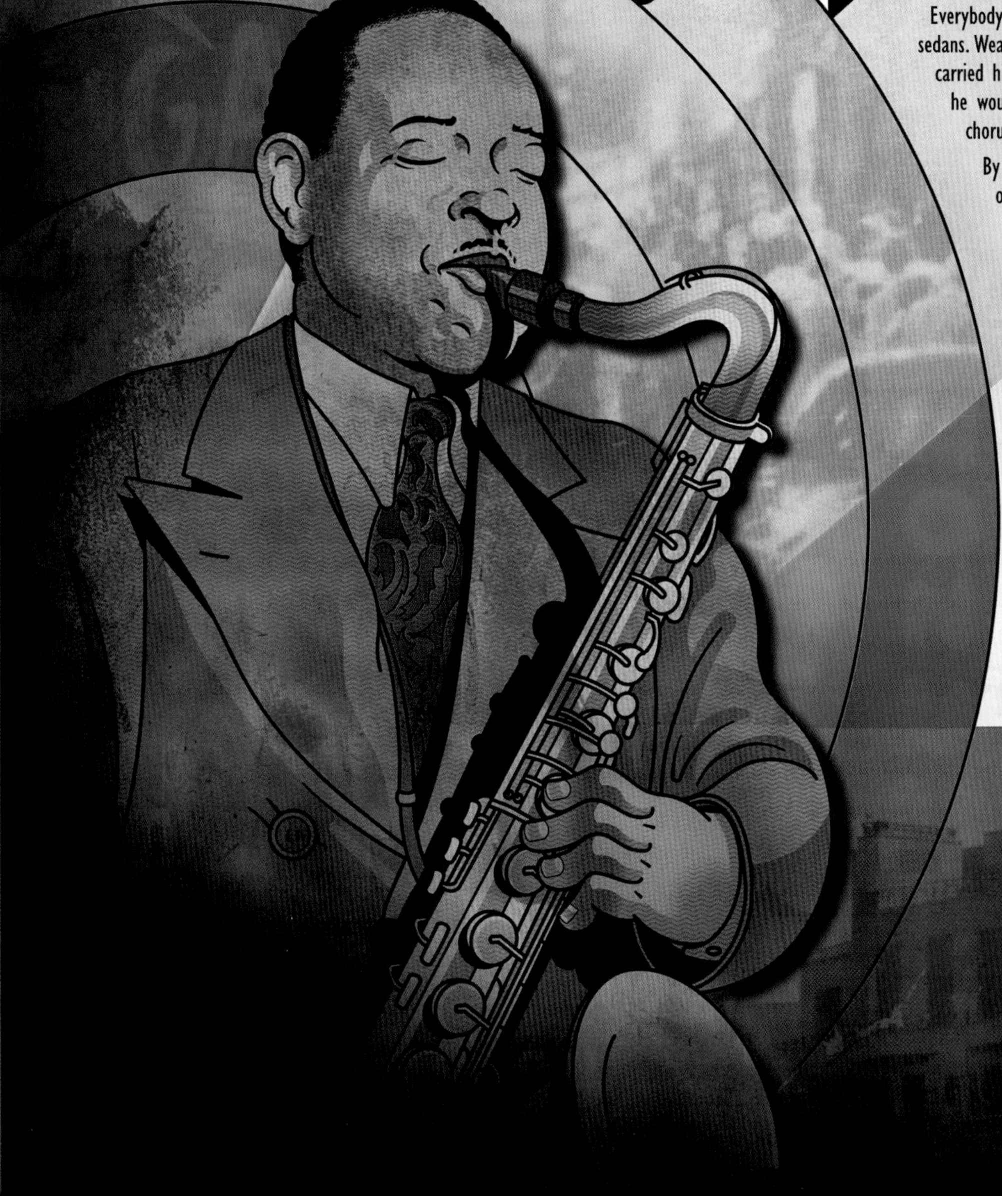

BROTHER, CAN YOU SPARE A FRANC?

The American stock market collapse of 1929 threw the United States and much of the world into an economic depression. France, however, with its high tariffs and still-intact colonies, was relatively immune to the global downturn. The nightclubs of Paris were booming and American hot jazz was all the rage. Starting as a trickle in the 1920s and accelerating as the Depression ground on through the '30s, black American musicians began showing up in France, playing the fancy nightclubs and gritty *bal-musettes* alike. They were playing jazz alongside another group of outsiders: the Manouches, French-speaking gypsies.

BORN JEAN BAPTISTE REINHARDT, January 23, 1910, into a family of Manouches Gypsies camped outside Liverchies, Belgium, "Django," as he came to be called, traveled with the Manouches through France and Belgium, putting on musical performances at country fairs and dance halls. He took up the guitar and six-string banjo early, impressing the other Gypsies with his prowess.

The extended family traveled continuously, circling their horse-drawn wagons into camps outside towns and cities. By the age of 13 Django was playing professionally with his Gypsy clan. Being illiterate, he relied on keen memory to recall the melodies; a skill he was to make use of for the rest of his life.

In 1928 a disaster struck that would change everything. The caravan of the Reinhardt clan was bivouacked on a vacant lot in suburban Paris, the wagons filled with artificial flowers that were to be taken to a cemetery the next day. Made of highly flammable cellulose, the rosettes burst into a fireball when Django knocked over a candle. Engulfed in the inferno, the badly burned guitarist barely escaped with his life. His left hand got the worst of it, with the pinkie and ring finger rendered almost useless.

It took him 18 months to recover, and even longer to relearn the guitar. Having only two fingers to fret with forced him to develop a new way of playing, influenced by the jazz music he was starting to hear. When Django resumed playing in Paris cafes, his new style began to attract attention from musicians outside the Gypsy community. Saxophonist Andre Ekyan and violinist Stephane Grappelli both saw him for the first time in the early 1930s. Tall, dark and handsome, with large expressive eyes and a rakish mustache, Django had the look of a movie star and a temperament to match. Extremely proud and easily slighted, he would put down the guitar and walk off stage if he felt the audience was not paying close enough attention.

Various club promoters, record producers, and musicians tried working with Django and discovered how difficult it could be. He would be booked for shows and recording dates only to turn up missing. Indeed, he would disappear from Paris, leaving on Gypsy caravans for weeks at a time. When he returned from his trip he'd casually resume the cafe circuit.

It was at this time, in 1934, that Django jumped into the jazz world full time. He would join "Le Quintette du Hot Club de France," and he would meet Coleman Hawkins.

NEW FACES IN THE CITY OF LIGHT

By the mid-1930s, the Paris of Hemingway's "movable feast" had largely moved on. The financial downturn in the U.S. had many of the American Lost Generation sailing back to New York. Taking their place was a different kind of lost community: Jewish refugees from Nazi Germany. They settled alongside the White Russians, Spanish anarchists, and a vast array of European political asylum seekers. Paris was still the cultural capital of the world, but the lights in Europe were fast going out.

DJANGO REINHARDT

LE QUINTETTE DU HOT CLUB DE FRANCE

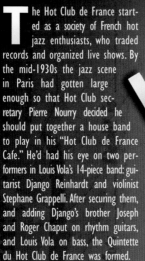he Hot Club de France started as a society of French hot jazz enthusiasts, who traded records and organized live shows. By the mid-1930s the jazz scene in Paris had gotten large enough so that Hot Club secretary Pierre Nourry decided he should put together a house band to play in his "Hot Club de France Cafe." He'd had his eye on two performers in Louis Vola's 14-piece band: guitarist Django Reinhardt and violinist Stephane Grappelli. After securing them, and adding Django's brother Joseph and Roger Chaput on rhythm guitars, and Louis Vola on bass, the Quintette du Hot Club de France was formed.

They were not a hit right away. Record executives found their playing too modern, and their Gypsy influences too rough. But if French audiences shied away, American musicians were quick to pick up on their unique sound. As jazz critic Ralph Gleason described them, "They were European and they were French and they were Jazz."

On February 25, 1935 one of their early fans, Coleman Hawkins, had them open for him at the Theater Salle Pleyel in Paris. This was their breakthrough performance; thereafter they were headliners.

STARDUST

One week after their big show, the Quintette and Hawkins recorded together for the first time. As nominal members of the Michel Warlop Orchestra, the Quintette played out the rhythm section while Hawkins sat in as the star. They did three rather unremarkable songs with full orchestra, but for the last number, "Stardust," it was just the Quintette and Hawkins. There was sparkle in that version, with both Coleman and Django soloing on top of the Quintette. They went their separate ways after the recording, but something special was there, something they would later return to.

I'se A Muggin'

Nobody knows just how it started,

Somebody blew it through a horn,

Somebody played it on a fiddle,

Somebody sang it and a song was born.

Now it's the craze, the new sensation,

Now it's the song the bands all swing,

Now it's the phrase that rocks the nation,

Don't try to stop me, 'cause i'm going to sing.

I'se a-muggin', boom doddy doddy,

I'se a-muggin', boom doddy doddy,

I'se a-muggin', boom doddy doddy.

Be-bop, be-bop, be-bop, be-bo!

Recorded by Le Quintette du Hot Club de France with Freddy Taylor singing, May 4, 1936

The hot jazz of the 1920s took deep root in Paris. So when American jazz styles migrated to swing in the mid-1930s, the French version retained some of its hot jazz style. One of those who pushed this emerging scene along was Charles Delaunay, publisher of *Le Jazz Hot* magazine. Delaunay was a tireless promoter of jazz music in France; his enthusiasm for the new sound was shared by the musicians in the Quintette. When the swing craze enveloped Europe in the late 1930s, they were ready.

In 1937 Charles Delaunay had branched out from magazine publishing to producing jazz records with Hugues Panassie's new Swing Disque label. For his first release he decided to do a recording with Reinhardt and Hawkins. Delaunay arranged an informal setting for the recording, more like a jam session than a typical studio affair. Knowing how competitive Hawkins was, he enlisted Coleman's friend, trumpeter and alto saxophonist Benny Carter, to keep the creative pressure on. French altoist Andre Ekyan and tenor Alix Combelle were added to fill out the reed section. Stephane Grappelli switched to piano. Django Reinhardt was on guitar. Delaunay scheduled the session to start at 9 PM, figuring the late-rising musicians would all arrive by 11 or so.

When Delaunay showed up at 9 o'clock, everyone was there and playing. He rushed to get the recording equipment rolling. The four songs they waxed, "Honeysuckle Rose," "Crazy Rhythm," "Out of Nowhere," and "Sweet Georgia Brown," were propelled by the bouncing rhythm set down by the Hot Club Quintette. With the massed guitars strumming crisply through the song changes, Carter and Hawkins floated above, weaving in and out of the melody. The session dynamic was crackling. As Alix Combelle later said: "It was a wonderful slice of luck for us. Needless to say we were right on our toes. I can remember that after the first take of 'Crazy Rhythm,' Benny said to Coleman, 'Man, that ain't the way it should go,' as if to make him realize he'd have to get down to it. Obviously, neither of them had anything to gain from the encounter, and we had nothing to lose. That's why the record came off so well."

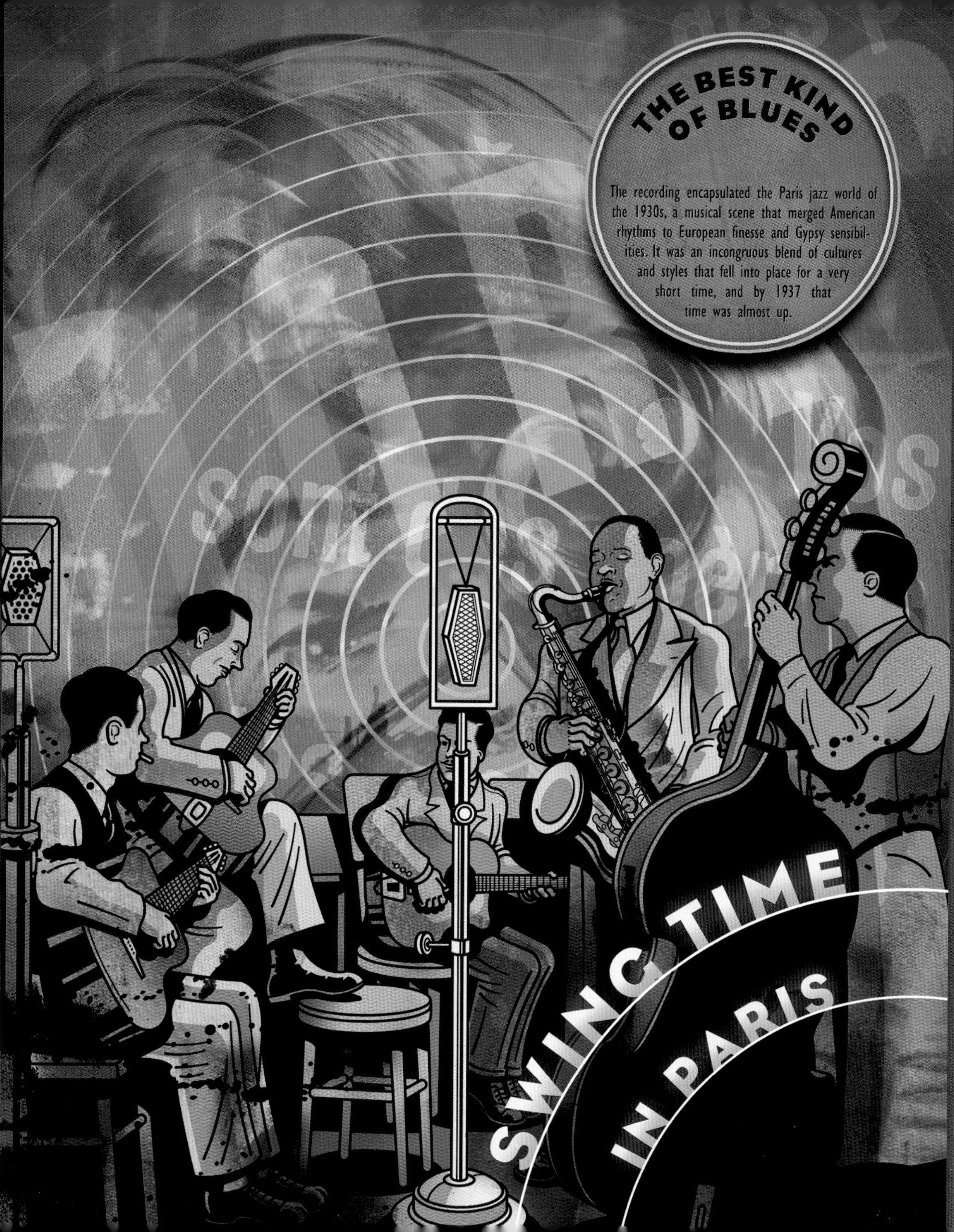
SWING TIME
IN PARIS

THE BEST KIND OF BLUES

The recording encapsulated the Paris jazz world of the 1930s, a musical scene that merged American rhythms to European finesse and Gypsy sensibilities. It was an incongruous blend of cultures and styles that fell into place for a very short time, and by 1937 that time was almost up.

THE GIDDY MOOD OF PARIS IN THE 1930S HAD TURNED DECIDEDLY GLOOMY BY 1939. Refugees from the Spanish Civil War were flooding into the city. French governments continued to veer between Left and Right while the coming war with Nazi Germany loomed ever nearer. The mood of the population tumbled into despair.

By late spring 1939, both Coleman Hawkins and the Quintette had embarked on separate tours of Britain. Coleman had resumed playing with the Jack Hylton Orchestra, but with the political crisis worsening by the day he decided to return to the U.S. Hawkins departed England on July 9, went to Holland to collect his belongings, and sailed immediately for New York.

The Quintette du Hot Club de France continued playing engagements in London, with band members noting that their dressing-room windows were blacked out for air raids. The mood in the city was increasingly grim. When air raid sirens sounded on September 3rd announcing the declaration of war, Django disappeared. Stephane and the band were stuck in England after the borders were sealed. Two weeks later, Reinhardt rather mysteriously turned up back in Paris. They were not to play together until after the war.

Django would restart the Quintette with clarinetist Hubert Rostaing replacing Grappelli; he continued to live in Paris through the German occupation. His music enjoyed a resurgence during the war, especially "Nuages" with its melancholic guitar, for many Parisians a nostalgic balm through those difficult years.

LATER THAN YOU THINK

BODY AND SOUL

Coleman Hawkins announced his return to New York by having the biggest hit of his career, "Body and Soul." Released in 1940, the song captured the imagination of the public with its trembling, overheated tenor spiraling around the simple melody. It was a song that became intrinsically linked to Hawkins, one he would have to play for the rest of his life. In a career that would span over 40 years, this period was his most fruitful. Coleman Hawkins was still in the driver's seat.

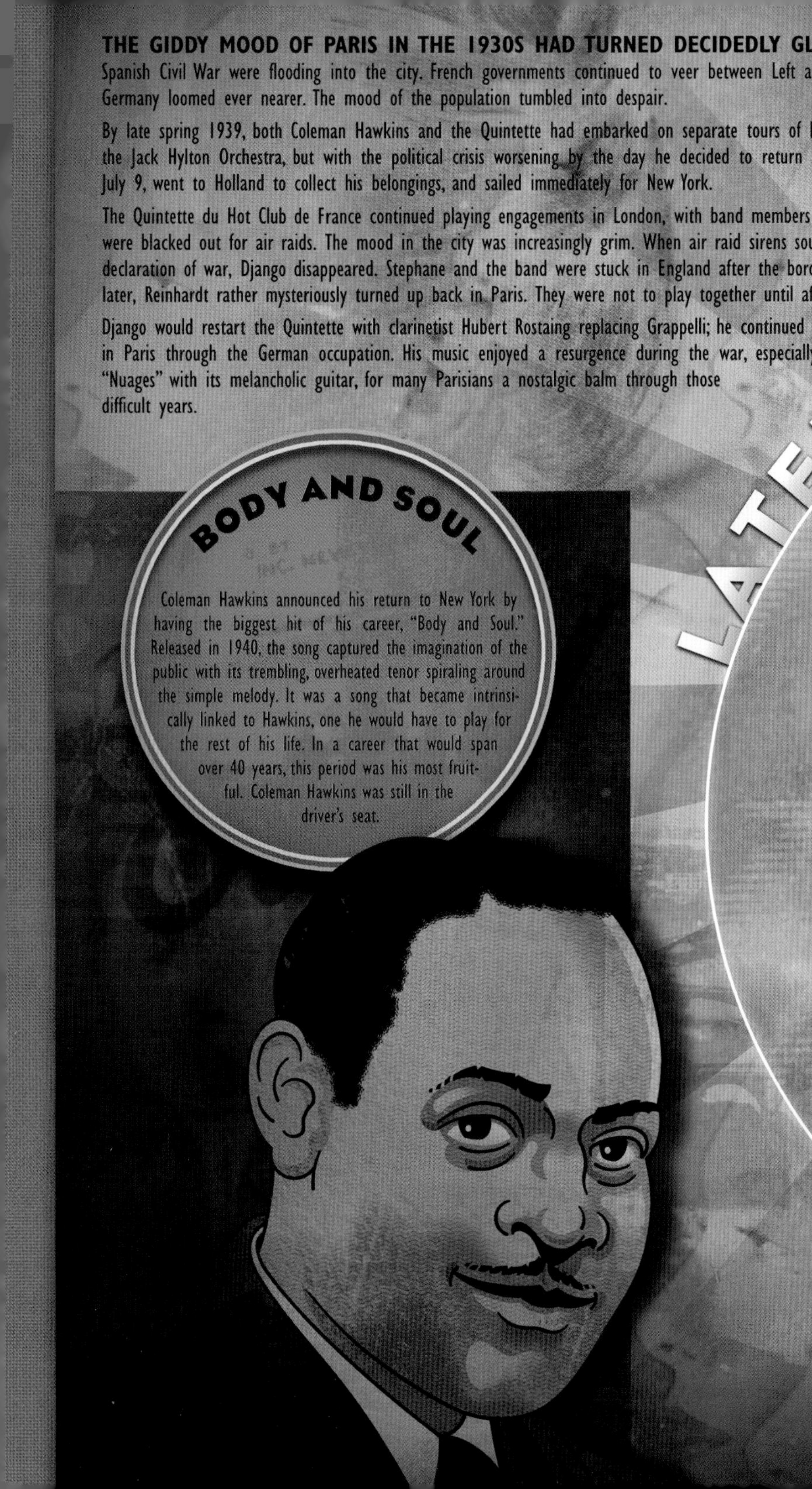

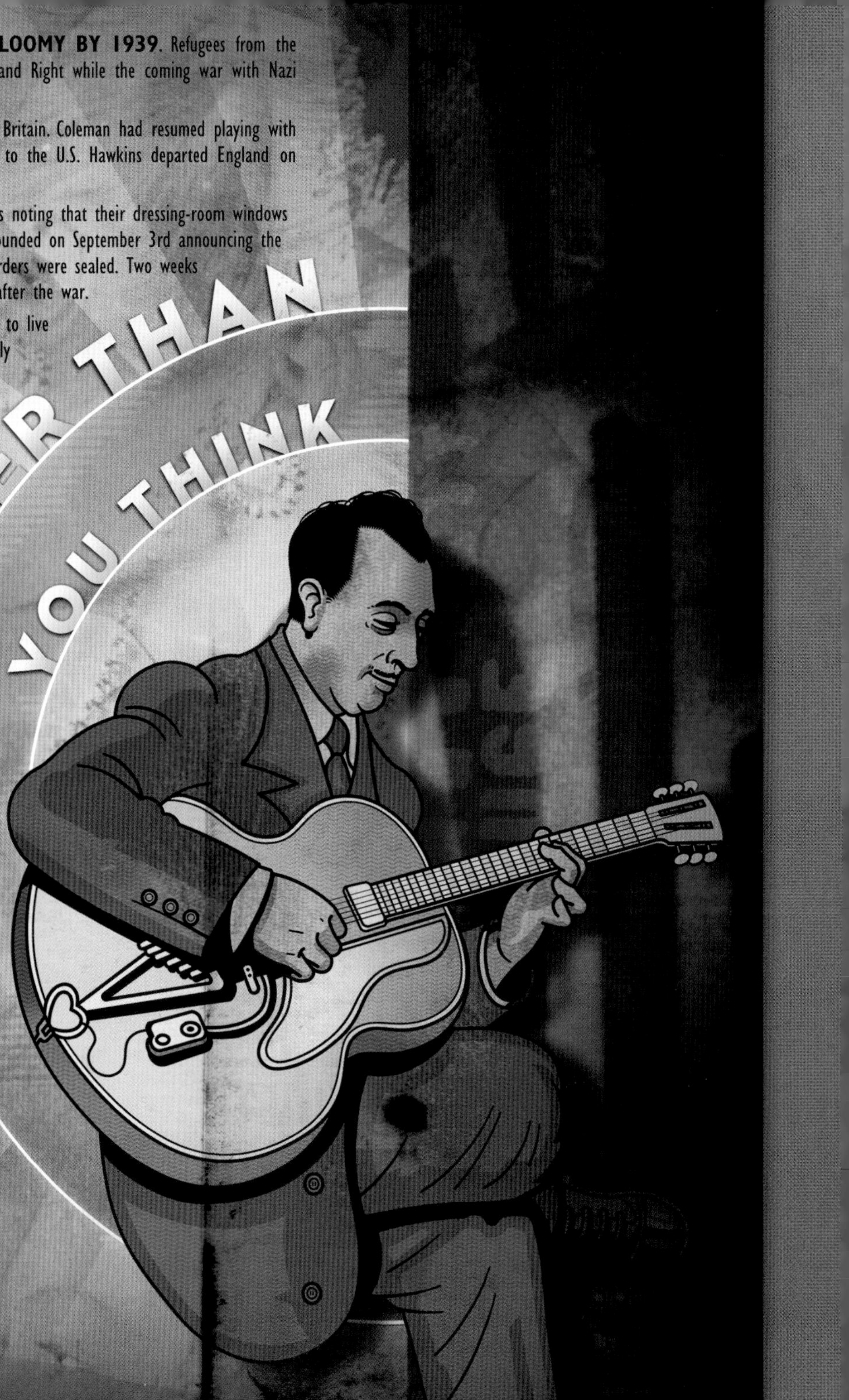

THE POSTWAR YEARS FOUND DJANGO REINHARDT OUT OF STEP WITH THE TIMES. A tour of the U.S. with the Duke Ellington Orchestra was poorly received, plans for a Hollywood career went nowhere, and young fans of Be-Bop regarded Django's swinging style as old-fashioned. He played the occasional reunion with Stephane Grappelli, trying to recapture the old magic, but found himself increasingly sidelined by severe headaches. On May 15, 1953, Django suffered a stroke while sitting at a Paris cafe along the Seine. He was carried upstairs and laid out on a bed, with his friends sending for help. When a doctor finally showed up, Django uttered his last words: "You've come now, have you?"

AFTER YOU'VE GONE

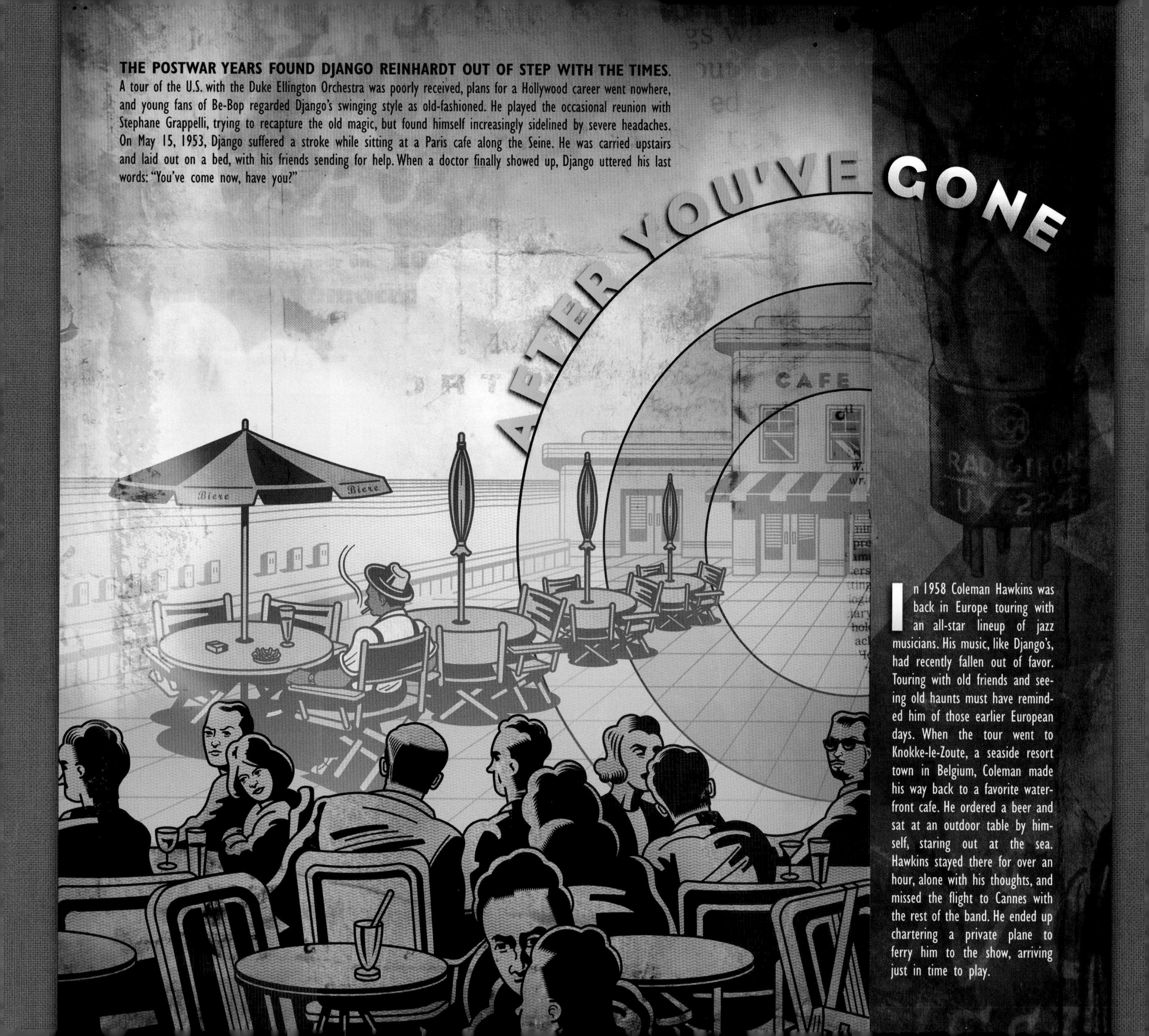
Biere
Biere
CAFE

In 1958 Coleman Hawkins was back in Europe touring with an all-star lineup of jazz musicians. His music, like Django's, had recently fallen out of favor. Touring with old friends and seeing old haunts must have reminded him of those earlier European days. When the tour went to Knokke-le-Zoute, a seaside resort town in Belgium, Coleman made his way back to a favorite waterfront cafe. He ordered a beer and sat at an outdoor table by himself, staring out at the sea. Hawkins stayed there for over an hour, alone with his thoughts, and missed the flight to Cannes with the rest of the band. He ended up chartering a private plane to ferry him to the show, arriving just in time to play.

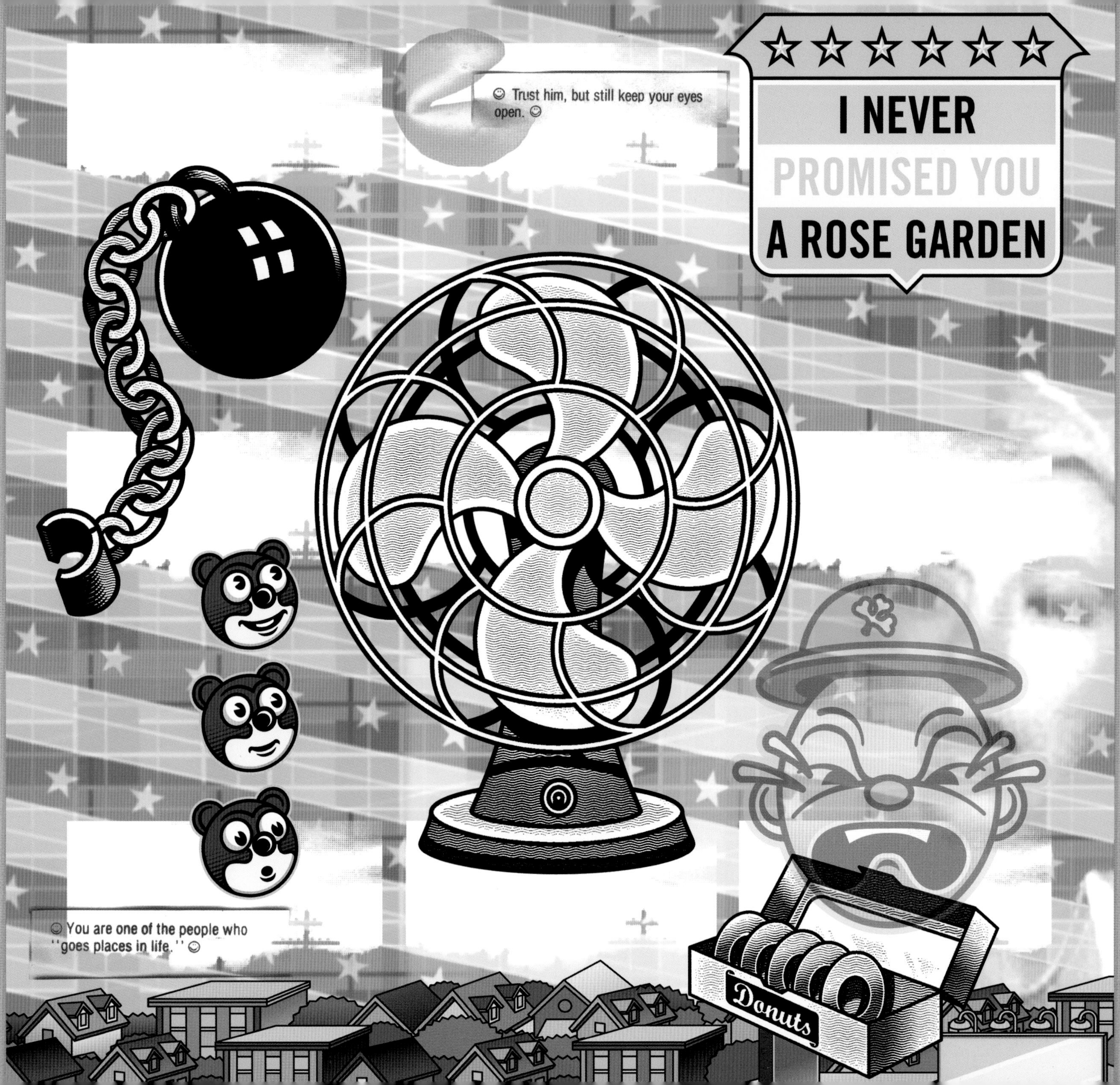
☺ Trust him, but still keep your eyes open. ☺
I NEVER
PROMISED YOU
A ROSE GARDEN
☺ You are one of the people who ''goes places in life.'' ☺
Donuts

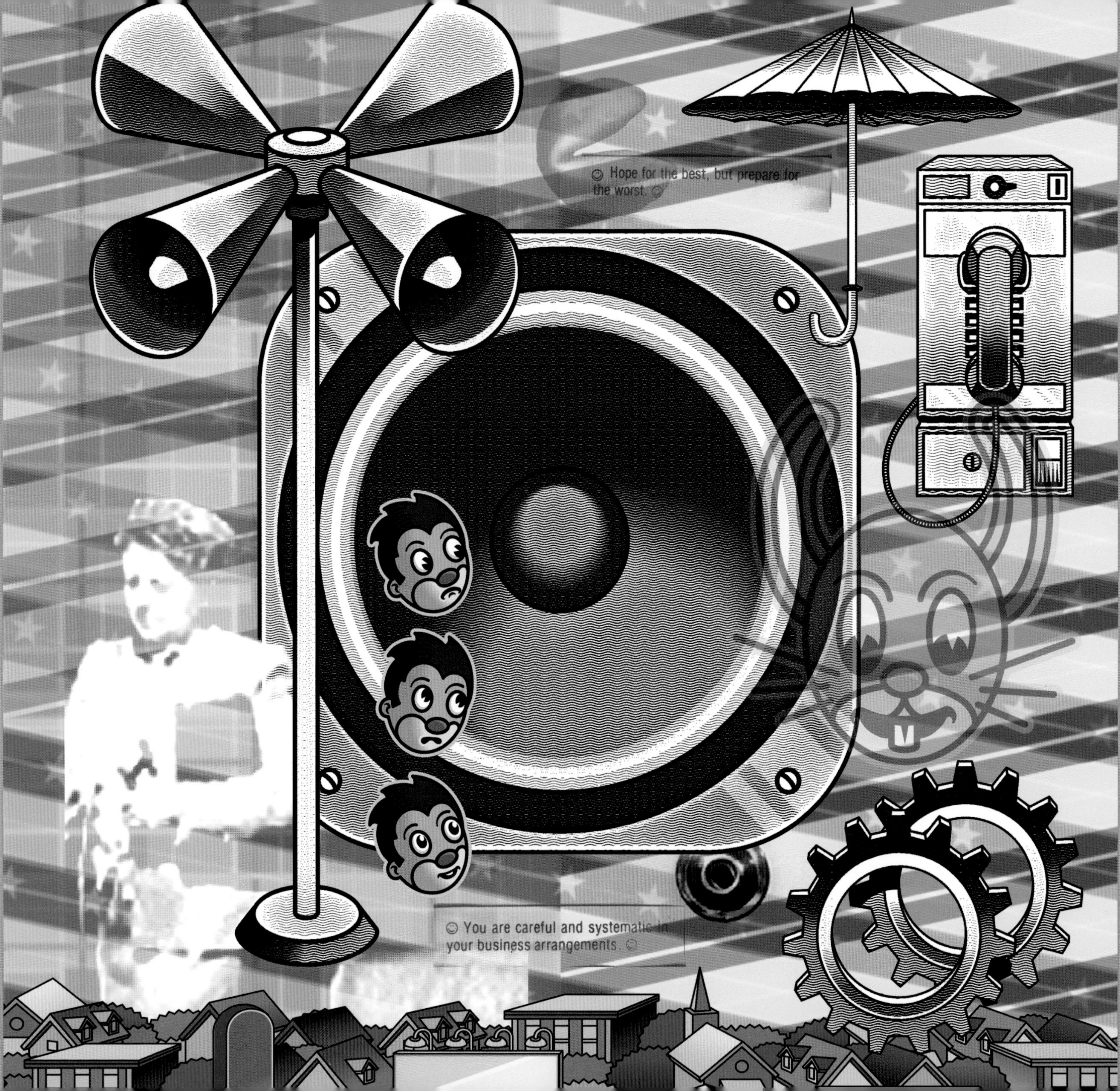
☺ Hope for the best, but prepare for the worst. ☺
☺ You are careful and systematic in your business arrangements. ☺

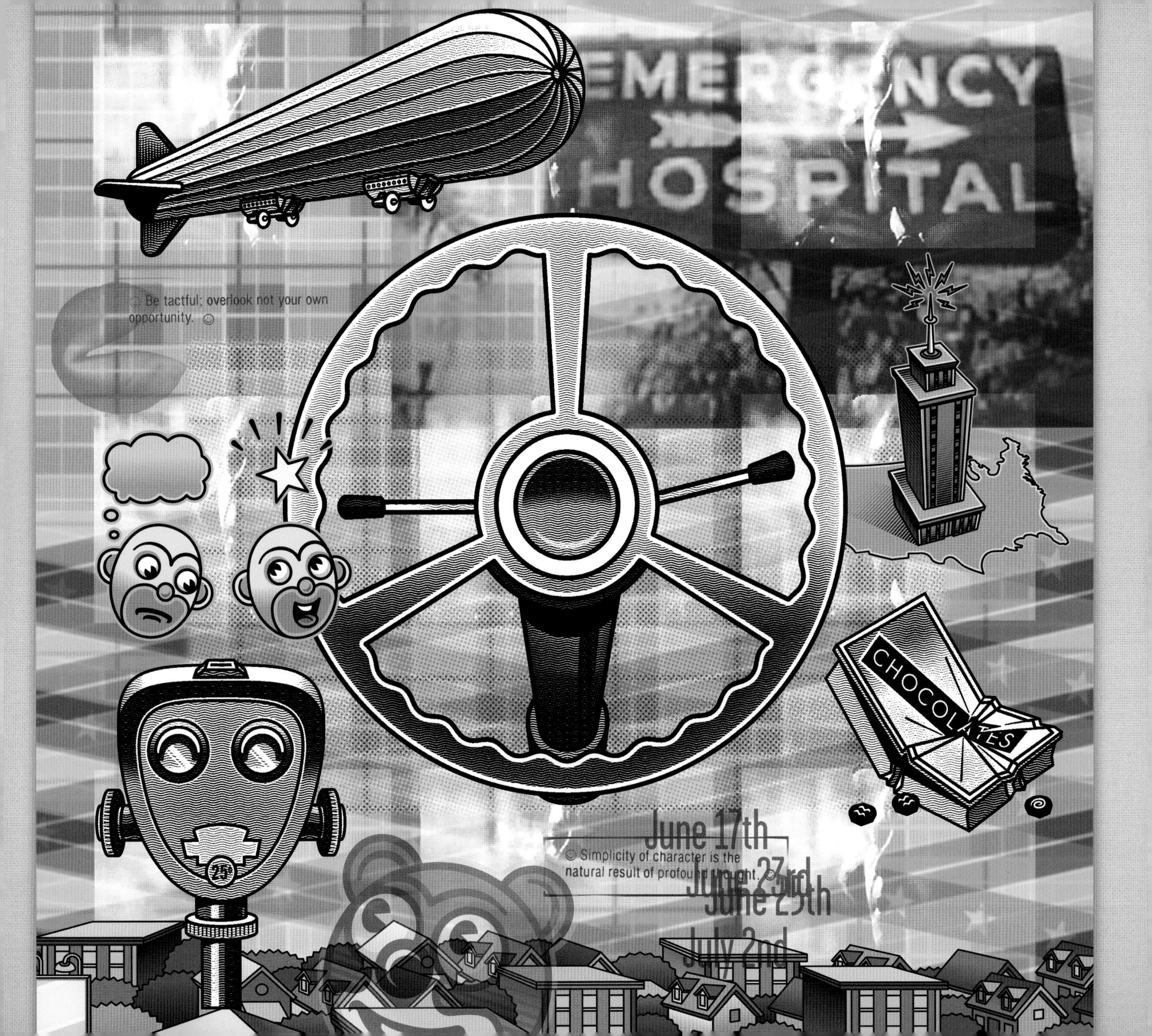
EMERGENCY
HOSPITAL
☺ Be tactful; overlook not your own opportunity. ☺
CHOCOLATES
25¢
June 17th
☺ Simplicity of character is the natural result of profound thought. ☺
June 23rd
June 25th
July 2nd

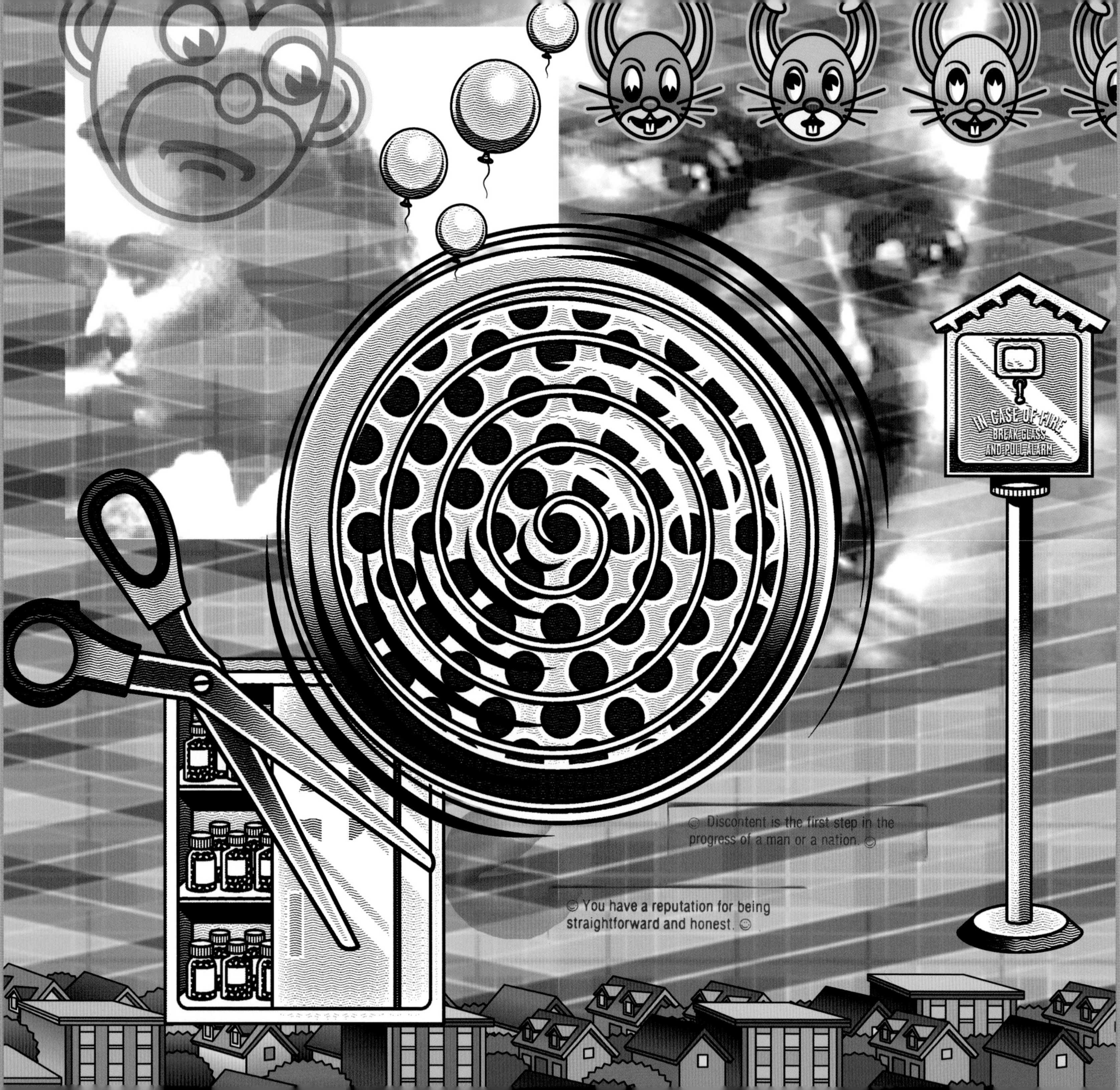
IN CASE OF FIRE
BREAK GLASS
AND PULL ALARM
☺ Discontent is the first step in the progress of a man or a nation. ☺
☺ You have a reputation for being straightforward and honest. ☺

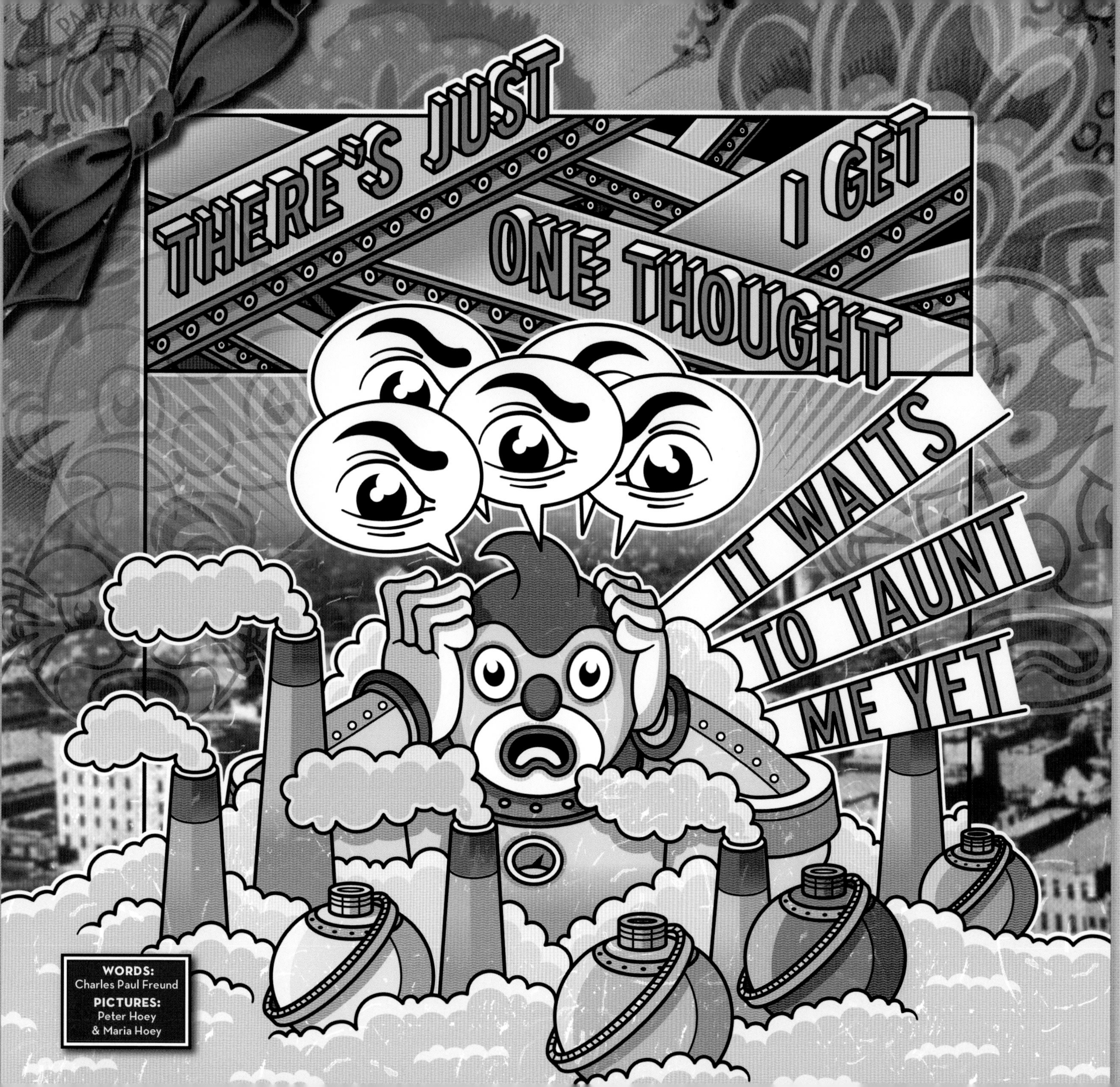
THERE'S JUST
ONE THOUGHT
I GET
IT WAITS
TO TAUNT
ME YET
WORDS:
Charles Paul Freund
PICTURES:
Peter Hoey
& Maria Hoey

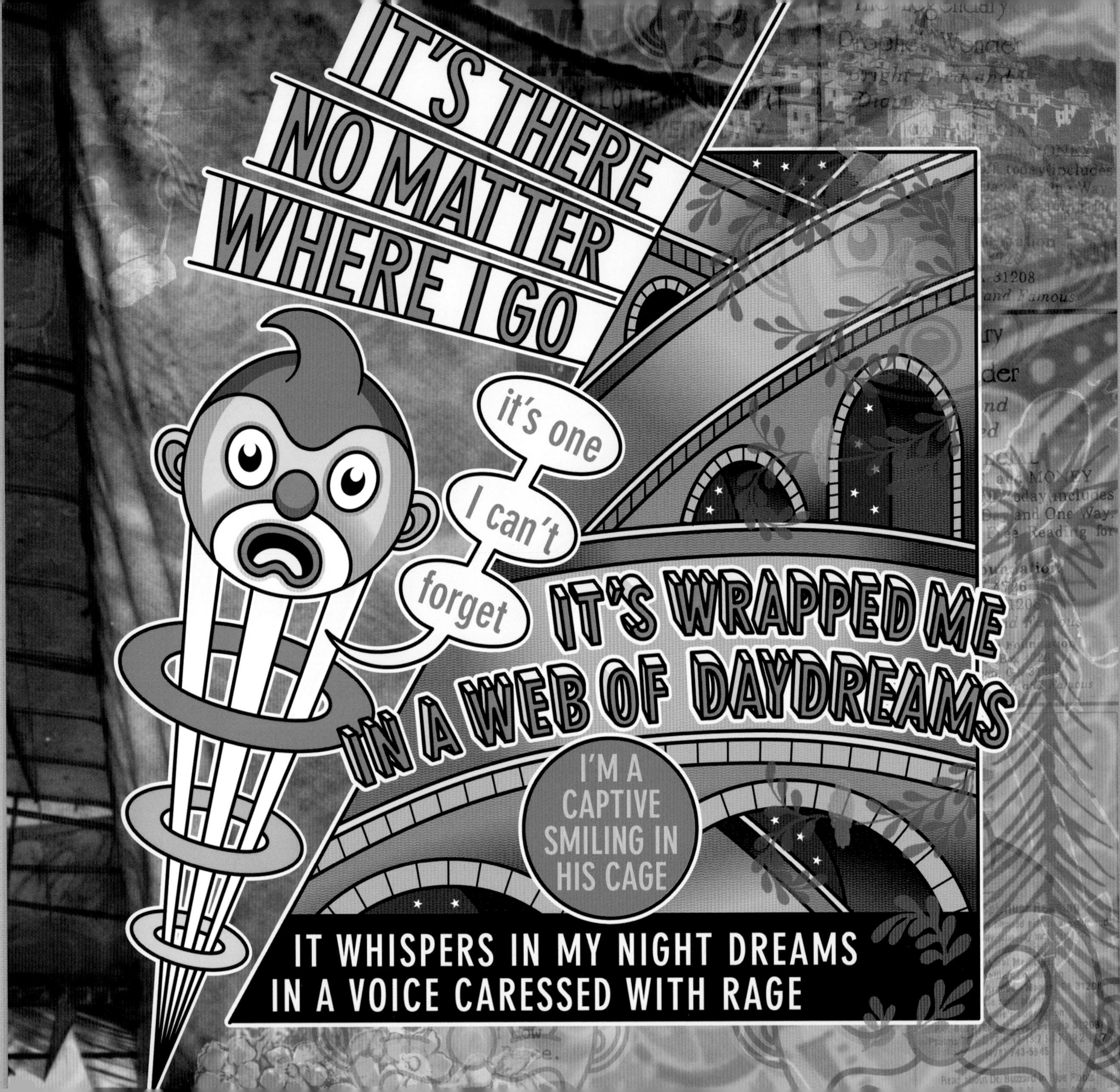
IT'S THERE
NO MATTER
WHERE I GO
it's one
I can't
forget
IT'S WRAPPED ME
IN A WEB OF DAYDREAMS
I'M A
CAPTIVE
SMILING IN
HIS CAGE
IT WHISPERS IN MY NIGHT DREAMS
IN A VOICE CARESSED WITH RAGE

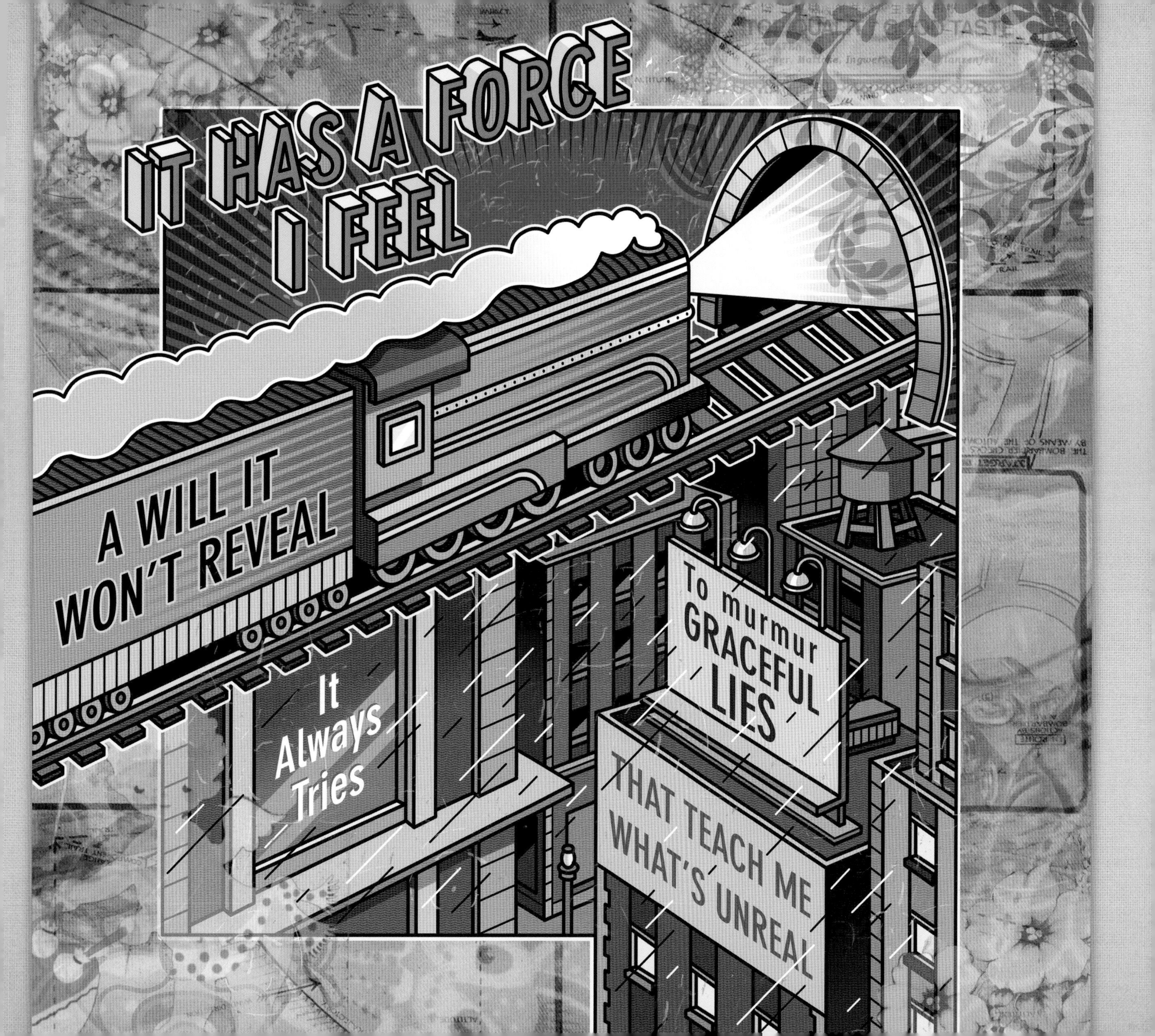
IT HAS A FORCE
I FEEL
A WILL IT
WON'T REVEAL
It
Always
Tries
To murmur
GRACEFUL
LIES
THAT TEACH ME
WHAT'S UNREAL

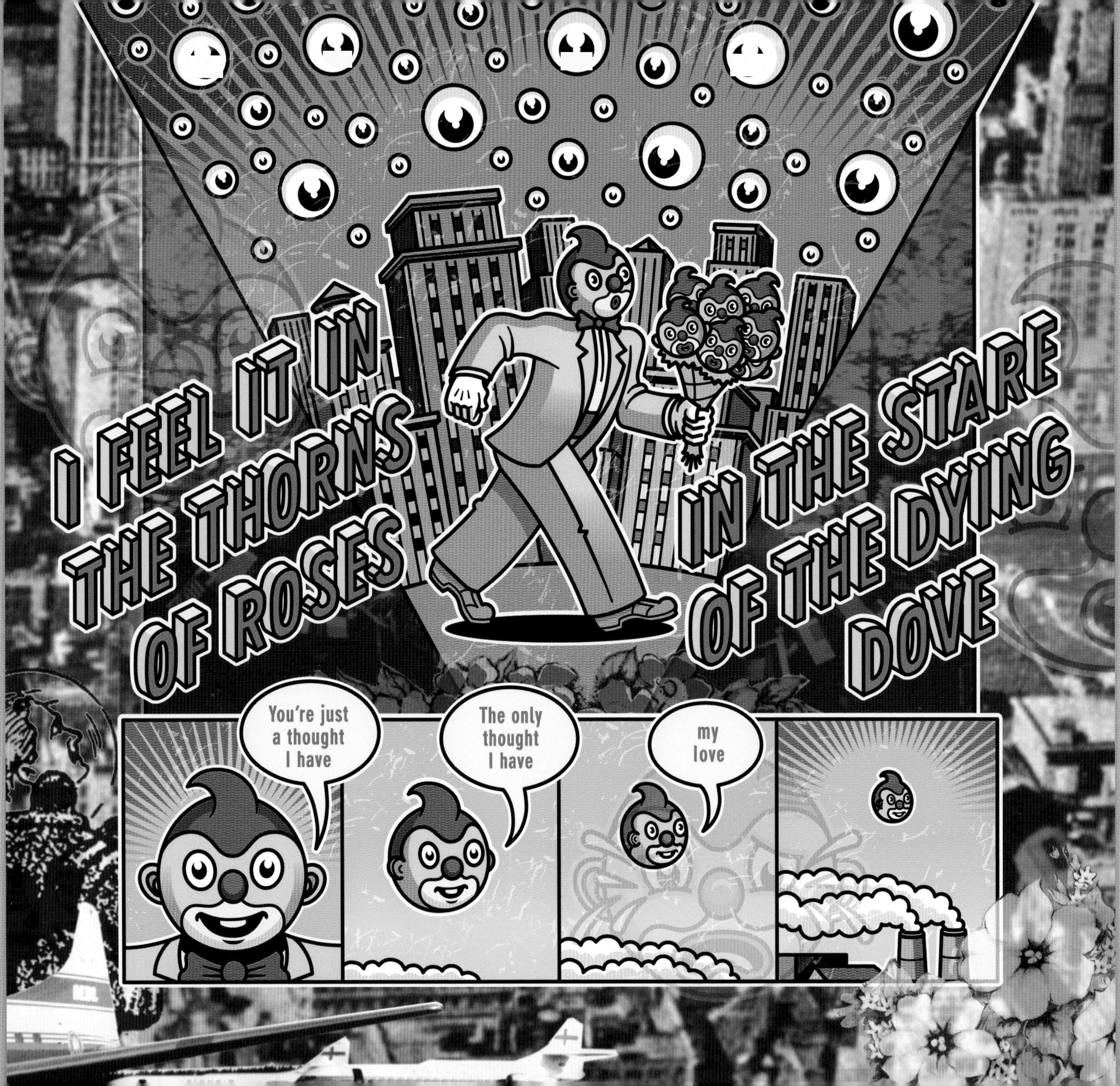
I FEEL IT IN THE THORNS OF ROSES
IN THE STARE OF THE DYING DOVE
You're just a thought I have
The only thought I have
my love

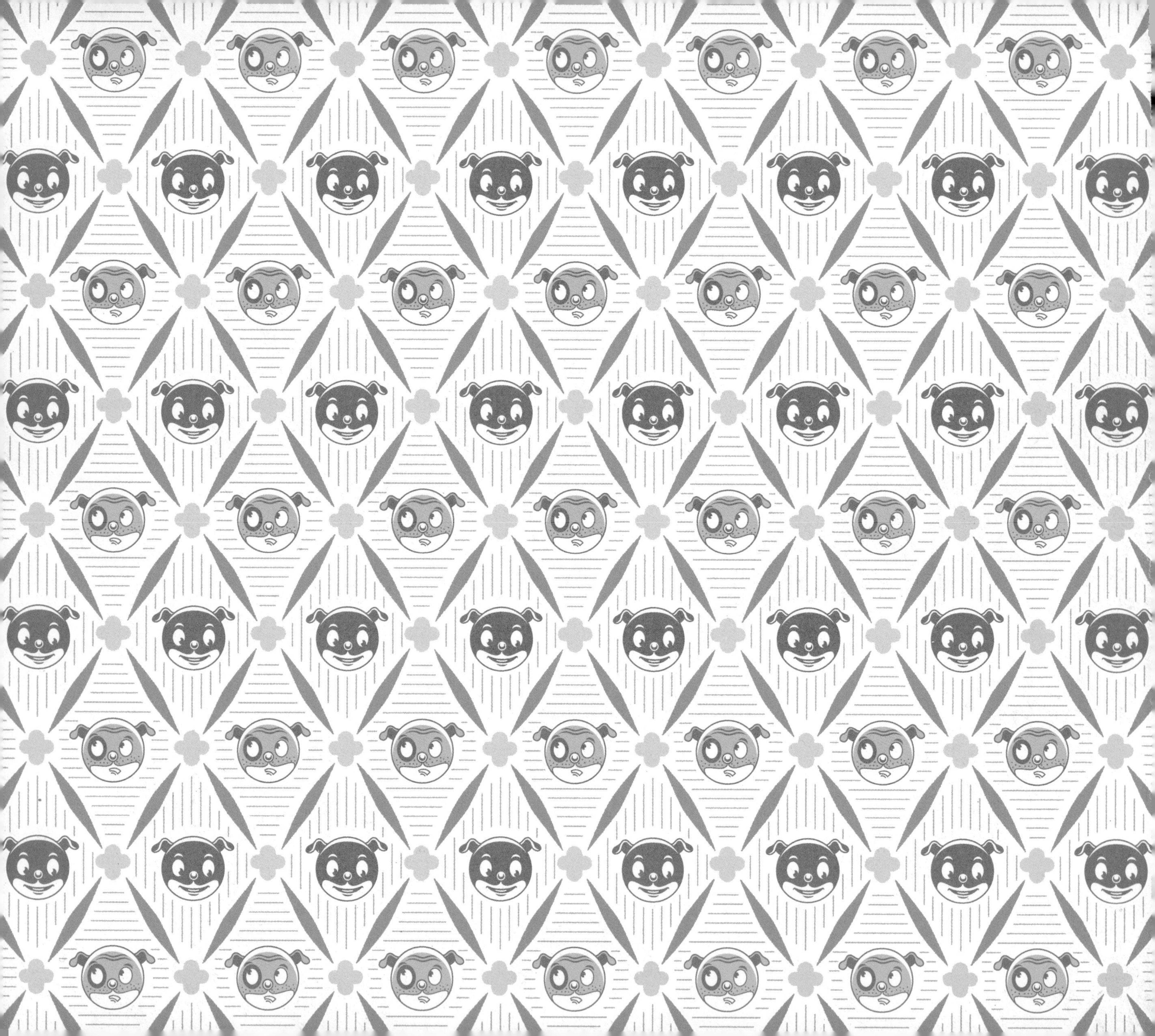